ESSAYS IN ECONOMIC ANALYSIS

ESSAYS IN ECONOMIC ANALYSIS

The Proceedings of the Association of
University Teachers of Economics
Sheffield 1975

EDITED BY

M. J. ARTIS
University College of Swansea

A. R. NOBAY
University of Southampton

CAMBRIDGE UNIVERSITY PRESS
CAMBRIDGE
LONDON · NEW YORK · MELBOURNE

Published by the Syndics of the Cambridge University Press
The Pitt Building, Trumpington Street, Cambridge CB2 1RP
Bentley House, 200 Euston Road, London NW1 2DB
32 East 57th Street, New York, NY 10022, USA
296 Beaconsfield Parade, Middle Park, Melbourne 3206, Australia

© Cambridge University Press 1976

Library of Congress catalogue card number: 75-46207

ISBN 0 521 21154 9

First published 1976

Typeset by EWC Wilkins Ltd, London and Northampton
and printed in Great Britain at the University Printing House, Cambridge
(Euan Phillips, University Printer)

CONTENTS

List of contributors	*page* vii
AUTE Executive Committee	viii
Editors' introduction	ix

PART ONE: THE FRANK PAISH LECTURE

1 The stability of general equilibrium: results and problems *Franklin M. Fisher*	3

PART TWO: MONEY, MACROECONOMICS AND WELFARE

2 Unemployment, inflation and the micro foundations of macroeconomics *Takashi Negishi*	33
Discussion *Michael Parkin*	42
3 Real cash balance and the optimal tax structure *A.L. Marty*	51
Discussion *R.E. Bailey*	62
4 Monetary expansion and the revenue of the monetary authority: a geometric exposition *David Laidler*	67
5 An analysis of monetary and fiscal policy in a quantity theory model of wealth adjustment *Gordon R. Sparks*	79
Discussion *Marcus H. Miller*	92
6 The movement of factor shares under conditions of rapid economic growth *John Sutton*	99
Discussion *D.C. Rowan*	123

PART THREE: TRADE AND THE BALANCE OF PAYMENTS

7 The effects of the oil price rise on the international economy *W.M. Corden*	129
Discussion *John Williamson*	147
8 A monetary model of an open economy with particular reference to the United Kingdom *M.D. Knight and C.R. Wymer*	153
Discussion *G.R. Fisher*	166

9	The international transmission of inflation *Russell S. Boyer*	173
	Discussion *David Laidler*	188
10	Effective rates of protection for United Kingdom manufacturing in 1963 and 1968 *P.D. Kitchin*	193
	Discussion *Dermot McAleese*	203

PART FOUR: UTILITY, VALUE AND THE FIRM

11	Tricks with utility functions *W.M. Gorman*	211
12	Whatever happened to the labour theory of value? *Ronald L. Meek*	245
13	The firm, finance and equilibrium in economic theory *S.J. Moss*	261
	Index of names	277
	Subject index	280

LIST OF CONTRIBUTORS

M.J. Artis (University College of Swansea)
R.E. Bailey (University of Essex)
Russell S. Boyer (International Monetary Project, London School of Economics and Department of Economics, University of Western Ontario)
W.M. Corden (Nuffield College, Oxford)
Franklin M. Fisher (Massachussetts Institute of Technology)
G.R. Fisher (University of Southampton)
W.M. Gorman (London School of Economics)
P.D. Kitchin (University of Sheffield)
M.D. Knight (London School of Economics)
David Laidler (University of Manchester)
Dermot McAleese (Trinity College, Dublin)
A.L. Marty (City College, New York University)
Ronald L. Meek (University of Leicester)
Marcus H. Miller (London School of Economics)
S.J. Moss (University of Southampton)
Takashi Negishi (University of Tokyo and London School of Economics)
Michael Parkin (University of Manchester)
D.C. Rowan (University of Southampton)
Gordon R. Sparks (Queen's University, Kingston, Ontario and University of Southampton)
John Sutton (University of Sheffield)
John Williamson (University of Warwick)
C.R. Wymer (London School of Economics)

AUTE EXECUTIVE COMMITTEE

M.J. Artis (*ex officio*), University College, Swansea
I.C.R. Byatt, HM Treasury
G. Clayton (Treasurer), University of Sheffield
B.A. Corry (Secretary), Queen Mary College, London
N.J. Gibson, New University of Ulster
H.G. Johnson, University of Chicago
D.E.W. Laidler, University of Manchester
E.T. Nevin, University College, Swansea
A.R. Nobay (Assistant Secretary), University of Southampton
J.M. Parkin, University of Manchester
D.C. Rowan (Chairman), University of Southampton
R. Shone (1975 Local Conference Secretary), University of Sheffield
R. Turvey, Scientific Control Systems, London
P. Vandome, University of Edinburgh
K.F. Wallis, London School of Economics

EDITORS' INTRODUCTION

This volume brings together papers presented to the Conference of the Association of University Teachers of Economics, held at Sheffield in April 1975. It represents the fourth published collection of the proceedings of this Conference. The volume displays the catholicity of interests of contemporary professional economists, and represents a cross section of the research that is currently undertaken at various universities, both in the United Kingdom and abroad.

Professor Franklin M. Fisher delivered the Frank Paish lecture. He dealt with some of the exciting and pressing issues of stability in general equilibrium. In their introduction to *General Competitive Analysis*, Arrow and Hahn persuasively pointed out that we need to know not only whether an economy characterised by general equilibrium theory with price signals operating to establish competitive equilibrium *is* true, but also whether it *could* be true. Professor Fisher's paper focuses upon the robustness of stability conditions in general equilibrium and the determination of prices in that system.

The second invited paper, by Professor W.M. Gorman, has an engaging title, 'Tricks with Utility Functions'. Professor Gorman's contribution provides an important synthesis of work in the area of consumer demand analysis, and draws upon the existing literature and his own important contributions in that area over a number of years. The third invited paper by Professor R.L. Meek, addresses itself to the classic transformation problem and its attendant controversies. Professor Meek has made a major contribution to the literature on the transformation problem and his return to it provides us with a stimulating reflection on that issue.

The contributions to the volume have been divided into three broad sections, money, macroeconomics and welfare; trade and the balance of payments; and a final section containing papers concerned with the theory of a firm, value theory and characteristics of utility functions. The largely analytical bias of the papers is no bar to topicality. There are papers which deal with current issues such as the analysis of the impact of oil price rise (Corden), and the framework for analysing the transmission of inflation across national boundaries (Boyer). Nor is applied economics unrepresented; the volume includes papers on the measurement of effective protection (Kitchin), the analysis of movements of factor shares in conditions of fast industrial growth (Sutton), and the econometric analysis of money in an open economy (Wymer and Knight). A number of papers are devoted to exploring the analytics of money and inflation (Marty, Laidler and Sparks). Papers by Negishi and Moss, although in different ways, are both concerned with the implications of proper microeconomic analysis for the interpretation of certain macroeconomic questions.

As is usual, the papers presented at the Conference generated a lively discussion from the floor. Space, however, precludes us from including a record of these comments in the volume, but in many cases authors have revised their papers for publication in the light of them.

We are immensely grateful to the many colleagues in the profession who have generously provided refereeing services and have greatly facilitated the tasks of the Programme Committee and ourselves.

We also acknowledge the generous financial support of Shell International in making possible the Frank Paish lecture (delivered this year by Franklin Fisher).

Finally, we acknowledge the secretarial and administrative help of Mrs Jan Gerrard and Miss Olwen Cornell, and the facilities provided by the Universities of Southampton and Swansea, Mr R. Ward for preparing the index and the staff of the University Press for their patience and generous help.

Michael Artis
Robert Nobay

PART ONE
THE FRANK PAISH LECTURE

1 THE STABILITY OF GENERAL EQUILIBRIUM: RESULTS AND PROBLEMS

FRANKLIN M. FISHER[1]

INTRODUCTION: THE IMPORTANCE OF THE PROBLEM

This is a paper about an important subject which is not in good shape — the study of the stability of general equilibrium. In it, I shall give a partial survey of the important developments in the history of the subject and then go on to discuss my own recent work. Unfortunately, my opening characterisation of the state of the art applies to that work at least as much as to anything else and much of my time will be spent discussing the all too evident problems which remain to be solved.

There was a time, about fifteen years ago or so, when the stability of general equilibrium was a hot topic among mathematical economists. Spurred on by important results of Arrow and Hurwicz, in particular,[2] there was a flurry of papers, some of them of lasting value, some of them, it now seems, not very interesting minor extensions of rather restricted results. Nowadays, however, the subject, if not actually disreputable, is at least not very fashionable. Since, as I have indicated, the subject is not in good shape, it may well be that this fall from favour is due to the considerable difficulty with which even small useful results are to be obtained; others may be more adept than I at making marginal maximising calculations in the allocation of effort. Nevertheless, I am convinced that the problems involved in stability analysis are of central importance to economic theorists, and, indeed, to economists generally. The fact that we know so little about the answers should not blind us to the importance of the questions. This should be kept in mind throughout this paper, which will mostly concern the inadequacies of our knowledge. It seems appropriate, therefore, that I take some space at the outset in reminding you why the subject is an important one.

There are, I think, three related reasons for such importance (all, of course, closely derived from reasons which make general equilibrium analysis as a whole an important subject). In the first place, consider what might be called the central policy prescriptions of microeconomics. Much of what economists have to say about the results of competition, the usefulness or lack thereof of government intervention, and the role of the price system is based on propositions about general equilibrium. These are chiefly what have in modern times been rigorously formulated as the central propositions of welfare economics concerning the relations between Pareto optima on the one hand and competitive equilibria on the other. Usually implicitly, to be sure, the propositions which may be the single most important set of ideas which economists have to convey to laymen are based on propositions about the optimality of competitive equilibrium and, therefore, on its attainability, for there is something odd about advice which is implicitly based on how good or efficient some equilibrium point would be if there is no way to get there from here.

This sort of implicit reliance on stability propositions, however, is not confined to microeconomic policy prescriptions. Important issues of macroeconomics are also, at bottom, general equilibrium issues and therefore also involve stability questions. Let me give just two examples.

The central question which concerned Keynes in the *General Theory* was that of how there could be a stable equilibrium with less than full employment. That is pre-eminently a question of general equilibrium analysis and of general equilibrium stability analysis, in particular. The fact that Keynes and later macroeconomists (undoubtedly quite wisely) did not use general equilibrium tools to answer it ought not to obscure the fact that a rigorous answer must surely be in general equilibrium terms. I yield to few economists in my ignorance of the causes of or cures for the situation of combined recession and inflation which has troubled our economies in recent years, but I cannot help suspecting that the apparent partial failure of macroeconomic analysis to cope with it may stem from the attempt to go on dealing at an aggregate level with general equilibrium questions involving detailed relatively microconsiderations.

To take a different example, consider the economic issues surrounding the question of Britain's continued membership of the EEC. The alternative fates of the British economy depending on staying in or pulling out are obviously questions of displacement of general equilibrium and hence of stability, even if we are hardly able to analyse them as such.

The third reason that the study of the stability of general equilibrium is important is closely related to the first one and, nowadays, probably applies to stability analysis more than to other, better understood branches of general equilibrium analysis. An extremely prominent economist long ago remarked to me in passing that the study of stability is unimportant because it is obvious that the economy is stable and, if it isn't, we are all wasting our time. I pass over the question of whether it really is obvious that the economy is stable and observe that the issue of time-wasting by economists is not one of whether the economy is stable but rather of whether the *theory* is. A principal reason for studying general equilibrium in the first place is to examine the consistency of partial equilibrium analyses. Having powerful theories of the firm, the household, and the market, may not be very useful if all those theories cannot be true at the same time.

Clearly, the heart of this important consistency question lies in the existence of general equilibrium, and existence theory, fortunately, is a subject which is in pretty satisfactory shape. Nevertheless, there is a sense in which the consistency question cannot be regarded as settled without a satisfactory analysis of stability. It is no use knowing that there exist points at which all partial equilibrium propositions can be jointly true, if such points are not attainable. Hence the question of the stability of general competitive equilibrium is a vital one for economic theorists, particularly if the economy is stable, but not only then. If general equilibrium turns out to be stable only under a very restrictive set of assumptions, then, indeed, we will all have been wasting our time, for there will be something wrong with the partial theory that we think we understand.

Hence, for a number of reasons, the stability of general equilibrium is a question of great importance. As I go on to consider what we know about it and as you are tempted to grow impatient with the sorry state of that knowledge, please bear in mind that every economist continually behaves as though the unsolved questions I am addressing had long ago been satisfactorily answered.

TÂTONNEMENT: LOCAL STABILITY

In my view, there have been four really important developments in the history of modern stability analysis. These are: the realisation that the subject was one which had to be studied in a context with a formal dynamic structure; the realisation that global, rather than simply local results could be obtained; the introduction of non-tâtonnement processes; and, closely related to this, the insight that attention paid to specifying the disequilibrium processes involved could lead to far more satisfactory results than could be obtained by restricting the excess demand functions. In some ways, the analyses resulting from each of these steps have made increasing use of the economic underpinnings of the stability problem (largely, but not exclusively, Walras' Law) and have led to correspondingly more and more satisfactory results.

The history of modern stability analysis begins with Samuelson (1941) and (1947) who, in considering what Hicks (1939) had called 'perfect stability' observed that the subject could only be rigorously studied in a framework specifying the equations of motion of the system when not in equilibrium. He proposed as a formalisation of Walras' idea of 'tâtonnement' a set of price adjustment equations that have formed the basis for nearly all later work.

I write those equations in an anachronistically general form as:

$$\dot{p}_i = H^i[Z_i(p)] \quad \text{unless } p_i = 0 \text{ and } Z_i(p) < 0,$$

$$\text{in which case } \dot{p}_i = 0. \tag{1}$$

Here, p_i is the price of the ith commodity, Z_i is the total excess demand for that commodity, taken as a continuous function of the prices, and H^i is a continuous, sign-preserving function, bounded away from zero except as Z_i goes to zero. The dot denotes a time derivative.

In other words, the price of the ith commodity adjusts in the same direction as excess demand for that commodity, the exact adjustment being a continuous function of excess demand (and therefore of price). The exception to this occurs where such a rule would require that a good which is already free and in excess supply be given a negative price, whereupon the price is simply left at zero.

This formulation, which forms at least part of practically all later work, already raises some technical and some economically substantive problems. The first of these is easy to overlook. It is the assumption that excess demands can be taken as continuous functions of the prices. (Of course, this is to be interpreted as a continuous function of the prices given endowments, technologies, and so forth.) The problem is not that there are other variables held constant; it is that there are plausible circumstances in which excess demands *cannot* be taken as functions of the prices, let alone continuous ones. If there are constant returns to scale, for example, a continuous increase in the price of the product, other prices constant, will cause firms to go from wishing to produce zero to wishing to produce an indeterminate amount to wishing to produce an infinite amount. Such cases are ruled out. One need not be a fanatic believer in the universality of constant returns to scale to be troubled by a formulation which cannot handle constant returns. Yet the assumption that excess demands are continuous functions of price is essential if we are to use the kind of mathematics which is embodied in (1), not only because it is hard to see what kind of adjustment process is reasonable in the absence of such a functional relationship but also because the very existence of solutions to (1) depends on such continuity.[3]

Thus we encounter important problems even in the building blocks from which the price-adjustment equation is constructed. When we come to that equation itself, we encounter another problem of even greater importance. Whose behaviour does the equation represent? It seems very plausible, to be sure, that price should adjust upwards when demand exceeds supply and downwards in the opposite case, but just how does this happen? To put it sharply, in a world in which all participants take prices as given, who changes the price?[4] Indeed, in the centre of a subject which deals with individual behaviour, how does there arise a behaviour equation (not an identity) based solely on aggregates? The familiar story which goes with equation (1) of the auctioneer who adjusts prices until demand equals supply is at best an inconvenient fiction.

I shall return to these problems below. For the present, I add three remarks:

First, the difficulty arises directly with the price-adjustment equation used. It has nothing to do with the question of whether or not trade, consumption, or production takes place out of equilibrium.

Second, the difficulty arises because we have an excellent theory of equilibrium behaviour and know very little about how individuals do or ought to behave when equilibrium is not present; hence, the resort to an aggregate equation.

Finally, despite this fact, we have already made an implicit assumption about disequilibrium behaviour in the formulation of equation (1) that will have to be considered explicitly later on. It is one which is relatively harmless in the unrealistic world of no trading out of equilibrium but very irksome otherwise. Implicit in the assumption that excess demand influences price is the assumption that individuals take action to make their excess demands effective. This involves the assumption that they *can* take such action which, as we shall later see, implies that they have something of value which they can and do sell so as to have something to offer when they buy. It also involves, however, the assumption that they *do* take such actions and take them now, so that, even though the excess demand involved may be for a good dated in the far future, 1990 toothpaste, for example, individuals who will want that good in the far future begin *immediately* to attempt to acquire it.[5]

I shall refer to this as the 'Present Action Postulate'. It is implicit in all stability analyses, although explicit in almost none, possibly because it has little objectionable content so long as we remain in a world in which the adjustment of prices to equilibrium can be safely supposed to take place before the dates on any commodities (future or otherwise) come due.

Note that, even if we were to adopt a more individualistic and plausible price-adjustment equation than (1), the problems involved in the Present Action Postulate would still present themselves. Stability analyses which take off from the economics of individual behaviour by way of deriving unsatisfied or excess demands must concern themselves with the question of when and how the participants attempt to exercise those demands. It is hard to see how to escape from the assumption that they do so when the demands occur, even though this involves implausible behaviour as regards future commodities. I shall return to this below.

As indicated, however, this last set of problems can be ducked if one is willing to separate the time in which adjustment takes place from that in which commodities are dated and consumption and production occurs. This is essentially guaranteed if we suppose that no trading (let alone consumption and production) takes place before equilibrium is reached, so let us now return to a consideration of the historical development in which that assumption played an important role. It is, in fact, that assumption and not just the price-adjustment process (1) that characterises the processes known as tâtonnement in the literature.

The early literature, beginning with Samuelson,[6] was primarily concerned with the local stability of the tâtonnement process, following Samuelson's observation that local stability properties could be studied by approximating the right-hand side of equation (1) linearly and considering the question of when the eigenvalues of the resulting matrix (essentially the Jacobian matrix of the excess demand functions) could be shown to have negative real parts. These discussions made little or no use of Walras' Law, but rather considered the excess demand functions as if they were pretty well unrestricted. Partly as a result of this and partly because of what now seems the rather peculiar origin of the subject — the relations between what Hicks (1939) had called 'perfect stability' and the local stability of the truly dynamic equation (1) — these investigations did not really get very far. They ended up in essentially the rather unfinished place of showing that, provided all commodities were gross substitutes,[7] the local stability of (1) was equivalent to the not very revealing condition that Hicks had found to be necessary and sufficient for his 'perfect stability', namely, that the principal minors of the Jacobian of the excess demand functions alternate in sign.

Such a result was obviously only a very partial one. This was so even in the narrow terms of the relations between Hicks' concept and dynamic stability where it remained for a much later paper of McFadden (1966) to elucidate the matter in terms of relative speeds of adjustment. Even more partial was the result in terms of stability analysis on its own grounds, since the alternation of the principal minors is not particularly interpretable in any natural way. Such a result is best thought of as a lemma rather than as a theorem, and, accordingly, we should not be surprised to find that by the end of the 1950s Hahn (1958) and Negishi (1958) had independently proved, using Walras' Law and the homogeneity of degree zero of the excess demand functions, respectively, that the assumption of gross substitutes itself implied the alternation of the principal minors and hence that, under the gross substitutes assumption, the tâtonnement process was invariably locally stable.

TÂTONNEMENT: GLOBAL STABILITY

These papers, however, were superseded by the results of a pair of pathbreaking papers by Arrow and Hurwicz (1958) and Arrow, Block, and Hurwicz (1959) which contained a demonstration of the fundamental point that global rather than local stability results might be available (and, indeed, might be easier to obtain than local ones). Among the specific stability results was that of the global stability of tâtonnement under the gross substitutes assumption.

This breakthrough rested on the use of a mathematical device known as Lyapounov's Second Method. Since practically all the work that followed has been based on that device and since my later discussion requires some understanding of it, I shall digress at this point, give some not-very-rigorous definitions, and discuss Lyapounov's Second Method and the role it plays in analyses of stability.[8]

An equilibrium of an adjustment process such as (1) is said to be *globally stable* if the system converges to it from every set of initial conditions. This, of course, is a very strong property. In particular, if there is more than one equilibrium, then no particular equilibrium can be globally stable in this sense, since if the process begins at some other equilibrium it will never leave it. Since we know that uniqueness of general equilibrium requires extremely strong assumptions, it is unreasonable to require equilibria to be globally stable. Instead, we need a somewhat weaker notion of global stability.

That notion is provided by the idea of the global stability of an *adjustment process*. An adjustment process, such as (1), is said to be globally stable if, for any set of initial conditions there is an equilibrium to which the system converges. The difference, of course, is that it doesn't have to be the same equilibrium for all initial conditions. If equilibrium is unique (as it is in the gross substitutes case), then the two notions of global stability coincide.

Finally, it is useful to distinguish this from the definition of the *quasi-stability* of an adjustment process.[9] For convenience of language, let us suppose that the variables involved are prices only, as in (1). Starting with any initial condition, consider an infinite sequence of prices. Such a sequence may not have a limit (unless prices converge to some equilibrium), but it may nevertheless have one or more limit points (roughly, points to smaller and smaller neighbourhoods of which the sequence keeps returning). If every limit point of every such sequence is an equilibrium, the adjustment process is said to be quasi-stable.

Obviously, the quasi-stability and the global stability of an adjustment process are closely related. Indeed, it is not hard to show that if an adjustment process is quasi-stable and the variables involved remain in a compact set, then that process is also globally stable provided either of two things are true. They are, first, that every equilibrium is locally isolated (which includes uniqueness as a special case), or, second, that every limit point of every sequence starting from a given set of initial conditions is the same.

Accordingly, modern stability proofs tend to be in three parts. First (and usually hardest) is a proof of quasi-stability. (This is where Lyapounov's Second Method comes in.) Second is a compactness argument which often amounts to an argument that the variables remain bounded. Third is either a demonstration of local uniqueness of equilibrium or a demonstration that all limit points (starting from the same initial conditions) are the same.[10]

I shall have some occasion to mention the latter two steps in my later discussion, but our principal focus will be on the first one, the proof of quasi-stability and the use of Lyapounov's Second Method.

Continue to think in terms of prices. Lyapounov's result is as follows. Suppose that we can find a function, $V(p)$, continuous in the prices, bounded below, and monotonically decreasing through time except in equilibrium. Then the adjustment process is quasi-stable. Lyapounov's Second Method consists of finding such functions $V(p)$. This is not a simple task and forms the heart of most stability investigations. As time has gone on, such Lyapounov Functions have tended to go from geometrically interpretable measures of the distance from equilibrium to economically more interesting functions such as (as we shall see) the sum of the utilities which households would expect to get if their mutually inconsistent plans could be realised.

Let us now return to the tâtonnement literature. Arrow, Hurwicz, and Block were essentially able to prove that the adjustment process (1) is globally stable provided that one is willing to place very severe restrictions on the excess demand functions. One such restriction — that of the gross substitutes assumption — has already been mentioned. Somewhat surprisingly, it turns out that this, as well as most of the other cases successfully investigated in the papers under discussion, are special cases of the assumption that the *aggregate* excess demand functions satisfy the Weak Axiom of Revealed Preference (at least in comparisons between equilibrium and other points), an axiom which makes excellent sense in terms of individual behaviour but which there is no good reason to impose on aggregate demand functions.[11]

Despite this, because all the special cases involved turned out to imply global stability, the authors ventured to conjecture that the tâtonnement process was always globally stable, given only the restriction that the excess demand functions be consistent with underlying economic considerations such as Walras' Law. Not surprisingly, this rather wishful conjecture was soon exploded when Scarf (1960) provided a counterexample.[12]

Tâtonnement stability was in an awkward corner. The process was not invariably stable; interesting necessary conditions for stability were clearly not to be had; and sufficient conditions for stability appeared to involve wildly restrictive conditions on individual (or aggregate) demand functions. Despite the fact that two other major developments were taking place at about the same time (the early 1960s) and would lead to what are (in my opinion) far more fruitful results, it is not surprising that the flurry of interest in the stability of general equilibrium more or less died out at about this time.

TRADING PROCESSES: PURE EXCHANGE

Both of the new developments had in common the fact that, unlike the work just discussed which can be thought of as largely drawing implications for stability by considering properties which are just as true in equilibrium as out of it, they were based on further specification of the disequilibrium adjustment processes themselves.

One such development was the abandonment of the tâtonnement assumption of no trading out of equilibrium which had wound up in a dead end and the introduction of what are rather inelegantly called 'non-tâtonnement' processes. Since that is not a very informative name, I shall refer to them as 'trading processes'.

It is important to remember that, while this stage of development permits trading out of equilibrium, most of the work to be discussed does not permit consumption or production to take place until equilibrium has been reached. One must think of participants as swapping titles to commodity stocks while prices (and, of course, possessions) adjust. Only after the music stops do people go home and enjoy what they have. Such a model is obviously most suited to pure exchange with no firms. While a step in the right direction, it clearly calls out for extension both to firms and to a model which permits production and consumption to take place during adjustment.

For the moment, however, let us put such extensions aside and restrict our attention to the case of pure trading processes and pure exchange. At this level, a rather surprising result occurs. Since we have added to the price adjustment process (1) some set of equations describing how individual stocks of commodities change hands, we might expect that we have made stability less likely than in the tâtonnement case, since the system is now more complicated than before. This turns out not to be true, however, provided we stay with pure exchange and are willing to make the reasonable assumption that nobody can change his wealth by trading at constant prices. That latter assumption might be called one of 'no cheating', for it amounts to saying that one cannot get anything by trading except by giving up something of equal value.

If one is willing to make that assumption (which I shall henceforth do), then it turns out that in essentially every case in which tâtonnement is known to be stable, exchange trading processes are also. The basic reason for this lies in Lyapounov's Second Method. Suppose that we have a Lyapounov function which depends on prices and on aggregate excess demands. The time derivative of that function in a trading process differs from the corresponding time derivative in tâtonnement by terms which depend on those parts of the time derivatives of the aggregate excess demand functions which come from the changes in individual commodity stocks induced by trading with prices fixed. An individual's demand for any commodity, however, is affected by constant-price changes in his holdings only insofar as these changes affect his wealth, and, by the No-Cheating Assumption, his wealth is not affected. The change in an individual's *excess* demand, for a commodity brought about in this way is therefore merely the negative of the change in his actual holdings of that commodity. Since, in pure exchange, the aggregate stock of any commodity is fixed, there are no such effects on *aggregate* excess demand. Hence the time derivative of any such Lyapounov function is the same in tâtonnement as in exchange trading processes, so that if such a function was decreasing out of equilibrium in the former case, it is still doing so in the latter.

Unfortunately, this rather pleasant and general result does not take us very far. The difficulty with the tâtonnement results which might be said partially to have prompted the study of trading processes in the first place is that tâtonnement can be shown to be stable only under very restrictive conditions. So it is not a great help to know that those same restrictions will generally ensure the stability of general exchange trading processes too. Something more is needed.

That something more is provided by the fourth of the major developments which, in my opinion, have marked the history of the subject, the perception that relatively reasonable restrictions on the adjustment processes themselves could lead to stability proofs involving essentially no restrictions on utility or production functions. While, as we shall see, that insight was closely and naturally associated with the development of the trading process literature, it is logically separate from that development. Credit for it (although they never enunciated it quite this way) belongs to Uzawa and to Hahn. (Indeed, one might say that it was Hahn (1962) who saw it most clearly, since he gave a *tâtonnement* example in which the specification of (1) was restricted and quasi-stability proved under quite general circumstances.)

The result of this insight was the development of two special trading processes, the Edgeworth Process (so named because it was discovered by Uzawa, 1962) and the Hahn Process (so named by Negishi, 1962). I happen to believe that it is the Hahn Process which is the more interesting and fruitful by far, and most of the remainder of this paper will be based on it. Let me then take a little time to discuss the Edgeworth Process, which is also of importance.

The central assumption of the Edgeworth Process[13] is that trade will take place if and only if there is some group of people who can all be made better off by trading among themselves at the current prices. With some complications, due to the fact that at some non-equilibrium prices no such Pareto-superior move may be possible until prices change, this leads to the use of the negative of the sum of actually achieved individual utilities as a Lyapounov function and hence to quasi-stability.

Unfortunately, this powerful and appealing result is not so helpful as it first appears. This is so for more than one reason.

First, while it is obviously innocuous to assume that individuals will not trade unless they can better themselves by so doing, it is not nearly so simple to assume that trade actually will take place whenever such a situation arises. This is because of the possibility that the only coalitions which can better themselves by mutual trade consist of very large numbers of people. Thus it is possible that there is no mutually advantageous bilateral or trilateral or quadrilateral trade and that the only mutually advantageous trade involves a very complicated swapping of commodities among millions of people. To require, as the Edgeworth Process does, that such a trade must take place is to put very heavy requirements on the dissemination of information and to assume away the costs of coalition formation.[14]

Second, the Edgeworth Process does not appear to lend itself readily to the important extension of allowing production and consumption to take place out of equilibrium. A crucial feature of disequilibrium consumption, for example, is surely that individuals take irreversible actions which they would not have taken had they correctly anticipated the future. This means that utilities turn out to be lower than anticipated. It is not easy to see how this phenomenon can be accommodated in a model whose central result relies on the increase of utilities out of equilibrium, although whether that can actually be done remains an open question.

It happens that the Hahn Process is strong on exactly these points. It requires much less information than does the Edgeworth Process; and it is particularly suited to accommodating irreversible mistakes. In addition, it lends itself easily to the introduction of firms and its central assumption is almost compelled when we start considering individuals as adjusting prices. Accordingly, I now turn to an examination of the Hahn Process.

THE HAHN PROCESS

The central assumption of the Hahn Process[15] is as follows. At any one time, there may of course be either unsatisfied demand or unsatisfied supply for some commodity, say apples. However, we suppose that markets are sufficiently well organised that there are not both. In other words, there may be people who wish to sell apples at the current prices and cannot or there may be people who wish to buy apples at the current prices and cannot, but there are not simultaneously both unsatisfied sellers and unsatisfied buyers. Markets are sufficiently well organised that willing buyers and willing sellers can and do come together and consummate a trade very quickly, relative to the rate at which the disequilibrium adjustment equations operate (in the idealised abstraction, such deals are to be thought of as consummated instantaneously or outside of time). This requirement, while severe, seems to be a moderately reasonable one on information flows in a competitive economy; it is much less severe than the corresponding requirement in the Edgeworth Process.

Given this assumption, it follows that any individual who has a non-zero excess demand for a particular commodity finds that the aggregate excess demand for that commodity is of the same sign. Since prices adjust in the direction of aggregate excess demand, he finds that, outside of equilibrium, the things which he wishes to buy and cannot buy are getting more expensive, while the things which he wishes to sell and cannot sell are getting cheaper unless they are already free. Accordingly, he finds himself getting worse and worse off in the sense that his *target* utility, the utility which he expects to get if he can complete all his transactions, is going down. Accordingly, the sum of such target utilities will serve as a Lyapounov Function and quasi-stability can be proved.

Note the different roles played by utilities in the Edgeworth and Hahn Processes. In the Edgeworth Process the utilities actually achieved by individuals (that is, the utilities which they would attain if they now stopped trading) rise while trading is going on. In the Hahn Process, target utilities — the utilities which they would achieve if they could complete their transactions — fall out of equilibrium. One way of looking at it is to say that in disequilibrium plans are not all compatible and that, in the Hahn Process, the adjustment is such that people have to lower their expectations until equilibrium is reached and everyone can in fact attain the utility which he targets for.

One can go on from this to prove the global stability of the Hahn Process in pure exchange by establishing or assuming the boundedness of prices and then showing that all limit points of any sequence starting from a given set of initial conditions are the same. The latter point is proved rather nicely by using strict quasi-concavity of the indifference maps,[16] but I shall not linger over the details now.

So far, so good. Unfortunately, there are problems with this simple version (beyond those common to all such processes, which I discuss below). Thus, suppose that there are at least three commodities, say apples, bananas and carrots (the need for at least three arises from Walras' Law). Suppose that, at current prices, apples and bananas are both in aggregate excess supply. There may be an individual who would like to buy bananas but has nothing to offer for them but apples. If he is one of the unlucky ones who cannot find a buyer for his apples, then, regardless of how easily he can find a willing banana seller, no trade will be consummated, for he can offer that seller nothing which the seller regards as having value. Out of equilibrium, this can occur even if apples have a positive price. No amount of efficiency in market organisation will get around this and the Hahn Process depends on it not occurring.

This possibility, which depends on the need to sell before you can buy, was first recognised by Clower (1965) among economic theorists working in a somewhat different context. It is well known to historians, however, that economies which rely on the Hahn Process can run into this difficulty. As the ancient document has it:[17]

Simple Simon met a pieman going to the fair.
Said Simple Simon to the pieman, 'Let me taste your ware.'
Said the pieman to Simple Simon, 'Show me first your penny.'
Said Simple Simon to the pieman, 'Indeed, I haven't any.'

It was not enough for Simple Simon and the pieman to be able to find each other. Trade still did not take place.

You will note, however, that the Simple Simon economy already had in it one feature which distinguished it from the models I have been talking about, the use of one commodity as the sole medium of exchange. No doubt reflecting on this, Arrow and Hahn (1971) were able not so much to solve as to isolate the Simple Simon problem by constructing a rather more satisfactory version of the Hahn Process model in which one commodity (which they happened to call 'money') serves as the only such medium. In that version, 'target' excess demands — the excess demands which would obtain without a money constraint — are distinguished from 'active' excess demands — the excess demands which are expressed by actual offers to buy or sell, offers to buy requiring money to back them up. It is aggregate *active* excess demands which then influence prices in equation (1). It is natural to take the Hahn Process assumption as applying to active demands since it then really does become merely one of market organisation. Arrow and Hahn were able to show the global stability of the resulting Hahn Process, provided that nobody ever runs out of money and that every individual who has money actively tries to satisfy some non-zero fraction of every non-zero target excess demand that he has.

The No Bankruptcy Assumption is, of course, very strong; moreover, it appears indispensable and it is hard to know how to ensure that it holds,[18] although, as we shall see, it becomes more palatable when we start to let individuals rather than auctioneers control prices. Moreover, the Arrow and Hahn treatment points up two more difficulties which are common to the entire literature but which now begin to surface more explicitly. While we have referred to them once, it is useful to mention them in the present context.

The first such difficulty concerns what I called the Present Action Postulate. Households in this model must act *now* to make some non-zero part of every non-zero target excess demand an active excess demand. Money must *now* be allocated to an attempt to buy a non-zero amount of every commodity which the household does not have enough of, even though the household may already have a large amount of that commodity and relatively little of another one which it also wants to buy. Note that it would be harder to get away with this if the household were simultaneously consuming its existing commodity stocks.

The Present Action Postulate seems as innocuous as it does in this context, however, mainly because we have already implicitly swallowed the camel of assuming that the household believes its transactions will be consummated before consumption time comes and is therefore indifferent about the order in which it attempts to complete them. This is a part of assuming that the household really does not notice that it is out of equilibrium, that it formulates its demands on the assumption that prices will not change, and that it rather stupidly does not notice what is really going on. Such problems are the natural consequence of having a good equilibrium theory and not knowing much about individual reactions to disequilibrium.

Nevertheless, the Arrow–Hahn introduction of money as a sole medium of exchange is a considerable step forward. It clarifies and isolates the Simple Simon problem in the No Bankruptcy Assumption; it begins to bring forward the problems just discussed; it has a modicum of realism, if not of monetary theory; and it is probably indispensable for the introduction of firms into trading processes.

This last point is true for the following reason. Without the introduction of money, firms would value their holdings the same whether or not they sold them. A firm which produced a large stock of toothpaste, for example, would feel it was doing well in terms of profits if toothpaste had a high price. There would be nothing (absent further assumptions) to make it interested in selling the toothpaste as opposed to holding it and therefore no reason why the presence of that stock of toothpaste should affect the price any more than the presence of target demands which are not active. Requiring firms to keep score in money which is needed by themselves and especially their owners to back up demands assures that firms actively participate in the market process.

As it happens, the Hahn Process Model can be fairly readily extended to acommodate firms (but not yet production). To this I now turn.

FIRMS (BUT NO PRODUCTION) IN THE HAHN PROCESS[19]

The obvious first question that occurs when one seeks to introduce firms into a model which permits trading but no other economic activity to take place before equilibrium is reached is that of what it is that firms are to trade. In pure exchange, the stocks of commodities are fixed and one can think of households swapping titles to various amounts of them; with firms in the picture, however, one has to think of the transformation of inputs into outputs as at least envisioned by the participants in the economy, even if we do not allow that transformation to take place during the adjustment process.

The answer (which will continue to be helpful when production is introduced) is to think of firms as trading in commitments to buy inputs and sell outputs. Each firm has access to a production technology which describes the efficient ways in which inputs can be turned into outputs. While trading is going on, the firm contracts for inputs and commits itself to deliver outputs. Payment for all such contracts and commitments is made when they are signed, but delivery and production do not take place until equilibrium is reached. The firm trades in such commitments at current prices, seeking to maximise profits while ending up in a technologically feasible position. Since, out of equilibrium, a firm may not be able to complete all the transactions which it attempts, it will sometimes be the case that the firm finds it has committed itself to sell outputs without in fact having acquired the inputs which would enable it to do so. In that case, it must go back on the market and either acquire the needed inputs or buy up output commitments, whichever is most profitable at the ruling (presumably changed) prices. Similarly, a firm which has overacquired input commitments will wish either to sell them off again or to sell further output commitments, whichever is most profitable.

Firms in this model pay out some or all (but not more than) their actually realised profits as dividends to their owners, although they may (and sometimes must) keep some retained earnings for transactions purposes so long as equilibrium has not been reached (the No Bankruptcy Assumption). Since everyone continues to believe that all transactions will be completed at current prices, however, households maximise their utilities and formulate their *target* excess demands on the basis not of received dividends but of the expected total earnings of the firms they own. Dividends only matter in providing some of the cash which backs up target demands and makes them active. Indeed, it is easy to see that Walras' Law only holds in terms of target demands and target profits and not in terms of active demands and actual profits. It is also not hard to show that Walras' Law requires that all profits be paid out to owners in equilibrium, so that any apparent tension in these matters, important as it is, is a disequilibrium one.

Now, what about stability in such a Hahn Process model? A crucial feature of firms which differentiates them from households is that their maximand, profits, involves prices as well as quantities directly. Nevertheless, it remains true of the firm, as of the household, that everything which it wishes to buy but has not yet bought is getting more expensive while every non-free good which it would like to sell is getting cheaper. Accordingly, target profits are going down out of equilibrium.

Given this fact, one can go on to consider the target utility of the household. So far as its trading is concerned, it too is caught in the same Hahn Process trap of wanting to buy goods whose prices are going up and wanting to sell goods whose prices are going down. The only way it can be getting better off (in terms of target utility) is for the firms it owns to be becoming more profitable. We have just seen, however, that firms become less profitable rather than more and accordingly, it is still the case, as it was in pure exchange, that the target utilities of households are falling out of equilibrium. This means that one can once again take the sum of target utilities as a Lyapounov function and establish quasi-stability.

A full proof of the global stability of the adjustment process, however, requires two more steps, as remarked above: first, a proof of compactness; and second, a proof either that all limit points are locally isolated or that, given the initial conditions, all limit points are the same. I have rather slighted these steps in my earlier discussion, and it now seems appropriate to spend a little time on them since the introduction of firms begins to make them rather more complicated.

First, let us consider the issue of compactness. Since we have so far been working in Euclidean space, this is basically an issue of boundedness, for, if we can show that the variables remain in a bounded set, there is no harm in taking them to lie in its closure. The basic variables here are the prices and the stocks or commitments of the commodities held by individual households and individual firms.

The problems involved in assuring that prices remain bounded are basically unaffected by the introduction of firms and, indeed, are the same for trading processes as they are for tâtonnement. (This is largely because the same price-adjustment process (1) is used in both cases.) Aside from the alternative of assuming directly that prices are bounded — which is not all that unappealing — there are two known ways of going about it. The first of these is to consider the classic case in which the price adjustment functions, $H^i(\cdot)$, which appear on the right-hand side of (1) are linear through the origin. Whether we work in terms of absolute prices or in terms of prices relative to that of the numéraire (money in the Hahn Process model), it is not hard to show that (provided the numéraire would be in excess demand if it were priced at zero — an innocuous assumption) there is a hyperellipsoid in the space of the prices, outside of which prices cannot go. If the units in which quantities are measured are appropriately chosen, this amounts to showing that the sum of squares of the prices is bounded above. The same result can be extended to the case in which the price adjustment functions, $H^i(\cdot)$, are not necessarily linear themselves, but are bounded above by rays through the origin.

This is a strong result which basically depends on limiting speeds of adjustment in a particular way. Boundedness of relative prices can also be accomplished without such a limitation if one is willing to restrict demands. Thus, it is possible to show boundedness if one is willing to assume that whenever any subset of prices become high enough relative to all others, then the highest-priced good is in excess supply. Such an assumption attempts to capture the notion that it is possible to price oneself out of the market, but it is pretty strong.[20]

Boundedness of individual commodity or commitment holdings is a potentially more delicate matter than that of prices, although it is relatively simple in the contexts we have so far considered. Under pure exchange there is, of course, no problem since total commodity stocks do not change. Once we introduce firms, however, there is at least the large potential difficulty that firms may wish to undertake unbounded commitments, even though they cannot in fact do so. This would occur, for example, under constant returns since firms are not supposed to take resource limitations into account directly. As it happens, however, constant returns have already had to be ruled out of the models we have been discussing because of the necessity of having excess demands continuous functions of the prices and, indeed, in the context of the Hahn Process model with firms but no production, it is in any case necessary to assume that each firm has a unique profit-maximising position continuous in the prices. Since prices are to be bounded, such an assumption already implies boundedness of commitments and gets us out of the problem.

It would be very shortsighted to let it go at that, however, both because an extension to constant returns is a clear direction for further work and because the introduction of consumption and production to be discussed below makes the problem one of bounding the integral of commitments rather than commitments themselves. The most attractive way to ensure boundedness of commitments (or their integrals) without the strong assumptions just mentioned seems to me to be to use what we know about the role of the price system in a world of limited resources. As resources become scarce, their prices ought to rise. Accordingly, it is undoubtedly possible to show that unbounded commitments cannot be profitable since the unit costs of production would rise above the price at which output can be sold. Such an argument would require both the boundedness of prices and a fairly careful specification of the technology, making limited or primary resources a non-negligibly required input for every good, either directly or indirectly. It also turns out to require care in restricting speeds of adjustment. Whoever works out the constant returns case is going to have to pay more detailed attention to this than I have, since I have hitherto been content with sketching out the way such an argument should go.

Returning now to stability in the Hahn Process model with firms (but no production), the final step is a proof that, given the initial conditions, all limit points are the same. In the case of pure exchange, Arrow and Hahn (1971) were able to do this by using the strict quasi-concavity of the utility function. I have adapted their proof to the present case. What is involved is essentially the use of the fact that, at equilibrium prices, households are minimising expenditure for given utilities while firms are maximising profits, given their technologies. However, since target profits and target utilities decline out of equilibrium, and since every limit point is an equilibrium (quasi-stability), each household has the same target utility and each firm the same target profits at any one limit point equilibrium as at any other limit point equilibrium. At the prices of equilibrium A, therefore, the commitments of equilibrium B would be worth less to firms than the commitments of equilibrium A itself. On the other hand, those same equilibrium B commitments must cost households more than would those of equilibrium A. Since the net commitments of the production sector are made only to the household sector, and vice versa, this establishes a contradiction in a rather pretty way unless the equilibria are the same as regards commitments. One can then go on and complete the proof by a fairly straightforward argument as to prices and marginal rates of substitution.

CONSUMPTION AND PRODUCTION OUT OF EQUILIBRIUM[21]

We now come to the obviously important step of allowing real economic activities other than trading to go on before equilibrium is reached. While, as I shall describe in a moment, I have produced a Hahn Process model in which disequilibrium consumption and production are allowed to take place, perhaps the most illuminating part of working on such a model turns out to be not the resulting stability proof, but the way in which a number of underlying issues are pushed into the open when consumption and production are to be included.

Let me begin, however, by describing the way in which the model just referred to operates. Every household has a utility function (it is convenient to work in continuous time) which is defined over its past and future consumption profiles of all commodities. At any given moment, however, the past is irreversible and the household can only attempt to optimise with respect to consumption yet to be undertaken. (In a sense, the utility function of the household is allowed to change as a result of its past consumption.) It performs such optimisation assuming that current prices will last forever and subject to a budget constraint which involves its share of the target profits which it expects to receive from firms.

Firms are analogously situated. The technological opportunities open to a firm at any given time depend in part on the input and output actions it has taken in the past. Given its own past actions, the firm attempts to maximise profits with respect to its planned pattern of inputs and outputs, also assuming that prices will be constant.

The essential difference between this model and the preceding one with firms but no production is that firms and households take irreversible actions which change their optimising actions later on. In the case of the household, such actions change the utility function; in the case of the firms, they change the set of feasible production points; in both cases, they change the stock of commodities available for trade. We know, however, that if such actions were reversible, then target profits for firms and target utilities for individuals would decline out of equilibrium, given the other assumptions of the Hahn Process model, for we would then be back in the previous case. However, profits for firms or utilities for households can never be higher given the restrictions imposed by irreversible actions than they would be could those actions be undone at will. It is therefore not hard to show that target profits for firms and target utilities for households are still declining out of equilibrium; indeed, the declining utility and profit feature of the Hahn Process makes it particularly adaptable to the case of disequilibrium consumption and production.

Given this result, it is possible to go on to prove the global stability of the adjustment process along the lines of the previous model, although there are some technically rather tricky details. These are related to two properties of equilibrium in this model which are of substantive interest and which I shall thus briefly describe.

The first of these properties is that trade actually ceases at equilibrium. In other words, equilibrium does not involve a situation in which everyone finds that he is able to go on trading as he planned to do at prices which he expected to rule, but rather a situation in which all trades have already taken place and the only remaining activities are the carrying out of consumption plans by households and the meeting of already paid for commitments by firms.

Second, because the optimising positions of households and firms change as a result of irreversible actions, the set of competitive equilibria at any moment depends not merely on current possessions and prices but also on past history. Hence the process converges to an equilibrium which is also moving.

As already stated, however, the interesting thing about this model may not be the results but the problems which it pushes to the fore. I have already discussed some of these in the context of earlier work, but it is now appropriate to consider them again.

The first of these problems has to do with the dating of commodities. It is common and sensible to suppose that the same commodity at two different dates is to be treated as two different commodities. On this view, dates on commodities matter.

The question arises, however, of whether or not the dates on commodities are reached during the adjustment process. So long as we remain in the unreal world of tâtonnement and even so long as we permit trading but no other activity out of equilibrium, we can suppose that those dates are not reached, although this is a bit sticky in the latter case. As soon as we permit production and consumption to take place during the adjustment process, however, we are forced to assume that some commodity dates are reached before equilibrium. One cannot now consume tomorrow's toothpaste.

The reason that this creates a difficulty lies in the fact that trading in *past* as opposed to *future* goods does not take place combined with the assumption that participants expect their trades to be consummated and fail to realise the disequilibrium nature of their circumstances. Hence, at the moment that a particular commodity date is passed, trading in that commodity is suspended and, out of equilibrium, there will be individuals who expect to trade further in that commodity and now suddenly realise that they cannot do so. Such individuals will now have to reoptimise subject to the suddenly imposed constraint that they are stuck with whatever they have of the dated commodity in question. Since, out of equilibrium, that constraint will be unexpected and will generally matter, its imposition can easily cause a discontinuity in the excess demand functions. This violates Lipschitz Conditions and removes the mathematical foundation for most stability analysis.

Now we know perfectly well why this problem sounds somewhat contrived. It seems obviously unreasonable for someone to care at midnight on 31 December that he cannot buy last year's toothpaste when he can obviously buy a perfect substitute, namely, this year's toothpaste. A little reflection, however, reveals that this is not an adequate way out of the difficulty. The reason that I am generally indifferent between buying last year's and buying this year's toothpaste as of the transitional moment is that I generally find that they are trading for the same price as of that moment. There are, of course, excellent reasons why that should be so, but they are mostly *equilibrium* reasons. There is certainly nothing in the price adjustment mechanisms of the models so far discussed that guarantees that prices will come together by the time the transition takes place. It is not merely a matter of permitting arbitrage but also of building a model in which arbitrage is sufficiently effective to erase such discrepancies by the crucial times. No one has yet done this and it does not appear to be particularly easy.[22]

One way around this difficulty may be to look more closely at the price adjustment process which we have been using. Suppose we abandon the fictional auctioneer and allow sellers to fix their own prices with buyers searching for the optimal price, a class of models which I discuss below. Then it is natural to identify commodities not merely by physical description and by date but also by the name of the dealer who sells them. If we do that we run into other difficulties, but we may evade the dated commodity problem, for, with a single individual adjusting the price of today's and tomorrow's toothpaste and also seeking to trade in those goods, arbitrage will in fact be instantaneous. Such an individual will take care to see that those prices come together as today blends into tomorrow, for it will be to his advantage to do so.

I cannot say, however, that I have worked out such a model and, indeed, in the model described above, I assumed away the dated commodities problem by assuming that all transitional moments are smooth or, in the extreme case, that future and spot prices for the same commodity are identical so that there are no dated commodities. This is obviously unsatisfactory and it exacerbates another problem, that of the Present Action Postulate.

We have already seen that it is crucial in a model in which prices are driven by excess demands that such demands be expressed currently. Just as demands which are not backed up with purchasing power can have no effect on price, so too demands which remain merely gleams in the eye of the demander can have no effect. Yet all stability proofs assume that it is the excess demands derived from optimising calculations that the demander attempts to exercise at least to some degree. We must now examine this more closely.

Let us begin with households. In all the models we have considered, participants believe that current prices will rule forever, since they are not aware of disequilibrium. This means that a household believes that it can always trade toothpaste at the current price. If it currently has a sufficient stock of toothpaste to satisfy its needs for some time to come but expects to need toothpaste sometime in the future, why should it *now* begin to acquire the extra toothpaste rather than wait until it is needed? (I abstract from questions of perishability and storage costs.) This seems particularly strange if we allow the household sufficient consciousness of what is going on that it becomes aware that it has a cash constraint. Indeed, since the household expects to be able to trade at the same price forever, its purchase plans are not determined even though its consumption pattern is, since it can buy more toothpaste than it needs and sell off the excess later or do the reverse, acquiring cash in the process.

This problem is present whether or not commodities are dated but is worse if they are not than if they are. It is bad enough to require that a household which expects to need toothpaste in 1980 should immediately enter the futures market for 1980 toothpaste and attempt to acquire it; it seems even more unreasonable to require that such a household should attempt to make such acquisitions in a world without dated commodities or futures markets by immediately entering the spot market for toothpaste. The best that can be said for this is that it forces the household to take a particular one of a set of equally optimal actions, given the assumptions under which it operates. Some vague notions as to transactions costs can be imported from outside those assumptions to justify this.

Unfortunately, not even such handwaving will do for firms, if commodities are not dated. For firms, the Present Action Postulate requires that they look into the future and consider whether they will end up being a net supplier or purchaser of any given commodity. If they find that over all future time it is best for them to sell a particular commodity, then they have to begin to offer it for sale right away. This is unreasonable both because their output of that commodity may not become positive for a long time to come and because it rules out technologies in which a given firm can find it optimal at given stationary prices first to buy a good for use as an input and then later to produce more of it as an output. Such problems are less when commodities are dated but, even then, the problems remain the same as for households.

Clearly, a principal source of such difficulties is the continuing assumption that participants fail to realise that they are in disequilibrium. Indeed, the most convincing argument that I know of in favor of the Present Action Postulate depends on allowing some such realisation. In the presence of the Hahn Process, any participant hanging back from *full* present action (no matter how small) to satisfy each of his excess demands will quickly find that prices are changing perversely (from his point of view) and that he had better act before things get worse.

Nevertheless, such a way out of the problem requires us to step outside the model and allow consciousness of disequilibrium. Could we do this adequately, it would be a great advance. However, we have no adequate theory of disequilibrium behaviour and all these models impose equilibrium-derived behaviour on a disequilibrium process. This is obviously unsatisfactory wherever it appears.

INDIVIDUAL PRICE ADJUSTMENT

For my final topic, I consider the question of dispensing with the fictional auctioneer who lurks behind the price adjustment process (1) and allowing individuals to set prices. This is, I believe, a very deep matter, closely related to the problem of how to allow consciousness of disequilibrium to occur in the behavioural assumptions of stability models. For, as I have already remarked, in a world in which everyone assumes that prices are given, how do prices ever change? Indeed, it is a very serious question whether or not one can have individualistic price-setting models together with consciousness of disequilibrium and still end up at the competitive equilibrium. This is as much of a problem for analyses of single markets as it is for general equilibrium analysis, although we perhaps know more about it in the partial context.

The obvious thing to do, if one is going to have individual price adjustment, is to assume that participants on one side of each market set their own prices and then that participants on the other side search over prices to find the most advantageous one.[23] For convenience, I shall speak of the price setters as the sellers and of the searchers as the buyers, but there is no reason why it can't be the other way round in particular markets.

If one considers such a model in the general equilibrium context in which we have been working,[24] it becomes natural to deal with the wares of different sellers as different commodities, even if they are physically identical. This, of course, raises the issue of whether or not one can ensure that the prices of two such 'seller-differing' commodities (i.e. the prices charged for the same commodity by two different sellers) will be the same in equilibrium. Not surprisingly, they will be if buyers are good at searching and they will not be if some sellers have persistent locational advantages in terms of buyer search, in which case the difference between the commodities is in some sense real even in equilibrium.

The interesting thing about distinguishing commodities in this way, however, is that, if one does so, the Hahn Process assumption becomes so natural as almost to be compelled. In such a context, that assumption amounts to saying that, at any one time, if a given seller (who is the only one on the supply side of the market for the commodity he sells) finds that he cannot sell as much as he would like to sell at the price he sets, then there are not also buyers (with money) who know about him and would like to buy more from him at that price. Similarly, if there are such buyers, then the seller can sell all he wants. This is so clearly reasonable as to provide an independent very strong reason for interest in the Hahn Process.

There is another reason as well which stems from assuming individual price adjustment. Perhaps the most bothersome assumption in the Hahn Process model is that of No Bankruptcy, that participants do not run out of money before equilibrium is reached. Now, when prices are controlled anonymously, there are two ways that individuals can run out of money. First, they may have spent all their money and have for sale only things now valued at zero prices; second, they may have spent all their money and have for sale things which have positive prices but which are in oversupply. There is nothing about individual price adjustment which takes care of the case in which someone is offering a zero-priced good, but the other case, of goods with positive prices but in oversupply can be handled. The reason for this is that such cases are essentially ones in which a seller is pricing himself out of the market. When prices are anonymously controlled, the seller can do nothing about this, but when he has control over his own price he can lower it and can lower it the more quickly the closer he is to bankruptcy. Hence the No Bankruptcy assumption, while still strong, becomes more palatable when we allow individual price setting to take place.

Thus the Hahn Process, for two reasons, becomes an appealing one in an individualistic price adjustment context. Indeed, I have shown (Fisher, 1972a) that (with some complications involving the switching of buyers among sellers as search proceeds) the Arrow—Hahn version of the Hahn Process in pure exchange can be extended to allow individual price adjustment while still proving stability. There seems little doubt that the same can be done for the more complicated versions involving firms, consumption, and production which I have already discussed.

There is one big catch to this, however, and that is the issue of just how individuals set prices in disequilibrium. The extension of the Hahn Process results to individual price adjustment just mentioned depends on sellers being rather foolish about what is happening. It requires each seller to set a price believing that there is a market equilibrium price and then to adjust that price up or down depending on whether he finds he can sell more or less than he wished at that price. In other words, the seller behaves like a little auctioneer and adjusts his own price according to the excess demand which occurs on his own personalised market. While one can rationalise such behaviour in terms of a rule of thumb for finding an unknown equilibrium price, this really is not very plausible. As Rothschild (1973) has pointed out, not only is it unreasonable to make sellers act while setting such prices just as they would if they were certain that they had set equilibrium prices but also it is hard to suppose that sellers fail to notice that their demand curves are not flat and that the number of searching buyers who attempt to purchase from them depends on the prices they set.

These difficulties, of course, are but part of the general one to which I have already referred, namely, that all these models make the participants base their behaviour on the obviously erroneous belief that equilibrium has been reached and their transactions will be consummated. We simply lack a satisfactory theory of individual behaviour in disequilibrium which is powerful enough to give general equilibrium stability results. Nevertheless, the problem seems particularly acute as regards price adjustment behaviour, perhaps just because we do have some notion as to how price setters ought to behave in such a situation. Putting aside the uncertainty issue (which is very difficult) it appears evident that sellers facing a declining demand curve, as these do, ought to behave as monopolies.

What happens if they do? Is it nevertheless possible to get convergence to competitive equilibrium or does some residual monopolistic element remain in any search model?[25] So far as general equilibrium is concerned, this is an important but wholly open question. The problem, however, arises also in the context of a single market and here one seems able to make a little progress.[26]

Let me thus restate the problem in the context of a single market so as to emphasise how fundamental it is. Just about the first thing any new student of economics encounters is a demonstration that competitive markets end up where supply equals demand. He is told that, if price is such that supply exceeds demand, then there will be unsold goods and sellers will offer lower prices to get rid of them; similarly, if demand exceeds supply, unsatisfied buyers will bid up the price. This basic idea lies behind the price-adjustment process (1) which we have been discussing. Like that process, however, it presupposes a model of how price gets changed out of equilibrium and it is hard to come to grips with this in a context in which everyone takes price as given. Even at this level, we lack a satisfactory fully rigorous disequilibrium model of price adjustment.

Suppose then that we try to build such a model by allowing sellers to set prices and buyers to search for low prices. If sellers behave in the not very sensible way indicated above for general equilibrium, setting prices, behaving as though their demand curves were flat, and adjusting prices according to whether or not they sell out all their supplies, then it is not hard to show, given reasonable restrictions on the search behaviour of buyers that the process can be made to converge to competitive equilibrium.[27]

Suppose, however, that we allow sellers to realise what is happening and to know the declining demand curves they face. Can we nevertheless get to competitive equilibrium allowing sellers to use that information in a profit maximising way? It turns out to be possible to tell such a story with a competitive ending, but the only such story which has been successfully told, so far as I know, turns out to be very complex and perhaps something of a fairy tale. It depends on demand curves flattening out at low enough relative prices as buyers find firms with usually low enough prices and on buyers gradually learning where the minimum price they can find can be expected to be if it persists long enough.[28] Whether even such unsatisfactory results can be carried over into the analysis of general equilibrium stability is an open question.

I end then where I began. The analysis of the stability of general (and even partial) equilibrium is in a far from satisfactory state. Although considerable progress has been made, such results as we have depend crucially on assuming that participants behave as though they were in equilibrium and do not realise what is going on. We lack a theory of convergence to equilibrium based on more reasonable individual behaviour largely because we usually do not know what more reasonable individual behaviour is. It is questionable whether a satisfactory model of individual disequilibrium behaviour will in fact converge to competitive equilibrium.

Nevertheless, the issue is one of great importance to economists. We all continually behave as though the subject had long ago satisfactorily converged.

NOTES

1. This paper was supported by National Science Foundation Grant GS 43185 to the Massachusetts Institute of Technology. Research on this paper was financed by the National Bureau of Economic Research, which is not, however, responsible for any of the statements made or views expressed herein. It forms part of an ongoing project which the Bureau hopes to publish when complete, pending the approval of its board of directors.
2. Arrow and Hurwicz (1958), and Arrow, Block and Hurwicz (1959). I discuss this work below. An excellent survey of work up to 1962 is given in Negishi (1962). Arrow and Hahn (1971) has a later discussion, also excellent.
3. Fortunately, a somewhat related technical problem involving the continuity of the adjustment process has recently been successfully handled. Claude Henry (1973a, b) has shown that the violation of Lipschitz Conditions involved in restricting prices to the positive orthant will still (under reasonable condtions) allow the existence of a continuous solution to (1), a matter which had previously to be taken on faith.
4. This important issue was raised by Koopmans (1957), among others.
5. Or that individuals who will want to sell that good in the future begin immediately to attempt to sell it. The problems involved are particularly nasty as to firms, as I shall later discuss.
6. Samuelson (1941, 1947) and including especially Metzler (1945).
7. That is, that a rise in the price of any one good increases the demand for every other, including income effects. For an analysis of what utility functions generate individual demand functions with this property, see Fisher (1972b).
8. A more rigorous treatment can be found in Arrow and Hahn (1971). Lyapounov's original paper is Lyapounov (1907). The curious may wish to know that his first method (for proving stability) was to solve the differential equations being studied, an alternative that is never available at the level of generality involved in general equilibrium analysis.
9. So named by Uzawa (1961).
10. The work of Debreu (1970) has shown that, for appropriate differentiability assumptions, local isolation of equilibria is true almost everywhere in the appropriate space of economies. Hence the last step in the stability argument might be made in this way. In practice, however, more direct results have generally been available.
11. This can be said to be because of income effects. It is worth remarking that it is easy to see that at least local stability would be guaranteed if there were no income effects in view of the negative semi-definiteness of the substitution matrix. See Arrow and Hahn (1971) for a more extended discussion.
12. More recently, Sonnenschein (1972, 1973) and Debreu (1974) have shown that the underlying economic derivation of the aggregate excess demand

functions does not imply any restrictions beyond homogeneity of degree zero and Walras' Law, thus eliminating any last forlorn hope that stability for tâtonnement processes might be aided by general rather than very special restrictions on the excess demand functions.

13 The principal works are Uzawa (1961) and Hahn (1962b). See also Arrow and Hahn (1971).
14 The parallel to the theory of the core is obvious. David Schmeidler has shown (in an unpublished communication) that if there is any mutually advantageous trade there is one involving at most the same number of participants as there are commodities. While interesting, such a result does not really get out of the difficulty, especially when commodities at different dates are counted as different commodities.
15 The original published paper is Hahn and Negishi (1962).
16 Arrow and Hahn (1971) were the first to do this in their somewhat more satisfactory version discussed below.
17 M. Goose (n.d.).
18 For some discussion of this, see Arrow and Hahn (1971). See also Fisher (1972a) discussed below.
19 This discussion is based on Fisher (1974).
20 The possibility of proving boundedness of prices this way was first noticed in Fisher (1972a) but the first correct version is in Fisher (1974).
21 This section is largely based on Fisher (unpublished).
22 Dated commodities also bring to the fore a somewhat related problem which is as follows. If we allow firms to deal in promises as well as in actual deliveries, then there may be participants who find that they cannot carry out their plans because promised delivery of goods does not materialise. When commodities are dated, this means that we must face the very complicated problem of insuring that contracts to produce and deliver 1984 toothpaste, for example, can be feasibly satisfied before 1985.
23 There is a burgeoning literature on such search models, most of which are not directly concerned with the question of whether one can end up in competitive equilibrium but with the no less interesting question of where one does in fact end up. For a good critical survey, see Rothschild (1973).
24 The ensuing discussion of the general equilibrium issues is drawn from Fisher (1972a).
25 As suggested by Arrow (1958).
26 Indeed, practically all the search literature is about single markets. The ensuing discussion is based on Fisher (1970) and especially (1973).
27 See Fisher (1970).
28 See Fisher (1973).

REFERENCES

Arrow, K.J. (1958) Toward a theory of price adjustment. In *The Allocation of Economic Resources*. Stanford: Stanford University Press.
Arrow, K.J., H.D. Block and L. Hurwicz (1959). On the stability of the competitive equilibrium II. *Econometrica* 27, 82–109.
Arrow, K.J. and F.H. Hahn (1971). *General Competitive Analysis*. San Francisco: Holden–Day; Edinburgh: Oliver & Boyd.
Arrow, K.J. and L. Hurwicz (1958). On the stability of the competitive equilibrium I. *Econometrica* 26, 522–52.

References

Clower, R.W. (1965). The Keynesian counterrevolution: a theoretical appraisal. In F.H. Hahn and F.P.R. Brechling (eds.), *The Theory of Interest Rates.* London: Macmillan; New York: St Martin's Press.

Debreu, G. (1970). Economies with a finite set of equilibria. *Econometrica* 38, 387–92.

Debreu, G. (1974). Excess demand functions. *Journal of Mathematical Economics* 1, 15–21.

Fisher, F.M. (1970). Quasi-competitive price adjustment by individual firms: a preliminary paper. *Journal of Economic Theory* 2, 195–206.

Fisher, F.M. (1972a). On price adjustment without an auctioneer. *Review of Economic Studies* 39, 1–15.

Fisher, F.M. (1972b). Gross substitutes and the utility function. *Journal of Economic Theory* 4, 82–7.

Fisher, F.M. (1973). Stability and competitive equilibrium in two models of search and individual price adjustment. *Journal of Economic Theory* 6, 446–70.

Fisher, F.M. (1974). The Hahn Process with firms but no production. *Econometrica* 42, 471–86.

Fisher, F.M. (unpublished). A non-tâtonnement process with production and consumption.

Goose, M. (n.d.). *Nursery Rhymes.* Various dates.

Hahn, F.H. (1958). Gross substitutes and the dynamic stability of general equilibrium. *Econometrica* 26, 169–70.

Hahn, F.H. (1962a). A stable adjustment process for a competitive economy. *Review of Economic Studies* 29, 62–5.

Hahn, F.H. (1962b). On the stability of pure exchange equilibrium. *International Economic Review* 3, 206–13.

Hahn, F.H. and T. Negishi (1962). A theorem on non-tâtonnement stability. *Econometrica* 30, 463–9.

Henry, C. (1973a). An existence theorem for a class of differential equations with multivalued right-hand side. *Journal of Mathematical Analysis and Applications* 41, 179–86.

Henry, C. (1973b). Problèmes d'existence et de Stabilité pour des processes dynamiques consideris en economie mathematique. Laboratoire d'Econometrie de L'Ecole Polytechnique.

Hicks, J. (1939). *Value and Capital.* Oxford: Clarendon Press.

Koopmans, T.C. (1957). *Three Essays on the State of Economic Science.* New York: McGraw-Hill.

Lyapounov, A. (1907). Problème général de la stabilité du mouvement. *Annales de la Faculte des Sciences de l'Université de Toulouse* 9, 203–474.

McFadden, D. (1966). Cost, revenue and profit functions: a cursory review. Working Paper 86. Berkeley: Institute of Business and Economic Research.

Metzler, L. (1945). The stability of multiple markets: the Hicks conditions. *Econometrica* 13, 277–92.

Negishi, T. (1958). A note on the stability of an economy where all goods are gross substitutes. *Econometrica* 26, 445–7.

Negishi, T. (1962). The stability of a competitive economy: a survey article. *Econometrica* 30, 635–69.

Rothschild, M. (1973). Models of market organization with imperfect information: a survey. *Journal of Political Economy* 81, 1283–308.

Samuelson, P.A. (1941). The stability of equilibrium. *Econometrica* 9, 97–120. Continued in 10 (1942), 1–25.

Samuelson, P.A. (1947). *Foundations of Economic Analysis*. Cambridge, Mass.: Harvard University Press.
Scarf, H. (1960). Some examples of global instability of the competitive equilibrium. *International Economic Review* **1**, 157–72.
Sonnenschein, H. (1972). Market excess demand functions. *Econometrica* **40**, 549–63.
Sonnenschein, H. (1973). Do Walras' identity and continuity characterize the class of community excess demand functions? *Journal of Economic Theory* **6**, 345–54.
Uzawa, H. (1961). The stability of dynamic processes. *Econometrica* **29**, 617–31.
Uzawa, H. (1962). On the stability of Edgeworth's barter process. *International Economic Review* **3**, 218–32.

PART TWO
MONEY, MACROECONOMICS AND WELFARE

2 UNEMPLOYMENT, INFLATION AND THE MICRO FOUNDATIONS OF MACROECONOMICS

TAKASHI NEGISHI[1]

INTRODUCTION

As is well recognised, neoclassical general equilibrium theory has not succeeded in effectively integrating microeconomics and macroeconomics. Micro and macro remain two distinct theories and the propositions in the latter are not derivable from those of the former. On the other hand, facing the coexistence of unemployment and inflation, we have to reconsider the determination of the level of prices in Keynesian economics. This seems to be a problem of the so-called micro foundations of macroeconomics cannot be founded on Walrasian ever, to argue that Keynesian macroeconomics cannot be founded on Walrasian microeconomics, that a new microeconomics should be built on the basis of macroeconomics, and that the level of absolute prices may be indeterminate to Keynesian economics and therefore subject to such factors as expectations.

What is macroeconomics? We may say, following Keynes (1936, p.4), that 'it is the pure theory of what determines the actual employment of the available resources'. In classical economics, however, the total volume of employed resources is determined by demand and supply schedules, each being obtained by the mere aggregation of the decision making of individual units. 'The amount of employment is fixed at the point where the utility of the marginal product balances the disutility of the marginal employment' (Keynes, 1936, p.11). In other words, the problem can be solved, at least theoretically, within the sphere of microeconomics. Macroeconomics can be completely derived from microeconomics by the merely mathematical operation of aggregation and there exist no essential difficulties in the micro foundations of macroeconomics. Classical macroeconomics is already well founded on, and therefore not independent of, microeconomics.

The classical theory of employment, however, does not admit of the possibility of involuntary unemployment. If involuntary unemployment does exist, the aggregate supply of labour willing to work for the current money wage is greater than the existing volume of employment. In other words, the latter is not on the Walrasian supply curve which is obtained through aggregating the result of well defined individual experiments antecedent to any consequence of the interaction of transactors in the market.[2] The result of any individual experiment is determinate without any reference to the demand conditions in the Walrasian world, i.e. if it is on the Walrasian schedule. In the Keynesian world, i.e. if it is off the Walrasian schedule, however, it is indeterminate, unless the demand conditions in the market are given in advance. Microeconomics is not antecedent to the imposition of demand conditions, and therefore not independent of macroeconomics. In contrast to classical macroeconomics, Keynesian macroeconomics cannot be founded on the aggregation of the Walrasian microscopic analysis of individual behaviour. We must rather start from macro analysis of the level of the employment determined by effective demand. Only then, may we 'micronise' it, i.e. develop a non-Walrasian analysis of individual behaviour which is based on the given data of macroeconomic conditions, the aggregate level of employment, output and effective demand.

THE PERCEIVED DEMAND CURVE AND THE KINKY DEMAND CURVE

The microeconomics which emerges in the micronisation of macroeconomics cannot be Walrasian, since Walrasian individual experiment is overdetermined when effective demand is introduced (see Leijonhufvud, 1974). In recent discussion of the microeconomic foundations of macroeconomics, the usual resolution of this overdeterminacy has been to replace the Walrasian individual experiment under given prices by constrained individual experiment under given prices and realised sales.[3] The introduction of given realised sales to the individual experiment, however, is not new in the neoclassical theory of prices and allocations. As a matter of fact, it is only in the case of perfect competition that the individual experiment is independent of the demand conditions, so that it can be carried out without introducing the constraint of realised sales. When competition is not perfect, individuals must perceive demand curves which should be based on the observation of the realised price and realised sales.[4] Only in the limiting case where the perceived demand curve is perfectly elastic, is it independent of the realised sale – the case of perfect competition.

The classical example of the perceived demand curve is the kinky demand curve in the theory of oligopoly. It was advanced independently and almost simultaneously by Hall and Hitch (1939) and Sweezy (1939) to explain observed price rigidity in oligopolistic industries. Sweezy clearly admitted that the perceived demand curve, which he called the imagined demand curve, can only be thought of with reference to a given *starting point*, i.e. a price–output combination which depends upon the previous history of the case. Since then, text books on price theory have been emphasising that fluctuations in marginal cost are not likely to affect output, and therefore price, since the marginal cost curve passes between the two parts of the discontinuous marginal revenue curve at the level of output corresponding to the point of the kink.[5] Oligopolistic price rigidity means, however, not rigidity at a fixed level of output but rigidity with a changing level of output. What is more important, therefore, is the fact that shifts in demand, i.e. the *starting point*, are considered not to affect the price at which the kink occurs but to shift the kink to the right or left. If marginal cost is not increasing rapidly, the equilibrium price remains unchanged while shifts in demand are absorbed in changes in the level of output.

If the product of each firm is differentiated and all the firms are oligopolistic ones to which the theory of the kinky demand curve can be applied, we can micronise macroeconomics on the basis of this theory of oligopoly. The level of output corresponding to the *starting point*, which Sweezy considered to be given historically, can be explained from the theory of effective demand in macroeconomics. Since prices remain unaltered in the face of changes in effective demand, fixprice in the sense of Hicks can be explained endogenously and need not be assumed.[6]

PERFECT COMPETITION AND DEMAND DEFICIENCY

Of course, we are not particularly interested in oligopoly.[7] As was pointed out by Arrow (1959), however, even in an objectively competitive market, individual firms are in the position of monopolists — as far as the imperfect elasticity of the perceived demand curves for their products is concerned — when the aggregate supply forthcoming at the market price exceeds the demand and individual firms cannot sell all they wish to at that price. Although Arrow did not mention it explicitly, the perceived demand curve must have a kink, since it should be infinitely elastic up to the level of output currently sold, i.e. the problem is whether to reduce the price or not. There is a formal similarity, therefore, between an oligopolistic firm and a competitive firm under demand deficiency, as far as the existence of a kink in the perceived demand curve is concerned. Since the product of the competitive firm in the same industry is not differentiated, however, the *starting point* of the perceived demand curve of the individual firm cannot be regarded as given, contrary to the case of an oligopolistic firm. We must, therefore, either assume that the aggregate demand for the industry is equally divided among identical firms, or equivalently, be concerned only with the case of the representative firm in our microeconomic analysis. Otherwise, microeconomic equilibrium of individual firms is indeterminate, since equilibrium conditions on the relation between marginal revenues and marginal costs are in the form of inequality rather than equality and therefore the equilibrium division of the given industrial output among firms is not uniquely determined. The microeconomics of the firm is not only dependent on the result of macroeconomics, i.e. the *starting point* of the industry as a whole, but also indeterminate except in the sense of the representative firm.

Analytically, the model of an individual firm is as follows. When y^* amount of output is being sold at the price of p^*, i.e. the *starting point* is (p^*, y^*), the firm perceives an inverse demand function for its output as

such that
$$p = f(y, p^*, y^*) \qquad (1)$$
$$p^* = f(y^*, p^*, y^*). \qquad (2)$$

Suppose the production function in the short run is given as
$$y = g(x) \qquad (3)$$
where x denotes the labour input. The firm will maximise its profits
$$py - wx \qquad (4)$$
with respect to x, being subject to the given w (the money wage rate) and to (1) and (3). When the market for the output of the firm is in equilibrium, i.e.
$$y = y^* \quad (p = p^*) \qquad (5)$$
the conditions which an equilibrium price and output must satisfy are given as
$$p(1 - e) \, dg/dx \leq w \qquad (6)$$
$$p \, dg/dx \geq w \qquad (7)$$
where e is the right-hand side elasticity of the inverse demand function perceived and defined as
$$e = -(\partial f/\partial y)(y/p) \qquad (8)$$
at the point of (p^*, y^*). Since the perceived demand function has a kink at (p^*, y^*), conditions (6) and (7) are derived respectively from the right-hand side and left-hand side conditions for profit maximisation.

As a matter of fact, what is given by the macroeconomic analysis of effective demand is not the individual values of y^*s, but the aggregate value to be supplied by all the firms (in the same industry). Since conditions (6) and (7) are inequalities, the distribution of the aggregate output among individual firms cannot be determined uniquely. It is less determinate, the less variable is (dg/dx) with respect to x. We shall assume, therefore, that all the firms are identical and the aggregate output is equally shared by each firm. In other words, each firm is a representative firm.

The readers may notice that the law of indifference is still assumed in the sense that each firm expects no possibility of price differentiation from other firms in the same industry. Generally speaking, this is a simplifying, but restrictive assumption in the case of demand deficiency, as was noted by Arrow (1959). In our case, however, it is not so restrictive since we have to assume that all the firms are identical in an industry. Then, each firm considers that others (in the same industry) will price the output in the same way.

If conditions (6) and (7) are satisfied with inequalities, p remains unchanged when aggregate demand changes, provided that changes are not large. Since (dg/dx) diminishes with the level of output, increases in demand will eventually bring forth the equality form of (7). Further increases in demand must result in an increase in p. On the other hand, decreases in demand bring forth the equality in (6) and the reduction of p, provided that $e < 1$. If $e > 1$, however, p remains unchanged.[8]

THE THEORY OF THE HOUSEHOLD UNDER INVOLUNTARY UNEMPLOYMENT

Although the theory of the kinky demand curve and the argument of Arrow were originally concerned with the case of firms, they must also be applied to the case of the household supplying labour services. In this case microscopic indeterminacy is still stronger, since the actual existence of the representative worker in the usual sense cannot be conceived when there exists involuntary unemployment, and part-time (un)employment is institutionally not allowed. Some workers are fully employed while the others are completely unemployed even though they are identically qualified. What we can assume is that those who are employed and those who are unemployed are chosen randomly, with an equal probability of employment for each identical worker. We can consider the actual existence of the representative worker only in such a probabilistic sense. In other words, we assume that the labour force is steadily turning over and no jobs are tenured at all. The level of aggregate employment, a macroscopic concept, is clearly determinate, but the actual employment of an individual worker, a microscopic concept, is indeterminate. Aggregate labour income is determinate but the income of a particular worker is indeterminate. We can talk only in terms of the expectation of individual employment and income, in so far as our model is purely an economic one and workers are assumed to be identical in economic qualifications.

Analytically, the model of the representative worker is as follows.[9] Let us suppose that those who are employed and those who are unemployed are chosen randomly, with the probability of employment for each worker being equal to the ratio of the number of employed workers to the total number of workers, i.e. $0 \leq k \leq 1$, which may be assumed to be a real number when the total number of workers is very large. When $100k^*$ per cent of workers are employed at the wage w^*, the inverse demand function for labour

$$w = F(k, w^*, k^*) \qquad (9)$$

such that

$$w^* = F(k^*, w^*, k^*) \qquad (10)$$

is perceived. If $k \leq k^*$, then $w = w^*$, irrespective of k. When the wage rate and the price of wage goods are respectively, w and p, the utility of employed workers is indicated by $U(w, p)$, the working hours being assumed to be institutionally fixed. On the other hand, the utility of being unemployed is denoted by $\bar{U}$. If workers are assumed to have no marketable assets, $U(w, p)$ is homogeneous of degree zero and $\bar{U}$ is constant with respect to p and w.

The condition for an underemployment equilibrium of the labour market and the household of the representative worker is obtained by the maximisation of the expected utility

$$kU(w, p) + (1 - k)\bar{U} \qquad (11)$$

with respect to k, being subject to given p and (9), when the expectation of the employment ratio is realised, i.e.

$$k = k^*(w = w^*). \qquad (12)$$

As a matter of fact, workers choose k indirectly by choosing w, i.e. by deciding whether to accept a wage cut in the face of unemployment. The wage cut will be accepted only when the loss of wage is compensated by the benefit of the increased opportunity of employment. If e is defined as

$$e = -(\partial F/\partial k)(k/w) \qquad (13)$$

at (w^*, k^*), the condition is

$$U(w, p) - \bar{U} \geq 0, \quad U(w, p) - \bar{U} - ew(\partial U(w, p)/\partial w) \leq 0, \qquad (14)$$

at (w^*, k^*). If the first condition is violated, workers are not satisfied with current w. On the other hand, a wage cut is not accepted in the face of unemployment, if the second condition is satisfied.

Let us assume that the wage elasticity of demand for labour is perceived constant for $k \geq k^*$, i.e. e is constant. Then, condition (14) on $w^*(= w)$ is independent of $k^*(= k)$. Since the left-hand side of (14) is homogeneous of degree zero with respect to w and p, employment can be increased with unchanged real wage by increasing effective demand. The unemployment considered here is, therefore, involuntary in the sense of Keynes.[10]

The money wage, however, rises when the first condition in (14) is violated by a rise in p, which is in turn caused by an increase in effective demand in (7), since depreciation in the depression makes the marginal productivity of labour low. A decrease in effective demand, on the other hand, causes a reduction in p in (6), if e is smaller than 1, and a fall in the money wage so as to keep the second condition satisfied in (14). This may partly explain the Phillips loop. The observations that changes in w do not, on average, compensate fully for changes in p can be explained by the fact that the conditions in (14) are inequalities and that e in (6) may be larger than 1 in some cases.

It may not be out of place to digress on the so-called disequilibrium theory of unemployment developed by Alchian, Clower, Leijonhufvud and Patinkin. Leijonhufvud (1967), following Alchian, explains unemployment as a disequilibrium phenomenon caused by the fact that an unemployed person in one industry does not accept the offer of a job in a different industry with a lower wage rate than in the previous job, until his notion of a normal wage level is adjusted downward in the process of search for jobs with wage rates higher than currently offered. Similarly, the speculative demand for money is explained as a disequilibrium phenomenon due to the fact that the level of the normal rate of interest is higher than the current rate. Unemployment of labour and unemployment of loanable funds are elegantly and consistently explained as the reserved demand of suppliers on the basis of a single assumption, i.e. the inelasticity of normal or reservation prices with respect to current prices.

As far as unemployment is concerned, however, I do not think the theory fully explains involuntary unemployment caused by a general reduction of the level of effective demand. It can certainly explain the frictional unemployment which is due to the slow adjustment of workers to changes in the composition of effective demand. It cannot explain involuntary unemployment in the case in which excess supply of labour exists in every industry, as then the problem is not that of the adjustment of workers to different jobs with lower wage rates but that of the choice for workers between the same job with a lower wage rate and unemployment. Unemployment cannot be called involuntary if it is due to that fact that workers are seeking the same job with a higher wage than the one currently offered. Such unemployment may disappear when information on the current (not equilibrium) level of wage rates is perfect. The policy required for eliminating such unemployment is not necessarily Keynesian effective demand policy but the creation of public agencies to supply free information on the state of the labour market. The involuntary unemployment to be explained is the unemployment which remains even if the law of indifference prevails in the labour market and cannot be cured by anything less than Keynesian effective demand policy.

THE INDETERMINANCY OF ABSOLUTE PRICES

Let us sum up by emphasising that, in a Keynesian world, microeconomics is not conceivable unless the *starting point* is given by macroeconomics and that even then microeconomic equilibrium is less determinate than macroeconomic equilibrium. We cannot found macro on the basis of micro. We rather have to found micro on macro.

Why, then, should we micronise macroeconomics? It is, I think, to rationalise, i.e. to give more plausible explanations of some *ad hoc* assumptions in macroeconomics. One of these assumptions is the rigidity of the money wage rate. In the post-Keynesian theory of unemployment, it is a basic assumption to explain the existence of involuntary unemployment, i.e. the excess supply of labour services in equilibrium. It is true that there exist some empirical observations, like Phillips' (1958) data, which seems to support this assumption. In spite of Keynes, however, many empirical studies seem to agree that the money wage rate, far from being rigid, does fluctuate, particularly when the price of wage goods changes and that the real wage, rather than the money wage, is the more stable through the process of trade cycles (see, for example, Bhatia, 1961). It seems to be the independence of the money wage rate from the conditions of demand and supply in the labour market, and not the absolute rigidity of the money wage rate, which is concluded from the micronisation of Keynesian economics and is consistent with empirical observations. In other words, absolute prices may be indeterminate in the equilibrium model, though relative prices are determined in a rather narrow range and are fairly rigid in the face of a changing level of output.

In a world of Walrasian tâtonnement, the level of absolute prices in the full employment equilibrium is determinate, irrespective of the level of initial money prices if exogenous variables (i.e. the level of independent investment, the quantity of money, etc.) are given in terms of money. Doubling of absolute prices, for example, is impossible without violating the equilibrium conditions. In the Keynesian world, however, the level of absolute prices is indeterminate in the sense that a proportional rise of equilibrium prices is possible under fairly general assumptions without violating equilibrium conditions, for the level of output can be reduced so as to be consistent with the exogenously given level of monetary variables. Since absolute prices cannot be determined by the equilibrium conditions and the exogenously given monetary variables alone, they must also be dependent on the initial conditions or the *starting point* (initial money prices) of the adjustment process towards equilibrium in the given period (Hicksian week). Such initial money prices in the process may not necessarily be equilibrium prices in the previous period. They may be subject to the influence of expectations and may be different from the previous equilibrium prices if equilibrium prices in the successive periods have been changing in the recent past.

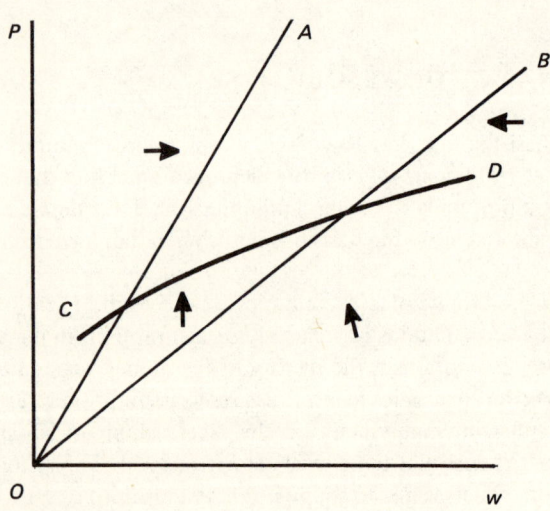

Figure 1

This can be shown by our model as follows. In figure 1, w is measured horizontally, while p is measured vertically. The level of the real wage which satisfies the equality form of the first condition in (14) is indicated by the line OA, and w will be raised in the labour market if the *starting point*, i.e. the combination of initial money prices (w, p) is located to the left of this line. The line OB indicates, on the other hand, the level of the real wage which corresponds to the equality form of the second condition in (14), and a wage cut will be accepted if the initial (w, p) is located to the right of this line.

To make the story simple, let us suppose that goods are malleable and can be used either to consume or to invest. Since workers have no assets, it is natural to assume that saving comes from profit. Then the equality of saving and investment is

$$s[pG(X) - wX] = I \qquad (15)$$

where s is the constant saving ratio, X is the aggregate level of employment, G is the aggregate production function corresponding to g in (3), and I is the level of investment exogenously given in terms of money. We can solve for the price level (p), the level of aggregate employment (X), and for the given wage level (w) by using (15) and the aggregate version of the equality form of (7),

$$p \, dG/dX = w. \qquad (16)$$

The curve CD indicates the values of p corresponding to different levels of w. The shape of this curve can be obtained by differentiating (15) and (16) with respect to w and solving for (dp/dw). In view of (16), we have

$$dp/dw = X/G, \quad (dp/dw)(w/p) < 1 \qquad (17)$$

i.e. CD is positively sloping with the elasticity being less than one. If the *starting point* is given below this curve, p must be raised.

If the elasticity e is less than one in (6), there will be another curve located above the curve CD which may impose a ceiling to the equilibrium values of p. If e is not less than 1 in (6), however, there will be no such curve, since (6) is always satisfied with inequality. Any combination (p, w) which is located to the right of OA, to the left of OB and above CD satisfies the equilibrium conditions (7) and (14). If for example, the starting (p, w) in the current period is proportionally above the unemployment equilibrium (p, w) in the previous period, other things being equal, the current equilibrium (p, w) will be proportionally higher than the previous equilibrium, since p is inelastic with respect to w along curve CD.

The same result will be obtained even if we consider that real investment I is given as a function of the rate of interest. Equation (15) is replaced by

$$s[pG(X) - wX] = pI(r) \qquad (18)$$

where r is the rate of interest. To determine the level of r, we add the equation which shows the equality of demand and supply of money,

$$L(r) \, pG(X) = M \qquad (19)$$

where M is the exogenously given supply of money and L corresponds to Marshallian k. We can solve (16), (18) and (19) for p, X and r when the value of w is specified. The correspondence between p and w is similar to the case of the curve CD, since we have

$$dp/dw > 0, \quad (dp/dw)(w/p) < 1 \qquad (20)$$

from the differentiation of (16), (18) and (19).

UNEMPLOYMENT AND INFLATION

The implication of this indeterminacy is that unemployment and inflation can coexist even if the market structure is ideal, i.e. perfectly competitive, when the pattern of expectations is unfortunate. The effect of traditional anti-inflation policy, i.e. the reduction of effective demand, is merely to reduce the level of output and not to mitigate the inflation due to expectations. An effect of expansion policy is, on the other hand, to accelerate the rate of inflation, since marginal cost is increasing.

Laidler (1973) insists, however, that there is nothing in recent experience of the coexistence of inflation and unemployment to contradict the orthodox view that inflation is caused by excess demand. 'Variations in the level of excess demand cause variations in the rate of inflation relative to the rate which is expected.' His theory can be written as

$$\Delta P = g(E - Y^*) + \Delta P^e_{-1} \qquad (21)$$

where E is aggregate real expenditure, Y^* is the full employment level of output, ΔP is the actual rate of inflation, ΔP^e_{-1} is the rate expected to hold between the previous period and the current period, and g is a sign-preserving function.

The conclusion of our theory may be reformulated in terms of the theory of Laidler that $g(E - Y^*)$ is zero for $E - Y^* < 0$, if the elasticity e in (6) above is larger than one. If there is no demand deficiency, e is zero under perfect competition. It will be larger, if the demand deficiency is larger. If e is small, the existence of an unemployment equilibrium may not be guaranteed while full employment equilibrium may be possible. The level of real expenditure will be restored through the reduction of p in (6) and of w in (14), even if p and w are high at the *starting point*. If e is large, however, the existence of an unemployment equilibrium can be proved (see Negishi, 1974b) and inflation based on expectations cannot be checked by the demand deficiency. If the economy is not competitive, the case is stronger since e is large even if the demand deficiency is small.

Following Leijonhufvud (1973), we may sum up our arguments as follows. The economic system behaves differently for large than for small displacements from the full employment path. Within some range from the path, which is called the corridor by Leijonhufvud, the elasticity e is smaller than one and the neoclassical adjustment mechanism may work. Outside the corridor, the elasticity e is larger than one and we have not only Keynesian unemployment equilibrium but also the coexistence of unemployment and inflation.

DISCUSSION: MICHAEL PARKIN[11]

This discussion is organised around three questions: first, has Professor Negishi succeeded in his aim of showing 'that the level of absolute prices may be indeterminate in Keynesian economics'? Second, what are the alternative approaches to the simultaneous analysis of inflation and unemployment and how does Professor Negishi's contribution relate to these? And third, if it can indeed be shown that the absolute price level (and its rate of change – the rate of inflation) are indeterminate in Keynesian economics, does that indicate a problem for Keynesian economics or a problem for the 'real world'? These questions are taken up in order.

First a semantic detail: I take it that by 'Keynesian economics' Professor Negishi means the economics of involuntary underemployment equilibrium arising from price–wage downward rigidities rather than from a zero elasticity of aggregate demand with respect to the absolute price level.[12] To see how Negishi reaches his conclusion of indeterminacy we can consider a simplified version of this model which suppresses an explicit analysis of the labour market (but makes assumptions about that market so that its role in the analysis is clear) and uses a simpler version of aggregate demand determination than that presented in the paper. Of central importance in making this simpler analysis go through is Negishi's assumption that all firms are identical (the role of this assumption will be critically appraised below). The alternative simpler model is analysed diagrammatically in figure 2. The horizontal axis measures the output of both the

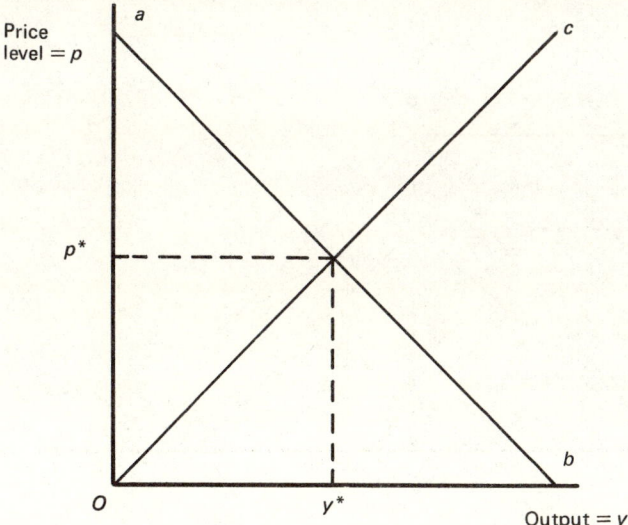

Figure 2

economy as a whole and that of an individual firm (by an appropriate scaling of units). The law of one price, implicit in the Negishi paper means that the vertical axis measures the money price level for the economy as a whole and as it faces each individual firm. The line ab is the aggregate demand function and, for simplicity, it is written 'eclectically' as:

$$p = F(y, z)$$

where **z** is the vector of shift parameters capturing monetary and fiscal policy and, if you wish, even 'animal spirits'. It is both the demand function facing the economy as a whole and that which, although not necessarily known to the individual firm, nevertheless determines the quantities that will actually be demanded from each firm at each price level. The line Oc is the aggregate supply function and the marginal cost function of the firm when the money wage rate is at the full Walrasian equilibrium level. The point (p^*, y^*) represents full equilibrium. Let the economy initially be in equilibrium and then let there be a cut in aggregate demand (a change in a z_i variable) so that ab moves to $a'b'$. Also, to focus only on the output market and to check the source of Negishi's underemployment equilibrium result, let the money wage rate instantly adjust to its new full Walrasian equilibrium level given the new level of aggregate demand. The aggregate supply (and marginal cost) curves move therefore to Oc'. Figure 3

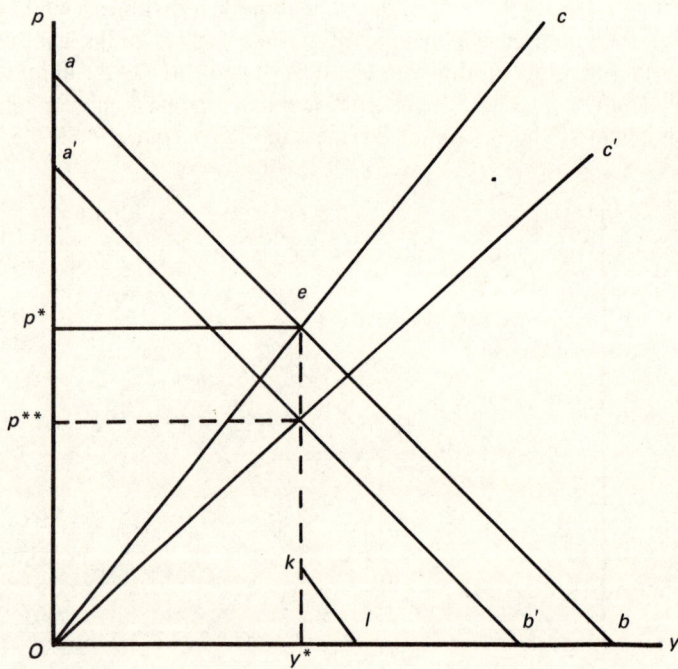

Figure 3

illustrates these shifts. The new full Walrasian equilibrium is (p^{**}, y^*). However, does the economy (and each firm in it) move to this equilibrium, given Negishi's assumption that, in the initial equilibrium situation, the firm perceives its demand function not as ab but as p^*eb, with a marginal revenue function ae, kl with a discontinuity at y^*? Under these assumptions, the firm will be facing a perceived demand function p^*eb and a marginal cost function Oc'. The firm's expected profit-maximising strategy is clearly to produce Oy^* since the new marginal cost curve cuts the break in the marginal revenue curve and this satisfies Negishi's conditions (6) and (7). However, with output remaining at y^* and demand at $a'b'$, the price level which clears the market will be p^{**} and a full Walrasian equilibrium will be reached immediately. What then is the source of Negishi's underemployment equilibrium results? It is clearly not his assumption of a kinked oligopoly type demand function. Rather, like all other versions of the Keynesian model, it is less than full adjustment of money wages. The simplest way to see this is to make the alternative extreme assumption that when aggregate demand falls from ab to $a'b'$, money wages remain constant at their initial level. With this assumption and the firms perceived demand function p^*eb the expected profit-maximising output level still remains y^*. However, the output market will now clear at price p_1 (Figure 4). At this price, the firm will believe it can sell as much as it likes up to the point d where the originally perceived demand curve becomes a constraint. The expected profit-maximising output, given p_1 is, however, y_1 and the firm is presumed to produce at that level. At that output the market-clearing price becomes p_2. Eventually, if the process is stable, the economy will settle down at (p_k, y_k) a stable underemployment equilibrium. Notice that there is no price level indeterminacy given the aggregate demand conditions and the money wage rate. If money wages react to prices (and excess demand) and if the process is stable, then full employment equilibrium is the only equilibrium. It is thus clear that the source of Negishi's underemployment equilibrium is his analysis of the labour market. It is also clear that indeterminacy arises only if we are not prepared to specify (and Negishi does not specify) how the kink points evolve through time from some initial disturbance of a full equilibrium position. It is particularly unfortunate that the underemployment equilibrium result depends so crucially on the labour market for the analysis of that market is, in my view, the least attractive aspect of Negishi's paper. It only seems to make sense if one monopoly union (acting paradoxically as if it were simulating a competitive solution) acts as the wage-setting agency on behalf of households.

The attraction of Negishi's paper is that it provides a story (if not an altogether convincing one) as to how involuntary underemployment equilibrium could arise. Its weakness is that it does not have a very convincing analysis of the labour market and it has no analysis of the microeconomics of wage and price *setting*. This stands in contrast to the main alternative strand in literature on the micro foundations of macroeconomics (of which, Phelps *et al.* (1970) still contains the best statement and summary), which is very strong on the microeconomics of price and wage setting but which is compatible only with voluntarily unemployed resources. The question arises therefore, as to which of the two approaches, that of Negishi, or that of the voluntary unemployment approach contained in the Phelps' volume, is the most promising, as a way forward for analysing the simultaneous determination of prices and output and employment. The Phelps *et al.* (1970) approach is clearly attractive in that it does specify precisely how firms set both wages and prices and how the quantities

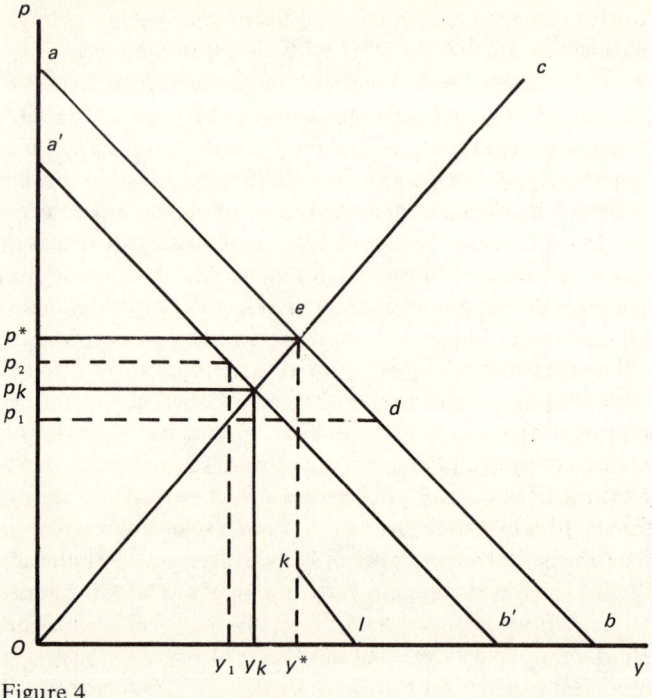

Figure 4

of output and employment respond to those prices and wages and further how the two sets of variables interact. It is noteworthy that in the Negishi approach firms simply make output decisions and households make labour supply decisions but markets in some anonymous sense determine both prices and wages. My own view is that the most fruitful way forward is to be found in what seems to be a natural extension of the Phelps et al. (1970) approach rather than the general equilibrium approach typified by Negishi's paper. Two primary reasons lead me to that conclusion. First, there already exists the beginnings of a literature stemming from the Phelps approach which seems capable of explaining both price and wage behaviour and rationing or involuntary quantity solutions. The best example of this approach in print is that of Barro (1972). By explicitly introducing stochastic demand for output (or stochastic supply of labour) and costs of price and wage setting and changing, it becomes optimal for the firm to enter into contracts for finite time periods and to set prices and wages on the basis of their expectations at the beginning of those periods. Should a situation develop during the period very differently from that which was originally envisaged then the firm will ration by not hiring as much labour as would like to work at the going wage rate or by not supplying as much output as households would like to buy at the going price level. Involuntary behaviour, therefore, ensues.

However, when the contract comes up for renewal the fact that a mistake was previously made affects the behaviour of prices and wages at the revision date.

This literature, in its infancy, seems to give rise to macroeconomic behaviour predictions which are different from those of Negishi and closer to the simple Laidler model which Negishi analyses in the final section of his paper. The second reason for suspecting this to be a more fruitful approach than that of Negishi is the critical way in which Negishi's results depend upon the assumption that all firms are identical. If there is a distribution of firms in the economy, and if in terms of Negishi's model, the kink point is not a single point common to all firms but one distributed across firms then there will be a price distribution across firms and an incentive for consumers to find the firm with the lowest price. Anything but a full Walrasian equilibrium seems inconceivable in such a world, although of course, it may take a very long time to arrive at it.

Finally, let me turn to the third question posed at the beginning, namely does the 'real world' appear to display price level indeterminacy? A full answer to this would require a great deal of space and the reader is referred to Parkin (1975) and Laidler and Parkin (1975). These papers summarise the state of the literature on the determination of wages and prices with a strong emphasis on the empirical literature. My own reading of that literature, as surveyed in those papers, is that prices and wages are by no means indeterminate and that it is difficult to see strong evidence for asymmetry in responses of prices and wages in excess demand and excess supply situations. Of course, expectations augmentation of price and wage reaction functions, which is now part of the standard way of modelling inflation, ensures that after a period of rising prices the rate of inflation will fall only sluggishly in the face of excess supply because of the lag in the response of expectations. However, it is important to identify this source of inertia correctly as an expectations lag and not an asymmetry or kink in the Walrasian price reaction function.

To conclude, Negishi has produced an extremely useful, clearly written, well argued analysis, showing that involuntary unemployment is a possible equilibrium state. It has not, however, convinced this critic that the general equilibrium foundation is the best foundation for the analysis of unemployment and inflation. The search literature and the so-called new microeconomics seems to be at least as and possibly more promising.

NOTES

1. The author is grateful for valuable comments given by J.M. Parkin, and participants in the AUTE Conference (1975), seminars in CEPREMAP, Universities of Cambridge, London (L.S.E.), Mannheim and Technische Hochschule Wein.
2. For the definition of individual experiment, see Patinkin (1964, p.12). See also Leijonhufvud (1974).
3. See Clower (1965), Barro and Grossman (1971), Morishima (1958, pp. 24–6).
4. On the perceived demand function, see Bushaw and Clower (1957, p. 181), and Negishi (1960–1). Dependence on realised sales is particularly necessary in a world of non-tâtonnement or non-recontract.

5   See for example, Baumol (1961, pp. 225–7), and Henderson and Quandt (1958, pp. 184–6).
6   See Hicks (1965, p. 78). 'Fixprice method has an inherent tendency to go macro.' Barro and Grossman (1971) assumes fixprice.
7   Leijonhufvud (1967) emphasised that Keynes (1936) was adamantly opposed to theories which blamed depressions on such obstacles to price adjustments as monopoly. We want to show that the market mechanism as such, even in its ideal form, does not resolve the problems of unemployment and inflation.
8   For details of a model of the firm under demand deficiency, see Negishi (1974a).
9   For the details of a model of the worker in unemployment equilibrium, see Negishi (1974a).
10 See Keynes (1936, pp. 14–16). It should be emphasised that the unemployment considered here is not the result of search for a wage higher than the current level. See also Leijonhufvud (1967) and Phelps (1970).
11 I am grateful to my colleages in the Manchester Inflation Workshop but especially to Malcolm Gray, William Peters and Michael Sumner for helpful discussions of Professor Negishi's paper.
12 This interpretation seems correct in view of equations (18) and (19) which indicate that Negishi does not want to do his analysis with a zero interest elasticity of expenditure and a 'liquidity trap'.

REFERENCES

Arrow, K.J. (1959). Towards a theory of price adjustment. In *The Allocation of Economic Resources*, pp. 41–51. Stanford

Arrow, K.J. (1967). Samuelson collected. *Journal of Political Economy* **75** 730–7.

Barro, R.J. (1972). A theory of monopolistic price adjustment. *Review of Economic Studies* **39**, 17–26.

Barro, R.J. and H.I. Grossman (1971). A general disequilibrium model of income and employment. *American Economic Review* **51**, 82–93.

Baumol, W.J. (1961). *Economic Theory and Operations Analysis*. Prentice Hall.

Bhatia, R.J. (1961). Unemployment and the rate of change of money earnings in the United States, 1900–1958. *Economica* **28**, 286–96.

Bushaw, D.W. and R.W. Clower (1957). *Introduction to Mathematical Economics*. Irwin.

Clower, R. (1965). The Keynesian counter-revolution: a theoretical appraisal. In *The Theory of Interest*, ed. F.H. Hahn and F.P.R. Brechling. Macmillan.

Hall, R.L. and C.J. Hitch (1939). Price theory and business behaviour. *Oxford Economic Papers* **2**, 12–45.

Henderson, J.M. and R.E: Quandt (1958). *Microeconomic Theory*. McGraw-Hill.

Hicks, J.R. (1965). *Capital and Growth*. Oxford.

Keynes, J.M. (1936). *The General Theory of Employment, Interest and Money*. Macmillan.

Laidler, D. (1973). The current inflation. In *After Keynes*, ed. J. Robinson. Basil Blackwell.

Laidler, D. and J.M. Parkin (1975). Inflation: a survey. *Economic Journal* **85**, 741–809.

Leijonhufvud, A. (1967). Keynes and the Keynesians; a suggested interpretation. *American Economic Review* **57**, 401–10.

Leijonhufvud, A. (1973). Effective demand failures. *Swedish Journal of Economics* **75**, 27–48.
Leijonhufvud, A. (1974). Keynes' employment function. *History of Political Economy* **6**, 164–70.
Morishima, M. (1958). *Shihonshugikeizai no Hendoriron (Dynamic Theory of Capitalist Economy)*. Sobunsha.
Negishi, T. (1960–1). Monopolistic competition and general equilibrium. *Review of Economic Studies* **28**, 196–201.
Negishi, T. (1974a). Involuntary unemployment and market imperfection. *Economic Studies Quarterly* **25**, 32–41.
Negishi, T. (1974b). Existence of an under-employment equilibrium. Conference on 'Equilibrium and Disequilibrium in Economic Theory' at the Institute of Advanced Studies, Vienna, 1974.
Parkin, J.M. (1975). The causes of inflation: recent contributions and current controversies. In *Current Economic Problems: Proceedings of the AUTE Conference, Manchester 1974*. Cambridge University Press.
Patinkin, D. (1964). *Money, Interest and Prices*. Harper and Row.
Phelps, E.S. et al. (1970). *Microeconomic Foundations of Employment and Inflation Theory*. Norton.
Phillips, A.W. (1958). The relationship between unemployment and the rate of change of money wage rates in the United Kingdom, 1861–1957. *Economica* **25**, 283–99.
Sweezy, P.M. (1939). Demand under conditions of oligopoly. *Journal of Political Economy* **47**, 568–73.

3 REAL CASH BALANCE AND THE OPTIMAL TAX STRUCTURE

A.L. MARTY

In recent years there has been an increasingly voluminous literature concerned with what tax minimises the welfare loss for a given government revenue.[1] However, this literature has not (with a few notable exceptions) dealt with the question of what is the optimal tax mix when one of the items which can be taxed is real cash balances.[2] That this is the case is somewhat surprising since considerable work in monetary theory is devoted to the measurement of the ratio of the marginal deadweight loss to the marginal increment to the revenue given an empirical specification of the demand function for real balances. It is the purpose of this paper to make explicit the relationships between the concepts used in these related areas of analysis. In the first part we show that a simple relationship, which depends only on the elasticity of demand for real balances, exists between the marginal deadweight loss and the marginal tax revenue. Since this relationship, which has been widely overlooked, avoids the necessity to evaluate a particular integral and holds for any general demand function for real balances, it is not only computationally convenient, but has the added advantage of facilitating comparison with optimal tax formulas which can also be couched in the form of elasticities.[3] The second section discusses the economic rationale for a recently proposed alternative definition of the tax revenue from the government's monopoly right to issue interest-free cash. Finally, in the third section, this new definition of the revenue is used to develop optimal tax rules when one of the items which can be taxed is real balances.

Let M = the nominal stock of money, ρ = the rate of growth of the nominal stock $(\dot{M}/M)$, P = the price level, $\Pi = \dot{P}/P$, Y = aggregate real income, $\dot{Y}/Y$ = the rate of growth of aggregate output, i = the money rate of interest, and r = the real rate. Under the assumption that the per capita income elasticity of demand for real balances is unity, it is well known that we can write $m = (M/P)/Y = \phi(i)$ and since $\rho = i - r + \lambda$, $m = \psi(\rho)$. The welfare loss taken as a ratio to income is

$$w = \int_0^\rho \psi(x)dx - \psi(\rho) + (r-\lambda)[\psi(0) - \rho\psi(\rho)],$$

where $\psi(0)$ is the stock of real balances held at the zero ρ. The marginal increment to the welfare loss is then

$$\frac{\partial w}{\partial \rho} = \psi'(\rho)(\lambda - r - \rho) = -i\psi'(\rho) = -i\phi'(i),$$

where i is the money rate equal to $\rho - \lambda + r$ at the given ρ. Since the traditional definition of the revenue is $G = \rho\psi(\rho)$, the marginal increment to revenue is

$$\frac{\partial G}{\partial \rho} = \rho\psi'(\rho) + \psi(\rho) = \rho\phi'(i) + \phi(i),$$

where i is the money rate equal to $\rho - r + \lambda$.

We note that the elasticity of demand for real balances with respect to i is $N_i = -i\phi'(i)/\phi(i)$ and the elasticity with respect to ρ is $N_\rho = -\rho\phi'(i)/\phi(i)$. It follows directly that

$$\frac{\dfrac{\partial w}{\partial \rho}}{\dfrac{\partial G}{\partial \rho}} = -\frac{i\phi'(i)}{\rho\phi'(i) + \phi(i)} = \frac{N_i}{1 - N_\rho}.$$

Clearly no integration is needed; all anyone needs to do is choose a particular ρ which given r and λ determines both Π and i, and evaluate the relevant elasticites.

There is, however, some reason for purposes of our analysis to use a definition of the revenue recently proposed by Phelps (1973) and Auernheimer (1974). The suggestion is that the proper measure of tax revenue is $(M/P)i$, rather than $\dot{M}/P$, so that maximum revenue is achieved when the elasticity of demand for real balances with respect to the money rate of interest is unity. Let us first consider Auernheimer's model and then turn to Phelps's more sophisticated rationale for reaching the same definition of the revenue.

Auernheimer points out that if the authorities want to implement a fully anticipated inflation, an 'honest' government must take steps to avoid the once-and-for-all jump in the price level associated with a movement from one equilibrium rate of price change to another. This 'blip' in the price level which is due to the once-and-for-all adjustment in real balances implies that over a finite time interval the rate of price change differs from that announced by the authorities. To avoid this change in the price level, the authorities buy (sell) nominal balances for goods when moving to a higher (lower) rate of inflation. The revenue is then taken as the sum of the stock adjustment in real balances at an instant of time and the flow into perpetuity $\dot{M}/P$; this flow, which is the traditional definition of the revenue, is discounted at the real rate to reduce it to a present discounted value. Thus, let m = real balances, Π = the anticipated rate of price change, r = the real rate, i = money rate, g_n = rate of population growth, g_y = the growth of output per capita, and finally define a growth factor $\gamma = g_n + \eta g_y$, where η is the per capita income elasticity of demand for real balances. Then

Real balances and the optimal tax structure 53

$$m_t = A \cdot e^{\gamma t} f(\Pi + r).$$

The present value of the revenue is

$$\underset{t=0}{R} = \int_0^\infty A \cdot e^{\gamma t} f(\Pi + r)(\Pi + \gamma) e^{-rt} dt + A[f(\Pi + r) - f(\Pi_0 + r)]$$

$$= A \cdot f(\Pi + r)(\Pi + \gamma) \int_0^\infty e^{-(\gamma - r)t} dt + A[f(\Pi + r) - f(\Pi_0 + r)].$$

If $r > \gamma$ the integral converges, then

$$R = A \cdot \frac{f(\Pi + r)(\Pi + \gamma)}{r - \gamma} + A[f(\Pi + r) - f(\Pi_0 + r)],$$

and

$$\frac{\partial R}{\partial \Pi} = A[(\Pi + \gamma)f'(\Pi + r) + f(\Pi + r) + f'(\Pi + r)(r - \gamma)] = 0$$

or

$$\frac{f'(\Pi + r)(\Pi + r)}{f(\Pi + r)} + 1 = 0,$$

i.e.

$$N_i = \frac{f'(\Pi + r)(\Pi + r)}{f(\Pi + r)} = -1.$$

Revenue is then maximised at a point where the elasticity of demand for real balances with respect to the money rate of interest is unity.

This model is open to logical objections. Why should the real rate which is treated as an exogenous constant be assumed greater than the growth factor γ so that the integral converges?[4] Why should the authorities take steps to prevent unanticipated changes in the price level? Why do they not take advantage of a lag in expectations in order to temporarily extract more revenue? Does the government stockpile goods which are sold (bought) when it chooses a higher (lower) rate of inflation? Are taxes changed to adjust real balances? It is a major advantage of the Phelps model that these matters of taxes, deficits and debt are explicitly part of the model and provide an economic rationale for the decision to offset the once-and-for-all change in prices when alternative rates of inflation are chosen. To this model we now turn.

Phelps claims that it is logically necessary to define the inflation tax within a context in which both wealth and income effects on the demand for consumption are held constant. In line with the modern treatment of differential taxation, we ask how the inflation tax can substitute for other taxes when income and wealth effects are held constant so that the time path of broad global variables such as net government expenditures and the ratio of investment to income are unaffected by the move to an alternate rate of inflation. Note that holding the ratio of physical investment to income constant as a matter of policy meets an objection to the traditional analysis, namely that it is improper to assume the real rate constant since a change in real balances produces a wealth effect. Unlike Phelps, I have couched the model in terms of comparisons between balanced growth paths as an aid to both verbal and geometrical exposition although the results hold fully along the transition from one steady state to another.

Define real disposable income as

$$Y_d/P = q_c/P + q_I/P + i_D D^*/P + v/P - T/P - \Pi D/P,$$

where q_c and q_I are the nominal output of consumption and investment goods equal to nominal national income (Y), D^*/P is the stock of government bonds held by the public, T/P is real taxes, v/P are transfers, i the money rate of interest, and D/P is the real stock of government debt held by the private sector — the sum of real cash balances and privately held government bonds. Since the real deficit $d/P = e/P + iD^*/P + v/P - T/P$ and the government purchases a proportion, h, of net national product, we get

$$Y_d/P = (Y/P)(1-h) + d/P - \Pi D/P = (Y/P)(1-h) + (d/dt)(D/P).$$

The gap between disposable income and net national product is the change per unit time in the real stock of government debt. Do policy instruments exist which enable the authorities to choose the rate of inflation (the level of liquidity) while holding invariant the gap between disposable income and net national product (the budget's contribution to income effects) as well as the real stock of outside wealth (the total of real balances, bond holdings and physical capital)? Let $g = D/L$, then

$$Y_D/PL = Y(1-h)/PL + (\dot{g}/g + \lambda - \Pi)g/P = \frac{Y(1-h)}{PL} + \frac{(\dot{g})}{P}\lambda,$$

where λ is the growth of real income (the growth of labour in efficiency units). In the steady state the growth of the per capita nominal debt $(\dot{g}/g)$ is equal to the rate of price change. Suppose the target is a lower rate of inflation; since the growth of the per capita nominal debt and the rate of inflation have been reduced by equal amounts, the real deficit has fallen by an amount equal to the depreciation of the debt and disposable income, on this account, is unchanged. It only remains for the authorities to impound wealth effects by keeping the real stock of debt, g/P, invariant at time zero when the lower rate of inflation is announced. To ensure this invariance, the central bank must make an open market purchase of cash for bonds of the requisite amount. Since the nominal stock of bonds in private hands declines by precisely the increase in nominal cash, the public acquires the extra real balances it desires to hold at the reduced money rate of interest and this acquisition is engineered by a rise in M rather than a fall in P. By offsetting the blip in the price level at time zero the authorities keep the real stock of debt constant and avoid disappointing expectations when the new rate of inflation is announced. Since consumption is a function of disposable income and wealth, and any effect of a lower rate of inflation on these variables is deliberately offset, the investment–income ratio remains unchanged which keeps the real rate of interest invariant. In this manner an economically meaningful rationale is provided for avoiding the blip in prices — a rationale which is absent in the Auernheimer model.

What happens to ordinary taxes, t/P, when the real deficit is reduced by an amount equal to the new lower depreciation of the debt? At first blush it may appear that since the deficit is lowered, ordinary taxes must be raised, but this would lose sight of the fact that, when a lower inflation rate is chosen, the authorities have exchanged non-interest-bearing cash for interest-bearing bonds; both the stock of bonds and the rate of interest paid on it are reduced. In the initial position the real deficit is

$$d^0/P_0 = \bar{e}/P_0 + \bar{v}/P_0 - t^0/P_0 + i_0(D/P_0 - M_0/P_0) = D/P_0(\Pi_0 + \lambda).$$

At the lower rate of inflation the real deficit is

$$d'/P_0 = \bar{e}/P_0 + \bar{v}/P_0 - t'/P_0 + i_1(D/P_0 - M_1/P_0) = D/P_0(\Pi_1 + \lambda),$$

where bars over the variables indicate unchanged time paths. Since the difference between the real deficits is equal to the unchanged real debt multiplied by the difference in the rate of depreciation of the debt, and noting that $i = \bar{r} + \Pi$, which we use to eliminate Π on the right of the above equations, we have

$$t_1/P_0 - t_0/P_0 = i_0 M_0/P_0 - i_1 M'/P_0.$$

It follows that if the elasticity of demand for real balances with respect to the money rate of interest is unity, ordinary taxes can remain unchanged, if the elasticity is greater (less) than unity, taxes can be reduced (increased) and still meet the requirements of a reduced deficit. In this model the inflation tax is simply the seignorage from the government's monopoly right to issue interest-free cash. $(M/P)i$ is the measure of the inflation tax and the maximum degree to which the inflation tax can substitute for ordinary taxes is at the point on the demand curve where the elasticity with respect to the money rate of interest is unity, precisely as in the previous model.

We are now in a position to illustrate the model graphically. Although the geometric technique is perfectly general, I have chosen the simplest possible case in which the authorities go from a constant price level to one in which prices fall at the growth of real output (a constant money supply). The analysis applies to alternative steady states so the per capita income elasticity of demand for debt is unity.

Along the x-axis, to the right of the origin, mark off the real value of total debt as well as the stock of real balances demanded as a function of the money rate of interest. The money rate is measured along the y-axis as is the real rate and the growth of output λ. To the left along the x-axis mark off the capital–labour ratio extant and draw the marginal productivity of capital schedule in the northwest quadrant as a function of the K/L ratio. The given K/L ratio sets the real rate and with prices assumed constant, the money rate is equal to the real rate. In this initial steady state, with constant prices, the growth of the nominal debt, as well as its components, money and bonds, is equal to the growth of output. Since $d/P = D/P(\Pi + \lambda)$ when $\Pi = 0$, the real deficit is equal to the rectangle $(AB)(AC)$ which is also the change per unit time in the real debt. Since national income is the integral under the marginal product of capital curve

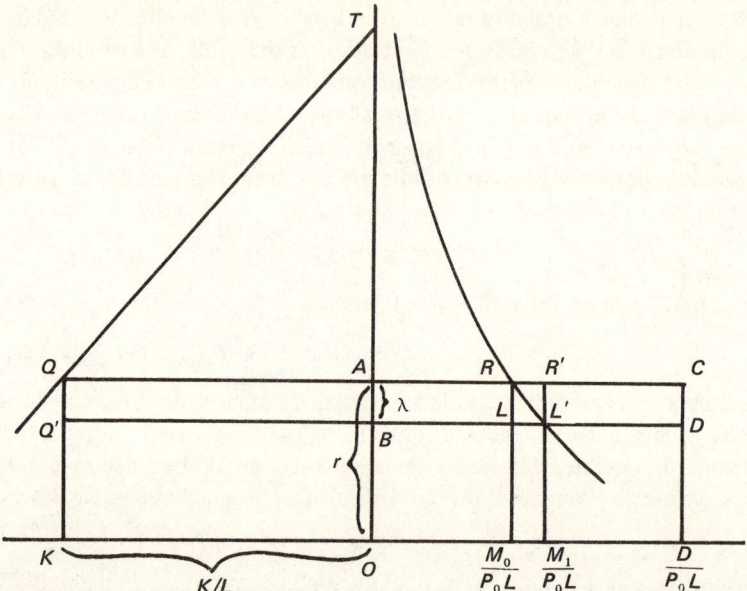

Figure 1

At point A:

$\Pi = 0$
$r = OA$
$d/P = (AB)(AC)$
$(d/dt)(D/P) = (AB)(AC)$
$K/L = OK$
$Y = TOKQ$
$Y_d = TOKQ + (AB)(AC)$

Savings per man

In physical capital = $\lambda K/L = \dot{K}/L = (QQ')(QA)$
In real cash balances $\lambda M/PL = \dot{M}/PL = (AB)(AR)$
In real bond holdings $\lambda D^*/PL = \dot{D}^*/PL = (RL)(LD)$

At point B:

$-\Pi = \lambda$
same as A
$d/P = 0$
same as A
same as A
same as A
same as A

Savings per man

same as A
$\lambda M/PL = (AB)(AR')$
$\lambda D^*/PL = (R'C)(R'L')$

$(KQTO)$ and the change per unit time in the real debt is $(AB)(AC)$ the sum of these two areas is disposable income.[5] Since total savings is $\dot{K}/L + \dot{M}/PL + \dot{D}/PL - \Pi(D/PL)$, when $\Pi = 0$, total savings per man is the rectangle $(QQ')(QC)$ which is the sum of $[\dot{K}/L = (QQ')(Q'B)] + [\dot{M}/PL = (AB)(AR)] + [\dot{D}^*/PL = (RL)(LD)]$, total savings plus consumption per man (the integral under the marginal product curve minus $\dot{K}/L$) exhaust disposable income per man.

Suppose the authorities now decide to achieve a decline of prices equal to the growth of output. If they can keep the total stock of debt constant at time zero when the switch occurs, income effects of the budget will, so to speak, automatically take care of themselves since the real deficit will fall percentage point for percentage point by the new lower depreciation of the unchanged debt and disposable income will remain unchanged. The decline in the money rate of interest causes an increase in desired real balances to M_1 which would cause a fall in prices and increase the real value of the debt. What the authorities must do is to purchase bonds equal to $M_0 M_1$ providing the public with these additional real balances thereby avoiding the blip in prices; this in turn allows both the real debt to remain constant and the new rate of inflation to be perfectly anticipated. Previously, when prices were constant, the real deficit was equal to the real debt times the growth of output; when prices are falling at the growth rate of output, the percentage point swing in prices is the growth of output, and the real deficit falls to zero. However, the change per unit time in the real debt, $(d/dt)(D/P) = \dot{d}/P - \Pi D/P$, remains equal to $(AB)(AC)$ since $\dot{d}/P$ falls to zero and $\Pi = -\lambda$. Both disposable income and real wealth remain unchanged, consumption is unchanged and the real rate remains constant. Total savings is still equal to the same $(QQ')(QC)$ and its components are $[\dot{K}/L = (Q'Q)(Q'B)] + [\lambda M/PL = (AR')(AB)] + [\lambda D^*/PL = (R'C)(DC)]$; note however, that savings in financial assets accrue solely through capital gains (prices decline at the growth of output) on an unchanged nominal debt of which a greater portion is held in the form of real balances.

In the initial steady state with constant prices, the differences between ordinary taxes and net government expenditure (this latter is to be held constant) is equal to the difference between the real deficit $(AB)(AC)$ and interest payments on the privately held debt $(RC)(RM)$. In the new state, the real deficit is zero and the difference between taxes and unchanged net real expenditures is $(L'M_1)(L'D)$, the interest payments on the outstanding debt. Thus the difference in the two levels of taxes is $(AB)(AR) - (LM_0)(LL')$. Clearly these areas are the same if the interest elasticity of demand for real balances is unity; ordinary taxes can then remain constant when the inflation rate is lowered. If the elasticity is greater (less) than unity ordinary taxes can be reduced (increased). The maximum degree to which the monopoly seignorage on issuing interest-free cash can substitute for ordinary taxes is at the point on the demand schedule where the interest elasticity is unity. This is equivalent to defining the revenue as $(M/P) \cdot i$.

The geometry also shows that there may be a maximum level of liquidity attainable through monetarising the public debt. If the demand curve cuts the perpendicular at D/PL at some positive money rate, the authorities would be forced to monetarise real assets in order to bring the interest rate still lower. This becomes a real possibility when it is recognised that not all of the government interest-bearing debt in private hands represents outside wealth since the taxes needed to pay the interest may be anticipated and capitalised into liabilities owed by the private to the government sector.[6]

Finally, we can compare the traditional definition of the revenue as $\dot{M}/P$ with the new concept $(M/P)i$. In the initial position with constant prices, $\dot{M}/P$ is $(AB)(AR)$ and the revenue on the new definition is measured by the larger area $(OA)(AR)$. Since the base for measuring the new concept of the revenue is lower along the demand function than for the old concept, revenue is maximised on the new definition at a lower rate of price change than for the old. It is also clear by inspection that the two definitions are equivalent when $r = \lambda$ since in this golden rule position the rate of monetary expansion is the money rate of interest.[7]

In what follows I shall use the new definition of the revenue as $(M/P)i$ which accrues to the authorities because of their monopoly seignorage on the issue of interest-free currency. A major point in its favour is that the tax on real balances is treated symmetrically with other taxes: the money rate of interest is the tax on liquidity driving a wedge between the price paid by consumers and the zero marginal cost of producing liquidity; the tax revenue is then the product of the tax rate and output (the stock of real balances). When the revenue is defined in this way, the reader can easily show as an exercise that the marginal increment to the welfare loss $(\partial w/\partial i)$ taken as a ratio to the marginal increment to revenue $(\partial G/\partial i)$ is

$$\frac{\partial w/\partial i}{\partial G/\partial i} = \frac{N_i}{1 - N_i}.$$

The economic meaning of this result is perhaps made most clear by noting that the elasticity of demand for real balances is the ratio of the marginal change in the deadweight loss to the marginal change in consumers' surplus. Since the sum of the deadweight loss and the tax receipts is equal to the consumers' surplus, the ratio of the marginal change in the deadweight loss to the marginal change in the revenue must clearly have the form given in the above equation. In the monetary literature this ratio is computed for alternative interest rates given an empirically specified demand function for real balances; the optimal tax is then taken as one which equates this ratio to some measure of the marginal increment to welfare loss taken as a ratio to the marginal proceeds due to other taxes.[8] In order to shed some light on the correctness of this procedure, I shall use the simple model of the structure of optimal taxes due to Dixit and reformulated by Sandmo as a basis for interpreting optimal tax rules when one of the items which can be taxed is real balances. I will heroically assume that real balances can be treated as a final commodity on all fours with Cournot's mineral spring although I am fully aware that this assumption puts to one side important conceptual problems about the nature of real balances, to which we shall return.

The objective of the authorities is to raise a given amount of tax revenue while minimising the damage done to the welfare of the private sector. Assume the private sector's preferences can be represented by a social utility function, that producer prices are given (this assumption is not seriously restrictive since it has been shown that the results carry over to the case of variable producer's prices if there are constant returns to scale). Let the social (i.e. the representative consumer's) utility function be

$$U = U(x_0, x_1, \ldots, x_m). \tag{1}$$

Consumers face prices $P_i = p_i + t_i$ where p_i are producers' prices and t_i are taxes. In the case of real balances, p_i is zero. Factors of production are treated as negative consumption goods; $t_i > 0$ for $x_i < 0$ then implies that the supply of factor i

is subsidised. By Walras's law

$$\sum P_i x_i = 0. \tag{2}$$

The authorities' revenue constraint is

$$\sum_{i=0}^{m} t_i x_i = T. \tag{3}$$

We assume, following Sandmo, that commodity 0 is not taxed and is used as the numéraire so that $P_0 = p_0 = 1$. For example, we may take commodity zero to be labour and other commodities (including real balances) are consumer goods. The first order conditions for maximisation by consumers is

$$U_i - \lambda P_i = 0. \tag{4}$$

Since the demand functions are $x_i = x_i(\mathbf{P})$ $i = 0, 1, \ldots, m$ where $\mathbf{P}$ is the price vector $(P_1, \ldots, P_m)$, we can define an indirect utility function as

$$V(\mathbf{P}) = U(x(\mathbf{P})). \tag{5}$$

Following Dixit, it can be shown that

$$\partial V/\partial P_k = -\lambda x_k. \tag{6}$$

Form the Lagrangian function

$$L = V(\mathbf{P}) - \mu \left(\sum_{i=1}^{m} t_i x_i - T \right) \tag{7}$$

then

$$\partial V/\partial P_k = \partial V/\partial t_k = \mu \left(\sum_{i=1}^{m} t_i \frac{\partial x_i}{\partial P_k} + x_k \right) \tag{8}$$

and from (6) we have

$$-\lambda x_k = \mu \left(\sum_{i=1}^{m} \frac{t_i x_i}{P_k} + x_k \right) \tag{9}$$

or

$$\sum_{i=1}^{m} \frac{t_i \partial x_i}{\partial P_k} = \frac{\lambda + \mu}{\mu} x_k = V x_k. \tag{10}$$

We can give an economic interpretation to this final equation. Consider the unlikely case in which all cross effects within the taxed sector are zero, i.e. $\partial x_i/\partial P_k = 0$ when $i \neq k$ (the shifting of resources is then from the taxed to the non-taxed sector). Then (10) becomes

$$-\frac{t_i \partial x_i}{x_i \partial P_i} = v, \tag{11}$$

so that the elasticities of output with respect to the tax rates are all brought into equality with a common γ.

But we have already shown that the elasticity of demand for real balances with respect to its tax rate (the money rate of interest) is the ratio of the marginal change in the deadweight loss to the marginal change in consumers' surplus — a result which holds for any commodity when the elasticity of demand is taken with respect to the tax, i.e. with a base taken at the level of constant marginal costs. Thus in the case where the shifting of resources is from the taxed to the untaxed sector, the optimal tax structure would equalise the tax elasticities; this is done by taxing more heavily those commodities for which the tax elasticity is least. It is this special case that fits most easily the rule suggested in the monetary literature: using an empirically specified demand function for real balances the ratio of the own marginal increment to welfare loss to the own marginal increment to revenue is calculated and the optimal tax on real balances brings this ratio into equality with the common ratio assumed to exist on other taxed commodities. Equalising the tax elasticities (i.e. equalising the marginal change in the deadweight loss to the marginal change in consumers' surplus) comes to the same thing as equalising the marginal change in the deadweight loss to the revenue.

It might be useful to deal with another special case: that in which a proportional tax structure is optimal. Differentiating equation (2) with respect to P, we have

$$\frac{\partial x_0}{\partial P_k} + \sum_{i=1}^{m} \frac{P_i \partial x_i}{\partial P_k} + x_k = 0.$$

Let $t_i/P_i \equiv \theta_i$ and substitute for x_k in equation (10) to yield

$$\sum_{i=1}^{m} \theta_i P_i \frac{\partial x_i}{\partial P_k} = \gamma \left(\sum_{i=1}^{m} P_i \frac{\partial x_i}{\partial P_k} + \frac{\partial x_0}{\partial P_k} \right) = \sum_{i=1}^{m} P_i(\theta_i - \gamma) \frac{\partial x_i}{\partial P_k} = \gamma \frac{\partial x_0}{\partial P_k}. \tag{12}$$

A sufficient condition for a proportional tax structure is that $\partial x_0/\partial P_k = 0$, i.e. the supply of labour is completely inelastic with respect to commodity prices. Then $\theta_i \equiv t_i/P_i = \gamma$. What of real balances which are produced at zero marginal cost? At first blush it might appear that $t_i/(t_i + p_i)$ is identically equal to unity when $p_i = 0$, but clearly this is the wrong route to take since it excludes the possibility that the optimal tax on real balances is zero and the limit of the ratio of two quantities both of which go to zero is not in general equal to unity. The correct solution is derived by noting that $t_i/P_i = \theta_i = \gamma = (\lambda + \mu)/\mu$ and utilising the definition of γ in terms of λ and μ. Then, $\mu t_i = (\lambda + \mu)(p_i + t_i)$ since $P_i = p_i + t_i$. Now in the case of real balances, $p_i = 0$, then $\mu t_i = (\lambda + \mu) t_i$, so $\lambda t_i = 0$. But λ is the marginal utility of money and must be greater than zero by non-satiation and the optimal tax on real balances is zero when a proportional tax structure is optimal.

Let us now turn to the general case in which shifting takes place within the taxed sector as well as between the taxed and untaxed sector. As is well known, the optimal tax structure is not, in general, a proportional one. Returning to equation (10) we have

$$\sum t_i \frac{x_i}{\partial P_k} = \gamma x_k.$$

Starting from an optimal tax structure consider a small change in the kth tax rate t_k and the kth price P_k by ΔP_k (p_k is by assumption fixed). For the kth good the change in consumers' surplus is given by $x_k \Delta P_k$, the change in total tax revenue is

$$\left(x_k + \sum_{i=1}^{m} t_i \frac{x_i}{\partial P_k} \right) \Delta P_k$$

since the change in price P_k causes a change in the amount bought of all goods $\Delta x_i = (\partial x_i / \partial P_k) \Delta P_k$. The change in the deadweight loss is then $-\Sigma t_k (\partial x / \partial P_k) \Delta P_k$ and the ratio of the change in the deadweight loss to that in the surplus is

$$\sum_{i=1}^{m} t_i \frac{\partial x_i}{x_i} \partial P_k = \gamma.$$

This is equivalent in an optimal tax structure to equalising the marginal loss/revenue ratio $= \gamma/(1-\gamma)$. This is in contrast to what is done in the monetary literature; there when the tax on real balances is altered only the own tax yield on money is considered. Any repercussions this alternation has in changing revenues elsewhere when a shift of resources takes place within the tax sector is ignored. This is quite unexceptional when there is no shifting of demand within the taxed sector so that all cross-elasticities are zero and we equalise tax elasticities, but this is clearly a special case. Put differently, the tax on real balances is treated in terms of a partial equilibrium analysis rather than in a truly general equilibrium framework.

The model could be extended to the case in which supply prices are variable and formulas for the optimal tax structure interpreted in a manner similar to those previously specified. However, since the comments made about the optimal tax mix in the presence of real balances carry over when supply prices are variable, it hardly seems worthwhile to pursue this exercise. Rather, what must be faced up to is the inadequacy of treating real balances as equivalent to a Cournot mineral spring; this lack of equivalence raises fundamental theoretical problems.

Thus, consider the case in which an optimal tax structure prevails, and let the amount of net government expenditures fall to zero. Assume for simplicity that the outstanding stock of government interest bearing debt is zero and that the real rate stands above the growth of aggregate output. In these circumstances it might appear that the government's revenue constraint falls to zero and with it all taxes so that full Pareto optimality would be attained. This would be the case if real balances were on all fours with a Cournot mineral spring and the tax on real balances identical with other commodity taxes. But, the tax on real balances is the money rate of interest which the government can influence only by altering the policy parameter it directly controls, namely the growth rate of the *nominal* money supply. When the real rate stands above the growth of aggregate output, full liquidity requires that taxes become positive (the real deficit becomes negative by the identical amount); the excess of taxes above the (zero) level of net expenditures is used to buy nominal balances which the authorities confine to the furnace. But, since we have ruled out lump sum non-distorting taxes, we are back in the second best world of optimal tax mix and full liquidity satiation should not be sought.

DISCUSSION: R.E. BAILEY

Professor Marty's paper focuses attention on the integration of two strands of literature which for the most part have developed along separate routes. The tax-like effects of inflation have largely been the provinces of the monetary theorist whilst the analysis of the optimal structure of taxes has been studied in the context of models which abstract entirely from monetary phenomena. In a paper by Phelps (1973) the two areas were brought together and Professor Marty's principal contribution is to illuminate this treatment in terms of an elegant diagrammatic analysis. The purposes of this note are two-fold: firstly, to comment on the structure of the models within which the analysis is posed; and, secondly, to discuss the nature of the optimality problem in this branch of monetary theory.

The models employed in these analyses fall into two broad categories, both of which make their appearance in Professor Marty's paper. Firstly, there are the macroeconomic growth models which are specified in terms of economic aggregates and in terms of behavioural relationships which, for the most part, leave implicit the optimisation activities of individual agents in the economy. Secondly, there are microeconomic models which focus on market equilibrium in which individuals explicitly optimise according to some preference ordering subject to the relevant budget constraint. In spite of formidable research efforts in recent years it remains the case that the most familiar and well-worked-out theories of money fall into the former class. Alternatively, the analyses of efficiency and optimal taxation being phrased, as they so often are, in terms of the notion of Pareto optimality are more appropriately studied in the context of the latter class of models.[9] Some of the reasons for this apparent split will perhaps be evident if we pause to consider the framework of the micro-oriented models in a little more detail.

The formulation which is possibly the most familiar, and in which optimal taxation is usually analysed, is the Arrow–Debreu general equilibrium model.[10] The version employed in the optimal taxation literature is not, I think, meant to be interpreted as the full-blown Arrow–Debreu model with a complete set of contingent futures markets. Rather the features of uncertainty and future time are ignored, an abstraction with some justification if the sole object is to study taxation amongst commodities rather than across time. This simplification, however, must obviously be made with much more circumspection when money (and along with it general asset choice decisions) are introduced into the analysis.

One class of models which do attempt to incorporate monetary phenomena, albeit in a rather crude fashion, are the temporary equilibrium theories,[11] which postulate the existence of spot markets but include a very limited set of futures markets. These models are formulated with money entering principally as a store of value, although some attempts may be made to pay heed to the role of money in effectuating transactions. Unfortunately, it is the case that, except for the stationary variant of these models, very few efficiency results can be derived.[12] One of the main reasons for the paucity of interesting efficiency theorems in this approach may be thought to be that expectations of prices and plans may not be fulfilled and, indeed, are likely to differ amongst individuals.

A third class of models has been developed in which not only are spot markets in equilibrium but also the plans and expectations of individual agents are also in equilibrium.[13] However, it seems that the optimality results are almost as scarce here as in the temporary equilibrium models.

Since many of the contemporary macroeconomic models may be thought of as being based on models of temporary equilibrium[14] it would appear that we should treat with reservation the implications of such models with respect to the optimal inflation tax on money balances. Similarly, models which include real money balances as simply one commodity in a utility function should be treated with caution, as emphasised by Professor Marty towards the end of his paper.

Turning now to the formulation of the optimal taxation problem in the monetary literature it must be noticed that the analysis is conducted in terms of 'differential tax incidence', a concept in the theory of public finance with a long and illustrious history going back to Wicksell and Ramsey.[15] The differential incidence approach is one way of making explicit what is being 'held constant' when some tax change is being studied. In terms of the Phelps (1973) model this amounts to holding constant the difference between potential pre-tax income and disposable income and also holding the fiscal effects on wealth constant as changes occur in the rate of inflation. If this approach is adopted, the intuitive plausibility of the definition of the inflation tax rate as the nominal rate of interest on government debt should be quite clear. For an increase in the rate of inflation substitutes for other taxes by raising the rate of seignorage on money balances, this latter rate being the saving of interest on debt which is not now having to be issued (since it is replaced by a faster growth of the money stock which is inducing the increase in the inflation rate).

A related notion of the impact of tax changes may be mentioned at this point. This is the concept of balanced-budget incidence which involves the evaluation of changes in taxes instigated in order to finance changes in government expenditure. Whilst the distinction between such an approach and that of differential incidence is quite straightforward its recognition may help to clarify the discussion in the monetary literature since in the macroeconomic literature there tends to be more discussion of changes in taxes and expenditures than of offsetting changes in different taxes.

To the non-specialist in the areas under review it may appear surprising that there is precisely one type of money in these models, no mention being made of the possibility of different varieties of money produced by banks. This latter situation could be handled on the demand side by simply interpreting other arguments of the utility function as being other types of money, thus incorporating the possibility of substitution amongst different types of money. However, on the supply side we must conjecture that the production technology for these alternative monetary assets will not be as simple as that for producing money balances as postulated in Professor Marty's paper. Indeed this provides an additional reason for his dissatisfaction with the 'Cournot mineral spring' assumption employed to characterise the supply of real balances.

Finally, we must reiterate the well known stricture that the analysis of the welfare implications of the inflation tax relies entirely on the postulate that the rate of inflation is perfectly anticipated; from the remarks made earlier on the microeconomic foundations of the theory this is hardly surprising. It has occasionally been argued that some such assumption of complete accuracy is essential for any analysis of optimal pricing and that the study of inflationary finance should hardly be singled out for criticism on this score. But in response to this view we would contend that some of the most important aspects of inflationary finance result from imperfect foresight and to ignore this is to impose a very serious limitation on the validity of the analysis.

In one of his contributions to this subject Phelps (1973, p. 67) has ruefully observed that 'the results of the analysis are as attractive as the method', and, one might add, as attractive as the models to which the method is applied.

NOTES

1. See, for example, Baumol and Bradford (1970), Lerner (1970), and especially Dixit (1970). See also Sandmo (1974).
2. The most notable exception is Phelps (1973).
3. The concept of the ratio of the marginal increment to deadweight loss to the increment to revenue is found, for example, in Tower (1971), Cathcart (1974), Marty (1973), Frenkel (forthcoming). The average ratio of welfare loss to revenue was first derived for the Cagan function (which involves evaluating a particular integral) and this average ratio is then used to compute the marginal ratio. This is mathematically cumbersome and economically misleading since the marginal ratio can be derived without evaluating a particular integral and holds for any general demand function. For an exception see Barro (1972) who does use a general demand function but restricts his results to the case of a stationary economy.
4. Although the integral is taken from time zero to infinity the model is not properly a steady-state solution unless the per capita income elasticity of demand for real balances is unity. To see this, note that $\dot{M}/P$ (which is total revenue in the traditional Chicago definition and the flow part of revenue in the present model) when taken as a ratio to income changes exponentially and without limit by $g_y(n-1)$. For example, if $n > 1$, the flow part of revenue as a ratio to income approaches infinity. This is economic nonsense;

the proper steady-state solution is one in which n is unity. In this case the convergence of the integral would be a consequence of this condition plus the assumption that in the steady state the real rate stands above the growth of aggregate output by some positive rate of time preference. This modified golden rule solution insures, as well, that the steady state is efficient in the Phelps–Koopmans sense.

5 This is not quite right since disposable income is equal to national product minus a constant proportion, h, that goes into government expenditure plus the change per unit time in the debt. However, it does no harm to treat the trapezoidal area $TOQK$ as equal to $Y(1-h)$.

6 Although in a society of mortal human beings it is unrealistic to suppose that the interest payments on privately held government bonds are completely offset by the discounted value of anticipated taxes, it is likely that some portion of the debt is so discounted which implies that the model as stated overestimates the real stock of privately held debt available for offsetting changes in real cash balances. It would be possible (and from a purist's viewpoint, perhaps desirable) to run the model so that when the inflation rate varies the monetarisation of physical capital is used to keep outside wealth constant.

7 When $\dot{M}/P$ is taken as the revenue we assume that the authorities produce a welfare loss only at positive rates of monetary expansion, so $\partial w/\partial G = N_i/1 - N_\rho$ becomes infinite when $N_\rho = 1$, which is on this definition the point of maximum revenue. Alternatively, when the revenue is defined as $(M/P)i$, we impute a welfare loss whenever $i > 0$ since the authorities are assumed to get revenue from seignorage which can accrue at $\rho < 0$ if $r > \lambda$. The revenue is then maximised and $\partial w/\partial G$ becomes infinite when $N_i = 1$, which occurs at a lower ρ (whenever $r > \lambda$) than in the previous case. The reason for this is that the base for measuring the revenue is $i = 0$ which is lower along the demand schedule than the point at which $\rho = 0$ whenever $r > \lambda$. At any given ρ, $\partial w/\partial G$ will then be higher when the revenue is taken as $(M/P)i$. When $r = \lambda$, the two interpretations are mathematically and economically equivalent.

8 The point is wrongly put by Mundell. He writes, 'Martin Bailey in "The Welfare Cost of Inflationary Finance", *Journal of Political Economy* 66 (April 1956) argues that inflation has a welfare cost, and using Cagan's data computes the points at which the marginal welfare cost balances the marginal revenue from the tax.' Not only did Bailey not compute such points (he computed the average ratio of welfare loss to revenue), but the procedure imputed to him is wrong. For balancing the marginal deadweight loss to the marginal tax receipts would constrain the elasticity to be exactly one-half. The 'proper' procedure equalises these ratios for alternative taxes. Note Mundell's procedure is wrong on either definition of the revenue (Mundell, 1971, p. 41, Footnote 9). It should also be noted that the 'proper' formulation implies that all other taxes are set at their optimal levels. The reader should also note that in the following section on optimal taxes, λ is used as the marginal utility of money and not the rate of growth of aggregate output.

9 We must, however, note that some efficiency type analyses have been attempted in terms of monetary growth models. See, for example, Hahn (1969) and Stein (1971) chapters 7 and 8.

10 The classical statement of this model is that of Debreu (1959).

11 See, for example, Grandmont (1974) and Grandmont and Younes (1972).

12 The main results are established in Grandmont and Younes (1973).

13 See Radner (1974) for a useful survey of his earlier work in this area.

14 A most explicit example of this is Patinkin (1965). For Patinkin *the* general equilibrium model is a form of temporary equilibrium analysis.

15 The relevant references are contained in Phelps (1973).

REFERENCES

Auernheimer, L. (1974). The honest government's guide to the revenue from the creation of money. *Journal of Political Economy* **82**, 598–606.
Barro, Robert (1972). Inflationary finance and the welfare cost of inflation. *Journal of Political Economy* **80**, 978–1001.
Baumol, W. and Bradford, D.F. (1970). Optimal departures from marginal cost pricing. *American Economic Review* **60**, 265–83.
Cathcart, C.D. (1974). Monetary dynamics, growth and the efficiency of inflationary finance. *Journal of Money, Credit and Banking* **6**, 169–90.
Debreu, G. (1959). *The Theory of Value*. New York: Wiley.
Dixit, A.K, (1970). On the optimum structure of commodity taxes. *American Economic Review* **60**, 295–301.
Frenkel, Jacob (forthcoming). Inflationary expectations and some dynamic aspects of the welfare costs. Forthcoming in University of Manchester Conference on World Inflation volume.
Grandmont, J.M. and Y. Younes (1972). On the role of money and the existence of a monetary equilibrium. *Review of Economic Studies* **39**, 355–72.
Grandmont, J.M. and Y. Younes (1973). On the efficiency of a monetary equilibrium. *Review of Economic Studies* **40**, 149–65.
Grandmont, J.M. (1974) On the short-run equilibrium in a monetary economy. In *Allocation Under Uncertainty: Equilibrium and Optimality*, ed. J. Dreze, chapter 12. London: Macmillan.
Hahn, F.H. (1969). On money and growth. *Journal of Money, Credit and Banking* **1**, 172–87.
Lerner, Abba (1970). Optimal taxes with an untaxable sector. *American Economic Review* **60**, 284–94.
Marty, Alvin L. (1973). Growth, satiety and the tax revenue from money creation. *Journal of Political Economy* **81**, 1136–52.
Mundell, Robert (1971). *Monetary Theory*. Goodyear.
Patinkin, D. (1965). *Money, Interest and Prices*, second edition. New York: Harper and Row.
Phelps, E.S. (1973). Inflation in the theory of public finance. *Swedish Journal of Economics* **75**, 67–82.
Radner, R. (1974). Market equilibrium and uncertainty: concepts and problems. In *Frontiers of Quantitative Economics*, vol. II, ed. M.D. Intriligator and D.A. Kendrick. Amsterdam: North Holland.
Sandmo, A. (1974). A note on the structure of optimal taxation. *American Economic Review* **64**, 701–706.
Stein, J. (1971). *Money and Capacity Growth*. New York: Columbia University Press.
Tower, Edward (1971). More on the welfare cost of inflation finance. *Journal of Money, Credit and Banking* **3**, 850–60.

4 MONETARY EXPANSION AND THE REVENUE OF THE MONETARY AUTHORITY: A GEOMETRIC EXPOSITION

DAVID LAIDLER[1]

It is widely recognised that analyses of money creation as a source of revenue to its issuer, or the so-called 'optimal quantity of money', as well as of the long-run neutrality of money, all involve different applications of essentially the same body of economic theory. However, there is no readily accessible and simple account of the basic results that have been achieved in any of these areas that exploits their inter-relationship. This paper seeks to do just that from the point of view of money creation as a source of revenue. Economists have a habit of treating questions about monetary optimality and the revenue from money creation as problems for partial equilibrium analysis while matters concerning the neutrality of money have inevitably been recognised as requiring general equilibrium analysis to handle them. The framework adopted here is explicity general equilibrium in nature. Though this paper's purpose is expository, and does not attempt to break new ground, this framework nevertheless enables us to raise and clarify certain questions that tend to be begged when partial equilibrium analysis is used.

Let us begin with the basic framework in terms of which the exposition of this paper will be carried out. This framework is an extension and generalisation of one which I first set out in 1969.[2] It consists of a neoclassical growth model in which saving behaviour is governed, not by a rule of thumb requiring savings to be some fraction of disposable income, but by the interaction of time preference and the marginal productivity of capital. Though there is, in effect, only a single production sector in the model, it also contains a money market. Here real cash balances are thought of yielding utility to their holders, utility that diminishes at the margin as the quantity of real cash balances held increases. As to the supply of real cash balances, the crucial assumption is that this can be increased at zero marginal cost in terms of output foregone but that no explicit interest payments are made to the holders of money. From the point of view of society, but not from the point of view of individual economic agents, cash balances are a free good.

The foregoing assumptions are commonly enough made and there is no novelty in the more detailed restrictions that we impose upon our model's structure to make it readily manageable. It is assumed that the growth rate of the population of the economy in question is exogenously given and that the supply of labour in this economy is proportional to the population. There is no choice to be made between work and leisure that might prove sensitive on the margin to variations in the relative costs and benefits to be realised from the two activities, nor is there any technical progress, so the economy is characterised by an exogenously given natural growth rate.[3] Labour and capital may be combined in varying proportions in the production process with diminishing returns to each of them. Returns to scale, on the other hand, are constant. Thus we can carry out all the analysis that follows on the basis that output per head of the population is uniquely related to the amount of capital per head of the population devoted to production, with output per head increasing at a decreasing rate as capital per head increases.

As to the demand for money, we have already remarked that we are concerned with a demand for real balances. Thus the demand for nominal balances is strictly proportional to the price level. Moreover, the aggregate demand for real balances is assumed to be strictly proportional to the population so that we analyse the monetary sector in terms of a per capita demand function for real balances. We assume the per capita income elasticity of demand for money to be positive and, because the marginal utility of real balances declines with the quantity held, the demand for money is inversely related to the opportunity cost of holding it. All these assumptions will be maintained throughout the analysis that follows. However, we will initially assume the rate of time preference to be constant and equal for every individual.[4] This assumption will be varied later in the analysis. It is adopted at the outset for the sake of simplicity but as we shall see, it turns out to be crucial as far as certain results are concerned.

Figure 1 is typical of the geometric representation of this model. On the horizontal axis we measure per capita stocks: capital from left to right from the origin O and real money balances from right to left from the origin Q. The units on the vertical axes are percentage rates of flow per unit of time. Thus rates of interest, rates of monetary expansion, rates of inflation, and rates of growth of real output, can all be and all are measured vertically. The marginal product of capital schedule, and the demand for real balances schedule are both drawn as straight lines simply to preserve geometric simplicity in the analysis that follows. The symbols used in figure 1, and throughout this paper, have the following meanings: K, capital per head; M, real balances per head; R, the rate of time preference; ρ, the rate of growth of population; λ, the rate of expansion of the nominal money stock; Π, the rate of inflation; and r the nominal rate of interest. Figure 1 itself depicts a special case of the general type of model under analysis, but a particularly simple one to begin from. It depicts an economy with a constant nominal money stock in which the real rate of return on capital is equal to the rate of time preference R, as it must be in any equilibrium situation, but in this case the rate of time preference is also equal to the rate of growth of population – the economy's natural growth rate ρ. Per capita real output in this economy is given by the area $ABCO$ which in turn is divided between per capita profits $DBCO$ and per capita wages ABD. If equilibrium is to be maintained over

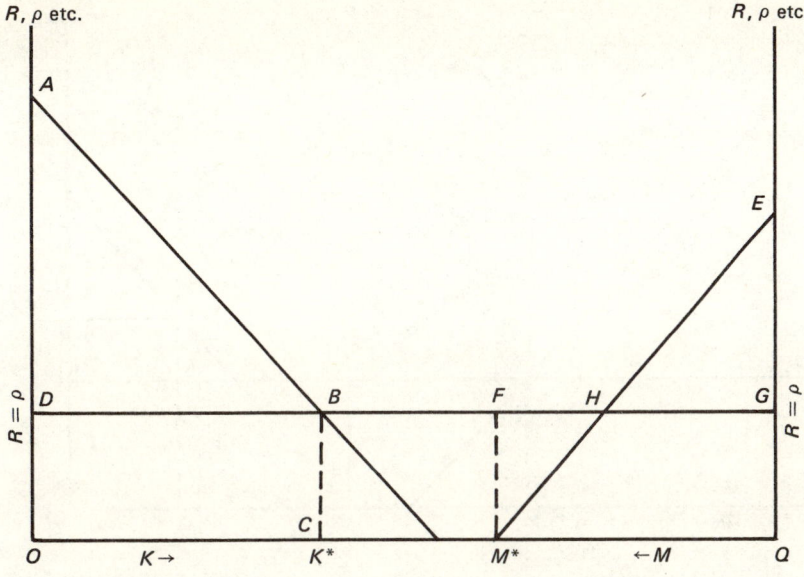

Figure 1

time, if the per capita capital stock is to remain constant, the overall capital stock must grow at the rate $R = \rho$. Thus per capita savings must be equal to *DBCO* and hence to per capita profits.

So much for the production side of the economy; what about the money market? When cash balances themselves bear no interest, the private opportunity cost of holding money is equal to the nominal rate of interest, which in turn is given by the real rate of return on capital plus the expected rate of inflation; moreover, analysis here deals with equilibrium situations in which the expected rate of inflation is equal to the actual rate. Because per capita output is constant, and because the elasticity of the aggregate demand for real cash balances with respect to population is equal to unity, the rate of inflation Π is in general equal to the rate of monetary expansion λ minus the natural rate of growth of the economy ρ. In the special case with which we are dealing here we have $\lambda = 0$, $R = \rho$, so that $r = R + \Pi = R - \rho = 0$.

The opportunity cost of holding money is zero and per capita holdings of real balances are therefore equal to QM^*. Their growth contributes $FGQM^*$ to disposable income, a sum that is all saved in order to ensure that per capita real balances remain constant over time. Per capita 'welfare' accruing from money holdings is equal to QEM^*. On the assumption that real balances are produced at zero social opportunity cost, the situation depicted in figure 1 has market forces leading to an optimal situation in the market for real money balances.

Let us now introduce some positive monetary expansion into this model. There is one special case in which such expansion has no effects whatever. That

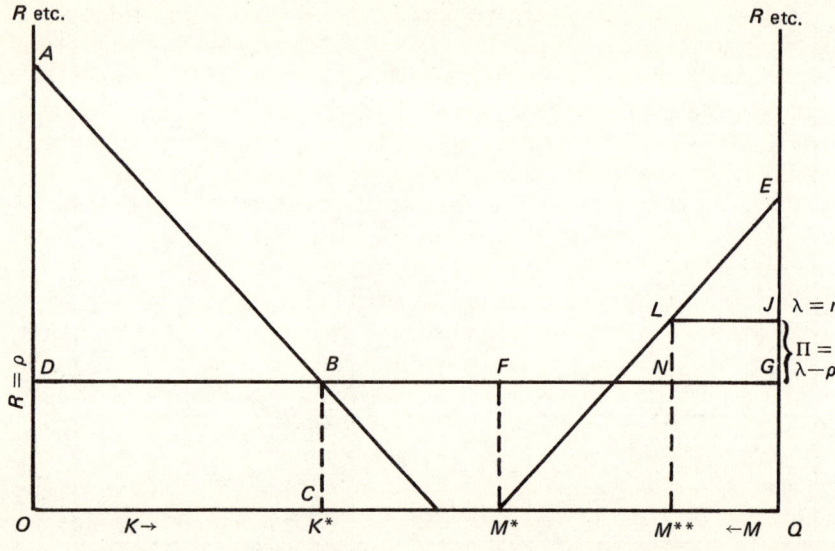

Figure 2

is when new money is put into circulation in the form of interest payments on existing money holdings, so let us dispose of this case first of all. If, in terms of the model depicted in figure 1, interest is paid on money at any rate λ per annum, two changes take place. First, price inflation at the rate $\lambda - \rho$ per annum will ensue. However, in calculating the opportunity cost of holding money we must make allowances for its own nominal rate of return, which is now λ. The overall opportunity cost of holding money would be given by $r - \lambda$. Since $r = R + \Pi = R + (\lambda - \rho)$ we have $r = R + (\lambda - \rho) - \lambda = 0$, for any value of λ, for any rate of monetary expansion. It should be noted that though I have started this particular analysis from a somewhat special case, there is a quite general conclusion to be drawn here. Interest payments on money financed out of nominal monetary expansion, or to describe the same activity in a different way, nominal monetary expansion implemented by paying interest on existing money balances, has no real effects.

Let us set aside this uninteresting special case then and introduce into the model set out in figure 1 a positive rate of monetary expansion λ implemented in some other way. We do this in figure 2. As the figure is drawn the rate of monetary expansion is set above the growth rate and a positive inflation rate of $\Pi = \lambda - \rho$ must occur for equilibrium to be maintained. Thus the nominal rate of interest will be $\lambda - \rho + R = \lambda$ and the demand for real balances will be given by M^{**}. What happened to per capita disposable income in this case and its division between saving and consumption? That might seem to depend upon how new money is put into circulation, and upon whether it is so-called 'inside' or 'outside' money, but this is not in fact so.[5]

Consider first monetary expansion implemented by the classic means of inducing an increase in the quantity of so-called 'outside money', namely having it dropped by a helicopter (piloted no doubt by a Walrasian auctioneer).[6] Those who pick up the money clearly have a windfall income gain equal in total to the rate of monetary expansion times the quantity of real balances in existence. This gain, averaged over the community gives a per capita gain in income equal to $LJM^{**}Q$. Against this must be set the inflation induced depreciation of per capita real balances already held, and that is equal to $JLNG$. Thus the money market contributes $GNM^{**}Q$ to disposable income an amount NFM^*M^{**} less than in the no-monetary-expansion case. Again, all of this must be saved, in order to keep per capita real balances constant over time. There are no effects running from the money market to the production sector in this model — money is neutral. Thus per capita disposable income is reduced overall by NFM^*M^{**} and, of course, a welfare loss of LM^*M^{**} is associated with this positive rate of monetary expansion.

Now suppose that new money comes into circulation through the monetary authority's buying assets from the public. It might at first sight seem as though the results of this for disposable income would be different from the 'helicopter' case. After all, monetary expansion at a rate of λ would now involve the sale of goods equal in value to $LJM^{**}Q$ to the monetary authority. Thus the area $LJM^{**}Q$ now becomes interpretable as a measure of the 'revenue from money creation', accruing to the monetary authority, and LM^*M^{**} a measure of the welfare cost associated with raising this revenue. Disposable income would now appear to be lower by $LJM^{**}Q$ as a result of monetary expansion but should we stop here? A partial equilibrium approach might tempt us to, but the general equilibrium framework being used here will not let us. $LJM^{**}Q$ of real output per capita is being given to the monetary authority in exchange for new nominal balances. What does the authority now do with the proceeds of this 'tax'?

Suppose it redistributes the revenue at random. It must then be added back into disposable income before we have completed the social accounting exercise associated with introducing and analysing the effects of this positive rate of monetary expansion. If it is, then it will be apparent that the end result is exactly that achieved by scattering money from a helicopter. Suppose instead the monetary authority uses the proceeds to provide public consumption goods. Then their value must be added to per capita income before our exercise is complete and normal social accounting conventions would then leave us yet again with the same solution for per capita income. Now suppose that the monetary authority in question is not a government agency but a private monopoly bank which distributes its revenue from money creation to its owners. Again we would have the same result as far as per capita disposable income is concerned so long as the bank's owners lived in the economy being analysed. In short, in all the cases considered, per capita disposable income will be equal to $ABCO + GNM^{**}Q$, and per capita savings will be equal to $BCOD + GNM^{**}Q$. In every case the revenue from money creation accruing to the monetary authority, whether it be public or private, is $LJM^{**}Q$. Differences between the foregoing cases might arise over the matter of who ultimately receives the revenue and perhaps over effects on the allocation of resources within the production sector, but not over the amount of revenue raised or over the effect of monetary expansion on per capita income, or savings, or anything else about which the model we are here analysing has anything to say.[7]

The mechanics of revenue raising from money creation are exactly the same, regardless of whether the emitter of the money is government or a private monopoly bank, but given those mechanics, one might expect the two agencies to act differently because they have different aims. One might expect a government to treat money creation as simply one source of revenue available to it, and hence to decide upon the amount of revenue it wishes to raise from money creation as a part of an overall taxation and expenditure strategy. A private bank might be expected to be interested in the more mundane matter of maximising its profits. Alvin Marty deals with the first of these issues in a related paper to this one, and so I will set this matter to one side here and concentrate on the second.[8] As it happens, virtually no attention has been paid to analysing money creation as part of an optimal tax strategy. Hence, it also is more in keeping with the mainly expository aim of this paper to stick to the analysis of the revenue-maximising rate of monetary expansion about which a good deal has been written. Although the work alluded to has all been written on the assumption that its results are relevant to the behaviour of government, they are more relevant to the behaviour of a monopoly private bank.

If our monetary authority is indeed a private monopoly bank, and if the marginal cost to it of producing real balances is zero, then its profit-maximising problem becomes a revenue-maximisation problem. It must pick the rate of monetary expansion that maximises an area such as $LJM^{**}Q$ in figure 2. Such a revenue-maximising solution will occur where the elasticity of the demand for real balances with respect to the rate of monetary expansion, or equivalently in terms of figure 2, with respect to the nominal rate of interest, is equal to unity. Given a linear demand curve, this will occur at a rate of monetary expansion (call it λ^*) half way between the horizontal axis and the intercept of the demand for money function with the vertical axis. The rate of inflation implicit in this solution will be given by $\lambda^* - \rho$, and it is obvious that the higher the natural rate of growth of the economy, the lower will this rate of inflation be. Indeed there is nothing in principle to stop the rate of inflation associated with a revenue-maximising rate of monetary expansion being negative.[9]

We have discussed the elasticity of demand for money with respect to the rate of monetary expansion and with respect to the nominal rate of interest as if they were equivalent concepts, but they are not equivalent. The rate of monetary expansion and the nominal interest rate do happen to be equal in the particular version of the model we have here analysed. Their equality arises from the property of the model that when the rate of monetary expansion is zero so is the nominal rate of interest or, to go to the root of the matter, from our having

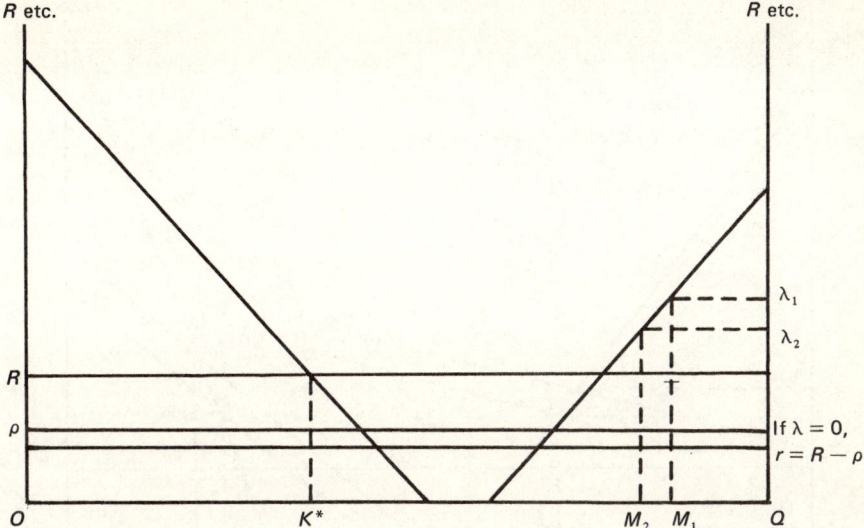

Figure 3

assumed equality between the natural rate of growth and the rate of time preference. If we let these two differ the nominal rate of interest and the rate of monetary expansion no longer take the same value. We must now ask which rule should the profit-maximising monopoly bank follow: set the rate of monetary expansion so that the elasticity of the demand for real balances with respect to the rate of monetary expansion is equal to unity, or so that its elasticity of demand with respect to the nominal rate of interest is unity? It is the latter rule that turns out to be correct as we shall now see.

Consider figure 3, where we depart from our initial assumptions by setting the rate of time preference R above the natural growth rate ρ.[10] The rate of monetary expansion that satisfied our first rule is given by λ_1 which lies half-way between the point at which $\lambda = 0$, and the vertical intercept of the demand for money function, so that $r = R - \rho$. The rate of expansion that satisfies the second rule is given by λ_2 which generates a rate of inflation that produces a value for r half-way between the origin and the vertical intercept of the demand for money function. Given that real balances are produced at zero marginal cost, it is geometrically clear that the bank's revenue is maximised by setting a rate of monetary expansion of λ_2. The economic interpretation of this result is simple enough. A bank's balance sheet must balance. It must hold assets equal in value to the quantity of real balances it has outstanding. If it were to finance its ownership of these assets by emitting bonds, it would have to pay to its creditors the nominal rate of interest in order to get the bonds in question held. The profit that it makes from being a provider of money is the difference between

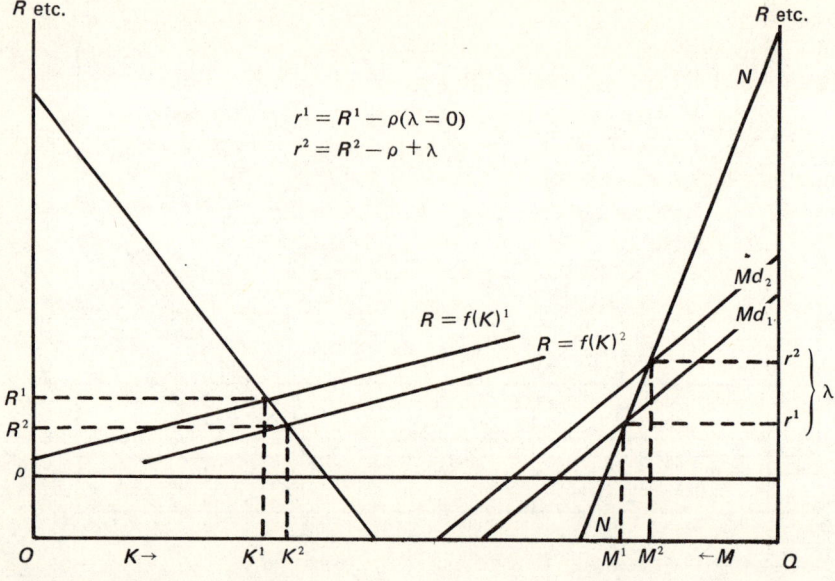

Figure 4

the interest bill it would have to meet in this case, and the zero cost it incurs in having non-interest-bearing money as its liability. To put the same point in another way, creation of new nominal balances is not the only source of revenue to any monetary authority be it a private bank or government agency. The assets held as a result of past issues of nominal money also yield a real return to the authority. Its total revenue is the sum of these two items and to maximise its revenue it must choose the rate of monetary expansion that maximises the sum of revenue arising from both sources, and not just the revenue arising from one of them.

One further matter ought to be analysed in this paper. So far we have dealt with a model in which money is neutral, in which variations in the rate of monetary expansion have no effect on the real side of the economy at all. This property is introduced into the model by two of its characteristics. First, the supply of labour is completely exogenous, and second, the rate of time preference is constant. By dropping this latter assumption, we can easily destroy the neutrality of money and complicate our analysis of the revenue arising to the emitters of money.

Figure 4 depicts a situation in which the rate of time preference rises with the level of non-human wealth.[11] Initially we start with zero rate of monetary expansion and hence in the real sector find ourselves with a capital stock per head of K^1 and in the monetary sector real balance holdings equal to M^1. Now consider implementing a positive rate of monetary expansion λ. We have seen that this produces a fall in the quantity of real balances held, and hence initially a fall in the level of wealth. But, if the level of real balances falls, and the rate of time preference rises with the overall level of wealth then the stock of productive capital that is consistent with a given rate of time preference increases. Thus the line $R = f(K)$ shifts to the right. As it does so the capital–labour ratio increases, the real interest rate falls, and per capita output increases. This in turn must have repercussions for the demand for real balances function. More per capita output means a greater demand for real balances at any nominal rate of interest, so the original demand for money function shifts out to the left. Equilibrium will be re-established at a higher level of output, a lower real rate of interest, and with the demand for money having moved not along the demand for money function per se but along a composite relationship $N-N$ that incorporates movements along and shifts of that function.

The implications of this extension of our analysis are straightforward. When money is permitted to be non-neutral, questions about revenue from money creation cannot be answered by considering the partial elasticity of the demand for money function with respect to the nominal rate of interest. One must consider instead the total differential of the demand for money with respect to the rate of monetary expansion when all interactions in the complete general equilibrium system are taken into account. $N-N$ is a geometric representation of this differential. Moreover, areas under the partial demand for money function may no longer be used as measures of economic welfare losses associated with various rates of monetary expansion. More powerful tools associated with the measurement of welfare changes when there are multiple price changes must be used.

Now the analysis of the non-neutral money economy which I have just presented is, of course a special case. There are many versions of our general model in which money is non-neutral but there is no point in analysing them case by case, for the basic analytic technique just exploited needs only minor modification to deal with them.[12] The reader who wishes to become familiar with the technique might himself apply it to a different case or two for himself in order to get to grips with it fully.

This paper needs no long concluding paragraph. I have tried to bring together in a simple and accessible way a number of results in monetary economics. The paper's main aim has been expository, and if it makes the task of the teacher, and student, of modern monetary theory a little easier, then it has fulfilled its purpose.

NOTES

1. I am deeply indebted to Alvin Marty for extensive disucssion of the matters dealt with in this essay.
2. In Laidler (1969) I dealt with a stationary economy and was concerned with the consequence of achieving an optimal quantity of money through the payment of interest on cash balances.
3. It would be possible to accomodate disembodied technical progress in the

analysis that follows by redefining the labour force in terms of constant efficiency units. However, it would be necessary to make the per capita income elasticity of demand for money unity in order to carry this analysis through.
4 This assumption ensures, of course, that the distribution of wealth within the economy is left undetermined, and indeed indeterminate. The problem is exactly analogous to that which arises in the analysis of perfect competition when all firms have the same constant returns to scale production function so that the distribution of output between firms is indeterminate.
5 This distinction is still widely utilised despite the fact that it was discredited in the course of the debate that followed the publication of Pesek and Saving (1968); cf. for example Johnson (1969), Marty (1969) and Laidler (1969). The appropriate line to draw is between interest-bearing and non-interest-bearing money.
6 The helicopter is, of course, Friedman's (1969) device.
7 This conclusion is an illustration of the general point already made above (n. 5) that the inside–outside money distinction is of no operational significance.
8 cf. Marty (1967).
9 This matter is extensively analysed in the exchange between Friedman (1971) and Marty (1973).
10 If we set the rate of time preference below the natural growth rate, we would make the real return to holding cash balances greater than that to holding productive capital. Unless we make the implausible assumption that the marginal utility of real balances became significantly negative as more and more of them were held, the model would not have an equilibrium solution in such circumstances. Real balances would be held in unlimited quantities and the productive capital stock would go to zero.
11 This is just one of many ways of making the time preference rate endogenous. One could make it depend upon human as well as non-human wealth, one could include the present value of the utility yield of cash balances in wealth, and one could make time preference decline rather than rise with wealth. Such variations as these were analysed in Laidler (1969) but there is nothing of substance to be gained from going through an extensive taxonomy here.
12 The reader who wishes to carry out such exercises will find it helpful to refer to Laidler (1969).

REFERENCES

Friedman, M. (1969). The optimal quantity of money. In *The Optimal Quantity of Money* chapter 1. London: Macmillan.
Friedman, M. (1971). Government revenue from inflation. *Journal of Political Economy* 79, 846–77.
Johnson, H.G. (1969). Inside money, outside money, income, wealth and welfare in monetary economics. *Journal of Money, Credit and Banking* 1, 30–45.
Laidler, D.E.W. (1969). Money, wealth and time preference in a stationary economy. *Canadian Journal of Economics* 2, 526–35.
Marty, A.L. (1969). Inside money, outside money, and the wealth effect. *Journal of Money, Credit and Banking* 1, 101–11.

Marty, A.L. (1973). Growth, satiety and the tax revenue from money creation. *Journal of Political Economy* **81**, 1136–52.
Marty, A.L. (1976). Real balances and optimal tax structure. Chapter 3 of these proceedings.
Pesek, B.P. and T.R. Saving (1967). *Money, Wealth, and Economic Theory*. New York: Macmillan.

5 AN ANALYSIS OF MONETARY AND FISCAL POLICY IN A QUANTITY THEORY MODEL OF WEALTH ADJUSTMENT

GORDON R. SPARKS[1]

The aim of this paper is to clarify some issues in the monetarist debate concerning the effects of monetary and fiscal policy in the short run and the long run. We attempt to construct an eclectic model which embodies on the one hand the important relationships emphasised in the neo-Keynesian income–expenditure approach, and on the other hand has the flavour of a modern quantity theory or monetarist approach. The principal feature of the model is that both consumption and asset demands depend on a broad measure of wealth that includes human wealth and allows for the effects of government expenditures and taxes on income streams. The effect over time of changes in monetary and fiscal policy is analysed with explicit account taken of the government's budget constraint. The long-run effects are seen to depend on the relative discount rates applied to income streams from human and non-human wealth, while the adjustment path depends, inter alia, on the speed with which changes in taxes are incorporated into perceived permanent income.

The paper begins with an outline of the model in equation form. We then analyse the effects of a one-shot increase in the money supply, a constant rate of growth of the money supply, and a change in government expenditures. The implications of the model are summarised in a concluding section.

THE MODEL

We begin by setting out the relationships in our model as a system of equations. The exact functional forms are not important since we use symbols primarily as a shorthand method of presentation rather than as a basis for formal mathematical analysis. An alphabetical list of definitions is given in an appendix.

Aggregate supply and investment

We use a one-sector model with output (x) determined by a Cobb–Douglas production function and inputs labour (l) and capital (k).

$$x = \xi l^\alpha k^{1-\alpha}. \tag{1}$$

The demand for labour is determined by the usual profit-maximising condition that the marginal products equal the ratio of the wage rate (W) to the price level (P).

$$\alpha \frac{x}{l} = \frac{W}{P}. \tag{2}$$

We assume that the supply of labour ($\bar{l}$) is fixed and that money wages are determined by a Phelps–Friedman variant of the Phillips curve (Phelps, 1967; Friedman, 1968).

$$\frac{\dot{W}}{W} = \eta(l - \bar{l}) + e. \tag{3}$$

$$\dot{e} = \mu\left(\frac{\dot{P}}{P} - e\right). \tag{4}$$

The expected rate of price inflation (e) is based on adaptive expectations so that there is a short-run unemployment–inflation trade-off. Long-run equilibrium on the other hand requires full employment but is consistent with any constant rate of increase of wages and prices.

Net investment is given by a simple stock adjustment process, with the desired stock (k^*) determined by the profit maximisation condition of the neoclassical investment theory (Jorgenson, 1963) which equates the marginal product with the user cost defined as the sum of the real cost of capital (r) and the depreciation rate (δ). Jorgenson's approach is modified by replacing actual output with 'permanent output' (y) and assuming the latter to be determined by an adaptive expectations process.

$$\dot{k} = \gamma(k^* - k). \tag{5}$$

$$k^* = \frac{(1-\alpha)y}{r+\delta}. \tag{6}$$

$$\dot{y} = v(x - y). \tag{7}$$

This formulation of the investment function together with equations (1) and (2) imply that full employment output is not fixed. To the extent that changes in exogenous variables alter the long-run equilibrium cost of capital, they will also affect the equilibrium capital–labour ratio and the level of output.

Wealth, permanent income and asset demands

Real wealth (a) is given by:

$$a = \frac{M}{P} + \frac{1}{P}\frac{B}{i} + d + \frac{y_k}{r} + \frac{y_h}{s}. \tag{8}$$

where the symbols are defined as follows:

M stock of money

B interest payments on government debt, assumed to be in the form of perpetuities
d stock of consumer durables
y_k expected future stream of property income
y_h expected future stream of labour income
i nominal interest rate on government debt
s discount rate applied to human wealth.

Different discount rates are applied to income from government bonds, real capital and human wealth because of differences in risk, marketability, etc. Permanent income streams are related to current income through adaptive expectations.

$$\dot{y} = \phi\left[(1-\alpha)x - \frac{T}{P} - y_k\right].\qquad(9)$$

$$\dot{y}_h = \psi\left[\alpha x - \frac{U}{P} + \theta g - y_h\right].\qquad(10)$$

Current incomes are defined by the distributive shares implied by (2) net of taxes, denoted by T in the case of property income and U in the case of labour income. In the latter case we also make an allowance for perceived income arising from government activities (g) and include this adjustment in consumption as well.

The rates of return are determined by market-clearing conditions for money and real capital together with a reduced form relationship for the discount rate applied to future labour income.

$$m(-e, i-e, r, a, x) = \frac{M}{P}.\qquad(11)$$

$$v(-e, i-e, r, a, x) = \frac{y_k}{r}.\qquad(12)$$

$$s = s(i-e, r, y_h).\qquad(13)$$

The arguments of the demand functions are real rates of return, current income and wealth, and follow closely Friedman's (1956) classic statement of the modern quantity theory.

The restriction on the supplies of financial assets arising from the government budget constraint is:

$$\dot{M} + \frac{\dot{B}}{i} = Pg + B - T - U.\qquad(14)$$

The importance of incorporating this relationship has been emphasised by Ott and Ott (1965) and Christ (1967, 1968), but these authors fail to take account of interest payments on government debt as an item in government expenditures. This deficiency is remedied by Blinder and Solow (1973), but their analysis of fiscal policy is marred by an inadequate treatment of the relation between fiscal variables and wealth as well as the relation between wealth and expenditures.[2] This problem is taken up further below.

Consumption and income determination

We define consumption (to be distinguished from current expenditure on consumption goods) as the sum of the following components:

- c current expenditures on non-durables and services
- $(\rho + \epsilon)d$ consumption of durables, represented by imputed rent[3]
- θ_g perceived income from government activities

On the basis of the life-cycle variant of the permanent income hypothesis developed by Modigliani and Brumberg (1955), we assume consumption to be proportional to wealth.

$$c + (\rho + \epsilon)d + \theta g = \beta a. \tag{15}$$

Net investment in durables is given by a stock adjustment process with the desired stock (d^*) determined by the rental price and wealth.

$$\dot{d} = \lambda(d^* - d). \tag{16}$$

$$d^* = d^*(i - e + \epsilon, a). \tag{17}$$

The equilibrium condition for the goods market is:

$$x = c + \dot{d} + \epsilon d + \dot{k} + \delta k + g. \tag{18}$$

Impact effects of policy

For the purpose of analysing the impact effects of policy, we make the usual Keynesian assumption that prices and wages are fixed, and that changes in aggregate demand are translated into changes in real income. Permanent income streams are assumed to be unaffected by changes in current income and feedbacks from lagged stocks to expenditures are ignored. Thus for purposes of analysing impact effects, we use (6), (11), (12), (13) and (17) and replace the remainder of the model with the following first difference equations:

$$\Delta a = \frac{1}{P}\left(\Delta M + \frac{\Delta B}{i}\right)$$
$$- \left(\frac{1}{P}\frac{B}{i}\frac{\Delta i}{i} + \frac{y_k}{r}\frac{\Delta r}{r} + \frac{y_h}{s}\frac{\Delta s}{s}\right). \tag{19}$$

$$\Delta M + \frac{\Delta B}{i} = P\Delta g - \Delta T - \Delta U \tag{20}$$

$$\Delta x = \beta \Delta a + \lambda \Delta d^* + \gamma \Delta k^* + (1 - \theta)\Delta g \tag{21}$$

Equations (19) and (20) are obtained from (8) and (14) while (21) combines (5), (15), (16) and (18). The endogenous variables are k^*, i, r, s, d^*, a and x and the model can be reduced to the usual two-equation IS–LM system with i and x as unknowns as follows. The LM curve can be obtained by substituting for wealth and the cost of capital in (11) using (19) (12) and (13) and the IS curve can be obtained by making the same substitutions into (21) and using (6) and (17) to eliminate the desired stocks.

Although our short-run model can be represented in an *IS–LM* framework, it differs from the conventional version in two important respects. First we view the impact effects as operating through changes in stocks of assets rather than through flows of income and expenditure. The direct effect on aggregate demand of an increase in government expenditures shifts our *IS* curve but there is no Keynesian multiplier effect since changes in current output do not affect permanent income. An increase in wealth also shifts the *IS* curve because of the wealth effect on consumption. We would expect the impact on consumption of non-durables and services, as measured by the parameter β to be relatively small, but the accelerator effect on durable expenditures may be substantial unless the speed of adjustment (λ) is slow. The emphasis on wealth rather than income effects also implies that when the government budget constraint is allowed for, the dichotomy that associates monetary policy with the *LM* curve and fiscal policy with the *IS* curve breaks down (Silber, 1970).

The second distinguishing feature of our *IS–LM* model is that it incorporates the theory of the monetary mechanism developed by Tobin (1961, 1963). Tobin argues that bonds and real capital are not perfect substitutes in the portfolios of investors and that the cost of capital relevant to the investment decision is not the bond rate of interest but the rate of return on the existing stock of real capital which he calls the supply price of capital. In our model this variable is represented by the variable r which enters into the investment function. Thus the influence of policy changes on investment is transmitted through the effects of changes in wealth and relative supplies of assets on the supply price of capital.[4]

Steady-state model

We define the steady state as an equilibrium in which all endogenous variables in the model are constant, but we also consider the existence of equilibria in which real variables are constant while nominal ones are changing at a constant rate. Equilibrium in the goods market is described by the following equations which replace (1)–(7) and (15)–(18).

$$x = \xi(\bar{l})^{\alpha}(k^*)^{1-\alpha}. \tag{22}$$

$$e = \frac{\dot{P}}{P}. \tag{23}$$

$$k^* = (1-\alpha)\frac{x}{r+\delta}. \tag{24}$$

$$d^* = d^*(i-e+\epsilon, a). \tag{25}$$

$$x = \beta a - \rho d^* + \delta k^* + (1-\theta)g. \tag{26}$$

By setting permanent income equal to current income, we obtain the following equation for wealth in which the combination of terms into the variable Z is done to facilitate consideration of the relationship between wealth and the government budget constraint.

$$a = \frac{M}{P} + \frac{Z}{P} + d^* + \left(\frac{1-\alpha}{r} + \frac{\alpha}{s}\right)x - (1-\theta)\frac{g}{s} \qquad (27)$$

where

$$Z = \frac{1}{s}Pg + \frac{1}{i}B - \frac{1}{r}T - \frac{1}{s}U.$$

Equilibrium in the asset markets is described by the following set of equations in which (14) and (11) are repeated as (28) and (29) for convenience.

$$\dot{M} + \frac{\dot{B}}{i} = Pg + B - T - U. \qquad (28)$$

$$m(-e, i-e, r, a, x) = \frac{M}{P}. \qquad (29)$$

$$v(-e, i-e, r, a, x) = \frac{1}{r}\left[(1-\alpha)x - \frac{T}{P}\right]. \qquad (30)$$

$$s = s(i-e, r, \alpha x - \frac{U}{P} + \theta g). \qquad (31)$$

ANALYSIS OF POLICY

The explicit recognition of the government's budget constraint somewhat complicates the usual taxonomy of monetary and fiscal policy changes. We can define pure fiscal policy as any combination of changes in the exogenous variables in equation (14) other than the money stock which is held constant. The meaning of pure monetary policy is somewhat ambiguous, so without considering this semantic problem further, we consider the following three policies. First we consider a one-shot increase in the money stock under various assumptions concerning the offsetting change implied by the budget constraint; second we consider the existence and properties of an equilibrium with a constant rate of growth of the nominal money stock; and third we examine the effects of pure fiscal policy.

A one-shot increase in the money supply

The short-run effects of an increase in the money stock are illustrated in figure 1 using the *IS* and *LM* curves defined above. The way in which the curves shift will depend on whether there is an increase in wealth as would be the case if the money is used to increase expenditures or reduce taxes. An increase in wealth

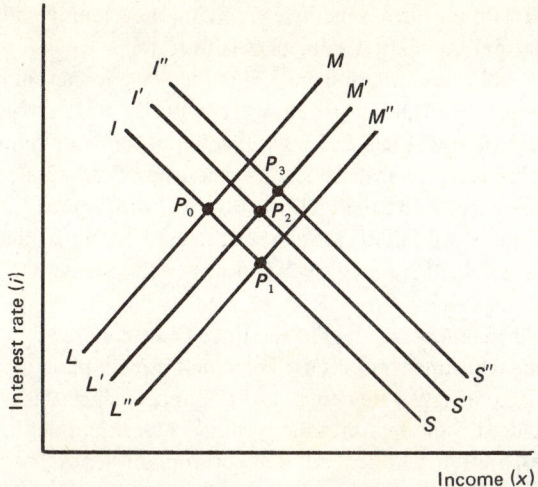

Figure 1 *Impact effect of an increase in the money stock*

reduces the shift in the *LM* curve to the extent that it increases the demand for money, and induces a shift in the *IS* curve through the wealth effect on consumption. We can distinguish three cases.

Open market operation. In this case there is no direct effect on wealth (as opposed to the indirect effect via changes in interest rates) so that we get a shift in the *LM* curve with no shift in the *IS* curve and a short-run equilibrium at P_1.

New money finance of a decrease in taxes. If the increase in the money stock is used to reduce taxes there is an increase in wealth so that we have a shift in the *IS* curve together with a smaller shift in the *LM* curve. The short-run equilibrium will be at P_2 which must be above P_1 but may be either to the right or left. Thus, compared with the open-market operation case, there will be a smaller fall in the interest rate but the increase in income may be larger or smaller.

New money finance of an increase in expenditures. Except in the case where government expenditures merely replaced private consumption ($\theta = 1$), we get a larger shift in the *IS* curve as a result of the direct impact on aggregate demand so that the new equilibrium is at P_3.

When account is taken of the complete model, the subsequent adjustments involve a conflict between expansionary and deflationary forces. Further growth of aggregate demand occurs as increases in real income are translated into increases in permanent output and permanent income, stimulating investment and consumption expenditures via the usual multiplier process. However, expansion of real income will be curtailed by the following influences:

1. Increases in income with no further increases in the money supply will cause interest rates to rise and the market value of wealth to fall.

2. Increases in income will cause inflation and consequently a reduction in the real value of financial assets. In the short run, wages will rise more slowly than prices so that the real wage will fall, and we will get increased employment at the expense of higher inflation. As inflationary expectations build up, however, wage inflation will accelerate and the Phillips curve will shift upwards.

3. Investment expenditures will fall as stocks of capital and consumer durables are built up and the accelerator process winds down to replacement demand.

At the same time the differences in effect in the three cases illustrated in figure 1 will narrow as the adjustment proceeds. The direct impact of an increase in government expenditures on aggregate demand will disappear since this is a one-shot change. Less evident is the fact that there will be a wealth effect in the case of an open-market operation. The reduction in government debt outstanding will lead to a reduction in government interest payments which will lead to a reduction in taxes if we assume taxes to be the residual item in the government budget constraint. Thus the reduction in bond holdings will be offset by an increase in human or other non-human wealth depending on the type of taxes reduced.

Turning to the steady-state version of the model, a basic question is the long-run neutrality of money; that is, do we ultimately get a proportional increase in the price level with no real effects? Clearly a necessary condition for neutrality is $s = r = i$. In this case the government budget constraint implies that in a steady state with a constant money supply and supply of bonds, the term in equation (27) denoted by Z is zero. In this case the only outside financial asset is money and a proportional change in the price level will restore total real wealth to its initial level. The speed with which real wealth is restored to its initial level in the case of an open-market operation will depend on the adjustment coefficients ϕ and ψ in equations (9) and (10), which determine the speed with which the tax reductions are incorporated into perceived permanent income.

Invariance of total wealth is not the only consideration since there will be changes in the composition of wealth if the money supply is increased by an open-market purchase of bonds. If the reduction in the government interest payments is offset by a reduction in taxes on labour income, there will be an increase in human wealth which enters into equation (31). Similarly if taxes on property income are reduced, the value of real capital on the right-hand side of equation (30) is increased. However, equality of discount rates implies perfect substitutability among non-monetary assets so that equations (30) and (31) drop out of the model. Thus we conclude that equality of discount rates is a necessary and sufficient condition for neutrality regardless of the method by which the money stock is increased.

Our conclusion concerning an open-market operation is at variance with those reached by Metzler (1951) and Mundell (1971, chapter 1). Metzler obtains non-neutrality because he considers an open-market purchase of equities and shows that this is equivalent to a capital levy on shares payable in kind. However, Metzler does not take account of the government's budget constraint and the income from government holdings of equities is not offset by an increase in expenditures or reduction of taxes. Furthermore, his analysis is short run: if the government buys existing capital goods and simply destroys them, we would get a fall in the interest rate but in the long run they would be replaced and the original equilibrium would be restored.

Mundell considers three cases. First, if the new money is used to finance an expenditure increase or a tax reduction, he obtains neutrality because he assumes that government interest payments are fixed in real terms so that money is the only asset whose supply is fixed in nominal terms. Second, Mundell concludes that an open-market operation combined with a reduction in income taxes is not neutral because he assumes that after-tax labour income is not capitalised and does not enter into wealth. Third, in the case of an open-market operation combined with a reduction in taxes on property income, he concludes there will be no direct effect on wealth because he assumes $r = i$. On the other hand he argues there will be an allocation effect if the *marginal rate* of tax on property income is reduced. Our analysis does not take account of the allocation effects of taxes.

In our view the assumption that labour income is not capitalized is not warranted particularly when the issue is viewed in the context of the permanent income theory of the consumption function, although we may wish to assume $s > i$. By the same token we may argue that $r > i$ so that departures from neutrality associated with tax discounting become a matter of degree.[5]

A constant rate of growth of the money supply

Under what circumstances will a constant rate of growth of the money supply combined with an equal rate of inflation be consistent with constant equilibrium values of all real variables? Again a necessary condition is $s = r = i$ since we will then have Z/P constant in equilibrium. This follows from equation (28) which (assuming $\dot{B} = 0$) implies that:

$$i\frac{Z}{P} = \frac{\dot{M}}{P} = \frac{\dot{M}}{P}\frac{M}{P}. \qquad (32)$$

However, in the present case with a non-zero rate of inflation, a problem arises from the fact that interest payments on government debt have been fixed in money terms so that i is a nominal rate of interest while r and s are real rates. In order to assume equality of discount rates, we must have indexed bonds with interest payments fixed in real terms so that i can also be interpreted as a real rate. Thus we can obtain a steady-state equilibrium by replacing $i - e$, i and s by r in (25), (27), (28) and (29), and dropping (30) and (31).

With these modifications, all real variables in the steady-state version of our model will be independent of the rate of growth of the money supply, with the exception of the demand for money. An increase in the rate of inflation will reduce the demand for money and lead to a one-shot increase in the price level so that real balances will fall.[6] The fall in real balances will reduce wealth and thus lead to lower real interest rates and a higher level of income. On the other hand this effect can be more than offset by the operation of the government budget constraint. Viewing inflation as a tax on real balances, the revenue in real terms is given by:

$$\frac{\dot{M}}{M}\frac{M}{P} = r\frac{Z}{P}. \tag{33}$$

If an increase in $\dot{M}/M$ increases the revenue, then it also increases Z/P and the net effect on wealth depends on the net change in:

$$\frac{M}{P} + \frac{Z}{P} = \left(1 + \frac{1}{r}\frac{\dot{M}}{M}\right)\frac{M}{P}$$

$$= \frac{1}{r}(r+e)\frac{M}{P}. \tag{34}$$

It follows from (34) that money will be neutral if the elasticity of demand for real balances with respect to the nominal interest rate is unity. In this case an increase in the rate of growth of the money stock will lead to a fall in real balances but will not affect any other real variables.

Fiscal policy

The question of the effectiveness of fiscal policy is at the heart of the monetarist debate. There seems to be general agreement that monetary policy affects real income and prices, but monetarists argue that fiscal policy is ineffective since increases in spending generated by the government sector 'crowd out' an equivalent amount of private spending.[7] Let us consider first the impact of an increase in real government expenditure financed by issuing bonds.

Figure 2 illustrates this case in terms of the *IS* and *LM* curves defined above. Complete crowding out will of course occur if the money demand function is interest-inelastic so that the *LM* curve is vertical. Tobin (1972) argues that this is the basis for the monetarist contention that fiscal policy is ineffective, but this interpretation is vigorously rejected by Friedman (1972). Friedman emphasises the importance of tracing through the subsequent adjustments rather than concentrating on 'first-round' effects, but there are a number of features of our model which reduce even the impact effect in comparison with the conventional *IS–LM* model.

1. The shift in the *IS* curve reflects the direct effect on demand plus the wealth effect but no multiplier process since permanent output and income are unaffected.

2. To the extent that government expenditure substitutes for private expenditure ($\theta > 0$), the effect on demand is reduced.

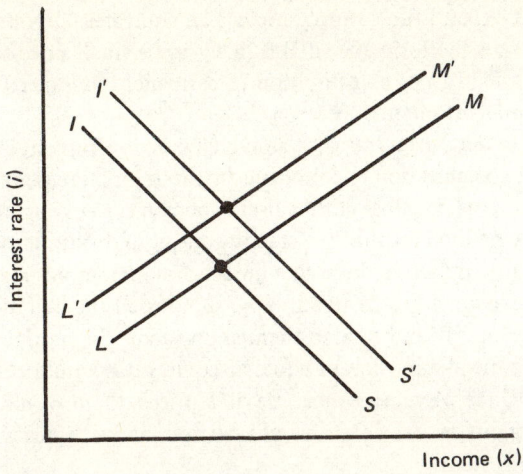

Figure 2 *Impact effect of a bond-financed increase in government expenditure*

3. As Silber (1970) has pointed out, the inclusion of wealth in the demand for money means that the *LM* curve shifts up, increasing interest rates and reducing income.

On the other hand it can be argued that Silber overstates the crowding out effect arising from the portfolio adjustment to an increase in the supply of bonds. Tobin (1963) has argued that an increase in the supply of bonds may lead to a *fall* in the supply price of capital, even though the bond rate rises, if real capital and bonds are poor substitutes in portfolios. This would be reflected in figure 2 in a larger shift in the *IS* curve.

If we assume the increase in real expenditures is maintained indefinitely, the subsequent adjustment path will be determined by the forces discussed above in the case of an increase in the money supply. In addition it will depend on the method of financing used in subsequent periods. Ultimately, in order to restore equilibrium, taxes must rise sufficiently to cover the expenditure increase plus the increased interest payments arising from temporary financing by bonds. As these tax increases are incorporated into permanent income, wealth will fall thus contributing to the crowding out of private expenditures.

If we neglect differences in discount rates the net effect in the steady state will depend on the extent to which government expenditures substitute for private consumption. From (27) we obtain the change in wealth as $-(1-\theta)\Delta g/s$ and substituting into (26) the net increase in aggregate demand is given by:

$$\Delta x = (1-\theta)\Delta g \left[1 - \frac{\beta}{s}\right]. \qquad (35)$$

The case in which $\theta = 1$ is the trivial one in which there is no impact or long-run effect because government expenditures simply replace an equivalent amount of private spending. In any event the term $1 - (\beta/s)$ is likely to be small since the ratio β/s is approximately the ratio of consumption to permanent income. This follows if we measure permanent income by $s \cdot a$.

Thus to a considerable extent, even if $\theta = 0$, an increase in government expenditures crowds out private consumption expenditures without an increase in the price level or interest rates. This conclusion that fiscal policy has a very small effect is not a consequence of the fact that the steady-state equilibrium in our model is at full employment, and would hold in a model of underemployment in which prices and wages are assumed to be fixed. If we suppressed the equations in our model determining P and W and treated them as constant, the net increase in aggregate demand under the assumption of equal discount rates would still be the amount given in (35). Once we reintroduced flexible prices, there would of course be further crowding out as real wealth would fall and interest rates would rise.

Our conclusions regarding the effects of fiscal policy are very much at variance with those of a number of previous analyses which take account of the government budget constraint. Ott and Ott (1965) and Christ (1968) derive the government expenditure multiplier as the reciprocal of the marginal tax rate. Blinder and Solow (1973) argue that when government interest payments are taken into account, this multiplier applies only to money-financed increases in expenditures while the multiplier in the case of bond finance is even larger.

We reject these conclusions on the grounds that the models used fail to incorporate properly the linkages between consumption, wealth and the government's budget constraint. For example, Blinder and Solow assume that consumption depends on disposable income, defined as total income plus government interest payments less taxes, and wealth, defined as holdings of money, bonds and real capital. Thus bonds, as well as real capital, are effectively counted twice, first as a flow of income and then as a stock of wealth. Human wealth, on the other hand, enters only as a flow and the whole question of discounted future tax liabilities is dismissed in a footnote (p.325). Their formulation implies that a one-shot increase in the supply of bonds with taxes raised to finance the interest will increase consumption since income will be unaffected but wealth will rise. We would argue that this involves an increase in non-human wealth offset by a decrease in human wealth.

The proposition that the multiplier is the reciprocal of the marginal tax rate (adjusted in the case of bond finance) merely reflects the fact already stated that taxes must ultimately rise by the amount required to cover the expenditure increase plus the increased interest payments. Since we argue that there is at most a small increase in income in the new equilibrium, tax *rates* must be raised to restore equilibrium. If the government attempted to finance an increase in real expenditures by a continual increase in the supply of bonds and no increase in the supply of money, the only way in which equilibrium could be restored (if indeed a stable equilibrium existed) would be through a fall in nominal expenditures brought about by a *fall* in the price level.

SUMMARY AND CONCLUSIONS

The major features and implications of our analysis can be summarised as follows.

1. The impact effects of policy are assumed to operate through changes in stocks of assets rather than flows of income and expenditure. Apart from the direct impact on demand of an increase in government expenditures, the influence of flows is felt with a lag through changes in permanent output and income.

2. On the basis of the permanent income theory of consumption, we use a broad measure of wealth that includes human wealth and allows for the effects of government expenditures and taxes on permanent income. The proper specification of the relationship between wealth and the government's budget constraint is seen to be crucial for the analysis of the long run effects of policy.

3. The impact effect of a one-shot increase in the money supply depends on whether there is a concomitant increase in taxes or expenditures, or reduction in the supply of bonds, but the differences narrow over time as the reduction in taxes associated with any fall in the supply of bonds is incorporated into permanent income.

4. A one-shot increase in the money supply is neutral only if the discount rates applied to bonds, property income, and labour income are equal.

5. A constant rate of growth of the money supply combined with an equal rate of inflation is consistent with constant equilibrium values of all real variables if government bonds are indexed and the discount rates are equal.

6. An increase in the rate of growth of the money supply will reduce real balances and leave other real variables unchanged if the elasticity of demand for real balances with respect to the nominal interest rate is unity.

7. The impact effect of an increase in government expenditures is lower than that obtained in conventional *IS-LM* models to the extent that an increase in wealth increases the demand for money or to the extent that government expenditure substitutes for private expenditure. The impact is also reduced by the assumption summarised in 1 above.

8. In the long run, there is a substantial crowding-out effect from an increase in government expenditures and a very small effect on real income, prices and interest rates. The speed with which the crowding out occurs depends, inter alia, on the speed with which the implied tax increases are incorporated into permanent income.

APPENDIX

The definitions of the symbols used are as follows. Upper case letters denote variables measured in money terms.

a   total real wealth
B   interest payments on government debt (perpetuities)

c expenditures on non-durables and services
d stock of consumer durables
d^* desired stock of consumer durables
e expected rate of inflation
g government expenditures
i nominal interest rate on government debt
k stock of real capital
k^* desired stock of real capital
l demand for labour
$\bar{l}$ supply of labour
M stock of money
P price level
r supply price of capital (cost of capital)
s discount rate applied to human wealth
T taxes on property income
U taxes on labour income
W wage rate
x real output
y permanent output
y_h permanent labour income
y_k permanent property income
$\dot{d}, \dot{k}$, etc. derivatives with respect to time
δ depreciation rate on capital stock
ϵ depreciation rate on consumer durables
ρ base year value of $i - e$

DISCUSSION: MARCUS H. MILLER

To construct an eclectic model which is designed to embody both neo-Keynesian and monetarist elements is liable to be a thankless task. Followers of either of the traditions drawn upon can be expected to cavil at the inclusion of elements reflecting the other tradition, and to emphasise any inaccuracies in the representation of their own views, so casting doubt on the value of the exercise. In my opinion, however, Professor Sparks deserves our gratitude for putting together in such short compass a construction which reveals clearly what assumptions are required to get characteristically monetarist results, and how these assumptions differ from those usually made by neo-Keynesians.

We are treated in the course of the paper to a brief survey of the literature on 'wealth effects' and to some criticisms of currently fashionable views of the long-run effects of bond financed fiscal policy; and we will here focus further on how Professor Spark's wealth effects relate to those discussed by Metzler and Mundell, and on the nature of his criticism of Blinder and Solow (1973).

For this purpose it is convenient to concentrate on the long run results, for which we need only consider the relationships given by equations (22) to (31). Using Spark's notation, with lower case letters denoting real variables, we first present the equivalent relationships based upon Mundell (1971, chapters 1, 2) in his development of Metzler's earlier work, as follows:

$$a = m + \frac{(1-\alpha)\bar{x} - t + b}{r},$$

$$L(i)(a-m) = M/P \equiv m,$$

$$S(r, a) = I(r),$$

where $\bar{x}$ is exogenously determined at full employment, and $r \equiv i - e$.

Thus the wealth variable includes real balances together with other 'non-human' wealth (real profits plus real bond payments less tax on such income, capitalised at the real rate r). Bonds are taken to be indexed, but money is not.

For Sparks's model, simplifying equations (22) to (31) by assuming $\theta = g = d^* = 0$ and $s = r = i - e$ and money financing, we can write

$$a = m + \frac{x - t - u + b}{r},$$

$$m(i, r, a, x) = M/P \equiv m,$$

$$x - \beta a = \delta k^*(r, \delta),$$

$$x = \xi \bar{l}^\alpha (k^*)^{1-\alpha},$$

$$\dot{M}/P = b - t - u,$$

where $\bar{l}$ is the exogenous supply of labour, and bonds are assumed to be indexed. The extra two equations make the level of output endogenous and make explicit the government's budget equation.

Sparks concludes that, for one-shot increases in the money supply (where in the steady state we therefore assume $\dot{M}/P = 0$ and $e = 0$), 'the equality of discount rates is a necessary and sufficient condition for neutrality regardless of the method by which the money stock is increased'. It is indeed evident that changing M and P in the same proportions will not affect the equilibrium values of all other variables, implying that an increase in money supply not offset by any reduction of bonds is 'neutral'. If there is an open market operation, so that bonds are reduced but real balances increase, then taxes must be cut to balance the budget. But if so, the open market operation will lead to no change in the real value of non-monetary wealth at the prevailing discount rate; hence, so long as the price level rises in proportion to the increase in money, equilibrium will prevail. So we would agree money is neutral here too.

So far so good: but when we turn to continuing increases in the money supply we come to a result which differs from Mundell's for reasons unconnected with the capitalisation of wage income. For Mundell the effect of increased monetary growth is clear; the rise in inflation will reduce the real rate of interest, as the rise in the nominal rate of interest reduces desired real balances and so the level of wealth (a). But Sparks postulates an offsetting effect, namely the fact that the inflation tax levied by the authorities on money $((\dot{M}/M)(M/P))$ allows them to *reduce* other taxes, and this latter *adds* to wealth. The suggestion is that the final result could go either way and depends on whether the fall in real balances exceeds the capitalised value of the inflation tax.

We would argue that this last named effect should not be included, so Mundell's result is not effectively set aside by Sparks's reasoning. In Mundell (1971, chapter 6), wealth is defined as the capitalised value of private disposable income — in so far as it *can* be capitalised, presumably. But in an inflationary environment, Solow (1970, p.60) has suggested that 'Disposable income in current prices is net national product less taxes plus transfers plus capital gains on money balances. These capital gains can be valued in current prices as $-M\dot{P}/P$.' We would thus argue that the stream of income which Sparks capitalises into wealth should include any deflation subsidy, or be net of any inflation tax, (so wealth should be modified to include the term $-me/r$). But if this is so, the reduction of other taxes consequent upon a rise in 'inflation taxation' will simply offset the fall in wealth caused by the inflation tax itself. We would thus argue that by redefining income and wealth as appropriate for inflationary conditions, the odd fact that inflation taxation has a positive effect on personal wealth will disappear, and leave Mundell's result to stand.

Ignoring, for reasons just given, this apparent discord between Sparks's results and those of Mundell, how do their general conclusions on monetary policy compare? First of all, Mundell grants the *principle* that 'if the private economy can capitalise [tax] liabilities [used to finance interest on the debt] there will be no change in wealth, and open market operations will have the same effect on prices and interest as a simple equal change in the quantity of money' (Mundell, 1971, chapter 1). But he also argues that 'in the real world some expected income streams are not readily capitalisable because of information costs, transactions costs, and various risks', and thus 'the rate of interest falls when open market purchases are combined with income tax reductions because capitalisable government interest payments are converted into non-capitalisable tax reductions'.

Sparks argues that labour income *is* capitalisable, through he grants that the discount rate may be higher than for government bonds; thus 'departures from neutrality become a matter of degree'. In support of his approach Sparks adduces the permanent income theory of the consumption function. While Sparks's position seems more consistent with much monetarist theorising than does Mundell's, it does carry some rather non-Keynesian implications which we mention below.

Another point of difference between the two authors is Sparks's neglect of the allocative effect of raising various taxes. Mundell has emphasised the effects of corporate taxes on corporate investment (and there could presumably be allocative effects attached to taxes on labour income even though the latter is not capitalised).

Before coming to fiscal policy, it is worth noting that deciding whether one capitalises various streams or not is distinct from deciding the degree of substitutability between the resulting components of wealth. Thus Tobin (1972), for example, has expressed the view that 'human and non-human wealth are not in general perfect substitutes for each other — indeed they are complements'.

Turning to Sparks's analysis of bond-financed government spending we see that he is critical of the results obtained by Blinder and Solow (1973). Insofar as the latter have a consumption function of the form

$$c = f(x + b - t - u, m + k + b/i)$$

it does seem fair to criticise them for double-counting bonds and capital, first as flows, then as stocks (though they are not without company in this; Foley and Sidrauski (1971) confess that in their book they 'introduce total wealth in the consumption function but without removing property income from disposable income, a procedure which suggests a kind of double counting'). But the implicit criticism, that the results of Blinder and Solow are not acceptable because they do not square with what is implied by the model specified here when all discount rates are equal, is much more difficult to sustain.

When all discount factors are equalised, bond financing has no wealth effects, and the expansion of aggregate demand which results from a parallel rise of taxes and government spending is simply the unit impact of the balanced-budget multiplier. But surely this is not being proposed as the most appropriate analysis of this issue?

Assuming that s and r exceed i will of course allow bond issues to have a net impact on wealth as the tax streams will be discounted more heavily than the bond coupons. Tobin (1972) has suggested that such a phenomenon may be ascribed to the monopoly which the government exercises over the issue of its bonds and bills, arguing that 'as long as the government does not expand the supply of these assets to the point where the public no longer pays an interest premium for their advantages, they will be valued more highly than the corresponding stream of taxes'. This effect can be captured in principle by the equations describing the asset markets (with an increase in b associated with a rise in i relative to other rates).

But is it enough simply to allow for different discount factors and to avoid double-counting? Will this provide a proper basis for analysing fiscal policy? Examining the resulting consumption function gives cause for doubt, for discounting labour income at a higher rate than property income while relating consumption solely to the aggregate measure of wealth implies that (at given discount rates) the marginal propensity to consume out of labour income (y_h) is *less* than that out of property income (y_k):

$$\text{if } c = \beta a = \beta \frac{y_h}{s} + \frac{y_k}{r}, \quad \text{then } \frac{\partial c}{\partial y_h} = \frac{\beta}{s} < \frac{\beta}{r} = \frac{\partial c}{\partial y_k}.$$

But surely those who put a high (even infinite) discount factor on human income are not likely to accept this restriction on consumption behaviour. (By way of empirical illustration, we note that the National Instiute of Economic and Social Research restricted UK marginal propensities to consume in such a manner as to imply long run values of 0.86 out of disposable 'wages and salaries' and 0.73 out of 'other disposable income' (see Surrey, 1971).

While the model is, with suitable restrictions on discount factors, capable of providing the monetarist analysis of the effects of fiscal policy spelt out in the paper, it is not clear that it is flexible enough to encompass a Keynesian position.

NOTES

1 This paper was completed while the author was a Visiting Fellow at the University of Southampton with financial support provided by a Canada Council Leave Fellowship. I am grateful for the facilities and assistance provided. I am also indebted to my discussant, Marcus Miller for his insightful comments in private discussions as well as in his formal presentation. However, responsibility for the contents remains that of the author and should not be attributed to any of the above.
2 A treatment of wealth and the budget constraint that is similar to ours is given by Brunner and Meltzer (1972). See also Rasche (1973).
3 The distinction between consumption of, and expenditures on, durables introduces an aggregation problem. We cannot assume the relative price of durable versus non-durable consumption is fixed since the imputed rental price of durables depends on the interest rate. To obviate this difficulty we use a base period value of the interest rate.
4 The importance of this mechanism as a component of a monetarist model is emphasised by Brunner and Meltzer (1972).
5 For a discussion of the tax discounting issue, see Barro (1974).
6 This process is analysed in detail by Friedman (1969).
7 See, for example, Spencer and Yohe (1970).

REFERENCES

Barro, R. (1974). Are government bonds net wealth? *Journal of Political Economy* **82**, 1095–117.

Blinder, A.S. and R.M. Solow, (1973). Does fiscal policy matter? *Journal of Public Economics* **2**, 319–37.

Brunner, K. and A.H. Meltzer, (1972). Money, debt, and economic activity. *Journal of Political Economy* **80**, 951–77.

Christ, C.F. (1967). A Short-run aggregate-demand model of the interdependence of monetary and fiscal policies with Keynesian and classical interest elasticities. *American Economic Review* **57**, 434–43.

Christ, C.F. (1968). A simple macroeconomic model with a government budget constraint. *Journal of Political Economy* **76**, 54–67.

Foley, D.K. and M. Sidrauski (1971). *Monetary and Fiscal Policy in a Growing Economy*. New York: Collier–Macmillan.

Friedman, M. (1956). The quantity theory of money: a restatement. In *Studies in the Quantity Theory of Money*, ed. M. Friedman, pp. 3–21. University of Chicago Press.

Friedman, M. (1968). The role of monetary policy. *American Economic Review* **58**, 1–17.

Friedman, M. (1969). *The Optimum Quantity of Money and Other Essays*. Chicago: Aldine.

Friedman, M. (1972). Comments on the critics. *Journal of Political Economy* **80**, 906–50.

Jorgenson, D. (1963). Capital theory and investment behaviour. *American Economic Review* **53**, 247–59.

Metzler, L. (1951). Wealth, saving and the rate of interest. *Journal of Political Economy* **59**, 93–116.

Modigliani, F. and R. Brumberg, (1955). Utility analysis and the consumption function: an interpretation of cross-section data. In *Post-Keynesian Economics*, ed. K. Kurihara, pp. 388–436. London: Allen and Unwin.

Mundell, R.A. (1971). *Monetary Theory*. Pacific Palisades, Cal.: Goodyear.

Ott, D.J. and A. Ott, (1965). Budget balance and equilibrium income. *Journal of Finance* **20**, 71–7.

Phelps, E. (1967). Phillips curves, expectations of inflation and optimal unemployment over time. *Economica* **34**, 254–81.

Rasche, R.H. (1973). A comparative static analysis of some monetarist propositions. *Federal Reserve Bank of St Louis Review* **55** (Dec.), 15–23.

Silber, W.L. (1970). Fiscal policy in *IS–LM* analysis: a correction. *Journal of Money, Credit and Banking* **2**, 461–72.

Solow, R.M. (1970). *Growth Theory*. Oxford University Press.

Spencer, R.W. and W.P. Yohe, (1970). The 'crowding out' of private expenditures by fiscal policy actions. *Federal Reserve Bank of St Louis Review* **52** (Oct.), 12–24.

Surrey, M.J.C. (1971). *The Analysis and Forecasting of the British Economy*. Cambridge University Press.

Tobin, J. (1961). Money, capital and other stores of value. *American Economic Review* **51**, 26–37.

Tobin, J. (1963). An essay on principles of debt management. In *Fiscal and Debt Management Policies*, Commission on Money and Credit, pp. 143–218. Englewood Cliffs, NJ: Prentice-Hall.

Tobin, J. (1972). Friedman's theoretical framework. *Journal of Political Economy* **80**, 852–63.

6 THE MOVEMENT OF FACTOR SHARES UNDER CONDITIONS OF RAPID ECONOMIC GROWTH

JOHN SUTTON[1]

The rapid growth of the postwar Japanese economy was accompanied by a marked decline in the share of wages and salaries in net output. This effect was observed for the non-agricultural sector as a whole (Ohkawa and Rosovsky, 1973) for manufacturing industry only (Minami and Ono, 1974), and for the 'modern' sector only (Minami, 1973). Furthermore, it has been noted that similar declines in the wage share occurred during the two earlier periods of rapid growth in the Japanese economy, from 1901 to 1911, and from 1931 to 1937 (Minami, 1973; Ohkawa and Rosovsky, 1973). These declines in the share of wages contrast with the long-run experience of a fairly constant share of wages noted by Ohkawa (1968).

This paper aims to explain the postwar decline in labour's share on the basis of a vintage capital model, which, it is argued, is more suitable for short-run analysis. It is shown that the response of factor shares to rising investment is critically dependent on the conditions of labour supply, and that the Japanese experience is easily explained in terms of the vintage capital model, once allowance is made for the availability of labour over the period studied. Comparisons are made with other economies experiencing rapid growth, and it is concluded that the model is consistent with the movements of factor shares observed.

THE MODEL

In dealing with short-run movements in factor shares, as opposed to long-run trends, the fact that opportunities for ex-post factor substitution are in practice likely to be severely limited becomes important. In particular, a model of the putty–clay type is clearly more appropriate than the putty–putty type model suitable for analysing trends over a period which is long compared to the lifetime of capital equipment. Moreover, a change in relative factor prices may take a number of years to affect the choice of technique, since expectations may not react rapidly to changes which possibly represent merely a temporary fluctuation from the underlying trend of factor price movements. This effect is likely to be further strengthened in the case of countries which, like Japan, tend to import their technology so that the choice of techniques does not always reflect domestic factor price ratios. This suggests the use of a model of the clay–clay variety for short-run analysis.

We begin by outlining in the present section some well-known results on the long-run behaviour of putty–clay models. These have been investigated by, in particular, Johansen (1959), Phelps (1963) and Bliss (1968). The recent study by Eltis (1973) is particularly valuable in the present context in that it provides some figures for the CES case which will be quoted below, and the present summary follows Eltis's treatment.

Firms are faced at each point in time with a production function which allows smooth substitutability of capital and labour. They anticipate that this production function will shift over time, reflecting technical progress, and wage costs will increase. Thus the quasi-rent they expect to earn on the equipment they construct in the current year, being the difference between output per man and the wage rate, will fall over time, becoming zero after some time T, the latter being the expected lifetime of capital.

In order to investigate the existence of a steady-state equilibrium path in such a model, we begin by taking the ratio of saving to national income, s, and the proportionate rate of growth of the labour force, n, as parameters. The existence of such an equilibrium requires the assumptions of constant returns to scale and Harrod neutral technical progress (at some rate a, say), so that the ex-ante production function is of the form

$$Y_t = F(K_t, L_t e^{at}); \quad \frac{Y_t}{E_t} = f\left(\frac{K_t}{E_t}\right); \quad E_t = L_t e^{at}$$

where E_t represents employment measured in 'effective labour units'.

The choice of technique problem is resolved by solving three equations to obtain the optimum capital–output ratio on new equipment, C, (the 'choice of technique'), the lifetime of capital, T, and the rate of return earned on equipment over its lifetime, r. We regard the savings ratio, s, the proportionate rate of growth of the labour force, n, and the elasticity of substitution on the ex-ante production function, θ, as parameters.

The three equations are as follows: firstly, the choice of technique decision is made by equating the capital cost of saving a worker on new equipment to the discounted cost of wages firms expect to pay over the lifetime of equipment; this yields an equation of the form

$$C = f(T, r, a, \theta).$$

Secondly, total savings equals the total volume of investment needed for a particular combination of a and T, which yields an equation of the form

$$s = f(C, T, a, n).$$

Finally, the operation of the capital market ensures that firms equate the cost of new plant to its discounted present value, where the discount rate is r, so that

$$C = f(T, r, a).$$

The above equations are given in explicit form by Eltis (1973), for the specific case of a CES production function. They serve to determine the characteristics of a steady-state equilibrium path, over which the rate of profit, the capital–output ratio, and the share of wages are constant.

The analyses of putty–clay models quoted above are concerned with comparisons between steady-state paths, and provide results showing, inter alia, the effect on the share of wages of a once-and-for-all increase in the share of national income devoted to investment. The economy can adjust to such a change by moving to a new equilibrium path on which the lifetime of equipment, T, the capital–output ratio, C, and the rate of return, r, will all, in general, be different. The effect of the rise in investment thus operates both on the choice of technique and on the lifetime of equipment. There is a critical value of the elasticity of substitution on the ex-ante production function, θ^*, such that if, and only if, $\theta < \theta^*$, a rise in the share of investment in national income will tend to lead to a rise in the share of wages, reflecting a fall in the lifetime or equipment T. Eltis calculates a value of θ^* in the region 0.7 to 0.83 for reasonable values of r and T. This result contrasts with non-vintage models, where the corresponding critical value of the elasticity of substitution is unity, but the two models are very similar otherwise. A rise in investment, with a given labour force, may lead to a rise or fall in the share of wages, depending only on the elasticity of substitution of capital and labour.

The present paper argues, however, that comparisons of long-run equilibria may not tell the whole story; the argument is that, as noted above, a rise in investment will not tend immediately to induce a change of technique. The analysis described below attempts to examine on a strictly short-run basis the movement of factor shares in response to a rise in the rate of investment above the levels achieved in the recent past. In the long run, it may or may not be the case that the economy moves towards the new equilibrium path specified above; if it does, the movement of the wage share is determined by the elasticity of substitution. However, the immediate impact, it is argued, will depend primarily on the elasticity of supply of labour. If the latter is zero, as assumed in the above model, the share of wages will rise, and this is the short-run factor price signal which must be relied on to bring the economy onto its new long-run path.

A RISE IN INVESTMENT

We suppose in the present section that the economy is initially on a steady-state equilibrium path. There is some captial–output ratio which is optimal and which reflects the expectations of entrepreneurs concerning future movements of wage rates over the lifetime of the capital equipment currently under construction. While the requirement that the economy be on a steady-state path will be relaxed below, this latter assumption will be retained: it essentially implies that the technology developed in the economy reflects experience of factor price

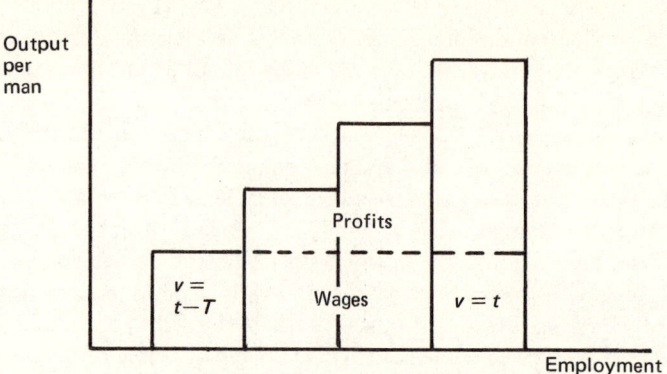

Figure 1 *The equilibrium path. Output per man increases by a factor e^a, while employment increases by e^n, on successive vintages*

movements over a period of time, and will not immediately respond to what are seen as short-run fluctuations in the factor price ratio.

The shares of wages and profits along a steady-state equilibrium path are illustrated in figure 1. The wage rate equals the level of output per man on the oldest vintage in use, denoted q_{t-T}, where T is the lifetime of equipment. Output per man is higher by a factor e^a on successive vintages, reflecting Harrod neutral technical progress; and the fact that employment rises at a proportionate rate over time, the lifetime of capital being constant, implies that the number of men, n_v, employed on vintage v rises by a factor e^n on successive vintages.

Thus the share of wages may be written as the quotient of total wages,

$$W(t) = q_{t-T} n_{t-T} (1 + e^n + e^{2n} + \cdots + e^{nT}),$$

and total output,

$$Y(t) = q_{t-T} n_{t-T} (1 + e^{n+a} + e^{2(n+a)} + \cdots + e^{(n+a)T}),$$

and is constant over time.

We now consider the effect of increasing the rate of investment above its equilibrium level at any point in time. Since the technique is assumed not to alter, an increase in investment at time t leads to a rise in employment on the current vintage.

It will be convenient to define two extreme cases, as follows; firstly, suppose that labour supply cannot be increased above its steady-state value; we then have the case corresponding to the usual assumption of a fixed rate of growth of labour supply.

Case 1: labour supply inelastic

An increase in employment on the most recent equipment now implies that labour must be drawn from the oldest vintages, so that the wage rate is bid up

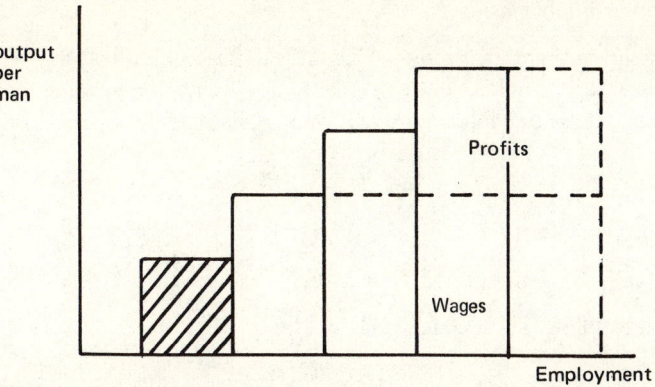

Figure 2 *A rise in investment above trend. Case 1: labour supply inelastic The shaded vintage now becomes obsolete*

and the lifetime of equipment declines. We will consider, for the sake of simplification, that the increase in employment is such as to draw all workers from vintage $(t-T)$ leading to the fall in a lifetime of capital to $(T-1)$ years, and the wage rate correspondingly increases to $q_{t-T}e^a$, being the output per man on vintage $t-(T-1)$. This is illustrated in figure 2.

Total wages now increase to

$$W_2(t) = q_{t-T}n_{t-T}e^a(1 + e^n + e^{2n} + \cdots + e^{nT})$$

while total output becomes

$$Y_2(t) = q_{t-T}n_{t-T}[(1 + e^{n+a} + e^{2(n+a)} + \cdots + e^{(n+a)T}) + (e^{aT} - 1)],$$

since n_{t-T} men have been transferred from vintage $(t-T)$ to vintage t, leading to a net increase in output of

$$q_{t-T}n_{t-T}(e^{aT} - 1).$$

It is easily shown from this that

$$S_2(t) = \frac{W_2(t)}{Y_2(t)} > \frac{W_1(t)}{Y_1(t)} = S_0(t).$$

Hence the upward movement of wage rates will now more than outweigh the rise in output, so that the wage share rises.

Suppose, however, that this is not the case, and that an increase in the wage rate above its steady-state path value can lead to a rise in labour supply. We then have the possibility that the increase in the wage rate required to expand employment above its steady-state value is small; this suggests considering the limiting case where the wage rate is not bid above its steady-state value, while employment expands.

Case 2: labour supply elastic

If, at any point in time, the supply of labour is perfectly elastic at the prevailing (steady-state) wage, employment expands from N_t to $N_t + \Delta n$, while the wage rate and the lifetime of capital are fixed. We thus have an increase in total wages to

$$W_1(t) = q_{t-T} n_{t-T} (1 + e^n + e^{2n} + \cdots + e^{nT} + \Delta n)$$

while output increases to

$$Y_1(t) = q_{t-T} n_{t-T} (1 + e^{n+a} + E^{2(n+a)} + \cdots + e^{(n+a)T} + \Delta n e^{aT})$$

from which it follows immediately that

$$S_1(t) = \frac{W_1(t)}{Y_1(t)} < \frac{W_0(t)}{Y_0(t)} = S_0(t)$$

so that the wage share declines. This follows essentially because the increased employment has occurred on the most recent vintage, on which the profit share is greatest. This is illustrated in figure 3.

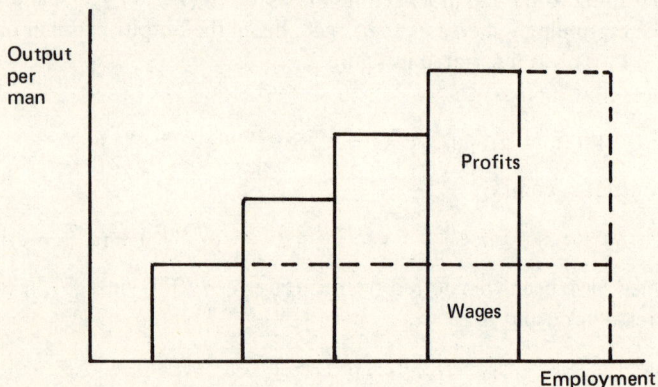

Figure 3 *A rise in investment above trend. Case 2: labour supply elastic*

The elastic supply case just considered might be a reasonable approximation in the following instances:

(a) where a flow of immigration occurs sufficient to provide the additional labour requirements,
(b) where a flow of emigration is occurring before the rise in investment takes place, so that employment rises in response to the appearance of job vacancies on the domestic market, while there is no induced increase in the wage rate,
(c) where an ongoing flow of labour out of the agricultural sector can be increased via more rapid mechanisation in agriculture, and/or the import of

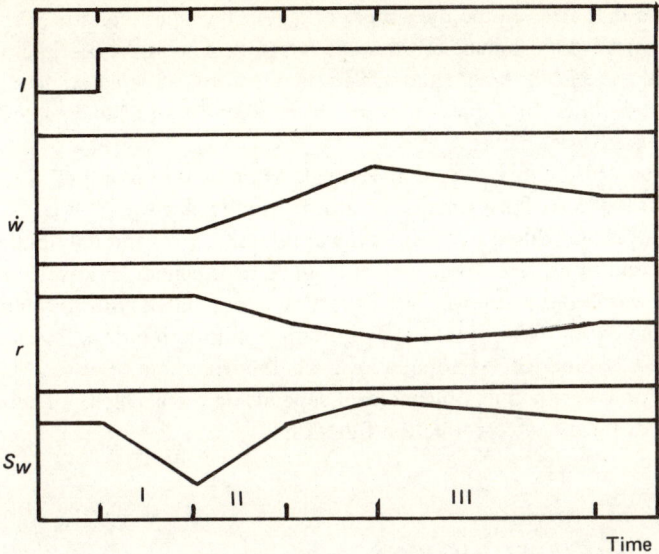

Figure 4 *The effect of a rise in investment above trend.*
Key: I: level of investment relative to steady-state equilibrium value
       S_w: wage share
       r: rate of return expected on new investment
       $\dot{w}$: year to year rate of increase of the product wage.

agricultural products so that employment in industry can be increased above its steady-state value in response to a small increase in the wage rate.[2]

We have thus established that if a rise in investment above the equilibrium level occurs at some point in time, the response of factor shares is critically dependent on conditions of labour supply, and, on our assumptions, will be such as to lead to an increase in the share of wages if employment can not be increased above its trend value.

It will be useful for the purposes of examining the empirical data presented later to sketch out the time path of the wage share on the assumption that the supply of labour is elastic up to a certain point, but that eventually labour shortages lead to a bidding up of wage rates and thus eventually lead to a rise in the wage share as described above.[3]

The time path of S_w, the wage share, is sketched in figure 4. We assume that at some point $t = 0$ the rate of investment increases above its orginal (steady-state) value. We now consider three phases, as follows:

I The initial effect is to expand employment, and assuming a perfectly elastic labour supply, real wages are unaffected, and the share of wages declines. The lifetime of capital remains fixed, so that the rate of return expected on new investment is unchanged.

II We suppose that after a time the supply of labour becomes inelastic. This will lead to an upward movement of the wage rate, a decline in the lifetime of capital and a rise in the wage share. The rate of return expected on new investment declines since quasi-rents are initially lower, and are expected to accrue over a shorter period.

III The reduced profitability of new investment will now lead to either
   (i) a fall in the rate of investment towards its trend value, or
   (ii) if investors are willing to accept a lower rate of return, and only under these conditions, rates of investment can be maintained. However, the higher wage rates and lower rate of return, as compared with the values associated with the original steady growth equilibrium path will induce a change of technique. As noted above, whether the share of wages will be higher or lower than its original level depends on the elasticity of substitution of the ex-ante production function.

RELAXING THE ASSUMPTIONS

The long-run trend

The above model is restrictive in that it assumes that the economy has been growing along a steady-state equilibrium path over time; this in turn necessitated the introduction of the assumption that the ex-ante production function exhibits constant returns to scale and Harrod neutral technical progress. This is unduly restrictive, however, since the implications of the model in the short run (phases II and III) require only a considerably weaker assumption, as follows. We assume that the lifetime of capital and the rate of increase in real wages, at full employment, have not fluctuated so much as to preclude a fairly stable expectation as to their future trends, and so allow a choice of technique to be based on past experience. It is also necessary to assume that the wage share at full employment has fluctuated about a fairly constant trend value — since we considered the movement of the wage share by comparison with the value it would have attained had investment not risen above its trend value. A slow secular rise of the wage share will modify the conclusions only slightly: the fall in which will accompany a rise in investment of the magnitudes cited below, if labour supply is elastic, will be such as easily to offset an underlying secular trend over the time periods considered.

The structure of the capital stock

It was assumed above that the rate of growth of the capital stock and employment on a given vintage was constant over time. If the capital stock is not balanced in this sense, the response of wages over time will be affected. In par-

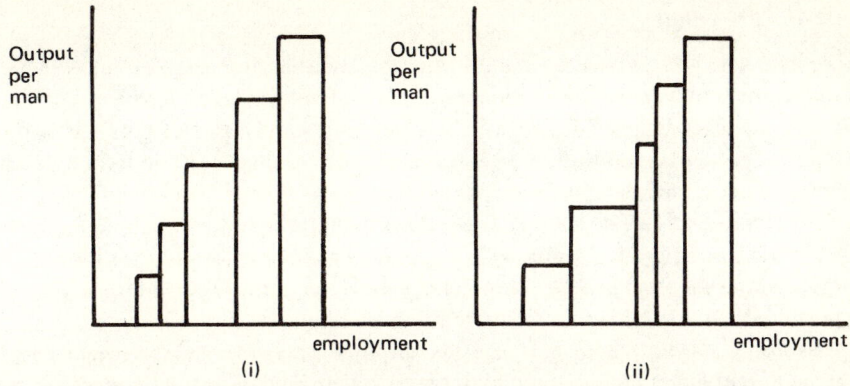

Figure 5 *Differences in the age structure of the capital stock*

ticular, the rate at which wages will rise in response to a given rise in investment at time t, the labour supply being fixed, will be affected. For the two cases illustrated in figure 5, for example, the immediate response of wage rates is sharper in (i) than in (ii).

However, once we assume that the new growth rate is higher than that attained over any period of a few consecutive years during the recent past, (the current lifetime of capital, to be precise), then the unevenness of the capital stock will merely be reflected in fluctuations in the wage share about the value predicted by the model.

Constant returns to scale

Insofar as investment rises, pressure on resources (the extractive industries, say) may lead to diminishing returns. This will be reflected in a lower output per man on new equipment, leading to a fall in the capital–output ratio, so that the rate of return anticipated on new equipment is depressed. This would tend to affect future investment plans adversely. Insofar as returns are increasing, the opposite effect may occur.

The machine–capital ratio

Ohkawa and Rosovsky (1973) note that all three phases of rapid growth in the Japanese economy have been marked by a rise in the ratio of plant and equipment relative to other types of capital stock (buildings etc.). Insofar as a temporary imbalance of the capital stock of this kind occurs, it will tend to reduce the capital–output ratio. This implies that the rate of profit will rise, if wage and profit shares are constant.[4] This effect is not of its nature likely to continue for a long period, but insofar as it operates, it may serve to prolong the high investment phase.

Capital utilisation

We have assumed above that there is full capacity utilisation throughout. While this is likely to be true during the period when investment is above its trend value, the preceding period may be characterised by less than full capacity working. Under these conditions, it is important to relax the assumption that, on each vintage, the capital–labour ratio is fixed. We divide workers into 'direct' (shop-floor labour likely to be laid off at the downswing) and 'indirect' labour (office staff, etc., who tend to be retained). A fall in demand is then associated with reduced output from each vintage. Taking the output from any vintage as proportionate to 'direct' labour, we have the following expression for the share of wages on vintage v, where q_v represents output per man (direct labour only), n_v^d, n_v^i represent direct and indirect labour respectively, and w_t is the (common) wage at time t,

$$\frac{W_t(v)}{Y_t(v)} = \frac{(n_v^d + n_v^i)w_t}{n_v^d q_v}$$

so that a fall in capacity utilisation, and so a fall in n_v^d, raises the share of wages. This is in accordance with the well-known observation that the wage share moves inversely with the cycle. The effect may be partially offset by concentrating direct labour on the newest available vintages within each firm; but the importance of this effect is not likely to be great except in the extreme case where all firms have a capital stock consisting of a wide spectrum of vintages.

Insofar as the rise in investment coincides with a recovery from less than full capacity utilisation, the associated fall in the wage share will accentuate the decline observed in phase I (assuming labour supply is initially elastic so that such a phase occurs). After full capacity utilisation is achieved, however, the approximation of a homogeneous labour force used in the basic model is a reasonable one.

We may summarise the above qualifications as follows. If we assume that expectations of relative factor prices are such as to produce, at a fairly steady trend value of the investment–national-income ratio, an approximately constant, or possibly slowly rising, wage share, then a rise in the rate of investment above trend will cause a decline in the share of wages if labour supply is (initially) elastic; otherwise the wage share will rise. The result does not depend on the assumption that the capital stock is initially balanced. The movement of the capital–output ratio will depend on the existence of economies or diseconomies of scale and the composition of new investment. The rate of return will, however, be adversely affected unless the capital–output ratio declines continually (assuming labour supply becomes inelastic after a time). Insofar as this is unlikely to occur, one of two consequences follow: either rising wages alter expectations and induce a change of technique, so that a transition to a new equilibrium path along which the rate of return is lower occurs, or else investment is reduced towards its original trend value due to the reduction in expected rates of return. Both of these effects will tend to offset further increases in the wage share.

THE JAPANESE EXPERIENCE

The Japanese economy expanded rapidly during the whole postwar period, with fluctuations in the growth rate coinciding with fluctuations in investment, which was, however, maintained at all times at levels which were high by international standards.

The dislocations which followed the war persisted through the late 1940s, but the boom of 1950–2 associated with the Korean War brought industrial output back to prewar levels in 1951. This boom led, however, to a deterioration in the initially strong balance of payments position, which provoked tight monetary controls, and a setback occurred in 1953–5. This was followed by a very rapid rise in investment up to 1962 (apart from a slowing down associated with tight monetary policy in 1957) and, after a 'stumble' from 1962–6, the growth rate again rose markedly between 1966 and 1970.

The serious problems posed by composition effects[5] in studying movements of factor shares suggest concentrating on the mining and manufacturing sector, in order to minimise such difficulties.[6] The level of investment as a percentage of net output in mining and manufacturing is shown in figure 6(a) while the

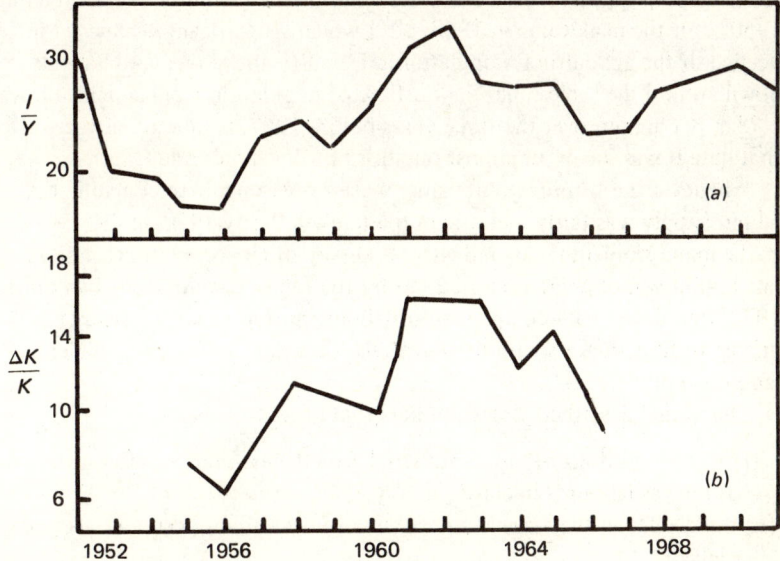

Figure 6 *Japanese mining and manufacturing*
    (a) Fixed investment ÷ net output
    (b) Year-to-year percentage change in the stock of capital

year-to-year rates of growth of the real stock of capital are shown in figure 6(*b*) for the same sector. It is clear that investment levels were high throughout, but reflect the setbacks of the post-Korean-boom years, of 1957, and of the period 1962–6.

The conditions of labour supply varied markedly over the two decades. In the immediate postwar period, severe dislocations in the industrial sector accompanied a high inflow of persons repatriated from overseas, and the population involved in agriculture increased rapidly to levels far in excess of those prevailing before the war, reflecting serious underemployment. This implied that a large reserve of labour was available to industry not only during the recovery phase up to 1951, but throughout the 1950s. The percentage of the population involved in agriculture fell from 46.7% in 1951 to 21.5% in 1967. This halving of the agricultural population, however, led to tight labour conditions in the late 1960s. The exact timing of the changed conditions of labour supply is arbitrary, since such a change is of its nature gradual, but Minami's suggestion that the change occurred in the early 1960s may put it too early. Minami measures the elasticity of supply of primary sector labour to non-primary sector industry. He takes agricultural wages as the supply price of agricultural labour, and estimates the elasticity of supply for the period 1959–68 as 0.4, compared with a value of 1.2 for the period 1897–1958. Whether labour was in inelastic supply in the early 1960s may be questionable; it seems certain, however, that by the late 1960s the changeover had occurred. The level of unemployment fell below unfilled vacancies for the first time in 1967. The postwar increase in birth rate led to a rising supply of school leavers entering the labour market in the mid-1960s, but the peak came in 1968, after which a significant decline set in. The decline of the agricultural population referred to above seems to have slowed down around the same time; the outflow of population from agriculture was 1.78 m per annum over the three years before 1967; for the three years after that date it was 0.6 m, or almost one-third of the earlier rate.

Whenever the turning point came, it seems reasonable to conclude that labour supply was fairly inelastic in the late 1960s; by 1970, in fact, it was seen as the main problem facing industry. A survey of all corporations capitalised at one billion yen or greater, carried out by the Japan Development Bank in July 1970, found that 61% complained of labour shortages, while a further 39% were unable to find workers with desired skills. Less than 1% had no problem of labour supply.

The model described above predicts that

(i) under conditions of rapid industrial growth, the share of wages will decline as long as labour is in elastic supply,
(ii) the decline in the wage share will be reversed if labour supply becomes inelastic,
(iii) the share of wages will fluctuate inversely with the cycle about the trend described by (i) and (ii).

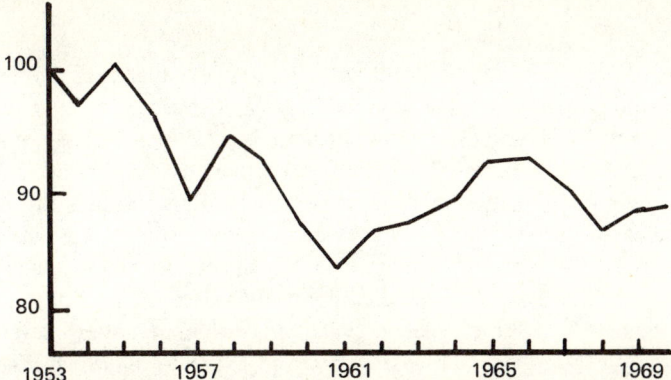

Figure 7 *Minami and Ono's estimate of labour's share[7] in mining, manufacturing, construction, facilitating industries and public utilities, Japan (1953 = 100)*

It was argued above that labour supply was highly elastic throughout the 1950s in Japan, but that it became less elastic during the following decade. On the basis of the present model we would therefore expect to find a downward trend in the wage share during the 1950s, but this downward trend should be offset during the 1960s as the supply of labour becomes less elastic. Moreover, changes in the rate of growth from year to year should lead to fluctuations above trend, a rise in the rate of growth being associated with a fall in the wage share below trend.

The share of wages, defined to include not only wages and salaries but also non-wage components of income, has been estimated by Minami and Ono (1974) and is shown in figure 7, for mining and manufacturing, construction, facilitating industries and public utilities. It is seen that the wage share declined markedly during the 1950s, as predicted on the basis of the model. Moreover, this trend is not evident after 1961, when the trend is slightly upward. The fluctuations about trend are of particular interest. Firstly, the setback of 1957 led to a rise in labour's share from 1957 to 1958. Secondly, the 'stumble' of 1962-8 was associated with a significant increase in labour's share. Thus the sharp turning point suggested by the graph may be somewhat misleading; the rise in labour's share in the early 1960s may be due primarily to the changing growth rate. However, the increase in the rate of growth which occurred in the late 1960s was associated with only a small decline in labour's share, as expected in the light of the tighter conditions then prevailing in the labour market.

The prediction of the present model, viz. that labour's share should decline markedly as the growth rate increases, but that this decline should be reversed over time as labour supply becomes less elastic, thus seems to be consistent with Japanese experience.

SOME COMPARISONS

While the model seems to be consistent with Japanese experience in the three periods of rapid growth which the economy has experienced, and in particular seems to account for the changed nature of the relationship after 1967, it is of interest to examine whether it is consistent with other countries during similar periods. A preliminary study of postwar experience in Europe and North America indicated that two countries enjoyed a steady period of rapid industrial growth over a decade or more.[8] Firstly, the German economy grew steadily over the postwar period as a whole. A good comparison is afforded by Denison (1967), as illustrated in Table 1. Secondly, the Irish economy, after a severe recession in the 1950s, grew rapidly from 1958 to 1968, during which time a rate of growth of capital stock in real terms of 9% per annum was achieved.

Table 1 *Denison's estimates of the rate of growth of capital stock, 1950–62*

USA	3.58	Germany	6.37
Belgium	2.61	Netherlands	4.72
Denmark	5.06	Norway	4.23
France	4.17	UK	3.35
		Italy	3.50

The rate of growth of capital stock in manufacturing industry is illustrated for the three countries in figure 8. The three countries differ considerably in growth rate (Japan), size (Ireland), and labour supply (Germany). Thus in spite of the small number of examples available, they do allow of some (fairly modest) conclusions concerning the validity of the model. The percentage of the occupied population involved in agriculture is illustrated in table 2. In spite of the rapid decline in the figures over the period 1951–67 the percentage remained high throughout in the Irish case.[9]

Table 2 *Percentage of occupied population involved in agriculture*

Year	Japan	Ireland	Germany
1951	46.7	40.3	21.4
1967	21.5	29.6	10.2

Sources: Stolper, Hanser and Borchardt (1967), Meenan (1970), Ohkawa and Rosovsky (1973).

The rate of growth of the stock of capital in Irish manufacturing is illustrated in figure 9, which shows clearly the recovery phase 1958–61. While some decline in labour's share might be expected to accompany the return to full capacity working, the present model (which is based on the assumption of full capacity

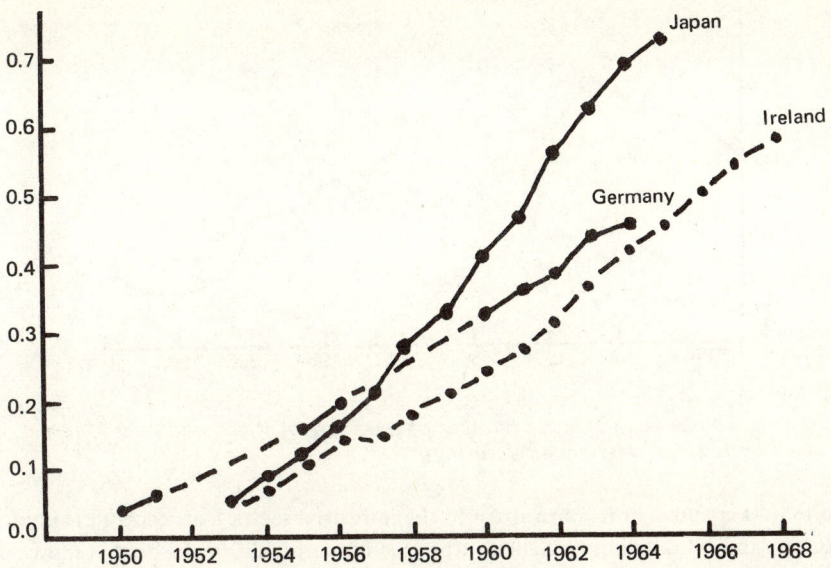

Figure 8 *Capital stock of manufacturing industry (for Germany, mining and manufacturing; German series incomplete): semilog scale*

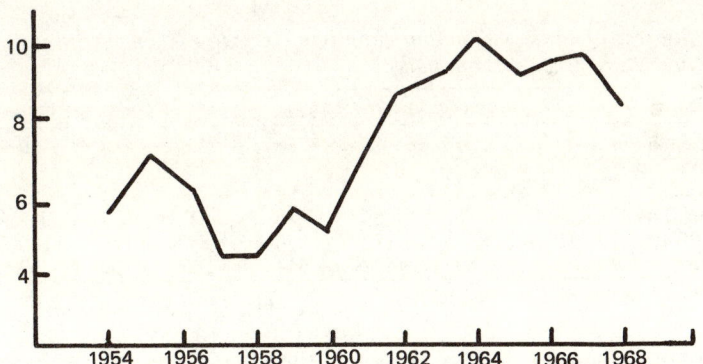

Figure 9 *Ireland: year-to-year rate of growth of the stock of capital (manufacturing)*

working), would suggest a fairly steady rate of decline of the wage share in the post-1961 period. That this in fact has occurred is illustrated in figure 10 which shows the index number to base 1957 of the share of wages and salaries in net output for manufacturing industry.

The German economy is of particular interest due to the different conditions of labour supply which prevailed in the first and second decades of the postwar

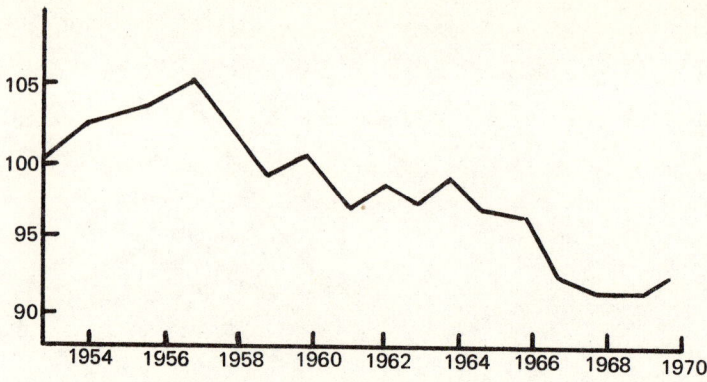

Figure 10 *Ireland: index number of the share of wages and salaries in net output (manufacturing)*

period. The course of labour supply to the industrial sector has been studied by Poncet, and his tabulation of the source of supply of additional labour is shown in table 3. During the 1950s, the combination of natural population movements and a very large inflow of immigrants from East Germany allowed a rapid growth of the industrial labour force, and the inflow to the labour market in the early 1950s was evidenced by a high level of unemployment. While unemployment figures for 1950 probably indicate not only the high level of structural

Table 3 *Sources of additional labour supply in Germany (change with respect to preceding year, in thousands)*

	1955	1960	1961	1962	1963	1964	1965
Natural population movements	+375	+18	−58	−33	−18	−50	−62
Unemployed	+293	+241	+90	+26	−31	+17	+24
Migrations (East Germany)	+161	+56	+116	+45	+2	+2	+2
Inflow of foreign labour	+8	+112	+196	+154	+144	+130	+210
Total	+837	+437	+344	+92	+192	+99	+174

Source: Poncet (1970)

unemployment (geographic misallocation of the workforce) and a significant fraction of unemployable persons, but also some underutilisation of capacity, Wallich's (1955) figures for 1952 suggest that over 80% of unemployment can be accounted for in terms of the first two categories. Thus the early 1950s were characterised by rapid growth at full capacity working and a continuous inflow of immigration which maintained a significant level of unemployment. This level of unemployment was continually eroded by the outflow to industrial employment, which Poncet's figures indicate to be of importance up to the late 1950s.

During the latter part of the decade, however, immigration from East Germany fell rapidly, becoming insignificant after 1960. This was immediately

Table 4 *Unemployment (U) and unfilled vacancies (V) in the German economy*

Year	U	V	Year	U	V
1952	1,385	129	1964	169	671
1956	765	236	1966	161	536
1960	270	539	1968	323	609
1962	154	607	1970	148	811

Source: Hallett (1973)

reflected in the labour market; while unemployment exceeded unfilled vacancies in the 1950s, the position was reversed from 1960 onwards. The tight conditions on the labour market were seen as the main barrier to growth in the 1960s, and led to the policy of allowing foreign immigration. The resulting inflow was never sufficient to allow more than a very slow expansion of the labour force in comparison with the levels attained in the 1950s, however, and the changed nature of labour supply is well illustrated by Helmstadter (1967) (see figure 11). The turning point came in the late 1950s, after which the supply of labour was severly curtailed.

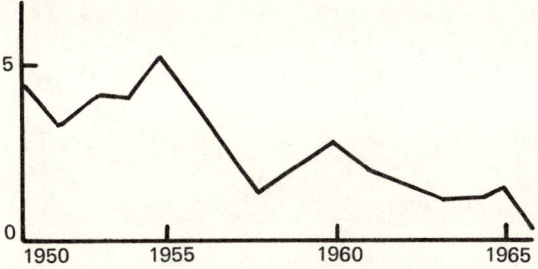

Figure 11 *Year-to-year percentage growth of the occupied population in Germany*

On the basis of the above model, it is to be expected that the wage share should decline during the 1950s, but that this decline should be checked during the 1960s. This is confirmed by reference to figure 12, which shows that while the wage share fluctuated considerably from year to year, it fell by 15 points up to the low of 1961, but subsequently remained fairly steady. The fall of 1958–61 is of some interest, as it coincided with an upswing in labour supply (see figure 11), while the rise of 1966–8 coincided with a temporary setback to the otherwise high rate of growth.[10]

SUMMARY AND CONCLUSIONS

The limitations of the above analysis require little comment. The scope of the article is limited to simple qualitative predictions, which rest on a model of an

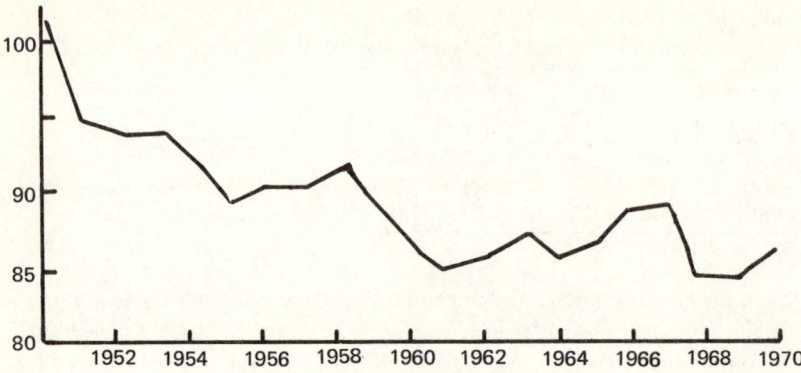

Figure 12 *Germany: index number of the share of wages and salaries in net output (mining and manufacturing)*

extremely simple kind. The fact that fairly satisfactory explanations of the main trends observed can be provided on the basis of a very elementary approach is of some interest, however, in indicating the value of using a vintage capital approach in short-run analysis. The differences between the predictions of such a model and the putty–putty approach are not so great as to constitute a serious criticism of the latter in long-run analysis, where factor substitution plays a key role. In the analysis of trends observed over, say, a decade, however, the predictions of the two models may differ widely, and the vintage approach must be preferred.

APPENDIX A

The aim of the present section is to describe the behaviour of certain variables over time, on the basis of the following assumptions:

(a) We consider a one sector model, of the economy as a whole, with constant returns to scale and Harrod neutral technical progress. We assume the model to be initially on a steady state growth path.

(b) Investment per unit time, which is initially given by $I_0 \exp(at)$ increases at time ζ to $kI_0\exp(at)$ and remains indefinitely on this latter path.

(c) During the interval from ζ to some time ζ_1 an exogenous inflow of labour occurs which is precisely such as to provide the excess of labour requirements over the steady-state growth path value. In general, total employment along a steady-state growth path increases according to $N_t = N_0\exp(nt)$; it will, however, simplify the present analysis considerably without materially affecting the conclusions if we take n as zero. Labour supply is then constant up to time ζ, increases by virtue of an exogenous inflow of labour from ζ to ζ_1, and is thereafter constant at its new value.

We may describe the initial steady-state equilibrium path as follows: the lifetime of capital, T, is constant at some value T_0. The capital–labour ratio increases at a proportionate rate a, as does the rate of investment, so that the number of men required to operate new equipment constructed during the interval $t, t + \Delta t$ is $n_0 \Delta t$ where n_0 is a constant. The total labour force is fixed, by virtue of our earlier assumption, and the $n_0 \Delta t$ men required are withdrawn from old vintages constructed during the interval $t - T_0, t - T_0 + \Delta t$, which now become obsolete.

Let output per head on the vintage constructed at time $t = 0$ be labelled w_0 so that the wage rate at time t is $w_0 \exp(t - T)$. Vintages constructed during any interval $\theta, \theta + \Delta \theta$ employ $n_0 \Delta \theta$ men, and output per head on this equipment is $w_0 \exp(a\theta)$. Thus total wages and total output at time t are given by

$$Y_t = \int_{t-T}^{t} n_0 w_0 \exp(a\theta) d\theta \tag{A1}$$

$$w_t = N_t w_0 \exp[a(t - T)] \tag{A2}$$

where N_t represents total employment at time t.

We consider the effect of increasing investment at time ζ as described above, assuming initially that no change of technique is induced by this increase. Employment on vintages constructed during the interval $\theta, \theta + \Delta \theta$ then increases from $n_0 \Delta \theta$ to $k n_0 \Delta \theta$. Total employment thus expands from $n_0 T_0$ to

$$N_t = n_0 [T + (k - 1)(t - \zeta)] \tag{A3}$$

while total output and total wages becomes

$$Y_t = \int_{t-T}^{\zeta} n_0 w_0 \exp(a\theta) d\theta + \int_{\zeta}^{t} k n_0 w_0 \exp(a\theta) d\theta \tag{A4}$$

$$W_t = N_t w_t = N_t w_0 \exp[a(t - T)] = n_0 w_0 [T + (k - 1)(t - \zeta)] \exp[a(t - T)]. \tag{A5}$$

Differentiation of (A4) and (A5) now yields – taking the second form of W_t

$$\hat{Y}_t = \frac{k \exp(aT) - (1 - \dot{T})}{k \exp(aT) - (k - 1) \exp\{a[T - (t - \zeta)]\} - 1} a \tag{A6}$$

$$\hat{W}_t = \hat{N}_t + a(1 - \dot{T}) \tag{A7}$$

(where we use the notation $\dot{x} = dx/dt$, $\hat{x} = (1/x)(dx/dt)$). The share of wages, S_t, is given by W_t/Y_t, from which it immediately follows that $\hat{S} = \hat{W}_t - \hat{Y}_t$, a relationship which will be found useful below.

We consider the time path of T, the lifetime of capital, and S_t, the share of wages, during phase I, when an exogenous inflow of labour occurs, and phase II, during which this inflow is no longer present.

Phase I: $\zeta < t < \zeta_1$: Employment on new equipment increases relative to its steady state equilibrium value, but the exogenous inflow of labour provides the increased requirements, so that the wage rate is unaffected. The lifetime of capital, T, is unchanged from its initial value T_0, so that $\dot{T} = 0$. Moreover, differentiation of (A3) yields an expression for the proportionate rate of change of labour supply,

$$\hat{N}_t = \frac{k-1}{(k-1)(t-\zeta) + T}$$

Substitution of the above values of $\dot{T}$ and $\hat{N}_t$ in (A4) to (A7) yields expressions for $W_t, Y_t, \hat{W}_t, \hat{Y}_t$ in phase I. The movement of the wage share may now be investigated as follows. From the expressions for W_t, Y_t, setting $t = \zeta$, we obtain the steady-state growth path values of these variables, and hence of S_t. Thus there is no discontinuity at time ζ. From the expression for $\hat{W}_t, \hat{Y}_t$, again setting $t = \zeta$, we find the initial values,

$$\hat{W} = \frac{k-1}{T} + a, \quad \hat{Y} = \frac{k-1}{T} + ka, \quad \hat{S} = -(k-1)a$$

so that $\hat{S}$ is negative, implying an initial decline in S during the interval from ζ to ζ_1. We rearrange the expressions for W_t, Y_t in phase I to obtain,

$$W_t = [W_0 + (k-1)n_0 w_0 \exp(-aT)t] \exp(aT)$$

$$Y_t = Y_0 \exp(at) + (k-1)\frac{n_0 w_0}{a} \exp(a\zeta)[\exp(at) - 1].$$

We examine the value of W_t and Y_t over time with respect to their steady state values $W_t = W_0 \exp(at)$, $Y_t = Y_0 \exp(at)$ by considering the shapes of the curves $W_t \exp(-at)$, $Y_t \exp(-at)$ whose quotient yields the wage share S_t (see figure 13). Since $W_t \exp(-at)$ increases linearly, but $Y_t \exp(-aT)$ increases at a diminishing rate, it follows that S decreases at a diminishing rate (and would eventually begin to increase).

Phase II: $\zeta_1 < t < \zeta_f$: (ζ_f is defined below). The supply of labour is now fixed, so that $\hat{N} = 0$. The number of men required to operate new equipment constructed during the interval $t, t + \Delta t$ is $kn_0 \Delta t$, and this is equal to the number withdrawn from old equipment, $n_0(\Delta t - \Delta T)$. Hence, equating these expressions, we obtain in the limit

$$\dot{T} = -(k-1)$$

and so the lifetime of capital falls linearly,

$$T = T_0 - (k-1)(t - \zeta_1).$$

Substituting these expressions into (A7), (A8) we have

$$\hat{W} = ka, \quad \hat{Y} = ka f(t),$$

where

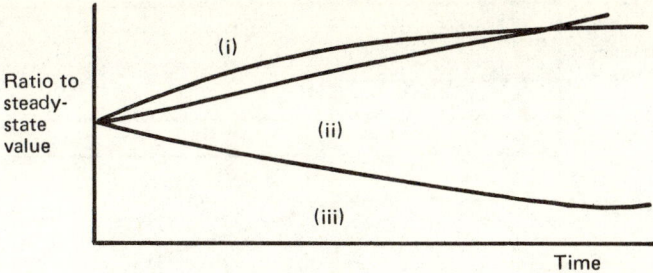

Figure 13 *The time paths of total wages (i), total output (ii), and the wage share (iii), expressed as a ratio of their steady-state growth path values in phase I*

$$f(t) = \frac{\exp(aT) - 1}{k\exp(aT) - (k-1)\exp\{a[T - (t - \zeta)]\} - 1}.$$

The term $f(t)$ represents the ratio of the steady-state value of output to its actual value; its initial value at $t = \zeta$ is unity and it subsequently decreases, though at a diminishing rate. We have

$$\hat{S}_t = ka[1 - f(t)].$$

Thus $\hat{S}$ increases at an increasing rate, so that S increases at an increasing rate also. If, and only if, no exogenous inflow of labour occurs, so that $\zeta = \zeta_1$ (no phase I) then $\hat{S}$ is initially zero; otherwise it is initially positive.

Phase III: The end of phase II occurs when $t - T = \zeta$, i.e. the oldest equipment in use is of vintage ζ, the number of men employed on new vintages during the interval $t, t + \Delta t$, is $kn_0 \Delta t$ while the number drawn from old vintages is $kn_0(\Delta t - \Delta T)$. Equating these expressions, $\Delta T = 0$, so that the lifetime of capital, and hence the wage share are constant at their new values.

The time paths of T and S_t are shown in figure 14. The equations of the wage rate and the expected rate of return on new equipment may easily be written down by reference to that of T (noting $w_t = w_0 \exp[a(t - T)]$).

The effect of a change of technique will now be considered. In phase II, the wage rate increases above its steady-state value. Suppose this induces a switch to a more capital intensive technique, from time ζ_2 onwards so that the capital–labour ratio on each vintage is increased by a factor c. Then the number of men required to operate new equipment is correspondingly reduced, so that the lifetime of capital is easily shown to decrease at the lesser rate $-(k/c - 1)$. This situation persists until time t such that $t - T = \zeta$; we label this time ζ_3. Thereafter, the number of men required to operate new equipment constructed during the interval $t, t + \Delta t$ is $kn_0 \Delta t/c$; equating this to the number of men withdrawn from old vintages, which is now $kn_0(\Delta t - \Delta T)$ we obtain $\dot{T} = (c-1)/c$ which is positive so that the lifetime of capital increases. This phase ends at time t such

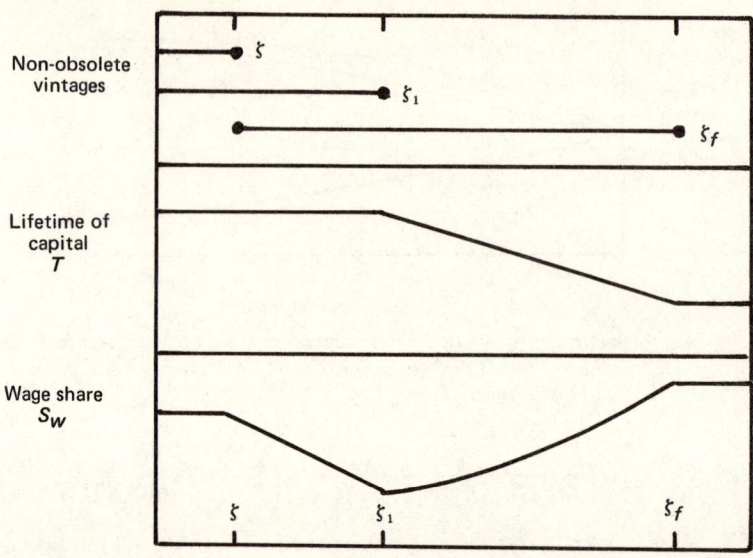

Figure 14 *The effect of an increase in investment (no change of technique induced)*

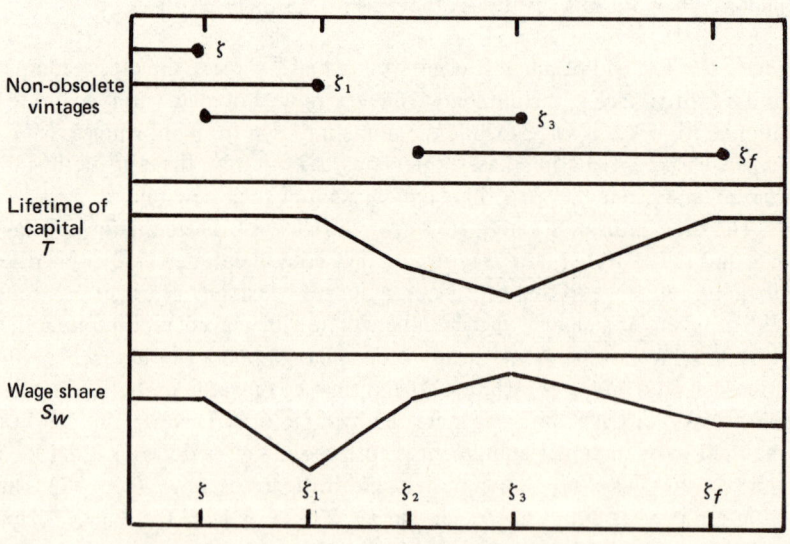

Figure 15 *The effect of an increase in investment (change of technique induced)*

that $t - T = \zeta_2$, after which T is constant. The time paths of T and S for this case are shown in figure 15.

The economy will then be on a new steady-state equilibrium path only in the rather fortuitous case where the technique chosen is such as to be optimal at the new (and lower) savings ratio now operative. A more realistic approach might assume a succession of switches of technique as the economy 'groped' its way to a new equilibrium: this, however, is outside the scope of the present paper. Insofar as the final path is a steady-state equilibrium path, whether the share of wages exceeds its original value depends, as noted above, on the elasticity of substitution of the ex-ante production function.

APPENDIX B: STATISTICAL APPENDIX

	Japan		Ireland		Germany	
	K	I	K	S	K	S
1951	–	33.6	–	–	104.0	94
1952	–	19.7	–	–	–	93
1953	100.0	18.4	100	100	–	93
1954	108.6	14.9	105.5	102.3	–	91
1955	115.4	15.9	113.1	102.7	124.7	89
1956	125.1	24.0	120.4	103.3	133.3	90
1957	141.3	25.6	125.4	105.0	–	90
1958	158.6	22.3	130.9	102.1	–	91
1959	176.0	28.3	138.4	98.5	–	89
1960	206.8	35.6	145.2	100.2	171.7	86
1961	224.5	40.0	155.3	96.6	184.6	85
1962	283.8	30.8	168.8	97.9	198.4	86
1963	321.7	30.0	184.0	97.1	211.4	87
1964	370.9	30.1	202.7	98.3	225.4	86
1965	408.3	23.2	221.1	96.0	–	87
1966	–	24.4	241.9	95.4	–	89
1967	–	29.8	265.0	91.6	–	89
1968	–	31.4	286.8	90.4	–	84
1969	–	33.1	–	90.4	–	85
1970	–	–	–	93.0	–	87

Key:
Japan: K: Capital Stock in mining and manufacturing (Okawa and Rosovsky, 1973, p. 314) (7-year moving average).
  I: Investment in fixed assets in mining and manufacturing (Okawa and Rosovsky, 1973, p. 295) as a fraction of net output in mining and manufacturing. (Okawa and Rosovsky, 1973, p. 283) (7-year moving average).
Ireland: K: Capital Stock in Manufacturing from Henry (1971).
  S: Share of wages and salaries in net output in manufacturing, calculated from the *UN Statistical Yearbook* 1973, p. 199, and corresponding tables in earlier issues.
Germany: K: Capital stock in mining and manufacturing. The index number shown (1950 = 100) was calculated from estimates due to Kirner and Krengel taken from Denison (1967, p. 420).
  S: Phelps Brown's estimates for *Produzierendes Gewerbe* (manufacturing, mining and construction) of the share of wages and salaries, including employers' contributions to social security, from Brown (1968, p. 439), was extended after 1960 using the figures published in the *Statistisches Jahrbuch der Bundesrepublik Deutschland*, 1971, p. 195, and the corresponding table in earlier issues.

DISCUSSION: D.C. ROWAN

The paper presented makes use of the framework of a vintage capital model to account for the observed behaviour of the share of wages in industrial output in three countries: Japan, Germany and Ireland. The periods covered by Sutton's data typically run from (approximately) the early 1950s to the late 1960s. Broadly speaking, Sutton's aim is to explain the observed *decline* in the share of wages (as defined), for example in Japan from the early 1950s until 1963, in relation to the observed *rise* in the proportion of output devoted to investment. Thus while Sargent (1968) employed the vintage framework to explain why a *rise* in the ratio of investment to output in the UK had been accompanied by a *rise* in the share of wages, Sutton employs it to throw light on the converse observation. In view of this reversal, it seems worthwhile to comment on the role of the vintage model in the analysis.

In the vintage model, given the exogenous rate of growth of the work force, a rise in the ratio of investment to output will be accompanied by a change in the share of wages determined by the elasticity of supply of labour with respect to the real wage and the elasticity of substitution of labour for capital in the ex-ante production function. Assuming the real wage clears the labour market in the sense that involuntary unemployment is zero, the elasticity of supply of labour is determined by the time profile of the capital stock and the rate of technical progress. If the economy has been moving along its long-term equilibrium path for a period equal to or greater than the lifetime of capital equipment, the long-term elasticity of labour supply is determined. The behaviour of the share of wages then depends upon the ex-ante elasticity of substitution exhibited by the production function. Sutton cites a calculation due to Eltis (1973) for a plausible range for the value of this elasticity at which the share of wages will be unaltered.

This, however, is a long-term equilibrium result of limited significance in Sutton's context since (a) he does not apply his vintage model to the whole economy but simply the industrial sector, (b) it cannot be assumed (in view of the Second World War) that the capital stock in Japan and Germany exhibited a long-run equilibrium time profile in the early 1950s and (c) the labour market was manifestly not clearing in the sense defined earlier in the first part of his observation period.

Sutton's method of adapting the long-term model to his shorter period analysis is as follows. Initially he argues that businessmen adapt techniques only very slowly. Hence capital–labour substitution can as a first approximation be ignored and the model, over the relevant period, treated as clay–clay rather than putty–clay. Next he argues that the fact that the rise in the ratio of investment did not occur in a position of long-term equilibrium, and hence that the initial (but unknown) time profile of the capital stock will influence the elasticity of labour supply, will simply result in very short-term fluctuations in the share of wages around a trend explained by the model. These can then be neglected as a first approximation. Finally he supplements the vintage model of the industrial sector by introducing an agricultural sector. The technology and role of technological change in this sector are not precisely defined. Presumably, however, agriculture has a technology of the putty–putty type. The analytical framework of the model thus approximates to that of a dual economy. For lack of time, however, Sutton does not present an analysis of this augmented model.

The short-term interpretation and the dual framework thus reduces the role of the vintage model to explaining the increase (net of labour released from marginal vintages) in the demand for labour by the industrial sector. Given this, the outcome, for the share of wages, must depend upon the elasticity of supply of labour. This shifts the emphasis of the analysis away from the vintage model element and on to the labour market.

This shift in emphasis is perfectly intelligible. It implies, however, the need to specify in some detail the behaviour of the labour market and, in particular, the way in which the real wage adjusts. Clearly the mechanism of the long-term vintage model will not do since the initial conditions, particularly in Germany and Japan in the early 1950s, were of a very considerable excess supply of labour: for example, in Germany unemployed were, in the early 1950s, around ten times as numerous as vacancies. Moreover, the agricultural model really requires the specification of two labour markets determining real wages in the industrial and agricultural sectors and *a fortiori* the relations between them. Sutton does not provide any clear account of these markets. He does not discuss their adjustment to disequilibria. Nor does he provide any data on the behaviour of real wages either at the aggregate level or in the two sectors. These omissions seem to me to be major gaps in the paper and to offer potentially fruitful opportunities for further work.

In Sutton's theoretical analysis, the crucial parameter is identified as the elasticity of supply of labour with respect to the real wage. Elasticities have meaning for economists only where they reflect choices by market participants who are not prevented from attaining, or moving towards, their preferred positions. Since this is so, it is difficult to apply the concept to Germany in the 1950s or to Japan in the early years of the same decade. The economic element in migration from East Germany may have been important. But this requires demonstration. Sutton essentially identifies large labour inflows and conditions of excess labour supply with a 'high' labour supply elasticity. This seems a misleading use of the term.

My conculusion is that Sutton's paper, though interesting, is essentially preliminary in that it focuses attention on the labour markets and the method of real wage determination. Work on these remains to be done. When it has been, my uninstructed intuition is that the characteristics of these markets will provide the major element in explaining Sutton's data and the role of the vintage capital model be of lesser significance.

NOTES

1 I would like to thank J.L. Ford, D.W. Anthony and the members of the staff seminar at Sheffield University for their helpful comments on an earlier draft. My thanks are also due to an anonymous referee whose suggestions I have incorporated.
2 Thus the present model is being applied for the purpose of short-run analysis to the industrial sector, essentially, as opposed to the agricultural. Equilibrium in the labour market demands that wage rates in the two sectors are equated, apart from quality differentials (which may be large). Thus in long-run analysis a two sector model is essential. However, while the main source of labour supply to Japanese industry derived from agriculture, migration was important in both other cases cited. Moreover, the gains to be had from using a dual model of the closed kind would be limited by the fact that the expected bidding up of agricultural prices which would follow an increase in industrial employment in excess of its steady-state value was in practice largely offset, not only by rising mechanisation in agriculture, but also an increasing inflow of imported agricultural products. All in all, it seems reasonable for the purpose of the present short-run study to embrace all sources of labour supply to industry in the single 'elasticity of supply' measure used above.
3 The derivations are provided in Appendix A.
4 Since $\pi/K = (\pi/Y)/(K/Y)$ where π = profits, K = capital stock, Y = output.
5 I.e. changes due purely to varying rates of growth in industries in which capital intensity, and so factor shares are initially different.
6 The series for labour's share in the Japanese case, shown in figure 7, refers to a larger grouping, which includes construction, facilitating industries and public utilities. This classification, due to Minami, is somewhat broader than we might wish. However, while wages and salaries figures are available for manufacturing only, they unfortunately seriously under-state labour's share, since non-wage income (which is included in Minami's figures) is unusally high in the Japanese case.
7 Based on the assumption that unincorporated enterprises earn the same rate of return as incorporated.
8 Defined, rather arbitrarily, as a doubling of industrial output in a decade, This corresponds to a growth rate of 7% per annum.
9 In the Irish case, a high flow of emigration which had persisted throughout the 1950s was halted by the upswing in activity at the end of the decade.
10 Hallett (1973, p. 74). This latter change was almost certainly accentuated by a fall in capacity utilisation, as unemployment figures for 1966 suggest.

REFERENCES

Bliss, Christopher (1968). On putty–clay. *Review of Economic Studies* 35, 105–32.
Brown, E.H. Phelps (1968). *A Century of Pay*. London: Macmillan.
Denison, E.F. (1967). *Why Growth Rates Differ*. Washington: Brookings Institution.
Eltis, W.A. (1973). *Growth and Distribution*. London: Macmillan.
Hallett, G. (1973). *The Social Economy of West Germany*, London: Macmillan.

Helmstadter, E. (1967). The trend of income distribution in the Federal Republic of Germany, from the standpoint of distribution theory. *German Economic Review* **5**, 278–92.
Henry, E.W. (1971). Estimation of capital stock in Irish industry, 1953–1968. *Journal of the Statistical and Social Inquiry Society of Ireland* **22**, 1–29.
Johansen, Lief (1959). Substitution vs. fixed production coefficients in the theory of economic growth: a synthesis. *Econometrica* **27**, 157–75.
Leacy, F.H. (1964). Supplement: short term fluctuations of wage shares. In *The behaviour of Income Shares*, Studies in Income and Wealth, vol. 27, Princeton: Princeton University Press.
Meenan, J. (1970). *The Irish Economy since 1922*. Liverpool University Press.
Minami, R. (1973). *The Turning Point in Economic Development: Japan's experience*. Tokyo: Kinokuniya Bookstore Co.
Minami, R., and Ono, A. (1974). Factor incomes and relative shares: long-term trends in Japan. mimeo. (Included in K. Ohkawa and R. Minami, *Economic Development in Modern Japan* (in Japanese). Tōyō Keizai Shinpō Sha.)
Ohkawa, K. (1968). Changes in national income distribution by factor share in Japan. In *The Distribution of National Income*, ed. J. Marchal and B. Ducros. London: Macmillan.
Ohkawa, K. and Rosovsky, H. (1973). *Japanese Economic Growth*. Stanford: Stanford University Press.
Phelps, Edmund, S. (1963). Substitution, fixed proportions, growth, and distribution, *International Economic Review* **4**, 265–88.
Poncet, J.F. (1970). *La Politique Economique da L'Allemagne Occidentale*. Paris: Sirey.
Sargent, J.R. (1968). Recent growth experience in the economy of the U.K. *Economic Journal* **78**, 19–42.
Stolper, G., Karl Hanser, and Knut Borchardt (1967). *The German Economy: 1870 to the Present*. London: Weidenfeld and Nicholson.
Wallich, H.L. (1955). *Mainsprings of the German Revival*. New Haven: Yale University Press.

PART THREE
TRADE AND THE BALANCE OF PAYMENTS

7 THE EFFECTS OF THE OIL PRICE RISE ON THE INTERNATIONAL ECONOMY

W.M. CORDEN

INTRODUCTION

The aim here is to sort out, at the level of simple theory, some implications for real incomes, the terms of trade, balances of payments and, more generally, international adjustment, of the rise in oil prices. The quantitative reduction in oil exports by OPEC, bringing about the price rise, is taken as given, and the concern is only with the effects on the oil-importing countries. This paper discusses only a few of the many issues presented by the rise in oil prices. One finds, without surprise, that simple and well-known theoretical techniques can be used for this problem and with respect to theory there is certainly nothing new here. The paper represents a stage in a continuing process of trying to think these matters through. It attempts to present somewhat more rigorously some ideas first published in 1974, but expounded more intuitively then.[1]

THE WELFARE EFFECTS OF THE OIL PRICE RISE: A SIMPLE MODEL

Let us, to begin with, suppose that the world consists of two countries, namely OPEC which exports oil and imports manufactures and OECD which does the opposite. Price flexibility and monetary policy maintain internal and external balance, so that a whole range of problems to which we shall come back later can be assumed away for the moment. We have, thus, a *real* model.

In figure 1 the vertical axis shows the price of oil in terms of manufactures and the horizontal axis shows the quantity of oil imports into the OECD world. The demand curve DD' allows for income and substitution effects in OECD. Over the relevant range it is assumed to have an elasticity less than unity. It indicates the marginal value in OECD of oil in terms of manufactures. The initial quantity of oil imports is OQ and the price is OP. The quantity is then reduced to OQ' so that the price rises to OP'.

What is the resulting welfare loss to OECD? This loss can be disentangled into three elements. (i) The area E is an approximate measure of the loss which would be incurred if there were no price rise — i.e. no terms of trade effect. It

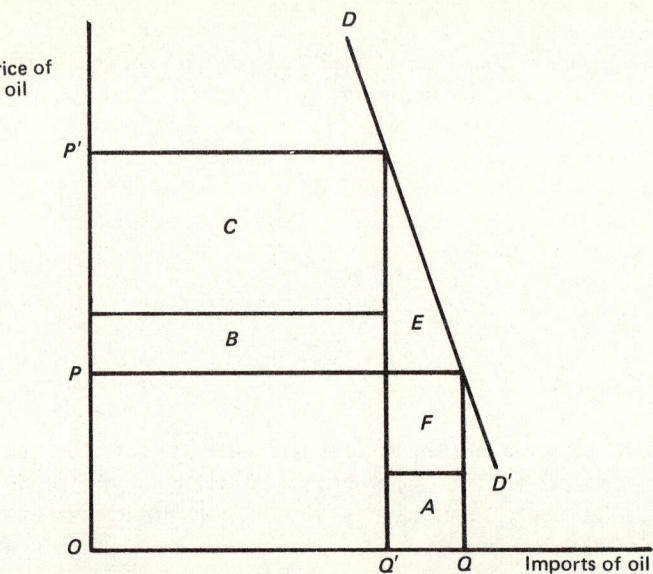

Figure 1

includes the excess cost over previously imported oil of the substitutes for oil imports developed in OECD, and also includes the cost of reducing consumption of oil-intensive goods. In other words, it is the welfare cost of the substitution effect. (ii) The area B is the extra loss which results from a price rise that is just sufficient to keep the value of imports constant; it would thus be the terms of trade loss if the import demand elasticity were unity. (iii) The area C is the additional loss resulting from the further rise in the price, causing the value of imports actually to increase. Thus the total cost to OECD is $(E + B + C)$.

How much of the OECD loss is a transfer from OPEC and how much is additional loss, and hence a world loss in the Pareto-efficiency sense?

The opportunity cost to OPEC of the oil exports QQ' is A. We need not go into details at this point as to what this opportunity cost consists of precisely. The main point is that it is much more than the current cost of production — which is, of course, quite tiny in the Middle East. It consists mainly of the value of oil in the ground — which depends, in turn, on expected future prices, and so on. Much of it consists of rent which could be reaped in later years. In addition, there is the area F, which represents the *current* rent (producers' surplus) received by OPEC. As we shall see below, it could be negative, though in figure 1 it is positive. The diagram has been drawn so that $(A + F) = B$. The gain to OPEC from the current rise in price (with the expected future price held constant) is then C (the rise in the value of its exports) plus A (the opportunity cost of the oil that was previously exported and is now kept in the ground). Thus there is a transfer of real income from OECD to OPEC of $(C + A)$ and an additional loss to OECD, representing the net world loss, of $(E + F)$.

As drawn in figure 1, it is assumed that initially output of OPEC oil was below the world optimum. The optimum would be where the marginal opportunity cost is equal to the demand price (disregarding taxes, externalities, and so on). At the optimum the area F would be much smaller and (if the opportunity cost curve were horizontal) would be zero. In fact, it might be reasonable to assume (in agreement with the Shah and the Club of Rome) that output had initially been *above* the world optimum. In that case F might actually be negative and there might possibly be a world efficiency gain from the reduction of supply.[2]

In spite of the simple diagram used, this analysis is *not* partial equilibrium. To verify this, the story is retold in terms of the general equilibrium box diagram in appendix 1.

It should be noted that we have *not* reproduced the standard analysis of the transfer problem. In the usual 'transfer problem' analysis one supposes that there is an income transfer — an 'unrequited transfer' — which leads, at constant prices, to a primary real income effect in each of the two countries. In addition, these income transfers lead to a price (terms of trade) effect. This terms of trade effect leads to secondary real income effects which have to be added to the primary effect. The central issue in the transfer problem discussion is to determine which way the terms of trade effect — and hence the secondary real income effects — will go. But here the analysis has been different. We start with a quantity change which leads to a price effect. Alternatively we could start with a price change that requires a validating quantity change. There are, at this stage, no unrequited transfers. As in the traditional transfer problem analysis we are interested in what the final real income effects are, but there is certainly no difficulty in deciding which way the price effect must go. The traditional transfer analysis only becomes relevant in the next stage of our story.

EFFECTS ON INDIVIDUAL COUNTRIES: THE SECONDARY EFFECTS

The next step is to distinguish the effects on different countries within the 'OECD' world (for this purpose the latter could be thought of as including also the LDCs). We continue to adhere to a *real* model, so that we are concerned with effects on the terms of trade, not balances of payments. The analysis required here is very familiar from international trade theory, so that one can be very brief.

Income effects

First, one has to distinguish income from substitution effects. To isolate the income effects, we suppose that initially there has simply been a transfer of income from different OECD countries to OPEC, this transfer not being associated at this stage with any relative price change (OPEC taxes OECD lump-sum). OECD produces many goods and, at constant relative prices, relative demands for these goods will change owing to the transfer. Why this should be so we shall see in a moment. These demand changes then give rise to imbalances which, in turn, lead to equilibrating relative price changes. The relative price changes, in their turn, have real income effects.

The position then is that the initial transfer created the adverse real income effects for different OECD countries described earlier. These were the *primary* income effects. But now there are, in addition, *secondary* income effects which represent redistribution within the OECD world. On balance, some OECD countries may actually gain in real income. In any case, the loss of some countries will be less and the loss of others greater than indicated by the primary effects alone. Let us now look at the elements that go into the secondary effects.

Essentially there are two elements. First, one needs to compare the ratios of the marginal propensities to spend on different goods in the OPEC countries with the *average* of these ratios for the OECD countries, assuming that this average stays constant. If, for example, the OPEC countries have a particularly high marginal propensity to spend on Japanese goods, relative to the OECD average, then this effect will tend to improve the Japanese terms of trade.

Secondly, the weighted average of the OECD marginal propensities will change. The reason is that the weights change, these weights depending on the relative sizes of the income losses incurred. Some countries – e.g. Italy, Japan and many LDCs – pay a higher proportional tax to the OPEC countries than others. They thus suffer higher proportional income losses owing to the primary effect. Compared with a weighting system based on an even distribution of the burden, their marginal propensities should then be given a higher weight in the analysis than those of countries where there has been little proportional income loss. Granting this, nothing more can really be said in general. One needs to specify the various propensities and income transfers to discover how the terms of trade of various countries will move because of this second effect. But if one wants to go on and talk about probabilities and presumptions one gets straight into the standard transfer problem analysis. The issue is whether there is some presumption that the terms of trade will turn against the countries which have incurred the relatively large primary income losses. If there is, then we have a presumption that a 'secondary burden' will reinforce the adverse effects of the primary burden just on those countries where the primary burden has been greatest.

As is well-known, this presumption follows from the standard analysis of the effects of a transfer in the presence of transport costs, non-traded goods and tariffs. The argument is that countries have marginal preferences for their own goods relative to foreign goods, so that (in a two-country model) the sum of the marginal propensities to import is less than unity. But here it should be noted that this effect could, conceivably, be overridden by taste differences. If trade were mainly explained by differences in tastes, the presumption would be that countries have marginal preferences for *foreign* goods.

Substitution effects

In order to isolate the income effect from the substitution effect we have assumed so far that the initial effect was the same as if OPEC had taxed OECD lump-sum. Let us now introduce the substitution effects. The relative price of oil has risen. Some goods are substitutes for oil, others are complements. Producers of substitutes will tend to gain and of complements will lose. Direct and indirect effects must be taken into account here. Thus activities producing goods which use oil or oil substitutes as inputs are complements for this purpose. These substitution and complementary effects lead to further relative price — and hence terms of trade and hence real income — effects.

We can thus summarise as follows. Apart from the primary real income effects, there are secondary real income effects which represent redistribution within the OECD world and which operate through relative price changes. These secondary effects have two components: those which result from the primary *income* effects (depending on relative marginal propensities to spend, and so on), and those which result from the primary *substitution* (and complementarity) effects.

There is one further point at this stage. We started off by treating the non-oil producers as if they consisted of one country — and, indeed, really as if they were one person. Now we have broken them up into countries, hence focusing on the relative terms of trade effects. But one should generalise this analysis. There will be redistributive effects within each country. The heavier primary burden will be borne by those people who, directly or indirectly, are relatively heavier consumers of oil or oil substitutes. Producers of oil substitutes, such as coal miners or oil companies owning non-OPEC oil, will benefit. Producers of motor-cars (complements) will lose. Each person, or family, can be thought of as a country, losing from the primary effect, and possibly gaining or losing from the various secondary effects. The redistributive effects *within* countries may be very important.

A SIMPLE EXTENSION: OPEC FUNDS INVESTED

Can one extend our analysis to allow for OPEC countries investing some of their funds in short or long-term bonds in the OECD world? We shall postpone some of the most interesting issues by (a) continuing to assume macroeconomic equilibrium (internal and external balance) and (b) supposing that all borrowing is for private investment, based on normal profit expectations.

OECD countries sell not only goods and services but also bonds (financial claims). OPEC countries can use some of their funds to buy bonds. When OECD countries lose income they reduce their purchases of new bonds and when OPEC countries gain income they increase their purchases. If the marginal propensity to save of OPEC is higher than that of OECD – as it clearly is – there will be a net increase in world demand for bonds, so that their prices relative to goods will rise (the rate of interest will fall). This means that there is a tendency for the terms of 'trade' of countries that are relatively large exporters of bonds to improve on this account. We define 'trade' here as including trade in bonds. Of course all the other factors affecting the terms of trade discussed earlier remain relevant.

A country is an exporter of bonds if it has more profitable private investment opportunities than can be financed from domestic savings. The general point is then the following. An aspect of the secondary income effect of a rise in oil prices is that the countries with significant investment opportunities may be gainers, while those that have few such opportunities lose. Capital importers gain; capital exporters lose. It should be added that a country may be a net capital exporter, and hence a loser from this effect, not so much because its investment opportunities are low but because it is an exceptionally high saver. This approach – thinking of bonds as particular types of commodities exported to OPEC – seems helpful if one wants to incorporate in standard transfer analysis the effects of OPEC countries lending their gains rather than buying goods and services.

One can also allow for different types of bonds, some countries selling or buying more of one than of another. If there were only one type of bond in the world with a single world price it would matter to an OECD country only whether it is a capital importer or exporter, and how much, and not whether the OPEC countries are buying *its* bonds. Indeed, its bonds could not really be differentiated. But in the presence of differentiation of bonds by country it matters to any particular country which bonds the OPEC countries buy. A country could be a net capital exporter and could nevertheless benefit if its own bonds are purchased.

The fact that OPEC countries will lend a significant part of their extra income while OECD countries will not reduce their lending to an equal degree means that the world 'production' of bonds will go up. Since we are assuming that extra bonds are issued only on the basis of extra private investment this means that resources in the OECD world will have to move out of consumption into investment on this account. This will have further terms of trade effects: countries that export investment goods will gain relatively.

There is another channel through which the country pattern of OPEC investment may affect the terms of trade. This channel becomes evident when one relates the investment effect to the standard transfer analysis. For this purpose let us grant the standard presumption that countries have a preference in their marginal spending patterns for their own goods and that this applies not only to consumption but also to investment spending.

Consider the simplest case of a country ('Canada') which initially did not suffer a real income loss, not having been an importer of OPEC oil and not suffering from any of the secondary effects. But it has exceptional investment opportunities. So OPEC buys its bonds, pushing up their prices and giving Canada a terms of 'trade' gain. To supply extra bonds Canada embarks on extra investment. There need be no fall in Canadian consumption since the extra resources can come through the current account deficit financed by the capital inflow. Now Canada's extra investment spending goes mainly on Canadian investment goods, so that their relative prices rise. Thus there is first a gain for the sellers of Canada's bonds – the industries in which OPEC invests, and so on – and then there is an additional terms of trade gain because Canadian real spending has risen in relation to other countries and has gone mainly on Canadian goods.

INTERNAL BALANCE

Behind the stories told so far lie the processes which maintain 'internal balance' and 'external balance'. First, let us think of the OECD group again as a single country.

The OECD group will have a current account deficit relative to OPEC. This will be balanced exactly by the export of bonds, and if this is described as capital inflow, then the capital account surplus exactly balances the current account deficit. The OPEC countries must deposit their funds somewhere in the OECD world. In that sense, OECD faces no balance of payments 'problem'.[3]

Is the oil price rise deflationary or inflationary? This has been much discussed, and most economists have sorted this out in their minds by now. The effect is likely to be cost-inflationary but demand-deflationary. So we can be very brief in dealing with the overall 'internal balance' story. It must be remembered that here we are only concerned with the effects of the oil price rise. Actual events have clearly been dominated by deeper forces, operative before October 1973.

If monetary policy kept the rate of interest constant the effect is likely to be demand-deflationary. World income has been redistributed towards countries with relatively high savings propensities so that the weighted average world propensity to save rises. The changed relative price and profitability pattern may also have raised the inducement to invest, but this is less certain. Investment in OPEC oil substitutes (such as North Sea oil, coal, etc.) will increase, but investment in complementary activities (e.g. the motor industry) will decrease. In any case, it seems likely that the oil price rise will – at a constant rate of interest – have increased world savings much more than world investment, at least in the short run.

The resulting deflationary gap could be eliminated by fiscal policy. In that case it would not be necessary for the rate of interest to fall. But we have been assuming so far that OPEC savings are borrowed only on the basis of private investment opportunities, so this solution is ruled out at this stage. Thus the rate of interest must fall. It must be stressed that the *real* rate of interest is meant here and in all further discussion. Monetary policy must ensure that the rate of interest falls until investment has increased to equal full employment savings. The lower rate of interest might also cause the savings propensity — including that of OPEC — to fall to some extent, so that the induced rise in investment may not need to be so great. In any case the change in the rate of interest is the mechanism of equilibrating adjustment.

The main concern of this paper is with real, rather than monetary, issues. But let us just note some of the monetary aspects. Suppose the world nominal stock of money stays constant initially. With prices of oil and substitutes having gone up, and, presumably, other prices rigid downwards, the average world price-level has risen and so the real money stock has declined. At the same time the changed world income distribution may have changed the average demand for money, probably raising the demand for liquidity. (One should really make distinctions here between claims of varying degrees of liquidity.) These two factors on their own actually make for an increase in the rate of interest. Clearly the nominal money supply has to increase to bring the rate of interest down sufficiently so as to bring real aggregate demand to the required full employment level.[4]

EXTERNAL BALANCE

What are the balance of payments implications of our analysis?

If exchange rates or domestic prices were completely flexible in each country so as to maintain full employment, and if governments did not borrow or lend, then we would have the outcome described earlier. OECD countries would be borrowing only on the basis of their private investment opportunities, and provided that private expectations of profit were reasonable, this would present no 'problem' — that is, there would be no balance of payments problems. Countries which export bonds to OPEC, or to other OECD countries, would have current account deficits, while countries which actually import bonds would have surpluses. A current account deficit would be a sign not of a 'problem' but of investment opportunities. The algebraic sum of the OECD deficits would, of course, be equal to the OPEC surplus (subject to the qualification about the definition of accommodating payments mentioned earlier). This approach makes the whole balance of payments issue disappear. Current account deficits would always be offset by capital account surpluses. To get a balance of payments 'problem' one has to introduce some kind of rigidity.

This is not the place to embark on a comparison of various types of balance of payments models. Broadly they can be classified into models which assume a rigidity in a monetary quantity (the monetarist models), those which assume a rigidity in a money price — which is usually the money wage and sometimes, explicitly or implicitly, the average price of non-traded goods (the standard

Keynesian models), and finally those which assume a rigidity in a real price or a real quantity. The third type of model is probably the most useful for the present purpose, and will be used here. The second and third types of models are compared in appendix 2.

In the full equilibrium outcome described earlier, with no government intervention, real consumption in many countries needs to fall as a result of the oil price rise. But the extent of the required fall would differ considerably between countries. We distinguished the primary from the secondary effects. The primary effects depended essentially on whether or not a country was a large importer of OPEC oil in relation to its total income, and also on the elasticity of substitution of domestic substitutes for this oil. The secondary effects depended on terms of trade changes – i.e. changes in price relationships of goods other than OPEC oil. The general point to be made now is that the governments of those countries where in the absence of intervention there would have to be a significant fall in real consumption may intervene to moderate or prevent this consumption fall. They will borrow from OPEC or from other OECD countries for this purpose. It is purely arbitrary to describe this borrowing as accommodating rather than autonomous, and so to measure the overall balance of payments deficit of these countries by such borrowing. But it is undoubtedly true that this type of borrowing cannot go on indefinitely, so in that sense it presents a 'problem' that is not presented by borrowing on the basis of profitable investment opportunities, private or public. This argument also applies when countries are running down their reserves – i.e. reducing their lending – rather than borrowing.

One can then relate our detailed earlier *real* analysis to the balance of payments issue as follows. Some countries are likely to require significant real income falls to achieve the full equilibrium outcome. These countries are also more likely to incur balance of payments deficits designed to modify or avoid these falls. Countries which would benefit from real income increases in the equilibrium outcome are likely to incur surpluses.

The objective of government borrowing may be seen in straightforward consumption maintenance terms, whether private consumption (subsidised by lower taxes or food subsidies, for example) or public consumption. Alternatively it may be seen in employment or anti-inflation terms. In the latter case, the real wage may be rigid downwards and the whole required fall in real consumption may not be bearable by the non-wage sector. Hence the maintenance of full employment – or the avoidance of a wage–price spiral – would require some form of subsidisation, direct or indirect, of wages.

ADJUSTMENT PROBLEMS

So far the impression may have been conveyed that the adjustment of the OECD countries to the oil price rise would be rather smooth. 'The market works.' Relative prices change, interest rates fall, real consumption falls as required. Yet one hears no end about problems, potential or actual crises, breakdown of the system, inability to cope, and so on. It should be recalled here that we are using the blanket term 'OECD' to embrace all the non-OPEC countries, including the LDCs, and it will be obvious that some of these, at least, have been placed in very severe difficulties, partly at least owing to the oil price rise.

Let us now list and examine the various points of possible difficulty and crisis.

The macro-problem

In the absence of government borrowing real incomes of some countries need to fall, in some cases significantly. If real factor prices are perfectly flexible, real incomes will indeed fall — so that there need be neither unemployment nor inflation (apart from a once-for-all price rise). If money wages are inflexible downwards, the necessary fall in real wages can be brought about by exchange rate adjustments. Even though unemployment could then be avoided, the essential problem of a fall in living standards would remain. This straightforward international income distribution effect of the oil price rise has, of course, been highlighted in our main analysis. It is that effect which presents the main problem to the countries adversely affected.

If real factor prices are not flexible downwards, this effect becomes transmuted into an inflation and macro-unemployment problem. In the absence of extra government borrowing or reduced lending — i.e. in the absence of a balance of payments deficit as usually defined — this transmutation causes output and hence aggregate real income to fall more, and in addition introduces a domestic redistribution against the unemployed. If these repercussions are avoided by government borrowing to sustain consumption at full employment, the problem becomes transmuted again, namely into the problem of the accumulation of foreign debt obligations and the need for eventual repayment.

The micro-problem

Within each country there are redistributive effects, as we have already stressed. Even if, in a compensation sense, the real income of the country as a whole hardly fell, some sections may lose a great deal to the benefit of others. Thus, calculations of the ratio which the increased OPEC oil bill bears to OECD GNP understate the extent of the income adjustments required. This micro-problem is really no different from the macro-problem except that it is more difficult for government intervention to avoid it in the short run. While the redistribution in itself represents a problem to the affected parties, with downward rigidity of real wages and immobility of labour it becomes transmuted into a micro (structural) unemployment problem. This is principally a short-run effect in activities complementary with oil and oil substitutes.

Reluctance to borrow

Countries may be hostile to foreign capital, especially OPEC capital, and hence may be reluctant to borrow. They may impose controls on foreign capital or they may tax the income paid to foreign lenders in order to discourage capital inflow. A picture is sometimes painted of a situation where OPEC funds have nowhere to go. In practice, if the governments of some countries reduce their countries' demands for these funds, this is equivalent to a reduction in their investment opportunities. The funds will then go to other countries, the interest rate falling in order to bring this about. One can then see the problem that the rate of return may fall so low — perhaps negative in real terms — that OPEC countries will choose to reduce their oil output. Without pursuing this issue in depth it might be noted that the OPEC reaction may be optimal from the OPEC point of view; the reaction of governments that do not like foreign capital and so discourage its inflow may also, from their points of view, be optimal, and it is by no means clear that the net result is non-optimal from a world point of view. If OPEC countries cannot usefully spend all their incomes, and if OECD countries do not want to borrow all the OPEC funds that are generated except at a very low rate of return, it seems sensible for OPEC countries to keep some of their oil in the ground until they do have need for the funds. On the other hand, countries currently heavily dependent on oil imports will certainly be losers; in other words, the international losers from restrictions that cause OPEC rates of return to fall may not only be the OPEC countries themselves.

The question one might ask is whether, literally, the OPEC funds might end up with nowhere to go. This is, of course, impossible. They must go somewhere, if only to lie idle with zero nominal rates of interest in New York banks (or negative rates in Swiss banks). If New York banks and all other OECD banks refuse to take any more funds belonging to OPEC countries then presumably the OPEC governments would have to ask the purchasers of their oil to keep their payments in OPEC credit accounts in the countries where the oil is sold. So the funds *would* go somewhere, though there would have been a slide into a regime of inconvertibility. If even this were not possible then, presumably, the OPEC countries would cease selling oil, since they could not be paid for it. But all this is fanciful. The funds must go somewhere. The question only is: at what rate of interest, and, finally, to which countries?

Breakdown of the banking system

The international financial intermediation industry has had a boom in business and clearly there is some problem in coping with this. If the whole population of Birmingham suddenly decided to shop at Marks and Spencer in Oxford there would also be a problem for Marks and Spencer, and some time for adjustment would be needed. In time the firm would expand, new firms would spring up, the firm would ferret out new suppliers, customers would adjust their demand patterns to the goods available, and some customers would choose to by-pass the excessively popular firm. This is what is happening in the international banking business. Adjustment is taking place before our eyes. This of course does not fully rule out the possibility of crises for individual banks if funds are shifted around and central banks fail to recycle these funds to counteract this.

There is a problem of determining who is to bear the risks of lending to governments that are borrowing for consumption maintenance. The potential international crisis is sometimes seen as a drying-up of funds for such governments, and so forcing them into a domestic crisis. In a sense this is a version of the macro-problem that was stressed earlier. Some governments may be willing, but not able, to borrow sufficiently for consumption maintenance. The risks could be borne by private banks, OPEC governments or other governments, notably the government of the US. When the borrowers are governments of large countries there is clearly a strong argument that private firms are unlikely to be large enough to carry the risks. One's first reaction is to argue that the OPEC governments should themselves carry the risks. Why should they be able to pass these on to anyone else? The counter-argument might then be that some governments would not be able to borrow at all. There is then implicitly an aid element in lending to governments that are not credit-worthy on the basis of normal risk-taking, and it is because of this need for what is in effect *aid* that OECD governments, including the US government, would be justified in acting as intermediaries.

Reluctance to run deficits

OECD countries may not be willing to run the current account deficits required if the sum of their deficits is to be equal to the given surplus of the OPEC countries. OPEC funds may indeed find a home in OECD countries, but some countries may choose to run overall balance of payments surpluses not matched by willing deficits run by other countries. The overall surplus must be distinguished from the current account. The latter would be in balance – that being the object of the policy – and the overall surplus would result from the export of securities to OPEC. The surplus would be matched by a budget surplus and would be a form of foreign investment, but not in profitable investment opportunities. If it were in such investment opportunities it would be embraced in our earlier analysis. It may not seem logical for governments to accumulate foreign assets yielding low and perhaps negative real rates of return because of the oil price rise. (For this purpose we should assume that their ratios of foreign exchange reserves to trade and to other assets were the desired ones initially.) But the policy may be explained not by any portfolio balancing process but rather by a reluctance to accept the domestic income distribution effects of a current account deficit.

In any case, such a country may succeed in the short-run in running an overall suplus if other countries are willing to accept the appropriate deficit. But when other countries react by trying to eliminate *their* deficits one would get an unstable competitive depreciation situation. We would have a world of unfulfilled balance of payments plans and disappointed expectations. In a world of fairly flexible exchange rates there is perhaps less reason to fear competitive deflations on these grounds. If countries behaved rationally they would only deflate sufficiently to make room for the demands for domestic resources which they expect to be generated by the depreciation. The current deflations in many countries need hardly be explained in 'competitive' terms. Furthermore, there is no rational argument why tariffs and import quotas should be preferred to depreciation on these grounds. A revival of such tariffs and quotas is more likely to be stimulated by the desire to avoid micro-unemployment generated directly or indirectly by the oil price rise. Early in 1974 there was a widespread fear that governments, partly out of ignorance, would seek to avoid the inevitable current account deficits, and so engage in competitive devaluations, deflations or trade restrictions. But so far there is evidence neither of competitive devaluations nor of a major revival of trade controls, while countries are deflating in order to restrain price inflation, or perhaps as a lagged effect of the oil price rise (for reasons discussed earlier) but not primarily and generally to improve their balances of payments.

APPENDIX 1: EFFECTS OF THE OIL PRICE RISE IN A BOX DIAGRAM

In figure 2 the initial quantity of OPEC oil exports is OQ. The initial price ratio is given by the slope of OR, so that the initial quantity of manufactures exports by OECD is OL and the initial equilibrium point is R. The consumption origin for OECD is at C and the OECD offer curve is OO'. It seems appropriate not to draw in an OPEC offer curve since we are analysing the effects of a given quantity decision – involving a given price decision – by OPEC.

The quantity of OPEC oil exports is then reduced to OQ'. Let us now represent the three welfare effects of this on OECD. (i) If the price stayed constant, the new consumption point would be at S. The welfare loss in moving from the indifference curve through R to the curve through S is the cost of the income-compensated substitution effect (income in terms of manufactures having stayed constant) and is roughly equivalent to the area E in figure 1. (ii) An oil price rise represented by the movement to the slope of the line OT is just sufficient to restore the value of imports in terms of manufactures, and so to keep manufactures exports constant. This inflicts an additional welfare loss (from the curve through S to the curve through T), and is equivalent to the area B in figure 1. (iii) Finally, we suppose the price to rise further, to bring the value of imports, and hence manufactures exports, up to OL'. The final equilibrium point is on the offer curve, at Z, and the additional loss which the movement from T to Z inflicts is equivalent to the area C in figure 1.

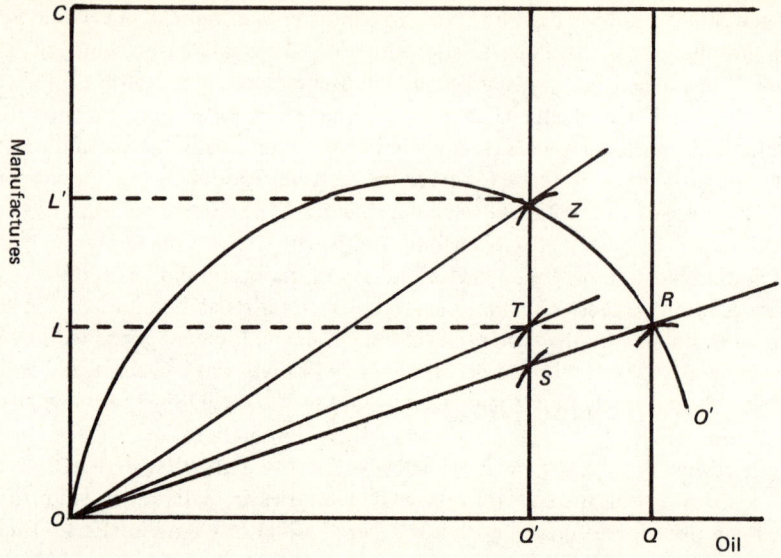

Figure 2

APPENDIX 2: THE EFFECT OF A DETERIORATION IN THE TERMS OF TRADE ON THE BALANCE OF TRADE

There was a certain amount of implicit theorising in the section of this paper on external balance. It may be helpful to clarify the issues in terms of a simple diagram used in an earlier article to analyse balance of payments policy (Corden, 1960).

Three assumptions will be made. (i) We consider a single country which cannot affect its terms of trade; (ii) the quantity and foreign currency price of its exports are fixed, so that the balance of payments problem is to adjust imports to the given export value; and (iii) the country is *not* a capital importer or exporter (so that it does not have investment opportunities leading to the export of bonds to OPEC). All these assumptions could be removed without affecting the main argument to follow.

The model is represented in figure 3. The vertical axis shows the quantity of home-produced goods (non-traded, import-competing, and export), and the horizontal axis the quantity of imports. Given the foreign price of imports and the exchange rate, the domestic price of imports is fixed, and given the average money price of home-produced goods, their price is fixed. (If home-produced goods were made by labour alone we could simply fix the money wage to get this result.) The initial domestic price ratio between the two categories of goods is given by the slope of FG, initial money expenditure (= income) is given by OF

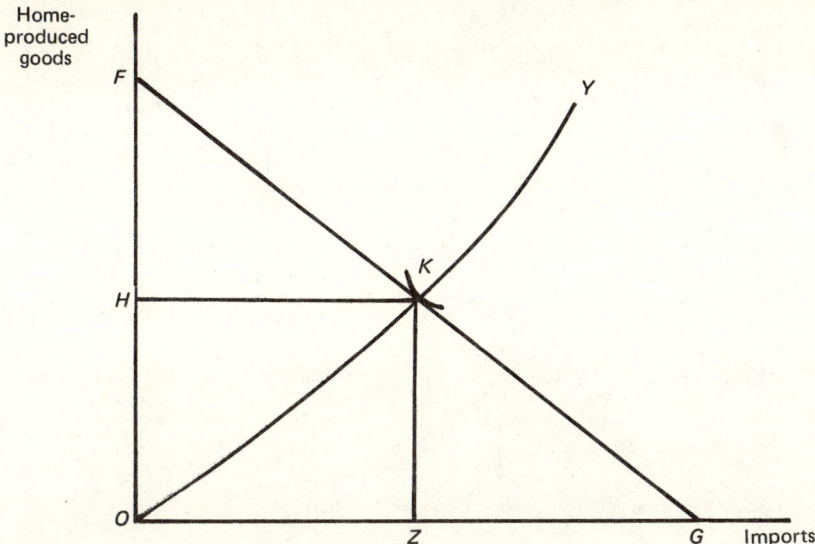

Figure 3

in terms of home-produced goods, and the chosen demand position is at the point K. We suppose that the home-produced goods purchased, namely OH, are just the right quantity for 'internal balance'. (The quantity of export production is HF, which is equal to imports OZ at the given price ratio.) The level of real expenditure (absorption) is indicated by the indifference curve through K, and the income–consumption line OY through K is also drawn.

Constant money expenditure case. In figure 4 the effects of a deterioration in the terms of trade are shown. The price of imports rises, so that with constant money expenditure and a constant price of home-produced goods, the new opportunity line shifts to FG'. The assumption of constant money expenditure is, of course, a very specialised one, but it is often made in this type of analysis. We shall consider other assumptions shortly. The assumption of a constant price of home-produced goods is crucial. If the wage share stays constant this implies a constant money wage even though import prices have gone up.

With the elasticity of demand for imports less than unity, the consumption point moves to L. This is on the income–consumption line OY'. Demand for imports falls by ZZ' and demand for home-produced goods falls by HH'. Measured in terms of home-produced goods or exports, the *value* of imports has risen from FH to FH'. This situation is only sustainable if expenditure (OF) is kept above the lowered level of income (OH' derived from sales at home plus HF derived from exports) by credit creation, borrowing, or running down of balances equal to HH'.

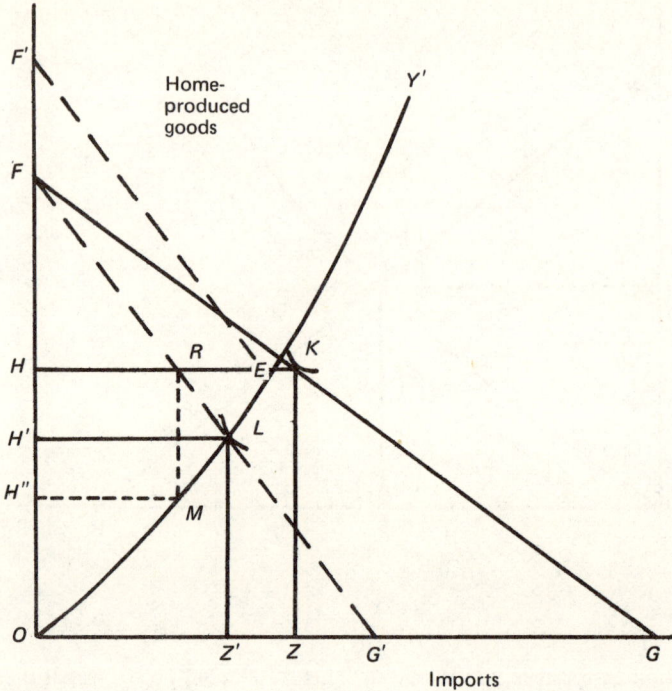

Figure 4

This case brings out the argument that the oil price rise is (a) demand-deflationary because it reduces the demand for home-produced goods and (b) creates a balance of payments deficit, because it increases the value of imports. It also brings out (c) that there has been a fall in real absorption, represented by the movement from the indifference curve through K to that through L.

We might regard this as the neutral case, though it implies a thoroughly non-neutral monetary policy, namely one designed to keep money expenditure constant. The next step is to consider various possible policy responses, involving departures from this 'neutrality'.

Full employment case. Government policy may be to restore full employment. Expenditure will then be increased to OF'. The new equilibrium will be at E, and the balance of payments deficit will increase, namely from HH' to FF'. The excess of expenditure over income is greater than before (being always equal to the balance of payments deficit).

Deflation case. Government policy may be to restore balance of payments equilibrium by deflation. Since the exchange rate is nowadays available as an instrument of policy, this is an improbable case. Expenditure will then be decreased until the point M is reached. The quantity of imports becomes HR, which is equal to the value of exports at the new price ratio. The demand for home-produced goods will then fall further (to OH''), thus increasing unemployment.

Devaluation case. Devaluation combined with expenditure adjustment is used to restore internal and external balance. This classic 'Meade' solution is represented in figure 5. The object is to get to the point R, so as to cut imports to HR while keeping the demand for home-produced goods at OH. For the expenditure

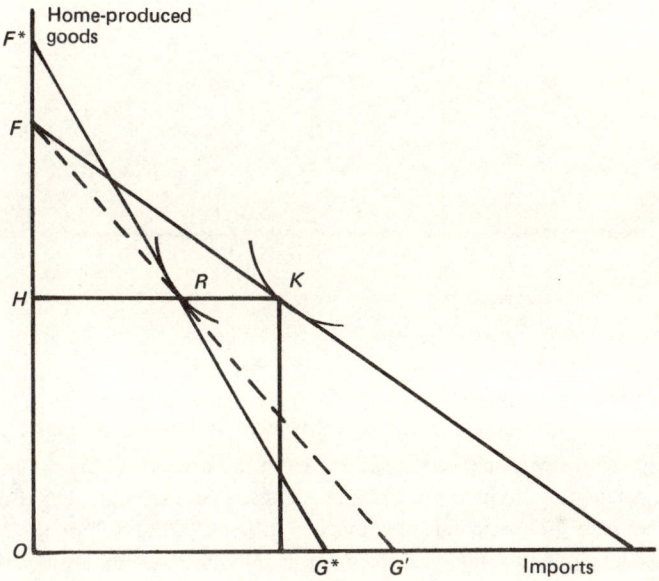

Figure 5

pattern to be at R, the budget line has to be F^*G^*. The devaluation raises the price of imports relative to home-produced goods, as represented by the steepening of the slope from FG' to F^*G^*. Expenditure on home-produced goods sold at home stays constant, and so expenditure out of income so derived stays constant. But domestic currency income derived from exports rises by FF^* as a result of the devaluation, so that total money expenditure increases by FF^*, as required. (The nominal money supply must be higher now, and in the export industries wages or profits must rise.)

Real-price rigidity case. Now consider the following interesting case. Suppose home-produced goods are made by labour alone (we can think of labour as the representative factor of production) and the real wage stays constant. Thus the price of home-produced goods rises in the same proportion as the price of imports, so that the relative price ratio does not change. Therefore, we stay on

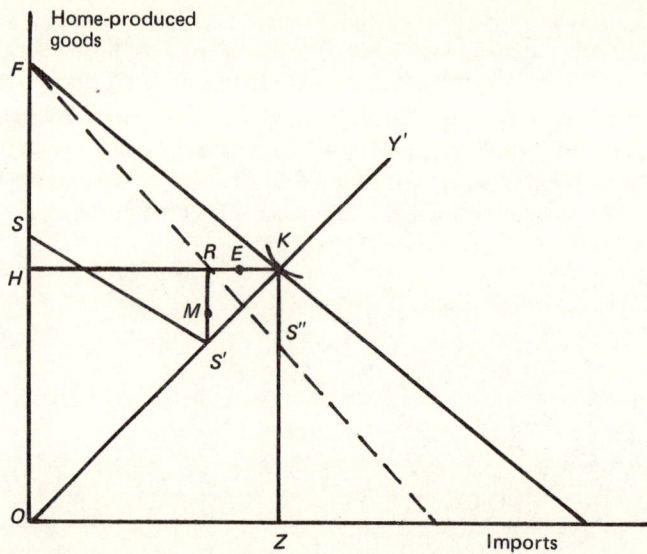

Figure 6

the income–consumption line OY' (figure 6). Note that a devaluation could not alter this. While it would raise the domestic price of imports it would lead to a compensating rise in the money wage and hence in the price of home-produced goods. If the balance of payments is to be brought into equilibrium, expenditure measured in terms of home-produced goods has to fall to OS, bringing the equilibrium to S'. Demand for home-produced goods falls short of full employment supply by RS'.

It is worth comparing this *real-price rigidity case* with the earlier *deflation case* where balance of payments equilibrium was also restored by deflation alone and we ended up at point M (figure 4, and also shown in figure 6). In both cases the quantity of imports has been reduced to HR, as required, but in the *deflation case* the demand for home-produced goods did not fall as much, thus there was less unemployment and less fall in real output. The reason is that the fall in real wages resulting from the rise in import prices was accepted, so that there was a relative price change bringing the economy to the income–consumption line OY'. By failing to devalue, the *further* fall in real wages required for full employment was avoided, and so some unemployment remained. In our *real-price rigidity case* a devaluation would, of course, be useless. One wonders whether this last case is not, regrettably, rather close to reality, 1974–5 style.

Constant absorption case. Finally, let us suppose there is both a real-price rigidity, as in the previous case, and a government commitment to full employment. Real absorption cannot then be allowed to change, and we must get back to the point K (figure 6). Expenditure in terms of home-produced goods stays at OF, the demand for home-produced goods stays at OH and the demand for imports stays at OZ. The balance of payments deficit is then RK (measured in terms of imports) or KS'' (in terms of home-produced goods). This is a bigger deficit than in our first case where expenditure policy maintained full employment. The deficit was then only RE (figure 6). In that case, of course, the fall in real wages created by the import price was not reversed.

In the main text of this paper it has been suggested that countries' deficits resulting from the oil price rise may be somewhat of this last kind: *some* governments, at least, will borrow to sustain the pre-oil-price rise level of real absorption so as to maintain full employment. Of course they may not go all the way. There is some flexibility of real wages, other things are not equal and, in any case, all countries cannot keep their real absorption constant since the aggregate full employment real absorption of the OECD countries must have fallen somewhat owing to the reduced supplies of oil (as explained by figures 1 and 2). Furthermore, these governments may not always find willing lenders or rescuers. But this *constant absorption case* can be regarded as a limiting case which sheds more light on the nature of balance of payments deficits than the earlier, more traditional, cases.

Perhaps one should add that, all the time, it has been assumed that the money supply is varied to achieve whatever result is desired. In several of our cases the nominal money supply will have to increase owing to the rise in the average price level, first because of the initial rise in import prices and secondly because of the devaluation or the rise in prices of home-produced goods at full employment. On the other hand, in the *deflation case* the money supply will have to decrease. One could, of course, present a model where domestic credit creation in nominal terms is constant or zero, where a price rise lowers the real value of the money supply, and where a payments deficit leads to a steady contraction of the nominal money supply until the deficit is eliminated. But there seems no need to add to the plentiful and elegant literature telling this sort of story.

DISCUSSION: JOHN WILLIAMSON

There has been a considerable convergence of views in recent months regarding the probable effects of the oil price increase, and Dr Corden's paper is in most respects representative of the consensus that has been emerging. There is, for example, very little with which one can quarrel in his admirable and elegant taxonomy of the various possible welfare effects, which includes one interesting novelty: the analysis of the welfare effects on capital-importing and capital-exporting countries of both the increased 'production of bonds' and of OPEC preferences for the bonds issued by particular countries. (One may, however, doubt whether the world capital market is so imperfect as to give the latter factor great quantitative significance.) His paper is also representative in arguing that the central 'problem' posed by the oil increase is not the creation of a threat of 'national bankruptcy', of an uncontrollable depression, or of a breakdown of the international financial system, but is the biggest sudden international redistribution of income in history. This problem is particularly acute because the international community lacks any mechanism for deliberately offsetting the loss suffered by those least able to bear it, such as exists within individual nations, so that although the OPEC members are proving to be rather generous aid donors there are likely to be severe consequences for some of the least developed countries. For the rest of the oil importers, the consequences are harsh but manageable.

I do not believe that, as is asserted in the section on 'External balance', it is undoubtedly true that this type of borrowing [for the maintenance of consumption] cannot go on indefinitely'. In 1974, the members of OPEC saved enough to finance roughly 12% of the net capital formation in the rest of the world. This proportion is likely to decrease in the future: while I suspect that some recent forecasts that the OPEC surplus will vanish by 1980 are as unrealistic as the earlier visions of a surplus that grew continually larger relative to all other economic magnitudes, it seems highly likely that the surplus will decline in real terms; while net investment will presumably continue to grow. Rough calculations suggest that OPEC will never come to own as much as 10% of the rest of the world's capital stock. This means that the oil importers could go on borrowing to finance consumption indefinitely, if they so chose, since they are already investing enough to provide ample debt-servicing capacity.

This is not to say that the oil importers could permanently avoid cutting consumption as compared to the level it would have reached in the absence of the income transfer to OPEC. Consider figure 7. The curve labelled *P* indicates

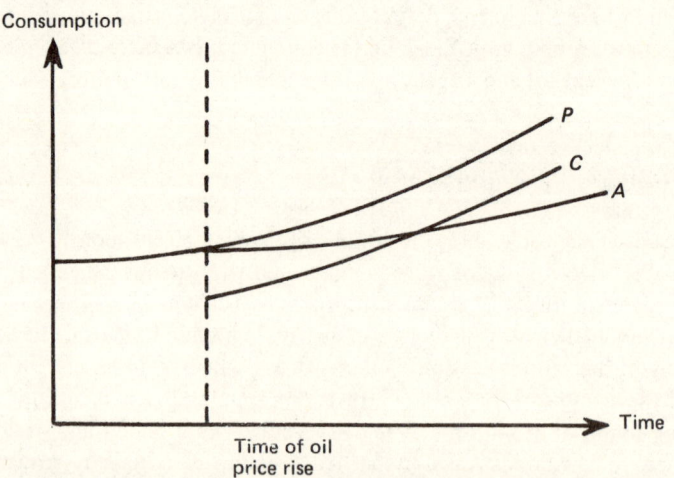

Figure 7

the time path that consumption would have followed in the absence of the oil price increase. The C curve (for Corden) indicates the time path implicitly recommended by Corden and Oppenheimer (1974), who advocated matching most of the increase in OPEC savings by an increase in investment in the oil-importing countries. What is being argued is that it would also be feasible to maintain investment constant and to curtail consumption only as and when OPEC import demand rises, as illustrated by path A. It is not of course being argued that this would be optimal; in fact, I would conjecture that a proper optimisation analysis would recommend a path intermediate between the C and A paths (assuming the P path to have been optimal under the conditions prevailing before the oil price rise).

I also have reservations regarding Dr Corden's suggestion that it may be perfectly rational — from the standpoint of OPEC, the oil importers, and the world — for the oil importers to curtail borrowing and OPEC to cut oil output correspondingly. Given the low short-run substitutability between oil and other products, a rapid move in this direction would in practice require the acceptance of substantial unemployment. In the longer run, there are also possibilities of substituting alternative sources of energy and of economising on energy, as is indeed already happening as a result of the oil price rise. The critical question seems to me to be whether it is rational to go beyond the point that is economical in the light of the current oil price. To do so would involve a sacrifice of real income and acceptance of a consumption path dominated by the C path. If there were rigidities — such as limited productive capacity in the investment goods industries — which made the C path infeasible, this lower path might conceivably ultimately rise above the A path, and might therefore be judged preferable on the customary welfare criteria. Otherwise, elimination of the collective oil deficit would impose an unambiguous sacrifice of consumption which could only be deemed rational if one admits xenophobic objections to foreign indebtedness to a place in the social welfare function.

Even if elimination of the collective oil deficit were judged desirable — on the basis of either rigidities which prevented investment rising or nationalistic dislike of foreign debts — there might be a problem in achieving it. This arises from the fact that each individual oil-importing country would find it nationally advantageous to eliminate its deficit by achieving a counter surplus with the other oil importers, rather than itself undertaking the uneconomic investment in oil substitutes or economy.[5] One would therefore have the 'reluctance to run current account deficits' discussed by Dr Corden in his final section. (This reluctance surely cannot be explained by 'the domestic income distribution effects of a current account deficit', since there is a presumption that domestic income distribution would be less affected by accepting a current deficit equal to the oil deficit rather than by adjusting to push more resources into the balance of trade.) I see no reason to suppose that this prospect could be faced with equanimity just because the world is floating: this fact makes it easier for countries other than the United States to depreciate against the dollar and concentrate the deficit on the United States, and such a result would surely strain American attachment to a liberal international economic order. That this has not yet happened is a reflection of the willingness that most countries have so far shown to go into international debt rather than sacrifice economic welfare on the altar of nationalism. The perpetuation of this desirable state of affairs would be more firmly assured if there were international agreement on how the collective deficit ought to be distributed. This might also reduce the danger, perhaps treated too lightly by Dr Corden, of some countries becoming uncreditworthy, since in the absence of such an agreement it may be too easy for some countries to evade their fair share of the deficit and for others — those with the least political will to avoid deficits — to end up carrying an unsustainable share.

NOTES

1 See Corden (1974) and Corden and Oppenheimer (1974). Both papers are reprinted, the latter paper in substantially revised form, in Rybczynski (1975). The present paper is essentially a development of the first of these two papers. It does not discuss a central theme of the second paper, namely that governments which borrow OPEC funds should do so primarily for socially profitable investment, rather than for consumption maintenance (other than in the short-term, to ease the transitional effects). These issues have given rise to some controversy, and we have amplified our argument somewhat in the forthcoming revised version of the paper. Some of the issues of the present paper are also discussed by Mussa (1974) and Posner (1974). I am indebted to discussions with Peter Oppenheimer, co-author of the second paper, and also to John Martin.
2 There are obvious difficulties in trying to represent the future price of oil by a simple supply (marginal cost) curve, especially as the expected future value depends on current price and output. The main point is that there will, in principle, be *some* area A and *some* area F, and the latter could be positive or negative. The size of A will not necessarily be invariant to the current price and output decision, as might be implied by the diagram. The thoughts in this note and the paragraph to which it is attached were inspired by a brief question at the conference by W.M. Gorman and by subsequent discussion with Peter Holmes.
3 If one nevertheless obtains a net deficit for OECD then the explanation is a matter of accounting. Exports of gold to OPEC might not be included in ordinary exports but regarded as 'accommodating'. The accumulation of liquid balances by OPEC might not be regarded as autonomous capital inflow into OECD, but, again, as accommodating. Then a deficit emerges. But the distinction between 'accommodating' and 'autonomous' loses its meaning here.
4 In *LM–IS* terms, define the rate of interest and expenditure (Y) in real terms. The *IS* curve moves to the left owing to the higher savings propensity, which outweighs extra investment at a constant interest rate. The *LM* curve also moves to the left owing to the fall in the real money supply and the (possibly) higher liquidity preference of OPEC. Supposing that the first effect outweighs the second, the rate of interest falls at this stage.

But to restore the initial level of expenditure, the *LM* curve needs to be moved to the right by an increase in the money supply until it cuts the new *IS* curve vertically below the original equilibrium. Since reduced world oil output has lowered current world real output at full employment somewhat it may not be necessary to fully restore the initial level of aggregate demand, but this is a minor point.

5 Dr Corden's discussion in appendix 2, while formally accurate, might mislead the incautious into overlooking the sort of collective inconsistency under discussion here. His assumption (iii) assumes away the problem. But the 'classic Meade solution' is of very limited relevance in the present context, because it is only available to the oil importers collectively if the definition of 'exports' is expanded to include the sale of bonds. The limited ability of OPEC members to spend their revenues on imports constitutes a constraint on the collective oil importers' current deficit which cannot be modified by the Meade mechanism.

REFERENCES

Corden, W.M. (1960). The geometric representation of policies to attain internal and external balance. *Review of Economic Studies* 28, 1–22. Reprinted in *International Finance*, ed. R. Cooper. Penguin Modern Economics, 1969.

Corden, W.M. (1974). Implications of the oil price rise. *Journal of World Trade Law* 8, 133–43.

Corden, W.M. and Oppenheimer, Peter (1974). Basic implications of the rise in oil prices. *Moorgate and Wall Street*, Autumn, 23–38.

Mussa, Michael (1974). Relative prices and macroeconomic policy in an open economy. Mimeo. University of Rochester Department of Economics.

Posner, Michael (1974). Energy at the Centre of the stage. *Three Banks Review*, no. 104, 3–27.

Rybczynski, T.M. (1975). *The economics of the oil crisis*. London: Macmillan for the Trade Policy Research Centre.

8 A MONETARY MODEL OF AN OPEN ECONOMY WITH PARTICULAR REFERENCE TO THE UNITED KINGDOM

M.D. KNIGHT AND C.R. WYMER

INTRODUCTION

This paper is a report on continuing research into the specification, estimation and analysis of a continuous disequilibrium model of a small open economy, and is one aspect of the work being carried out within the International Monetary Research Programme. The main purpose of the model is to investigate the short-run dynamic processes implicit in the monetary approach to balance of payments theory. The model describes interactions between the home economy and the rest of the world which arise from the behaviour of domestic and foreign residents in the markets for real goods and services and for financial assets. Excess demands in the markets for real output, labour services and financial assets lead to disequilibrium in the foreign exchange market and the balance of payments. Under a regime of fixed exchange rates, balance of payments disequilibrium induces accommodating transactions in official exchange reserves and changes in the domestic money supply. The resulting excess supply or demand for real money balances causes changes in interest rates and prices which feed back into domestic markets for goods and securities. This causes further changes in the balance of payments. The model includes policy functions for the fiscal and monetary authorities and thus shows the reaction of government policies to target variables and their feedback into the rest of the economy.

After a discussion of the basic assumptions of this study, the model is presented and briefly described in a deterministic form. The steady-state solution and the mechanism generating the transitory dynamics of the system will then be considered. The model presented here is designed to be used for econometric estimation and for policy analysis. Hence the paper ends with a discussion of the methods which are being used to estimate the parameters of the system and to determine its properties.

BASIC ASSUMPTIONS OF THE MODEL

The model contains two countries, the 'home' country and the rest of the world, and two composite real goods. Domestic residents produce a homogenous stream of domestic output. They use the income derived from production and funds from foreign borrowing to finance purchases of domestic goods, foreign goods (imports), and domestic securities, or to increase their holdings of money balances. Banks in the home-country borrow via domestic and Eurocurrency deposits and hold domestic securities and Eurocurrency claims on foreigners. Foreign residents purchase home-country output, government bonds, and Eurocurrency deposit liabilities of the banks.

The home country is 'small' in the sense that it cannot affect either the price level or the interest rate prevailing in world markets. Thus in long-run equilibrium the home-country price level and interest rate are determined by their levels in world markets. It is assumed, however, that sectors and markets do not adjust instantaneously to change, and further that the structure of markets is such that the excess demands of certain sectors have a predominant effect on market adjustment functions. The rates at which domestic output, prices, interest rates and financial holdings converge to their long-run equilibrium depend on the speeds of response of various sectors and markets. One purpose of the econometric estimation of the model will be to find out as much as possible about the nature of these lags and their implications for the disequilibrium behaviour of the economy.

In the current version of the model it is assumed that the spot exchange rate is perfectly fixed at ϵ and that all transactors expect it to remain at this level. Thus any change which leads to an autonomous balance of payments deficit or surplus will induce related changes in the domestic volume of money. The growth of domestic output is assumed to be a lagged response to excess demand created by the secular growth of intended expenditure on domestic output by both home and foreign residents. Increases in output are constrained, however, by the rate of growth of the capital stock and the labour force, as well as by the rate of technical change.

The model consists of four sectors: a domestic private sector, a domestic banking sector, the fiscal and monetary authorities, and a foreign sector. It incorporates a full (although highly aggregated) financial sector with policy functions for the Central Bank discount rate and for issues of government bonds. The government budget constraint is specified explicitly so that the connection between fiscal and monetary policy may be examined. This identity ensures consistency between monetary and fiscal policy, a relationship often absent from macroeconometric models.

The model is a non-tâtonnement system consisting of demand and supply functions, price and quantity adjustment functions, wealth identities and market identities. The adjustment functions are restricted to include only one or two excess demands. The behavioural functions are generally specified as linear in the logarithms of the variables so that they have constant elasticities. Most identities are linear in variables. The model is specified in continuous time so that it is a simultaneous system of stochastic non-linear differential equations.

THE MODEL

Definition of variables

Note: unless otherwise stated, all output and expenditure variables are valued in real terms and all variables representing financial holdings are valued in money terms.

Endogenous variables

   Output and expenditure variables
      C = real consumption expenditure of private sector,
      E = real exports of domestic goods and services,
      K = stock of fixed capital,
      k = proportional rate of increase of fixed capital,
      G = central government expenditure on current goods and services,
      I = real imports of goods and services,
      Y = net domestic output and income,
      V = inventories of goods and work in progress,
      p = price level of domestic output,
      L = employment,
      w = money wage rate.

   Financial variables
      R = official reserves of gold and foreign exchange,
      H = liquid assets held by commercial banks,
      B_p = commercial bank holdings of government bonds (market value),
      N = domestic banks' Eurocurrency loans to foreign residents,
      B_p = government bonds held by private sector (market value),
      A = commercial bank advances to private sector,
      T = tax receipts (valued in money terms),
      M = domestic money stock (commercial bank deposits),
      B = total stock of government bonds excluding official holdings,
      b = proportional rate of increase in volume of government bonds,
      S = net liabilities of private sector to foreign residents,
      r = market yield in long-term government bonds,
      r_0 = Central Bank discount rate,

Exogenous variables
      F = domestic banks' Eurocurrency deposits held by foreign residents,
      B_f = foreign holdings of domestic government bonds.
      r_f = foreign interest rate,
      ϵ = exchange rate (price of foreign currency in terms of domestic currency),
      q = price of foreign output in terms of the foreign monetary unit,
      t = time.

X^d refers to the desired demand for variable X and X^s refers to desired supply of of variable X. All variables are defined at time t and D is the differential operator d/dt.

$$D \log C = \alpha_1 \log (C^d/C) + \alpha_2 \log (M^d/M) \tag{1}$$

where

$$C^d = \gamma_1 \, e^{-\beta_5 (r - D \log p)}(Y - T/p),$$

$$M^d = p\gamma_2 r^{-\beta_6} r_f^{-\beta_7} Y.$$

$$D \log E = \alpha_3 \log (E^d/E) \tag{2}$$

where

$$E^d = \gamma_3 \left(\frac{p}{eq}\right)^{-\beta_1} e^{\lambda_3 t}.$$

$$Dk = \alpha_4 \{\gamma_4 [\beta_3 (Y/K)^{1+\beta_4} - r + D \log p] + \gamma_5 - k\}. \tag{3}$$

$$D \log G = \alpha_{18} \log (G/\gamma_{14} Y)_1 + \alpha_{19} \log \left(\frac{L}{\gamma_{15} e^{\lambda_2 t}}\right) + \alpha_{20} \, D \log \left(\frac{L}{\gamma_{15} e^{\lambda_2 t}}\right). \tag{4}$$

$$DI = \alpha_5 \left[\gamma_6 \left(\frac{p}{eq}\right)^{-\beta_8} (C + DK + E + G) - I\right] + \alpha_6 \left[\gamma_7 (C + DK + E + G) - V\right]. \tag{5}$$

$$DY = \alpha_7 \left\{\left[1 - \gamma_6 \left(\frac{p}{eq}\right)^{-\beta_8}\right] (C + DK + E + G) - Y\right\}$$

$$+ \alpha_8 [\gamma_7 (C + DK + E + G) - V]. \tag{6}$$

$$D \log p = \alpha_9 \log \left\{\frac{\gamma_8 \beta_2 w \, e^{-\lambda_1 t} [1 - \beta_3 (Y/K)^{\beta_4}]^{-(1+\beta_4)/\beta_4}}{p}\right\}. \tag{7}$$

$$D \log L = \alpha_{10} \log \left[\frac{\beta_2 \, e^{-\lambda_1 t}(Y^{-\beta_4} - \beta_3 K^{-\beta_4})^{-1/\beta_4}}{L}\right]. \tag{8}$$

$$D \log w = \alpha_{11} \log \left[\frac{\beta_2 \, e^{-\lambda_1 t}(Y^{-\beta_4} - \beta_3 K^{-\beta_4})^{-1/\beta_4}}{\gamma_9 \, e^{\lambda_2 t}(w/p)^{\beta_9}}\right]. \tag{9}$$

$$D \log r = \alpha_{12} \log (M^d/M). \tag{10}$$

$$D \log S = \alpha_{13} \log (M^d/M) + \alpha_{14} \log (B_p^d/B_p) \tag{11}$$

where

$$B_p^d = p\gamma_{10} r^{\beta_{10}} r_f^{-\beta_{11}} Y.$$

$$D \log B_b = \alpha_{15} \log (H^d/H) \tag{12}$$

where

$$H^d = \gamma_{11} r_0^{\beta_{12}} M.$$

$$D \log (N/F) = \alpha_{16} \log \left[r^{\beta_{13}} r_f^{-\beta_{14}} \left(\frac{N}{\gamma_{12} F}\right)\right]. \tag{13}$$

A monetary model of an open economy

$$D \log A = \alpha_{17} \log (A^d/A) \tag{14}$$

where

$$A^d = p\gamma_{13} r_0^{-\beta_{15}} Y.$$

$$D \log b = \alpha_{21} \log \left(\frac{R}{\gamma_{16}M}\right) + \alpha_{22} D \log \left(\frac{R}{\gamma_{16}M}\right) + \alpha_{23} \log \left(\frac{L}{\gamma_{15}e^{\lambda_2 t}}\right)$$

$$+ \alpha_{24} D \log \left(\frac{L}{\gamma_{15}e^{\lambda_2 t}}\right). \tag{15}$$

$$D \log r_0 = \alpha_{25} \log \left(\frac{r}{r_f}\right) + \alpha_{26} \log \left(\frac{R}{\gamma_{16}M}\right) + \alpha_{27} D \log \left(\frac{R}{\gamma_{18}M}\right). \tag{16}$$

$$D \log T = \alpha_{28} \log \left(\frac{T}{\gamma_{17}pY}\right). \tag{17}$$

$$D \log K = k. \tag{18}$$

$$D \log B = b. \tag{19}$$

$$DV = Y + I - C - DK - E - G, \tag{20}$$

$$DR = pE - pI + DF - DN + DB_f + DS. \tag{21}$$

$$DM = pG + pE - pI - T + DA - DB_p + DS. \tag{22}$$

$$DB = pG - T - DH + DR, \tag{23}$$

$$H = M + F - B_b - N - A. \tag{24}$$

Equation (23) could be replaced by the identity

$$B_p = B - B_b - B_f. \tag{23'}$$

which shows explicitly how the endogenous variable B_p is determined by the system. This is unnecessary, however, as equations (21) to (24) and (23') are linearly dependent and so one may be eliminated. We have decided to eliminate (23') rather than the wealth constraint of the authorities (23).

The parameters of the model are defined such that the αs are rates of adjustment, the βs are long-run elasticities and the γs are propensities, other desired proportions or expected levels or rates of change. $0 < \gamma_1 < 1, 0 < \gamma_6 < 1, \beta_4 > -1, \beta_8 < 1$ and all other parameters are positive except $\alpha_2, \alpha_{15}, \alpha_{16}, \alpha_{18}, \alpha_{19}, \alpha_{20}, \alpha_{21}, \alpha_{22}, \alpha_{25}, \alpha_{26}, \alpha_{27}, \alpha_{28}$, and possibly λ_3. The λs are exogenous rates of growth where:

λ_1 = rate of technical progress,
λ_2 = rate of growth of population,
λ_3 = rate of growth of foreign real income,
λ_4 = rate of growth of foreign volume of money.

OUTPUT EXPENDITURE AND THE LABOUR MARKET

The first part of the model specifies the behaviour of domestic residents and foreigners in the markets for two composite goods: domestic output with price p and foreign output with foreign currency price q. The demand for labour services is derived from a CES production function which is also implicit in several other equations of the model. The specification of the real sector, including the price and wage equations, is similar to earlier work by Bergstrom and Wymer (1974) except that the present system incorporates a central government expenditure function. The adjustment functions for production and expenditure are tightly interlinked and related to the level of inventories in the domestic economy.

The output and expenditure section of the model consists of eight equations. Equations (1) to (4) are adjustment functions for the various components of aggregate expenditure: consumption (1), exports (2), fixed capital formation (3) and government spending (4). In general, the rate of change of expenditure of each sector is an increasing function of the ratio of the partial equilibrium or desired expenditure to the current level of expenditure. Equation (1) assumes that consumption responds to an excess demand for either consumer goods or money. The rationale for including the latter excess demand is that if the private sector wishes to increase its holdings of real money balances it will do so by foregoing current consumption. As the private sector is an aggregate of the household and corporate sectors, the effect of any excess demand for money on consumption will be to increase money balances only to the extent that the decrease in consumption reduces imports, as in equations (5) and (22).

Equation (2) makes the simplifying assumption that exports respond with a lag to foreign demand. As output of domestic goods Y is constrained by the production function implicit in the model, for given terms of trade equation (2) determines the proportion of domestic output which is exported. The terms of trade will not remain unchanged, however, when an increase in the rate of growth of foreign income creates an excess demand for home goods.

Following Bergstrom and Wymer, equation (3) assumes that the investment accelerator depends on the difference between the partial equilibrium and actual proportional rate of increase in fixed capital k. The desired proportional rate of increase in the stock of capital is a linear function of the difference between the marginal product of captial $\beta_3(Y/K)^{1+\beta}$ and the real interest rate $(r - \text{D} \log p)$. The parameter γ_5 is equal to the rate at which entrepreneurs would expect output to grow if there were perfect competition and no risk. The marginal product of capital is derived from the CES production function

$$Y = \left[\beta_3 K^{-\beta_4} + \left(\frac{1}{\beta_2} e^{\lambda_1 t} L \right)^{-\beta_4} \right]^{-1/\beta_4}$$

where λ_1 is the rate of decrease, due to technical progress, in the amount of labour required to produce a given output with a given stock of capital. The elasticity of substitution is $1/(1 + \beta_4)$, and the elasticity of output with respect to capital is $\beta_3(Y/K)^{\beta_4}$. This equation is also used in deriving the price, wage and employment functions, giving rise to important across-equation restrictions on the output-expenditure sector of the model.

The determinants of government spending will be discussed below in the section on economic policy. The adjustment function for imports (5) states that when inventories are at their desired level, the partial equilibrium level of imports is some proportion of total sales, where the porportion $\gamma_6(p/eq)^{-\beta_8}$ depends on the terms of trade with an elasticity equal to $(1 - \beta_8)$. The rate of change in imports depends not only on the difference between the desired and actual level of imports, however, but also on the excess demand for inventories where γ_7 represents firms' desired ratio of inventories to total sales. The rate of increase in domestic output also depends on the difference between desired and actual output and the excess demand for inventories, where the partial equilibrium level of output is defined to be consistent with the partial equilibrium level of imports. The rate of change of inventories is given by the identity (20) which relates realised output and expenditure. Thus equations (1) to (6) and (20) determine all components of output and expenditure. Equation (7) determines the price level of domestic output. The proportional rate of increase of prices is an increasing function of the ratio of marginal labour cost to the current price level under the assumption that capital is fixed. The parameter γ_8 allows for imperfect competition in the goods market as discussed in Bergstrom and Wymer (1974); perfect competition corresponds to $\gamma_8 = 1$.

The behaviour of the market for labour services is given in equations (8) and (9). The model assumes that at the current price level each firm in the domestic economy takes its sales as given and maximises profits by minimising labour costs. Following Bergstrom and Wymer we assume in equation (8) that actual employment responds with a lag to the effective demand for labour which is derived from the production function as the minimum amount of labour required to produce a given output with a given capital stock. The proportional rate of change of the money wage rate is an increasing function of the ratio of effective demand and desired supply defined as a function of the labour force and the real wage.

An intuitive impression of the simultaneous dynamic structure implicit in the output and expenditure equations, and their relation to domestic monetary variables and the international sector may be obtained by tracing the implications of a single exogenous change. Consider the effect of an increase in the foreign inflation rate caused by a once-for-all rise in the rate of foreign monetary expansion, under the assumption that real income abroad continues to grow at a constant rate. Initially, the higher rate of inflation abroad leads to a deterioration of the home country's terms of trade. The excess demand for exports so created will cause a rise in the rate of growth of domestic exports (via equation 2) and, consequently, in the rate of growth of output (6), prices (7), and imports (5). However, monetary adjustments induced by the incipient balance of payments surplus on current account and the resulting expansion in the volume of money will cause a fall in the rate of interest (10), leading to a higher rate of gross capital formation (3) as well as an increase in the rate of growth of consumption via a dishoarding effect (1). Imports will now rise more rapidly, not only because of the faster rate of growth of domestic expenditure, but also due to the subsequent improvement in the terms of trade as the home country's inflation rate begins to rise. The terms-of-trade effect will also, of course, slow down exports. As imports continue to rise relative to exports the balance-of-payments surplus will eventually reverse itself until the terms of trade have returned to their initial level, and the domestic rate of inflation has risen to equal the inflation rate abroad. Accordingly, the rate of change of domestic money wages also increases (9), and when the system returns to the steady state the growth rates of all real variables will be back at their initial levels.

THE DOMESTIC MONETARY SYSTEM

Equations (10) to (16) together with identities (19), (22), (24), and (23'), specify the behaviour of various sectors in domestic and international financial markets. The portfolio behaviour of commercial banks and the private sector in the domestic monetary system is considered first, before proceeding to a discussion of the links between domestic financial markets and those in the rest of the world.

Banks in the home country issue money in the form of liabilities to the domestic private sector and hold liquid asset reserves H, government bonds B_b and domestic advances A. (Their holdings of Eurocurrency liabilities and claims will be discussed below.) If domestic money balances earn no interest, or if the rate on deposit accounts is tied to Bank rate r_0, the commercial banks cannot induce the private sector to increase its holdings of money by raising the rate on deposits. Thus total deposits are determined exogenously from the point of view of the banking system. Given the level of their deposit liabilities, banks can adjust their holdings of the remaining assets and liabilities in their portfolio in response to their excess demands and supplies. But since their wealth identity must always hold, the banks can only adjust four of their five holdings independently. It is assumed that once the banks have set the level of their interest earning assets, their holdings of high-powered money are determined as the residual of their wealth constraint (24). However, as the banking system is required to maintain a legal minimum reserve ratio against its domestic liabilities, banks have a demand for reserve assets which depends on the level of deposits and the opportunity cost of holding reserves. Equation (12) assumes that the banking system adjusts its holdings of government securities in order to achieve its desired level of reserve assets.

The domestic private sector holds bank deposits and government securities, and borrows from the banking system by means of advances. If bank advances are granted on an overdraft system, (as in the United Kingdom) with the interest rate on advances tied to the Central Bank discount rate r_0, the level of advances responds to the excess demand for borrowing by the private sector as in (14). The wealth constraint of the private sector is given in (22). Transactions in both real goods and services and financial instruments between the domestic private sector and all other sectors of the model must ultimately be settled by transfers of money. Thus the change in the volume of private sector cash balances equals the money value of all purchases and sales of goods and securities by private domestic residents. Although the actual level of cash balances is the residual of the wealth constraint, the private sector's desired demand for money plays a crucial role in the linkage between the financial and real sectors of the model. Equation (10) assumes a dynamic version of the liquidity preference theory of the rate of interest in which the financial interest rate adjusts to the private sector's excess demand for money. Changes in the financial interest rate then affect the desired levels of consumption and net investment in (1) and (3). Further, the private sector's excess demand for money has a direct effect on current consumption and on capital flows. These latter effects imply across-equation restrictions on equations (1), (10) and (11).

THE FOREIGN EXCHANGE MARKET AND THE BALANCE OF PAYMENTS

Since the behaviour of all sectors in the home economy leads to transactions with foreign residents, the equations which specify the foreign exchange market and the balance of payments are the focus of the structural model. Domestic markets for output, labour, and financial assets are influenced by what happens abroad through the foreign exchange market.

Although it is intended to extend the specification of the model to allow for both devaluation and periods of floating exchange rates, the present system is based on the assumption that the exchange rate is perfectly fixed. The balance of payments equation (21) states that the rate of change of official reserves DR must equal domestic residents' export earnings pE, minus payments for imports pI, plus the net capital inflow ($DF - DN + DB_f + DS$) which occurs as holders of financial assets at home and abroad readjust their portfolios in response to changes in domestic and foreign interest rates and changes in their wealth. Under the present assumption of a perfectly fixed exchange rate, the right side of (21) represents the excess private supply of spot foreign exchange. Thus (21) is a causal statement which describes how the authorities must respond with their reserves if they wish to keep the spot exchange rate perfectly fixed at ϵ. An excess supply of foreign exchange implies that the authorities will be accumulating reserves. Thus balance of payments disequilibrium is reflected in changes in official reserves resulting from imbalances between the total aggregate receipts and payments of private domestic residents.

Since domestic residents may hold goods and securities as well as money, the private sector wealth constraint (22) requires that the counterpart of an excess demand for real money balances is an excess supply of goods or securities, or both. A non-zero excess demand for commodities or securities by domestic residents implies a balance of payments deficit.

Traditionally, economic theory assumes that relative prices determine the equilibrium flows of real goods and services, while relative interest rates determine equilibrium stocks of financial assets and debts. This approach is reflected in the distinction made by Johnson (1965) between 'stock deficits' and 'flow deficits' in the balance of payments. Briefly, a flow deficit implies a decision by domestic residents to spend more than they are currently receiving, while a stock deficit results from an effort by wealth owners to alter the distribution of a given stock of assets between domestic and foreign securities. Since the stock deficit involves a once-for-all change in the composition of asset portfolios, it causes a temporary balance of payments deficit which endures only during the time that the portfolio adjustment is being made. Flow deficits, on the other hand, result in a continuing change in the level of official exchange reserves. It is tempting to associate flow deficits with the current account of the balance of payments and stock adjustment deficits with the capital account. However, this distinction is not generally tenable because of the private sector wealth constraint. A current account surplus reflects the fact that domestic output is greater than domestic expenditure. The determinants of the various components of output and expenditure have already been discussed. It is important to note, however, that in the model a current account surplus may result from either stock or flow disequilibrium. If the private sector has an excess demand for real balances, it will reduce consumption via (1). This tends to cause a surplus in the balance of trade until the stock adjustment in the level of cash balances has been completed. Alternatively, an increase in the foreign price level will raise the foreign demand for domestic exports, resulting in a flow surplus in the current account until the domestic price level has risen enough to restore the terms of trade to their initial level.

Foreign holdings of domestic government bonds B_f are exogenous to the model. Thus the capital account of the balance of payments is determined by the portfolio adjustments of the domestic private sector and the banks. Equation (11) states that home country residents tend to increase their liabilities to foreigners when they have an excess demand for money or domestic bonds, while (13) provides a simplified specification of the behaviour of domestic banks in the Eurocurrencies market. It is assumed that the acceptance rate which the banks pay on Eurocurrency deposits is determined exogenously in world market. Thus the level of their Eurocurrency liabilities F is also exogenous. Equation (13) states that given the level of their Eurocurrency liabilities, domestic banks adjust their Eurocurrency loans in order to attain their desired net Eurocurrency position $(N/\gamma_{12}F)$, thus inducing capital movements between the home country and the rest of the world.

POLICY FUNCTIONS OF THE AUTHORITIES AND THEIR BUDGET CONSTRAINT

Six equations describe the policy system operated by the central government and the monetary authorities. Real government expenditure on current goods and services G is determined in equation (4), while nominal tax receipts (net of subsidies) adjust to changes in money income (17). The difference between the money values of expenditure and tax receipts is the government's net borrowing requirement. This budget deficit may be financed either by creating high-powered money H, or by issuing government debt B. Since the level of high-powered money is assumed to be determined in (24), the flow of government borrowing is given by (23). Equation (19) defines the rate of change of government debt and (15) specifies that the authorities can adjust the rate of change of government borrowing as a policy measure. Finally equation (16) describes the criteria on which the authorities set the level of Bank rate.

In theoretical models the policy instruments of the monetary and fiscal authorities are usually assumed exogenous in order to show the effects of various policy alternatives on the behaviour of the system. In an econometric model, however, it is not appropriate to assume that the authorities fix the level of their policy instruments exogenously if there are direct feedbacks from endogenous variables in the system to the authorities' policy reaction functions. Government policy is determined by the authorities' objectives such as employment, the level of official reserves of gold and foreign exchange, the price level, and the rate of growth of output. In practice these general objectives are represented by a set of target variables which the government aims to influence in a known direction and to a significant extent by its policies. Thus the government's fiscal spending equation (4) assumes that the authorities have a desired level of employment ($\gamma_{15} e^{\lambda_2 t}$) and their spending is adjusted according to the ratio of desired employment to actual employment. The authorities respond both to the level of this ratio, and to its rate of change. Thus the reaction function for fiscal spending is based on the concept of proportional and integral control developed by A.W. Phillips (1954). This form of response has a simple rationale: if the ratio of actual employment to the desired level is less than unity but rising, the authorities will wish to increase government spending by a smaller amount than they would if this ratio were steady at the current level. The first term of equation (4) implies that when employment is stable at its desired level the authorities adjust so as to keep their spending a constant proportion γ_{14} of real income. Open market policy is specified in (15) which gives the determinants of the rate of change of government borrowing. In addition to the target employment level, the monetary authorities are assumed to have a desired ratio γ_{16} of foreign exchange reserves to the volume of money. When this ratio falls below the desired level, the authorities will sell gilt-edged stock at a more rapid rate in an attempt to drive up market interest rates. The response of the monetary authorities to a difference between desired and actual employment is analogous to that described above in the case of fiscal policy. Assuming that the authorities' policy targets for employment are consistent, across-equation restrictions must be imposed to ensure that γ_{15} has the same value in (4) and (15). The final policy equation of the model is (16), which says that the authorities adjust Bank rate in response to changes in the level of foreign interest rates and the ratio of official exchange reserves to the volume of money. Again across-equation restrictions must be imposed on equations (15) and (16).

THE STEADY STATE OF THE MODEL

Under certain conditions the non-linear differential equation system (1) to (24) has a particular solution, described as the steady state,

$$X_i(t) = X_i^* e^{\rho_i t}$$

where the $X_i(t)$ refer to the endogenous variables in the model, the X_i^* are the corresponding steady-state levels where $t = 0$ and the ρ_i the corresponding steady state growth rates. The formulae for the growth rates are:

Variable	Steady state growth rate
L	λ_2
C, E, K, G, I, Y, V	$\lambda_1 + \lambda_2$
p	$\lambda_4 - \lambda_3$
w	$\lambda_4 - \lambda_3 + \lambda_1$
$M, T, R, B, B_p, B_b, H, A, S, N$	λ_4
r, r_0	0

In order to obtain this solution it is necessary to assume that the steady-state paths of the exogenous variables are:

$$B_f(t) = B_f^* e^{\lambda_4 t}, \quad F(t) = F^* e^{\lambda_4 t}, \quad q(t) = q^* e^{(\lambda_4 - \lambda_3)t}$$

$$r_f(t) = r_f^*, \quad \text{and} \quad \epsilon(t) = \epsilon^*.$$

Moreover, for a full international steady state, the rates of growth of domestic and foreign output must be equal, that is $\lambda_1 + \lambda_2 = \lambda_3$. These steady-state rates of growth are consistent with international monetary theory. A condition for this steady state to exist, however, is that $\beta_9 = 0$.

The levels of the steady-state growth paths X_i^* may be expressed as explicit functions of the parameters $\alpha, \beta,$ and γ of the model, the rates of growth λ and the initial state of the exogenous variables B_f^*, F^*, q^*, r_f^* and ϵ^*. Thus the steady-state behaviour of the complete system may be calculated given numerical values of the structural parameters and rates of growth. Moreover, it is possible to determine definitely the effect of changes in certain parameters on the steady-state paths of some variables since the signs of many of the partial derivatives of the initial steady-state levels X_i^* are independent of the values of the parameters. In addition, the stability of the model in the neighbourhood of the steady state can be investigated. Work on these aspects of the model is continuing.

The prototype model of Bergstrom (1967) and the work of Bergstrom and Wymer (1974) shows that the steady state will exist only if certain conditions are satisfied. These involve the policy functions of the authorities and, in general, imply that the desired ratio of government expenditure to output and of foreign reserves to the volume of money will not be attained unless the authorities' desired level of employment has no influence on the steady-state employment level (or if the level aimed at is that which necessarily occurs in the steady state). The inclusion of the terms involving α_{19} and α_{23} in the policy reaction functions (4) and (15) has no effect on the steady-state employment level, prevents the attainment of the desired relationship between government expenditure and output (and possibly the desired ratio between foreign reserves and money balances), and is likely to be destabilising. The effect of including the rate of change in employment and the rate of change of foreign reserves and money balances in these functions may be stabilising if α_{20} and α_{22} are negative and α_{24} is positive, but these results have not yet been fully determined and must be regarded as tentative.

THE ESTIMATION PROCEDURE

Consistent estimates of a linear stochastic differential equation system may be obtained from a discrete sample but it is not yet possible to obtain such estimates for a non-linear system such as that specified above. Estimates may be obtained, however, by deriving a linear approximation to the non-linear system and treating this as if it were the true model. Although this assumption allows consistent estimates of the linear model to be obtained, these will be biased estimates of the structural parameters owing to the approximation involved in the linearisation.

The model (1) to (24) may be approximated by a Taylor series expansion, either about sample means of the logarithms of the variables, or about the steady state, to give a differential equation model linear in the logarithms of the variables. Initially, estimates of the former approximation are being calculated as it is easier to change the specification of the model when it is linearised about sample means. These estimates may be used to compute the coefficients of the model in terms of deviations about the steady state as that is the model necessary for studying the dynamic and long-run properties of the system.

The alternative procedure, which linearises the model about the steady state, has the advantage that its coefficients are functions only of the structural parameters and do not involve sample means. The complexity of these functions makes this model more difficult to estimate than the first approximation, and it would be expected to provide better estimates only if the system was close to the steady state during the observation period. Thus this approximation might be necessary where the sample period is particularly long, but it might not be superior to the approximation about sample means for the relatively short sample period used in this study. Estimates of the approximation about the steady state may be used directly for investigating the dynamic behaviour of the system.

Estimates of the parameters of the system may be calculated using the full information maximum likelihood estimator of the exact discrete model which is stochastically equivalent to the differential equation system in that it is satisfied by any set of equi-spaced observations generated by the differential equation system. This estimator is expensive to use, however, so preliminary estimates are being calculated using the discrete approximation to the linearised continuous model. Both of these estimators have been described in Bergstrom and Wymer (1974) and Wymer (1972).

As the present model is specified for a fixed exchange rate regime, the sample initially consists of quarterly UK data for the period 1955 to 1966. For estimation, the observations must be deseasonalised and transformed to eliminate the moving average inherent in the data generated by a first-order differential equation stock/flow model (Bergstrom and Wymer, 1974). Once maximum likelihood estimates of this model have been obtained, it will be modified to take account of the 1967 devaluation and re-estimated using the sample period 1955 to 1971. Finally, the structural model will be generalised to allow for floating as well as fixed exchange rate regimes. The study will conclude with an analysis of the dynamic properties of the system and the scope for its control by the authorities. This will include the calculation of the eigenvalues of the model, a sensitivity analysis, forecasting, and policy simulations.

DISCUSSION: G.R. FISHER[1]

This paper reports on interesting and sophisticated research which is potentially important for two reasons. First, it seeks to evaluate a vital area of contemporary economic affairs within the framework of a clearly specified theory. It thus has the potential to advance our knowledge of economic theory and of recent economic history. This is particularly important in respect of endogenous feedback on policy variables. Second, the research contributes to the growing body of knowledge on the application of continuous-time econometric models in an area which would seem appropriate for this sort of treatment. Since applications of such models have been rare, we have very limited knowledge of their ability to capture reality or about their practical advantages over corresponding discrete-time specifications with which we are more familiar. The research has the potential to increase our knowledge in these areas as well.

Yet despite the potential importance of the research, the paper itself is rather difficult to comment on, since it is primarily concerned with specification problems. There are no estimates available. To comment on or perhaps criticise the model is bound to evoke the response that we really ought to wait and see what the estimates look like. Moreover, there are no simulations on which to appraise the dynamic behaviour of the model, since it is not yet available in final estimated form, whence it is very difficult to assess how the whole model will perform in a real or an artificial situation.

It is usual to exploit discrete-time models in econometric work, principally perhaps because this is how the data are presented to us. While we know that such models are more or less inadequate, the alternative of using a continuous-time approach is fraught with difficulty. In particular, the mathematics involved are undoubtedly complicated and must include — at least in the present case — two substantial approximations: a discrete approximation to the continuous-time formulation, and a linear approximation to a non-linear system. One begins to wonder whether the additional complications are really necessary and whether the conclusions from such work will be substantially different from the conclusions that would have emerged from a corresponding discrete-time approach to the problem.

There would seem no way out of using one or other of the approximations just mentioned. Unfortunately, nature has not been sufficiently understanding as to provide us with a wholly linear world, and as already indicated, man typically provides economic observations in discrete time only. In discrete time we can make a reasonable attempt to estimate a non-linear system and some would argue that the most interesting and important aspects of behaviour are those which arise from, and hence require, a non-linear formulation; moreover, that the major purpose of econometric model-building is to explain the time-path of discrete observations. Given this background, it should be recognised in model building that we must squarely face the choice of which course it is better to take: whether we should linearise a non-linear, continuous-time model and estimate its exact discrete analogue (thereby throwing away an important element of behaviour), or whether we should stick with discrete-time models (even though though, in truth, the process generating the discrete observations may itself be continuous) and concentrate on estimating a non-linear model. Since, in any case, all econometric models must be approximations to reality, the choice comes down to a consideration of the comparative opportunity costs. Which are we more prepared to forego: the benefits of non-linear behaviour or the benefits of continuous-time specifications?[2] The authors — at least as witnessed by their own behaviour — prefer to forego the former. Unfortunately they do not tell us either that there is a choice or why they prefer to forego the benefits of non-linear behaviour in the case of a monetary model of an open economy.

I should emphasise that I have no wish to discourage a new development before it has had a chance to justify itself. In the end we must judge the continuous-time approach on its own merits, according to what is may contribute to the development of economic theory. And clearly we cannot make a reasoned judgement on this issue on the basis of the present paper. It falls to me, therefore, to encourage development at least to the point where experience is sufficient to consider the choice between alternatives in terms of their associated costs and benefits. In this respect, I must express disappointment that comparative work is not proceeding parallel with the mainstream development of continuous-time models. It would be nice, for example, to compare the results from an existing discrete-time model with the corresponding results of a continuous-time version of it; and would it not be possible to write explicitly, at this stage, what the linearly approximated discrete version of the Knight–Wymer model looks like?

I suspect that whatever comparisons are eventually made, it will not always be possible to think of discrete-time specifications as mere analogues of a corresponding continuous-time formulation. At least one would hope that this is the case, since otherwise there would be no essentially new behaviour embodied in the continuous-time approach. Take, for example, Knight and Wymer's equation (10):

$$D\rho = \alpha_{12}(m^d - m)$$

where $\rho = \log r$ and $m = \log M$. Here the rate of interest adjusts continuously according to the discrepancy between the logarithms of desired and actual money balances. Presumably the discrete version of such an equation would look something like

$$\rho_t - \rho_{t-1} = \lambda(m_t^d - m_{t-1}),$$

a formulation which it would be hard to describe as meaningful; moreover, if m_t^d is looked upon as the estimated value of m_t and we maintain the same subscript on m as on m^d (to get closer to the continuous-time version), then $\rho_t - \rho_{t-1}$ becomes a mere random walk, which can hardly be said to constitute interesting dynamic economic behaviour. It would appear difficult to find a meaningful discrete analogue to the continuous-time adjustment process given by equation (10).

The last point would seem to me to be not unimportant in respect of strategic issues like the lags in monetary policy. For the evidence from discrete-time models is that the lags in monetary policy are long and variable; moreover, empirical evidence also suggests that if we lengthen the time period of observations, we tend, in discrete dynamic models, to lengthen the estimated mean lags. One is led to ask if perhaps the existing evidence on the lags in monetary policy is more the result of the use of discrete-time specifications than it is a reflection of actual behaviour, and whether a continuous-time specification would change matters. To the extent that it would, we would still be left with the issue of principle, namely which formulation is a better approximation to reality and whether it would be better still to adopt a mixture of the two approaches. In financial markets, a convincing case can be put for limited application of continuous adjustment mechanisms, but it would seem unlikely, even if we restrict ourselves to these markets, that continuous responses to stimuli are universal, since many policy reactions are in reality discrete.

There has been some discussion of adding-up and other budget restrictions. These may be dealt with by the residual method, namely, that with m asset demand functions, $(m-1)$ can be estimated and the mth determined via the appropriate identity. This is all very well in a wholly linear system where, subject to certain conditions, the estimates may be invariant to the equation selected as the residual. However, in a non-linear system, the choice of the residual equation becomes important since it is required to soak up any discrepancies that a non-linear system might cause in respect of the budget restraint. Knight and Wymer can get around this problem by considering a linearised version of their non-linear model. In this case the residual equation method must be used since otherwise singularities are introduced into the covariance structure. But then it is hard to maintain *both* that the model is non-linear-continuous *and* that all adding-up and other budget restrictions are carefully satisfied; indeed, in a completely non-linear system this would be impossible and in a mixed-linear — non-linear system it places undue strain on the linear part, and thereby raises tricky questions about the interpretation to be placed on the resulting estimates. But the problem of restrictions is not alone one of ensuring that accounting constraints are satisfied, for there are usually behavioural restrictions as well, and these further complicate the issue. To the extent that the total set of restrictions is then so severe as to imply that, of m equations to be estimated, one is predetermined upon estimation of $(m-1)$ of them, the choice of the residual may have important behavioural implications, unless an invariance rule can be shown to apply.

Some mention has been made about the appropriate point around which to expand to obtain a linear approximation of the model: the steady-state solution or the sample mean. Presumably other points might also be relevant in particular circumstances, for it seems as if selection of the point ought to depend on the application in mind. For example, if the model were used for forecasting, perhaps expansion around the most recent sample point would be appropriate.

Knight and Wymer are working within a regime of fixed exchange rates. Their specification recognises this fact. To extend the model to devaluation ought to be fairly straightforward; a further extension to floating exchange rates would surely turn out to be a different kettle of fish. Nevertheless, may I encourage them to undertake such when the present part of their study has been completed?

Finally, may I congratulate the authors on a well-written paper?

NOTES

1 Thanks are due to D.C. Rowan and A.R. Nobay for helpful discussions.
2 I am grateful to Franklin Fisher for clarifying my mind on this issue.

REFERENCES

Works cited in the text

Bergstrom, A.R. (1967). *The Construction and Use of Economic Models*. English Universities Press.

Bergstrom, A.R. and C.R. Wymer (1974). A model of disequilibrium neoclassical growth and its application to the United Kingdom. Discussion Paper, International Monetary Research Programme.

Johnson, H.G. (1965). Towards a general theory of the balance of payments. In *International Trade and Economic Growth*. Also in R.N. Cooper (ed.), *International Finance*. Penguin Books.

Phillips, A.W. (1954). Stabilization policy in a closed economy. *Economic Journal* **64**, 290–323.

Wymer, C.R. (1972). A continuous disequilibrium adjustment model of United Kingdom financial markets. In A.A. Powell and R.A. Williams (eds.), *Economic Studies of Macro-economics and Monetary Relations*. North-Holland.

Additional references

Barro, R. and H.I. Grossman (1971). A general disequilibrium model of income and expenditure. *American Economic Review* **61**, 82–93.

Branson, W.H. (1970). Monetary policy and the new view of international capital movements. *Brookings Papers in Economic Activity*, No. 2, 235–70.

Brunner, K. (1973). The money supply hypothesis in an open economy. In A.K. Swoboda and M.B. Connolly (eds.), *International Trade and Money*. Allen & Unwin.

Christ, C.F. (1968). A simple macroeconomic model with a government budget constraint. *Journal of Political Economy* **76**, 53–67.

Clower, R.W. (1966). The Keynesian counter-revolution. In F.H. Hahn and F.P.R. Brechling (eds.), *Theory of Interest Rates*. Macmillan.

Friedman, M. (1968). The Role of monetary policy. *American Economic Review* **58**, 1–17.

Johnson, H.G. (1972). *Further Essays in Monetary Economics*. Allen & Unwin.

Johnson, H.G. (1973). The monetary approach to balance of payments theory. In A.K. Swoboda and M.B. Connolly (eds.), *International Trade and Money*. Allen & Unwin.

Knight, M.D. (1973). A continuous disequilibrium econometric model of the domestic and international portfolio behaviour of the U.K. banking system. In J.M. Parkin (ed.), *Essays in Modern Economics*. Longmans.

Mundell, R.A. (1968a). Capital mobility and stabilization policy under fixed and flexible exchange rates. In R.A. Mundell, *International Economics*. Macmillan.

Mundell, R.A. (1968b). The appropriate use of monetary and fiscal policy for internal and external stability. In R.A. Mundell, *International Economics*. Macmillan.

Mundell, R.A. (1968c). The monetary dynamics of international adjustment under fixed and flexible exchange rates. In R.A. Mundell, *International Economics*. Macmillan.

Patinkin, D. (1965). *Money, Interest and Prices*, 2nd edition. Harper and Row.

Swoboda, A.K. (1973). Monetary policy under fixed exchange rates: effectiveness, speed of adjustment, and proper use. *Economica* **40**, 136–53.

Swoboda, A.K. and R. Dornbusch (1973). International adjustment, macroeconomic policy and monetary equilibrium in a two-country model of income determination. In M.B. Connolly and A.K. Swoboda (eds.), *International Trade and Money*. Allen & Unwin.

Tobin, J. and W. Brainard (1968). Pitfalls in financial model-building. *American Economic Association, Papers and Proceedings* **58**, 99–122.

9 THE INTERNATIONAL TRANSMISSION OF INFLATION

RUSSELL S. BOYER[1]

INTRODUCTION

The recent acceleration in the rate of inflation in Western economies has provided a strong incentive for individual countries to alter their exchange rate policies. Under the fixed rate system of Bretton Woods a rise in prices abroad is quickly transmitted into an inflationary situation at home in spite of domestic policies. A flexible exchange rate regime, it is argued, offers better insulation from events abroad in that the exchange rate moves countercyclically to foreign prices.[2]

These views are widely held and have been enunciated with considerable frequency over most of the twentieth century. However, to this author's knowledge, the basic argument has never been submitted to a careful analysis. The contention may be represented plausibly enough in a purchasing power parity context. Nonetheless that doctrine has not had unqualified verification empirically and theoretically can be derived from only the most rudimentary model.[3]

In order to capture more fully the effects of greater exchange rate flexibility, this paper presents a general equilibrium model in which the exchange rate can be treated as either an exogenous or an endogenous variable. The small, open economy under consideration produces and consumes a non-traded good whose price is endogenous under either exchange rate regime so that purchasing power parity is not trivially satisfied.[4]

This framework enables us to analyse the consequences of a rise in the foreign-currency price of the traded good. Under fixed rates, the increased price of these goods impinges directly on the domestic economy so that the price level rises while the relative price of the non-traded good is reduced. In contrast, under flexible rates the exchange rate falls so as to provide insulation for the small economy. This movement of the exchange rate is shown to reduce both the relative price and the price index effects of the rise in foreign prices. However, in the general case where domestic citizens hold some foreign-currency-denominated assets, the insulation is less than perfect because of the drop in the value of these assets with the fall in the exchange rate. When this effect is included we demonstrate that the price level is higher than previously and the relative price of the non-traded good has deteriorated. Nonetheless,

173

these price changes are smaller with flexible rates than they are with fixed so that a flexible exchange rate regime does provide insulation for a small economy.[5]

THE MODEL

The model is derived from Mundell's formalisation of the Metzlerian framework for an open economy, but incorporates a portfolio balance view of the capital account.[6] The centre of the analysis is a small, open economy which has goods and financial capital mobility with the rest of the world. The asset markets are disaggregated into a money market and a bond market. Bonds can be disaggregated into a domestic bond (perhaps non-traded) and internationally mobile bonds, but this is not crucial to the argument. The country is small in the sense that the foreign-currency price of traded commodities and the rate of return on bonds are taken to be exogenous. All markets clear instantaneously so that the well-established techniques of comparative statics can be used. In particular, full employment obtains at all times.

The economy is in full equilibrium in the short run if two general conditions are satisfied: at prevailing prices the market for domestic (non-traded) goods clears, and portfolios are in balance. Under fixed exchange rates the price level and the quantity of nominal balances adjust to clear these markets. Under flexible rates the domestic-currency prices of both commodities and foreign exchange vary to bring about equilibrium.

The two market-clearing conditions are:

$$\text{non-traded goods:} \quad D(r, w) = S(r) \tag{1}$$

$$\text{assets}^7: \quad M = P_I l(w). \tag{2}$$

The functions D and S are respectively the demand and supply of non-traded goods and l is the demand for real cash balances. Denote the derivative of a function of a single variable with a prime (') and the partial derivative of a multivariate function, f, with respect to the ith argument by f_i. Assuming the usual signs of the partial derivatives we have $D_1 < 0, D_2 > 0, S' > 0$, and $0 < l' < 1$. Real income is not included as an argument in these demand functions on the grounds that it can be defined as a constant along a production possibilities curve so long as production is not specialised.[8]

The variables in these equations are: r, the relative price of the non-traded good in terms of the traded good, defined by the identity

$$r \equiv P_d/(eP_t);$$

w, the real value of nominal wealth; P_I, the domestic-currency price index; and M, the money supply. The variables in the identity are: P_d, the domestic-currency price of the non-traded good; e, the domestic-currency price of foreign exchange (the exchange rate using the North American convention); and P_t, the foreign-currency price of the traded good. Units are chosen so that all prices and the money supply are equal to one at the initial equilibrium.

The domestic-currency price index is a linear homogeneous function of the prices of traded and non-traded goods,

$$P_I = P_I(P_d, eP_t)$$

such that an increase in either price raises the value of the index. This assumption implies that P_{I1} and P_{I2} are both positive; furthermore, by homogeneity and the initial unit value of prices

$$P_{I1} + P_{I2} = 1.$$

This demonstrates that increasing both prices by the same percentage increases the price index by that percentage. For notational simplicity write P_{I1} as α so that P_{I2} equals $1 - \alpha$.

Nominal wealth, W, equals the sum of money and bond holdings, a portion of which, B, is denominated in foreign currency, with the rest, B_d, denominated in domestic currency. Expressing nominal wealth in domestic currency requires multiplying foreign-currency-denominated bond holdings by the exchange rate. That is,

$$W = M + eB + B_d$$

where W, M, and B are all assumed to be positive.[9] Dividing through by P_I defines the variables: $b \equiv B/P_I$, $w \equiv W/P_I$, and $l \equiv M/P_I$. This definition of wealth provides a constraint on the excess demand functions in the asset markets. In particular, since the disaggregation is only between money and bonds, when the money market is in equilibrium both asset markets are clearing.

Under fixed exchange rates the money supply is an endogenous variable, while only wealth, the foreign-currency price of the traded good, and the exchange rate are exogenous. Under flexible rates the only exogenous variables are M and P_t. Nominal wealth becomes an endogenous variable in that any exchange rate change alters the domestic-currency value of the foreign-currency-denominated assets.

The central endogenous variables, in terms of which the diagrammatic comparative statics is conducted, are the price index and the exchange rate for flexible rates, and the price index and the money supply for fixed exchange rates. The equilibrium values of these endogenous variables, two for each exchange rate regime, are determined from equations (1) and (2). The equilibrium values for all other endogenous variables can be determined by substituting these values into subsidiary equations.

The slope of the market-clearing locus for the non-traded goods market in price-level-exchange-rate space, denoted by XX in figure 1, is given by totally differentiating equation (1):[10]

$$\left.\frac{de}{dP_I}\right|_{XX} = \frac{(D_1 - S')/\alpha - D_2 w}{(D_1 - S')/\alpha - D_2 b}. \tag{3}$$

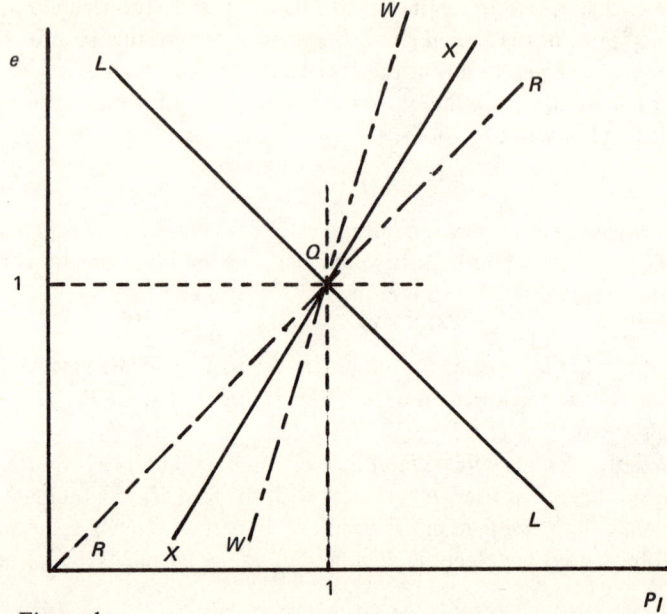

Figure 1

This derivative satisfies the inequalities:

$$1 \leq \left.\frac{de}{dP_I}\right|_{XX} \leq \frac{w}{b} \qquad (4)$$

and so clearly is a positive quantity. The explanation of the positive slope and the inequalities in expression (4) can be most easily phrased in terms of two additional loci. These loci are the points for which the real value of nominal wealth, and the relative price of the non-traded good in terms of the traded good, respectively, are constant.

The locus of points for which real wealth is constant, shown as WW in figure 1, has the slope:

$$\left.\frac{de}{dP_I}\right|_{WW} = \frac{w}{b}, \qquad (5)$$

an expression that is greater than one, approaching infinity (that is, a vertical line) when b goes to zero. The locus of points for which the relative price of the non-traded good is equal to one, shown as RR in figure 1, has the slope

$$\left.\frac{de}{dP_I}\right|_{RR} = 1.$$

This says that the relative price is constant when the exchange rate and the price index move in proportion. With an exogenous foreign-currency price of traded goods this means that purchasing power parity holds.'

An alternative way of writing the inequalities in expression (4) is:

$$\left.\frac{de}{dP_I}\right|_{RR} \leqslant \left.\frac{de}{dP_I}\right|_{XX} \leqslant \left.\frac{de}{dP_I}\right|_{WW}$$

This shows that the locus of points for which there is zero excess demand in the non-traded goods market is steeper than that for which the relative price is constant but flatter than that for which real wealth is constant.

The explanation for these limits on the slope of the non-traded goods market locus is quite simple. A rise in the exchange rate with an unchanged price index creates an excess demand for the non-traded good. It does this because it increases the real value of nominal wealth (that is, it moves the point under consideration northwest of the WW locus), and because it reduces the relative price of the non-traded good (that is, it moves it northwest of the RR locus). Therefore, from both the wealth and substitution points of view, a rise in the exchange rate creates an excess demand for the non-traded good. This excess demand can be eliminated by creating an equivalent excess supply by raising the price index while keeping the exchange rate constant. The rise in this price creates an excess supply through a reduction in real wealth (that is, a movement towards the area southeast of the WW locus) and in the relative price of the non-traded good (that is, a movement towards the area southeast of the RR locus). The rise in P_I must be sufficiently large so as to move the point under consideration past the WW locus, which from a wealth point of view creates an excess supply in the non-traded goods market due to the reduction in real wealth. However, the rise must not be so large as to increase the relative price of that good (that is, the movement can not be past the RR locus) because then the excess supply created from the relative price point of view would reinforce the excess supply due to the reduction in real wealth. Therefore, XX must lie between RR and WW so that starting from the initial equilibrium any reductions (increases) in the real value of wealth are just matched by reductions (increases) in the relative price of the non-traded good. When $B = W$ (so that domestic-currency-denominated assets sum to zero) all these loci coincide.

The derivative of the zero excess demand equation for the non-traded goods market with respect to the money supply with unchanged wealth is equal to zero. Therefore, with fixed exchange rates a change in the money supply through the balance of payments has no effect on the goods market equilibrium condition.

The slope of the asset-market-clearing condition, shown as LL in figure 1, is given by differentiating equation (2):[11]

$$\left.\frac{de}{dP_I}\right|_{LL} = -\frac{1 - l'w}{l'b}. \tag{6}$$

With the usual assumption that $(1 - l'w)$ is positive (see Patinkin 1965, p. 222) this derivative is negative. The explanation for this slope is that a rise in the exchange rate increases the domestic-currency value of foreign assets. This implies an excess demand for money, other things being equal. In order to satisfy this demand the real supply is increased by a reduction in the price index.

The derivative of the asset-market-clearing condition with respect to the money supply is given by:

$$\left.\frac{dP_I}{dM}\right|_{LL} = \frac{1}{1-l'w} \tag{7}$$

which is positive and greater than one. That is, an increase in the money supply shifts LL to the right by a greater proportion than that increase.

COMPARATIVE STATICS – A DISTURBANCE ARISING INTERNALLY

The curves in figure 1 are drawn in exchange rate, domestic-price index space and so are directly applicable to an analysis of flexible exchange rates. These are the two main endogenous variables under such an exchange rate regime. A comparative static experiment consists of a shift in either XX or LL or both loci so that at old prices some markets have non-zero excess demand. The new equilibrium under flexible rates is at the intersection of these two curves where all markets are clearing. The LL curve is drawn for a given value of the nominal money stock, which is appropriate for flexible exchange rates.

Consider an exogenous increase in demand for the non-traded good. This is shown in figure 2 as the movement of the zero-excess-demand locus for domestic goods into a region where previously there was excess supply. That is, this locus shifts from position XX to position X'X'. Under flexible exchange rates the equilibrium point moves from Q to V. Therefore, the domestic-currency price index rises and the price of foreign exchange falls. This implies that the relative price of the non-traded good rises.

The new position of equilibrium, V, depends upon the slopes of XX and LL. These slopes, in turn, are related to the proportion of foreign-currency-denominated assets in domestic portfolios. We showed above (equations (5) and (6)) that when there are no such assets in domestic portfolios the LL and WW curves are both vertical, and the XX curve is rather steep, with a slope distinctly larger than one. Under these circumstances, the increased demand causes a fall in the exchange rate and a rise in the relative price of the non-traded good which are quite substantial while the rise in the price index is very small. In the limit when b is equal to zero the price index does not change at all, vindicating Mundell's (1963) theorem on fiscal policy under flexible exchange rates.

As the proportion of foreign assets in domestic portfolios is increased XX becomes flatter, moving toward the unitary elastic position it attains when nominal wealth equals foreign-currency bond holdings. At the same time the LL curve becomes downward sloping with no definite limit (except the horizontal axis, of course, which it need never approach). This shows that the effects of the increase in demand for non-traded goods depend upon the proportion of foreign-currency-denominated assets in domestic portfolios. The larger is this proportion

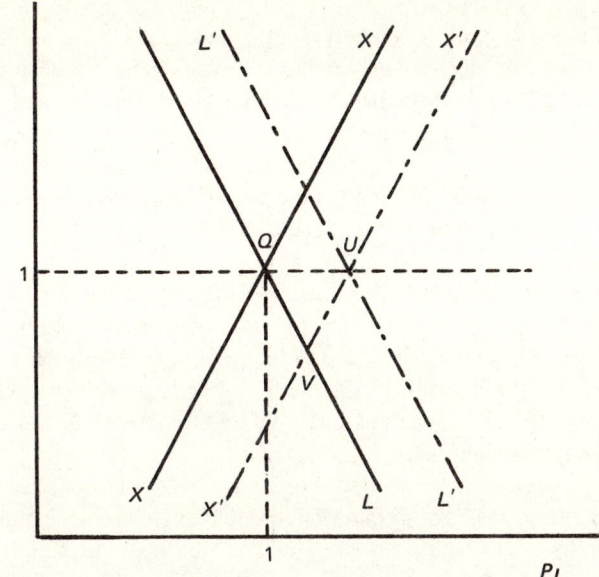

Figure 2

the smaller is the fall in the exchange rate and the rise in relative price of the non-traded good. However, the increase in the price index is larger the higher is this proportion for a given shock to the goods market. The way in which the comparative statics of flexible exchange rates depends upon foreign-bond holdings is a matter to which we return in the next section of the paper.

Under fixed exchange rates without sterilisation the diagrammatic technique is somewhat different. The impact effect of the increased demand is again a movement of the zero excess demand locus from its old position XX, to the new one, $X'X'$. The immediate tendency is for the exchange rate to fall. But the central bank is committed to a fixed exchange rate so it counters these forces with expansionary open market operations. Alternatively, through its foreign exchange operations it can act passively permitting the increased supply of money to come about from the foreign sector as domestic citizens rearrange their portfolios. The final equilibrium is the same so long as the central bank does not sterilise.

The final equilibrium is at U where the non-traded goods market clears and the exchange rate is unchanged. An increase in the money supply causes the asset locus to move so that at the new equilibrium exchange rate and price index the asset market clears. In other words, the increase in the money supply shifts the LL locus to the position $L'L'$, so it runs through point U. The proportion of foreign-currency assets has no influence on the fixed-exchange-rate equilibrium.

In this diagrammatic analysis the crucial point is that the increase in the money supply through an export of bonds, which shifts the LL locus upward to the right, takes place without any influence on the domestic goods market locus. This fact establishes the intersection between the impact *XX* locus and the horizontal line drawn through the old equilibrium as the new equilibrium for fixed exchange rates. In this particular conceptual experiment the rightward shift in *XX* causes a rise in the price level and the money supply under fixed rates.

This exogenous increase in demand for the non-traded good is a counter-example to the general contention that a fixed exchange rate regime is appropriate if disturbances arise within the economy.[12] The usual argument is that under fixed exchange rates the effects of this disturbance are spread to the rest of the world so that the price level does not change by so much as it would under flexible exchange rates. The analysis here shows that quite the opposite is true. It should be noted that this conjecture is in conflict with Mundell's theorem cited above. The error in the earlier analysis is the failure to consider the consequences of exchange rate changes on the asset markets.

Figure 2 shows that an increased demand for the non-traded good means a shift downward and to the right in the *XX* locus. Other things being equal, the exchange rate must fall or the price index rise to establish equilibrium in this market. The unshifted *LL* locus shows the division between exchange rate fall and price rise which maintains equilibrium in the asset markets under flexible exchange rates. Under fixed exchange rates the exchange rate is not permitted to fall so the price index must rise by more, and the money supply increases to keep the asset markets in balance.

On the other hand, a disturbance in the asset markets, through a shift in either asset supplies or demands, is completely offset under fixed exchange rates. The reason is that any disturbance in the asset markets shifts the *LL* locus. But equilibrium under fixed rates remains where the horizontal line at the exchange rate equals one intersects the *XX* curve. Therefore, any shift in the asset markets does not affect the price index or the exchange rate, but instead it changes the composition of portfolios. In contrast, under flexible exchange rates a shift in *LL* clearly does affect these price variables.

These comparative static exercises demonstrate that the choice of an exchange rate regime is not so simple as previous writers have led us to believe. We have argued here that the choice of the regime can be viewed in terms of the size of the change in the price index which arises when exogenous disturbances impinge on the economy. Even under these stylised conditions the conclusions are ambiguous. When disturbances arise internally, the appropriate exchange rate regime is : fixed rates if the disturbances are in the asset markets; and flexible rates if the disturbances are in the goods markets. Furthermore, the next section of the paper demonstrates that if the disturbances arise externally and are of a monetary nature (a rise in the foreign-currency price of the traded good) then a flexible exchange rate regime provides more insulation than does a fixed rate regime.

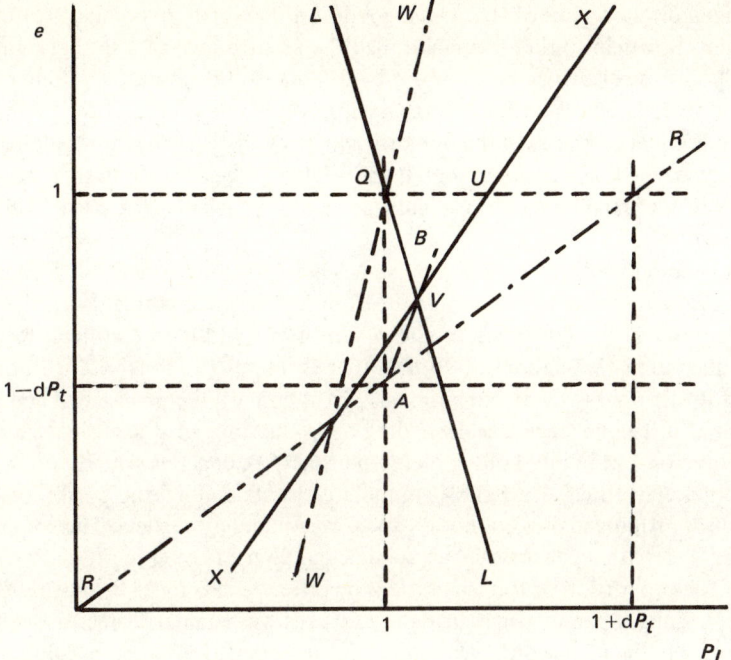

Figure 3

A RISE IN FOREIGN PRICES

The preceding sections of the paper give us the tools to analyse the consequences of a rise in foreign prices for this small economy under both fixed and flexible exchange rates. The diagram for this analysis is figure 3, in which the initial equilibrium is at point Q. At that point, before the price rise, there is a quadruple intersection (not shown) of the loci drawn in figure 1: the WW locus, along which the real value of wealth is constant; the RR locus, along which the relative price equals one; the LL locus, for which the demand for nominal balances equals unity; and the XX locus, for which excess demand for the non-traded good is zero.

A rise in foreign prices leaves WW and LL unshifted. The reason is that the equations represented by these two loci depend upon the price index and the exchange rate, and are independent of the other prices in the model. Therefore, if P_t rises but (P_d is adjusted downwards at the same time such that) the price index remains constant, then these two equations are not altered. In other words, at the old values of the exchange rate and the price index the same nominal quantity of money is required to clear the asset markets; in addition, the real value of wealth is unchanged.

An increase in foreign prices does shift the RR and XX loci. A rise in the foreign-currency price of the traded good of dP_t percent pivots the RR locus around the origin so that it runs through the point shown as A in that figure. At that point the exchange rate is lower by dP_t and so the domestic-currency price of the traded good is unchanged from its previous value there. If the price index remains equal to one then the domestic-currency price of the non-traded good is also unchanged, and so, therefore, is the relative price of the non-traded good in terms of the traded good. This argument demonstrates that RR passes through point A.

It is noted above that the XX curve lies between the RR and WW loci and runs through their intersection. The shift in RR, when combined with the stationarity of the WW locus, implies a shift in XX so that it continues to bear this diagrammatic relationship to the other two loci. The shift in XX is downward to the right (as with expansionary fiscal policy); the precise size and nature of the shift can be viewed as depending upon the slope of WW.

This slope, as pointed out earlier (equation (5)), depends entirely upon the proportion of foreign-currency-denominated assets in domestic portfolios. When this proportion equals zero the WW locus is completely vertical. This implies that under these circumstances XX passes through point A.

If the proportion of foreign assets is positive the WW locus is positively sloped. Thus, a parametric increase in b/w causes a parametric decrease in this slope while the locus continues to run through point Q. That is, rises in the proportion of foreign-currency-denominated assets in domestic portfolios can be viewed as causing a rotation of the WW locus around point Q in a clockwise direction but never past the position of unitary elasticity.

This rotation of the WW locus around point Q moves the intersection between WW and RR along the RR locus from point A towards the southwest, with the origin as the limit attained when the foreign-asset proportion equals one. The shift in XX with a rise in foreign prices is such as to maintain the triple intersection between RR, WW and itself, no matter what the value of this parameter. Therefore, XX's intersection with RR after the foreign inflation is closer to the origin the higher is the proportion of foreign assets.

In addition, any increase in this proportion causes the XX curve to become flatter as is shown by equation (3). Indeed, the southwesterly movement of the intersection between XX and RR, and the flattening of the XX locus are such that the position of XX at an unchanged exchange rate (point U) is unaffected by this proportion. Therefore, a rise in this proportion can be viewed as a clockwise rotation of the XX curve around point U. The reason that U does not depend upon the currency composition of the portfolio is that at that point the exchange rate is unchanged from previously so that no matter what this composition there are no capital gains or losses.

This is an appropriate juncture at which to summarise the impact positions of all these loci with a rise in P_t of dP_t percent. RR rotates clockwise around the origin by that percentage. XX shifts to the right and downward; in each direction the shift is less than dP_t percent. The horizontal shift is independent of the composition of portfolios, while the downward shift depends upon this composition, captured by the foreign-currency-asset proportion. When this proportion is zero XX shifts downward by the full amount of the price rise; when this proportion is greater than zero the shift is not so large. Finally, the WW and LL loci do not shift with this rise, although their slopes do depend upon the currency composition of the economy's portfolio. In particular, the higher is this foreign-currency-asset proportion, the flatter are both these curves: LL being negatively sloped, and WW positively sloped; both loci running through point Q.

Now that the impact shifts of these loci have been pinpointed it is a simple matter to establish the characteristics of the equilibria under both fixed and flexible exchange rates.

The comparison between the equilibria under fixed and flexible exchange rates is one between a single point and an infinity of points. For fixed exchange rates the new equilibrium is at point U no matter what the proportion of foreign-currency-denominated assets in domestic portfolios. For flexible exchange rates the new equilibrium does depend on this proportion, which is treated as a parameter in this analysis. The set of points of equilibrium for flexible rates is denoted by the locus AB. The specific point of equilibrium for a particular economy depends entirely on the foreign-currency-asset proportion. In other words, this locus is the set of points of intersection between XX and LL after the rise in foreign prices as the currency-composition proportion is varied parametrically between zero and one. The slope of this locus is greater than one (since it is steeper than RR); the general expression for the slope of this locus is given in the appendix. The point B is at the intersection of this locus with a unitary elastic line drawn from the origin to point U.

When the foreign-currency-asset proportion is zero the point of equilibrium for flexible exchange rates is point A. When this proportion is one the flexible exchange rate equilibrium is at point B. When this proportion is between zero and one the equilibrium lies in the interior of the AB locus, more than proportionally closer to B.

With these equilibria for fixed and flexible exchange rate regimes established, it is a simple matter to note their characteristics.

Under fixed exchange rates without sterilization the new equilibrium is at point U where the money supply increases (by less than the rise in foreign prices — see appendix) so as to run the LL locus through that point. At point U the price index is higher, but by less than the rise in foreign prices. That is, U is between the vertical lines drawn at $P_I = 1$ and $P_I = 1 + dP_t$. The fact that the price index does not rise as much as the increase in foreign prices implies that the non-traded good's price does not increase by so much. In other words the relative price of the non-traded good in terms of the traded good falls. It can be shown (see appendix) that this fall is within the limits

$$-1/\alpha < \left.\frac{dr}{dP_t}\right|_{\text{fix}} \leq 0.$$

Under flexible rates the exchange rate falls by an amount less than or equal to the rise in foreign prices, so as to establish a new equilibrium at point V. In other words V is between the horizontal lines drawn at $e = 1$ and $e = 1 - dP_t$. This fall is equal to the foreign price rise when the foreign-currency proportion equals zero. Under these circumstances flexible exchange rates provide complete insulation from foreign inflation because point V then coincides with point A. At that point the fall in the exchange rate obviates any change in the other price variables: the relative price of the non-traded good or the price index.

When the foreign-currency-asset proportion is greater than zero flexible exchange rates provide insulation which is less than perfect. However, the insulation is always present. This insulation can be outlined as follows. First, the fall in the exchange rate substitutes for the capital inflow which arises under fixed exchange rates. In addition, this fall causes the price index to be lower under flexible rates than it is under fixed rates. The higher is the foreign-currency-asset proportion the greater is the increase in the price index under flexible rates, but never so large as that which occurs under fixed rates. Finally, this movement in the exchange rate causes the relative price of the non-traded good to deteriorate by less under flexible rates than under fixed.

The specific results which come out of the matrix algebra in the appendix are these. The price index rises under both exchange rate regimes by less than the rise in foreign prices, with a smaller rise under flexible exchange rates:

$$\theta \leqslant \left.\frac{dP_I}{dP_t}\right|_{\text{flex}} < \left.\frac{dP_I}{dP_t}\right|_{\text{fix}} \leqslant 1.$$

The exchange rate falls under flexible exchange rates by an amount less than the rise in foreign prices:

$$-1 \leqslant \left.\frac{de}{dP_t}\right|_{\text{flex}} < 0.$$

The fall in the relative price of the non-traded good under fixed rates is less than $1/\alpha$ times the rise in foreign prices. The fall in this price under flexible rates conforms to the following inequalities:

$$-1/\alpha < \left.\frac{dr}{dP_t}\right|_{\text{fix}} \leqslant \left.\frac{dr}{dP_t}\right|_{\text{flex}} \leqslant \frac{b}{w} \left.\frac{dr}{dP_t}\right|_{\text{fix}} \leqslant 0. \tag{8}$$

This shows that the relative price under flexible rates deteriorates by less (in absolute terms) than its deterioration under fixed rates but greater than that amount times the foreign-asset proportion. When domestic-currency assets sum to zero all insulative power for flexible exchanges rates with respect to the relative price is lost.

CONCLUSIONS

This paper demonstrates that under very general circumstances flexible exchange rates do provide insulation for a small, open economy from foreign influences of a monetary nature. This insulation is perfect only when domestic citizens hold no foreign-currency-denominated assets.

The insulation is less than perfect when these holdings are greater than zero. In fact, when such assets predominate in domestic portfolios the insulatory power of flexible exchange rates for the relative price of the non-traded good is negligible. The price index is insulated from foreign developments no matter what proportion foreign-currency-assets make up of domestic portfolios.

APPENDIX

The model is a linearised system of excess demand functions so that a matrix **A** multiplies the endogenous variables vector, **N**, to yield the endogenously created excess demand function vector, **ED**. That is,

$$\mathbf{ED} = \mathbf{A}\mathbf{N}$$

where **ED** and **N** are vectors of differential changes. For equilibrium the endogenously created excess demand, **ED**, must equal the exogenously created excess supply, **ES**. Therefore, the vector equation for the system is

$$\mathbf{A}\mathbf{N} = \mathbf{ES}.$$

Solving for the endogenous variables yields

$$\mathbf{N} = \mathbf{A}^{-1}\mathbf{ES}$$

where $\mathbf{A}^{-1}$ is the inverse of the **A** matrix.

Independent excess demand functions are introduced for the goods market and the money market. In the case of fixed exchange rates the endogenous variables are the domestic-currency price index and the loss of money through the external sector. Under flexible rates the endogenous variables are the price index and the exchange rate. The endogenous variable vectors and excess demand coefficient matrices are:

$$\mathbf{N}_{\text{fix}} = \begin{pmatrix} dP_{I\text{ fix}} \\ -dM \end{pmatrix} \qquad \mathbf{A}_{\text{fix}} = \begin{pmatrix} \dfrac{D_1 - S'}{\alpha} - D_2 w & 0 \\ 1 - l'w & 1 \end{pmatrix}$$

$$\mathbf{N}_{\text{flex}} = \begin{pmatrix} dP_{I\text{ flex}} \\ de \end{pmatrix} \qquad \mathbf{A}_{\text{flex}} = \begin{pmatrix} \dfrac{D_1 - S'}{\alpha} - D_2 w & -\dfrac{D_1 - S'}{\alpha} + D_2 b \\ 1 - l'w & l'b \end{pmatrix}$$

The inverses of these matrices are

$$A_{fix}^{-1} = \Delta_{fix}^{-1} \begin{pmatrix} 1 & 0 \\ -(1-l'w) & \Delta_{fix} \end{pmatrix}$$

where

$$\Delta_{fix} = (D_1 - S')/\alpha - D_2 w < 0,$$

and

$$A_{flex}^{-1} = \Delta_{flex}^{-1} \begin{pmatrix} l'b & \dfrac{D_1 - S'}{\alpha} - D_2 b \\ -(1-l'w) & \Delta_{fix} \end{pmatrix}$$

where

$$\Delta_{flex} = (D_1 - S')[1 + l'(b-w)]/\alpha - D_2 b < 0.$$

The **ES** vector is equal to

$$\begin{pmatrix} \dfrac{D_1 - S'}{\alpha} \\ 0 \end{pmatrix} dP_t.$$

For the fixed rate case, multiplying A_{fix}^{-1} by **ES** yields

$$\begin{pmatrix} dP_{I\,fix} \\ -dM \end{pmatrix} = \Delta_{fix}^{-1} \begin{pmatrix} 1 & 0 \\ -(1-l'w) & \Delta_{fix} \end{pmatrix} \begin{pmatrix} (D_1 - S')/\alpha \\ 0 \end{pmatrix} dP_t$$

$$= \Delta_{fix}^{-1} \begin{pmatrix} \dfrac{D_1 - S'}{\alpha} \\ -\dfrac{D_1 - S'}{\alpha}(1-l'w) \end{pmatrix} dP_t$$

This shows that under fixed rates

$$0 < \left.\frac{dP_I}{dP_t}\right|_{fix} \leq 1$$

$$0 < \left.\frac{dM}{dP_t}\right|_{fix} \leq 1$$

so that the domestic-currency price index and the money supply both rise by less than the increase in foreign prices.

Under flexible exchange rates the changes in the endogenous variables are:

$$\begin{pmatrix} dP_{I\,flex} \\ de \end{pmatrix} = \Delta_{flex}^{-1} \begin{pmatrix} l'b & (D_1 - S')/\alpha - D_2 b \\ -(1-l'w) & \Delta_{fix} \end{pmatrix} \begin{pmatrix} (D_1 - S')/\alpha \\ 0 \end{pmatrix} dP_t$$

$$= \Delta_{flex}^{-1} \begin{pmatrix} bl'(D_1 - S')/\alpha \\ -(1-l'w)(D_1 - S')/\alpha \end{pmatrix} dP_t$$

Thus, under flexible exchange rates

$$0 \leqslant \left.\frac{dP_I}{dP_t}\right|_{\text{flex}} < 1$$

$$-1 \leqslant \left.\frac{de}{dP_t}\right|_{\text{flex}} < 0.$$

Subtracting the changes in the price indices from each other under the two exchange rate regimes, we find

$$\left.\frac{dP_I}{dP_t}\right|_{\text{fix}} - \left.\frac{dP_I}{dP_t}\right|_{\text{flex}} = \frac{(D_1 - S')}{\Delta_{\text{fix}} \Delta_{\text{flex}}} (D_1 - S' - D_2 b)(1 - l'w)$$

which is a positive expression. Therefore

$$\left.\frac{dP_I}{dP_t}\right|_{\text{flex}} < \left.\frac{dP_I}{dP_t}\right|_{\text{fix}}.$$

The change in the relative price of the non-traded good is given by:

$$\frac{dr}{dP_t} = \frac{dP_d}{dP_t} - \frac{de}{dP_t} - 1$$

under either exchange rate regime. We have solved for the change in the price index and need to find the relationship between this and changes in the domestic-currency price of the non-traded good, the foreign-currency price of the traded good, and the exchange rate. This is given, under either exchange rate regime, by

$$\frac{dP_I}{dP_t} = \alpha \frac{dP_d}{dP_t} + (1 - \alpha) \left(\frac{de}{dP_t} + 1\right).$$

Combining these equations we find that

$$\left.\frac{dr}{dP_t}\right|_{\text{fix}} = \frac{D_2 w}{D_1 - S' - D_2 w \alpha}$$

and

$$\left.\frac{dr}{dP_t}\right|_{\text{flex}} = \frac{D_2 b}{(D_1 - S')[1 + l'(b - w)] - D_2 b \alpha}$$

Algebraic manipulation of these expressions yields

$$-1/\alpha < \left.\frac{dr}{dP_t}\right|_{\text{fix}} \leqslant \left.\frac{dr}{dP_t}\right|_{\text{flex}} \leqslant \frac{b}{w} \left.\frac{dr}{dP_t}\right|_{\text{fix}} \leqslant 0,$$

which is equation (8) in the text.

The slope of the *AB* locus in figure 3 is given by

$$\left.\frac{de}{dP_I}\right|_{AB} = \frac{\left.\frac{de}{dP_t}\right|_{\text{flex}} + 1}{\left.\frac{dP_I}{dP_t}\right|_{\text{flex}}} = \frac{\frac{-(1-l'w)(D_1-S')/\alpha}{(D_1-S')[1+l'(b-w)]/\alpha - D_2 b} + 1}{\frac{bl'(D_1-S')/\alpha}{(D_1-S')[1+l'(b-w)]/\alpha - D_2 b}}$$

$$= -\frac{D_2 \alpha}{l'(D_1-S')},$$

which is greater than one.

DISCUSSION : DAVID LAIDLER

I have three comments to make on Boyer's paper, one rather specific and the other two more general. In judging them, it should be remembered that they come, not from a specialist in international economics, but from a monetary economist. To some extent then, they may represent a difference in perspective between Boyer and myself, rather than any more fundamental disagreement.

First, I am a little puzzled as to how to interpret the exercise in which we follow through the effects of a change in the demand for the non-traded good. Boyer suggests that we treat this change in demand as arising from an expansionary fiscal policy, but I wonder if it is quite that easy. What kind of government expenditure is it that can be directed solely to non-traded goods, and how do we ensure that ensuing multiplier effects do not spill over into the market for tradables? Moreover, if we are dealing with an increase in aggregate demand originating in the government sector, how is that increase to be financed? Surely we ought to look carefully at the way in which the government budget constraint it satisfied in a model such as the one Boyer analyses. Its main purpose, after all, is to enable us analyse the interaction between (flow) goods markets and (stock) financial markets, and government finance provides an important linkage between the two. If we are interested only in impact effects we can perhaps ignore this issue, but if the increase in demand under analysis is a permanent one then I do not see how its implications for financial markets can safely be neglected.

Second, I think that Boyer stops too soon in his analysis of the consequences of a change in the price of the tradable good. He analyses the transmission of a once-and-for-all change in a price into an open economy, not the transmission of inflation, and it is far from clear to me how relevant the answers generated in the one exercise are to the other. The reasons for this are as follows. In a model such as this, in which one is dealing with equilibrium relationships, one would have to treat inflation as fully anticipated, as indeed Boyer implicitly does here, albeit at a zero rate. Inflation expectations affect the level of nominal interest rates; they also get built into the behaviour of exchange rates under a flexible system; and so on. Thus one might expect a change in a fully anticipated inflation rate to have far more pervasive effects on a model such as the one that Boyer analyses than a once-and-for-all change in the price level that leaves the expected inflation rate equal to zero. This is not to criticise Boyer for a sin of commission. However, there is a rather serious sin of ommission in this paper of which I hope its author will repent in future work.

Third, and finally, I wonder whether a framework of the type that Boyer here uses is as well adapted as it might be to dealing with questions about the relative merits of fixed and flexible exchange rates. It is widely agreed that, in a world of complete price flexibility, fixed exchange rates are to be preferred since the system yields advantages similar to those yielded to an individual country by having a single currency. When we have less than complete price flexibility, however, these advantages can only be fully exploited in a situation of long-run equilibrium. A flexible exchange rate, it is frequently argued, is an institutional device that enables an economy to enjoy more short-run price flexibility than a fixed rate would permit. To the extent that those shocks which cannot be absorbed in price changes instead result in fluctuations in income and employment, exchange rate flexibility comes to look more desirable when short-run price rigidities are allowed for. It is not my purpose here to pronounce any judgement on the relative merits of fixed and flexible exchange rates. However, it does seem to me that a major element in the choice between them is the trade off between the undoubted long-run advantages that a fixed rate regime yields and the short-run advantages that are supposed to arise from flexible rates. Thus I do not see how the regimes can be compared fairly except in a model that permits short-run fluctuations to be analysed. Boyer's model, dealing as it does with comparative static equilibria does not do so. Nor would its extension to deal with comparative dynamic equilibra meet this problem. An explicit analysis of disequilibrium behaviour would be called for to deal fully with these issues.

NOTES

1 Financial assistance from the Social Science Research Council while the author was a Research Fellow with the International Monetary Research Programme is gratefully acknowledged. He would like to thank A.R. Nobay, H.G. Johnson, R. Jackman, A. Swoboda, M. Knight, P. Jonson, and B. Hindley for comments on an earlier version of this paper. J. Nixon and J. Sheen were kind enough to proofread a number of drafts of the typescript.
2 See the discussion of this point in Nobay (1975). The long quotation from Cassel (1922) in his paper is an explicit statement of this assertion. There has been some work recently on the channels through which inflationary pressures from abroad impinge on a small economy. See Turnovsky and Kaspura (1974) and Shinkai (1973). Swoboda (1974) provides an excellent summary of the prevailing theories of the transmission mechanism.
3 The purchasing power parity theorem has had a long history but the recent empirical work is most pertinent to our point. See Balassa (1964) and Yeager (1966).

4   There has been a great deal of work with models including non-traded goods. See Dornbusch (1973), Berglas and Razin (1973), and Boyer (1975).
5   Therefore Cassel's contention is correct only when domestic citizens do not hold foreign assets or when foreign assets are denominated in foreign goods. See note 9 below.
6   For a full discussion of the fixed exchange rate case without sterilisation see Boyer (1975).
7   The asset market condition takes the expected values of relevant returns to be exogenous. This is justified by our assumption that foreign inflation consists in an unanticipated and expected-never-to-be-repeated, once-for-all increase in the foreign-exchange price of the traded good.
8   The assumption that real income is constant, independent of the exchange rate, is a drastic departure from the usual analysis of flexible exchange rate systems. See Laursen and Metzler (1950) and Johnson's (1958) comments on their results.
9   We assume throughout that B and $M - B_d$ are both greater than or equal to zero. That is, that the small country is a creditor in both foreign-currency and domestic-currency assets. This seems like a reasonable assumption in a world in which domestic central banks are indebted to the private sector in domestic currency while holding claims, denominated in foreign currency, on the reserve centers. R. Jackman has observed in private correspondence that if foreign bonds are denominated in traded goods (as foreign equities might be) so that $B = Pt\bar{B}$, then a rise in the price of foreign goods is precisely the same as a devaluation. Under these circumstances flexible exchange rates provide full insulation no matter what the foreign-asset proportion.
10 In taking this derivative the exchange rate is varied while the price index is held constant and the price index is varied while the exchange rate is held constant. For both cases the domestic-currency price of the non-traded good must move appropriately.
11 A. Swoboda has pointed out at a seminar the similarities between this diagram and that used by Mundell (1971). The reader should remember that the LL curve here is a portfolio schedule, whereas in Mundell the curve so denoted is the locus along which income equals expenditure. The XX curves in our analyses are equivalent; the other two curves in Mundell's diagram are subsidiary loci left out of figure 1 for tidiness.
12 A. Laffer (1973) has suggested that this an appropriate rule for choosing an exchange rate regime. See Johnson's (1975, pp. 9–10) discussion of this rule.

REFERENCES

Balassa, B. (1964). The purchasing power parity doctrine: a reappraisal. *Journal of Political Economy* 72, 584–96. Reprinted in R. Cooper (ed.), *International Finance*, chapter 8. Harmondsworth: Penguin Books, 1969.

Berglas, E. and A. Razin (1973). Real exchange rate and devaluation. *Journal of International Economics*. 3, 179–91.

Boyer, R. (1975). Commodity markets and bond markets in a small, fixed-exchange-rate economy. *Canadian Journal of Economics* 8, 1–23.

Cassel, G. (1922). *Money and Foreign Exchange after 1914* London: Macmillan.

Dornbusch, R. (1973), Devaluation, money and nontraded goods. *American Economic Review* 63, 871–80.

Johnson, H. (1958). The transfer problem and exchange stability. In his *International Trade and Economic Growth*. Chapter 7. London: Allen and Unwin. Originally published in *Journal of Political Economy* **64**, 212–25 in a slightly shorter form. Reprinted in R. Cooper (ed.), *International Finance*, chapter 3. Harmondsworth: Penguin Books, 1969.

Johnson, H. (1975). The monetary approach to the balance of payments. *International Monetary Research Programme Discussion Paper.* London School of Economics

Laffer, A. (1973). Two arguments for fixed rates. In H. Johnson and A. Swoboda (eds.), *The Economics of Common Currencies*, chapter 1. London: Allen and Unwin.

Laursen, S. and L. Metzler (1950). Flexible exchange rates and the theory of employment. *Review of Economics and Statistics* **32**, 218–99.

Mundell, R. (1963). Capital mobility and stabilization policy under fixed and flexible exchange rates. *Canadian Journal of Economics and Political Science* **29**, 475–85. Reprinted in adapted form in his *International Economics,* chapter 18. New York: Macmillan, 1968.

Mundell, R. (1971). Devaluation. In his *Monetary Theory: Interest, Inflation and Growth in a World Economy*. chapter 9. Pacific Palisades, California: Goodyear Publishing.

Nobay, A. (1975). International aspects of the economics of inflation. In J.M. Parkin and G. Zis (eds.), *Inflation in the World Economy* (forthcoming).

Patinkin, D. (1965). *Money, Interest and Prices*. New York: Harper and Row.

Shinkai, Y. (1973). A model of imported inflation. *Journal of Political Economy* **81**, 962–71.

Swoboda, A. (1974). Monetary approaches to the transmission and generation of worldwide inflation. Paper presented to the Brookings Conference on Worldwide Inflation, 21–3 November 1974.

Turnovsky, S. and A. Kaspura (1974). An analysis of imported inflation in a short-run macroeconomic model. *Canadian Journal of Economics* **7**, 355–80.

Yeager, L. (1966). Exchange rates and price levels. In his *International Monetary Relations,* chapter 10. New York: Harper and Row.

10 EFFECTIVE RATES OF PROTECTION FOR UNITED KINGDOM MANUFACTURING IN 1963 AND 1968

P.D. KITCHIN[1]

INTRODUCTION

This paper investigates changes in the effective protection of UK manufacturing industry arising from tariffs and excise taxes and subsidies. Estimates of the effective protection arising from tariffs and excise taxes/subsidies are made for the UK for 1963 and 1968 using the theory of effective protection developed since the mid-1960s by Corden, Grubel, Johnson and others.[2] Other forms of protection such as quotas and exchange rate changes are not considered in this paper. The estimates made are based on data taken from the *UK Input–Output Tables 1963 and 1968*.

The results confirm the findings of previous papers[3] that there is a high but incomplete correlation between tariff rates (and excise tax/subsidy rates) and the resulting effective protection.[4] This finding, in conjunction with the finding of Guisinger and Schydlowsky (1971) that the correlation falls as the degree of aggregation is reduced, points to the importance of not relying on nominal tariff and excise tax/subsidy rates in considering trade and development policy.[5]

The investigation of the changes between 1963 and 1968 shows that there were marked changes in effective protection. These resulted mainly from changes in tariff rates and excise tax/subsidy rates and not from changes in the structure of inputs into UK industries. There was, however, no overall pattern of falling protection or of rising protection. The changes showed both rises and falls in protection resulting from rises and falls in nominal tariff and excise tax/subsidy rates. *A priori* reasoning, however, suggests that nominal tariff rates would predominantly have fallen, as a result of the first stage of the Kennedy Round cuts in July 1968. The absence of such a pattern throws doubt on the method of estimating nominal tariff rates used in this and earlier papers.

The results are reported for the forty-seven commodity groups which constitute manufacturing output, excluding those industries predominantly producing services, for example, 'textile finishing'. As published, the *UK Input–Output Tables 1963 and 1968* show the economy aggregated into seventy sectors (1963) and ninety sectors (1968). In order that the maximum number of direct comparisons could be made between the years the published data were further aggregated into sixty-nine commodity groups for each year.

The *Input–Output Tables* are published in such a form that the effective rates of protection estimated are not for industries but for commodity groups.

In the next section of the paper the estimating equation and attendant assumptions are set out. There follows a discussion of how the estimates were made for the paper and an exposition of and a commentary on the results. The paper concludes with a discussion of some of the limitations implicit in the estimating method employed, and a summary of the results appears in conclusion.

EFFECTIVE PROTECTION

The estimating equation used in this paper embodies the following assumptions: domestic and imported inputs are perfect substitutes for one another; all inputs are importable; the supply of imports is perfectly elastic; there is no tariff redundancy (i.e. all domestic prices are dependent on the level of tariffs); the input coefficients for a product are fixed in physical terms;[6] the analysis is partial equilibrium and does not take into consideration the working out of production and consumption changes resulting from the imposition of nominal tariffs on inputs and final products.

Notation

g_j = the overall level of effective protection of commodity j;
p_j = value of output of commodity j in the absence of tariffs;
a_{ij} = the free trade input coefficient, the fraction of the output of j formed by the input i;
t_j = the overall nominal tariff rate chargeable on total imports of commodity j;
t_i = the nominal tariff rate chargeable on imports of commodity i for use as an intermediate product;
X_j = the overall rate of excise tax/subsidy chargeable on the value of product j in a tariff-ridden economy;
D_j = the total of excise taxes *minus* subsidies;
V_j = the value added in industry j in the absence of tariffs and excise taxes/subsidies;
V_j^1 = the value added in industry j in the presence of tariffs and excise taxes/subsidies.

The overall effective protection arising from tariffs and net excise taxes/subsidies is,[7]

$$g_j = \frac{V_j^1 - V_j}{V_j}. \qquad (1)$$

That is,

$$g_j = \left(\frac{t_j - \sum_i a_{ij} t_i}{1 - \sum_i a_{ij}}\right) - \left(\frac{X_j(1 + t_j)}{1 - \sum_i a_{ij}}\right) \qquad (2)$$

where

$$X_j = \frac{D_j}{p_j(1 + t_j)} \qquad (3)$$

In equation (2) the effective *tariff* protection (g_j^1) is the first bracketed term and the effective *excise tax/subsidy* protection (g_j^2) is the second bracketed term. Thus $g_j = g_j^1 + g_j^2$.

ESTIMATION

As in almost all estimation, the formal exactness of the theory has to suffer in order that the available data may be used. This section briefly indicates the source and/or method of estimation of each of the variables required in equation (2).[8]

(1) The input coefficients (a_{ij}) were based on tables I, K and M in the *UK Input–Output Tables* (*1963 and 1968*). The published coefficients were adjusted for an element of double counting and then deflated to their free trade values. Both adjustments are as in Barker and Han (1971). In order to maximise the number of one-to-one commodity comparisons between 1963 and 1968 the deflated coefficients were aggregated for both years to sixty-nine commodity groups each with sixty-nine potential inputs.

(2) The nominal tariffs on final goods (t_j) were estimated by dividing tariff revenues (provided by the CSO) by the value of imports (taken from table B, *I–O Tables 1963, 1968*). Separate estimates were made if rounding errors in the data were significant. The tariff rates were aggregated to sixty-nine using free trade production totals as weights (derived from table B, *I–O Tables 1963, 1968*). Estimation using *totals* of tariff revenues and imports implies the averaging of individual tariff rates using imports as weights.[9,10]

(3) The nominal tariffs of intermediate inputs (t_i) were estimated by dividing tariff revenues on intermediate imports by totals of imports of intermediates. The data sources were as for t_j above. When aggregating to sixty-nine values the weights were the free trade input coefficients. As these differ for each commodity group (e.g. $a_{11} \neq a_{12}$, except by chance) a square matrix (69 × 69) of tariff rates was derived.

(4) The composite net excise tax rate (X_j) was estimated by dividing net excise taxes for j (derived from tables B and C, *I–O Tables 1963, 1968*) by the production of j (table B, *I–O Tables 1963, 1968*). Aggregation used production totals as weights.[11]

Seven estimates were made using equation (2):
(a) The full seventy (ninety) sector model for 1963 (1968).[12]
(b) The 1963 (1968) data aggregated to sixty-nine commodity groups.

Table 1 *Nominal and effective protection rates, 1963 and 1968*

All figures are percentages

	Overall nominal tariffs (t_j)		Effective tariff protection (g_j^t)					Excise tax/ subsidy rate (X_j)		Excise tax/subsidy protection (g_j^x)				Overall protection ($g_j = g_j^t + g_j^x$)			
	1963	1968	a_{ij}^{1963} t_j^{1963} 1963	a_{ij}^{1968} t_j^{1968} 1968	a_{ij}^{1963} t_j^{1968} 1963	a_{ij}^{1963} t_j^{1968} 1963	a_{ij}^{1968} t_j^{1963} 1963			a_{ij}^{1963} X_j^{1963} 1963	a_{ij}^{1968} X_j^{1968} 1968	a_{ij}^{1963} X_j^{1968}	a_{ij}^{1968} X_j^{1963}	a_{ij}^{1963} X_j^{1963} t_j^{1963} 1963	a_{ij}^{1968} X_j^{1968} t_j^{1968} 1968	a_{ij}^{1963} X_j^{1963} t_j^{1968}	a_{ij}^{1968} X_j^{1963} t_j^{1963}
	(1)	(2)	(3)	(4)	(5)	(6)	(7)	(8)	(9)	(10)	(11)	(12)	(13)	(14)	(15)	(16)	(17)
Mineral oil refining	0.2	0.1	−2.9	−2.8	−2.8	−3.9	−2.4	−0.7	−2.0	−7.2	−14.6	−20.4	−5.1	−10.1	−17.4	−23.2	−7.5
Paint and printing ink	12.1*	11.0*	30.5	23.5	26.9	26.9	26.4	−1.5	−2.2	−5.5	−6.9	−8.0	−4.7	25.0	16.6	19.0	21.7
Coke ovens	0.0	0.0	−2.7	−1.3	−2.4	−2.7	−2.4	−0.9	−1.1	−6.8	−6.4	−8.3	−5.3	−9.5	−7.7	−10.7	−7.7
Pharmaceutical and toilet preps.	2.4	5.0	0.1	7.8	7.3	6.7	0.1	−1.4	−1.3	−3.6	−3.5	−3.5	−3.7	−3.6	4.4	3.8	−3.6
Soap, oils and fats	2.2	2.6	1.8	3.4	4.3	4.1	−0.6	−1.0	−1.6	−5.7	−8.9	−9.2	−5.5	−3.9	−5.5	−4.9	−6.1
Synthetic resin and plastic materials	8.0	3.3	15.7	2.6	2.2	1.6	14.9	−0.7	−0.6	−2.3	−1.7	−18.5	−2.1	13.4	0.8	0.3	12.8
Other chemicals and allied industries	5.0	8.7	8.3	20.9	17.7	17.7	9.1	−1.4	−2.1	−3.7	−7.3	−5.8	−4.7	4.6	13.7	12.0	4.4
Iron and steel	6.0	9.4	10.0	21.4	17.4	20.4	11.7	−1.4	−1.1	−4.5	−4.2	−3.7	−5.2	5.5	17.2	13.8	6.5
Light metals	1.5	1.4	0.8	0.8	0.8	0.6	0.3	−1.1	−1.0	−3.1	−3.5	−2.8	−3.9	−2.2	−2.7	−1.9	−3.6
Other non-ferous metals	0.2	0.3	−4.1	−2.7	−3.6	−3.7	−3.7	−0.7	−0.6	−3.2	−2.4	−2.8	−2.8	−7.4	−5.2	−6.4	−6.6
Agricultural machinery	7.8	9.7	11.2	16.7	17.3	16.2	11.6	−1.0	−1.3	−2.8	−3.8	−3.7	−2.9	8.4	12.9	13.6	8.7
Machine tools	8.4	10.1	10.6	13.9	13.0	13.8	11.5	−1.1	−1.1	−2.2	−2.5	−2.3	−2.5	8.4	11.4	10.7	9.0
Engineers' small tools	12.9	14.0*	19.6	20.7	21.8	21.6	18.6	−1.2	−1.2	−2.5	−2.4	−2.5	−2.4	17.2	18.3	19.4	16.2
Industrial engines	2.3	5.1	−2.4	3.2	3.6	3.9	−3.0	−0.9	−0.7	−2.1	−1.8	−1.7	−2.2	−4.5	1.4	2.0	−5.3
Textile machinery	5.9	19.9	7.3	39.4	37.8	38.3	6.5	−0.8	−0.8	−1.9	−2.3	−2.1	−2.0	5.5	37.2	35.7	4.4
Contractors' plant and mechanical handling eqpmt.	6.3	12.5	6.8	21.7	21.6	21.4	7.8	−0.9	−0.8	−2.3	−2.2	−2.1	−2.3	4.5	19.5	19.5	5.5
Office machinery	11.6	6.5	18.8	8.7	7.8	8.4	16.0	−1.0	+0.2	−2.3	+0.4	+0.4	−2.3	16.5	9.2	8.3	13.7
Other non-electrical machinery	8.9	5.9	13.1	6.2	6.8	6.7	13.7	−1.1	−0.8	−2.6	−1.8	−1.8	−2.6	10.6	4.4	5.0	11.1
Other mechanical engineering	8.3	3.2	11.2	1.4	1.7	1.4	11.7	−1.1	−0.7	−2.3	−1.4	−1.4	−2.3	8.9	0.1	0.4	9.5
Scientific instruments etc.	15.1	11.2	22.6	14.7	16.0	15.0	21.2	−1.4	−1.2	−3.2	−2.7	−2.6	−3.3	19.5	12.0	13.4	17.9
Electrical machinery	9.5	20.9	13.6	40.3	36.6	37.6	14.3	−1.3	−0.6	−3.0	−1.7	−1.5	−3.4	10.6	38.5	35.0	11.0
Insulated wires & cables	10.0	16.7	36.8	132.0	67.2	68.5	72.2	−1.0	−1.1	−5.2	−12.2	−6.1	−10.5	31.6	119.9	61.1	61.7
Radio & telecommunications	12.6	12.9	18.5	19.9	20.6	19.1	17.7	−1.0	−0.5	−2.4	−1.3	−1.2	−2.6	16.1	18.6	19.3	15.0
Other electrical goods	10.8	13.6	18.5	26.4	27.1	25.6	18.4	−0.9	−1.3	−2.5	−3.9	−3.7	−2.6	16.0	22.5	23.4	15.8
Cans and metal boxes	3.7*	11.0	−0.1	27.7	23.4	26.9	−1.3	−0.9	−0.8	−3.5	−4.0	−3.3	−4.2	−3.6	23.7	20.2	−5.5
Other metal goods	8.4	5.9*	15.2	9.4	9.1	8.7	15.6	−1.2	−1.2	−3.4	−3.6	−3.3	−3.7	11.8	5.9	5.8	11.9
Shipbuilding and marine engineering	7.5	0.0	7.9	−3.9	−5.9	−9.2	7.1	−1.0	+1.1	−2.5	+2.1	+2.5	−2.0	5.5	−1.9	−3.4	5.1
Motor vehicles	20.1	15.3	55.1	29.4	34.3	35.4	47.8	−0.8	−1.1	−3.9	−4.6	−5.2	−3.5	51.2	24.8	29.1	44.2
Aircraft	2.2	0.7	0.0	−2.6	−2.5	−2.9	−1.0	−1.1	−0.3	−2.2	−0.7	−0.6	−2.5	−2.2	−3.3	−3.1	−3.5
Other vehicles	21.8	6.4	47.0	6.7	7.2	7.3	41.7	−0.8	−0.3	−2.5	−0.7	−0.8	−2.2	44.5	6.0	6.3	39.5

Table 1 (*continued*)

All figures are percentages

	Overall nominal tariffs (t_j)		Effective tariff protection (g_j^1)					Excise tax/ subsidy rate (X_j)		Excise tax/subsidy protection (g_j^2)				Overall protection ($g_j = g_j^1 + g_j^2$)			
	1963	1968	a_{ij}^{1963} t_i^{1963} 1963	a_{ij}^{1968} t_i^{1968} 1968	a_{ij}^{1963} t_i^{1968}	a_{ij}^{1963} t_i^{1968} t_i^{1963}	a_{ij}^{1968} t_i^{1963} t_i^{1963}			a_{ij}^{1963} t_j^{1963} X_j^{1963} 1963	a_{ij}^{1968} t_j^{1968} X_j^{1968} 1968	a_{ij}^{1963} t_j^{1968} X_j^{1968}	a_{ij}^{1968} X_j^{1963} t_j^{1963}	a_{ij}^{1963} X_j^{1963} t_j^{1963} 1963	a_{ij}^{1968} t_j^{1968} X_j^{1968} t_j^{1968} 1968	a_{ij}^{1963} X_j^{1963} t_j^{1968} t_j^{1968}	a_{ij}^{1968} X_j^{1963} t_j^{1963} t_j^{1963}
	(1)	(2)	(3)	(4)	(5)	(6)	(7)	(8)	(9)	(10)	(11)	(12)	(13)	(14)	(15)	(16)	(17)
Production of man-made fibres	12.7	6.8	22.1	12.1	10.4	9.2	25.7	−1.0	−0.6	−2.5	−1.6	−1.4	−2.9	19.6	10.4	9.0	22.8
Cotton, etc., spinning and weaving	6.1	5.4	5.3	5.9	6.7	2.9	3.4	−0.7	−0.4	−2.6	−1.5	−1.5	−2.6	2.7	4.4	5.2	0.8
Wool	2.7	4.6	6.1	8.9	10.9	15.9	3.5	−0.6	−0.7	−3.2	−2.8	−3.8	−2.4	2.8	6.1	7.1	1.1
Hosiery, lace and other textiles	7.3	7.2	17.9	12.8	14.3	12.9	16.4	−0.9	−0.7	−3.1	−2.2	−2.4	−2.9	14.8	10.6	12.0	13.4
Leather, leather goods & fur	4.9	4.0	13.0	7.6	8.3	9.2	10.4	−1.0	−1.4	−4.4	−5.0	−6.1	−3.6	8.6	2.6	2.2	6.8
Clothing	6.7	4.5	10.2	3.8	4.2	4.2	9.3	−1.5	−1.1	−4.4	−3.1	−3.1	−4.2	5.8	0.8	1.0	5.0
Footwear	6.7	5.9	8.8	7.9	8.3	6.7	6.8	−0.9	−1.8	−2.5	−4.3	−5.0	−2.2	6.3	3.6	3.3	4.6
Cement	1.4*	5.6	0.7	13.1	10.1	10.1	0.7	−4.4	−3.7	−10.0	−11.9	−8.8	−13.6	−9.3	1.3	1.3	−12.8
Other building materials etc.	7.5	5.1	14.1	9.0	7.3	8.7	16.8	−2.6	−3.2	−6.4	−9.2	−7.7	−7.6	7.8	−0.2	−0.4	9.1
Pottery and glass	13.6	12.2	21.9	20.6	19.4	19.2	23.1	−2.1	−2.2	−4.6	−5.2	−4.7	−5.0	17.3	15.4	14.6	18.1
Furniture, etc.	9.5	12.5	17.1	28.7	24.9	24.5	18.9	−2.0	−3.0	−5.5	−9.9	−8.4	−6.4	11.6	18.8	16.5	12.4
Timber and miscellaneous wood manufactures	2.1	1.5	1.4	0.5	0.6	−0.3	1.1	−1.8	−1.8	−4.9	−5.6	−4.9	−5.6	−3.5	−5.0	−4.3	−4.5
Paper and board	2.6	1.1	2.4	−0.1	−0.7	−2.5	2.5	−1.3	−1.4	−4.4	−4.2	−4.7	−4.0	−2.0	−4.4	−5.4	−1.5
Paper products	9.9	12.9	23.7	36.5	34.8	32.9	24.8	−1.3	−1.3	−4.4	−4.7	−4.5	−4.6	19.3	31.7	30.3	20.2
Printing and publishing	2.3	2.4	1.8	2.7	2.9	2.0	2.1	−1.3	−1.2	−2.6	−2.3	−2.4	−2.4	−0.8	0.4	0.5	−0.3
Rubber	7.9	5.8	14.8	8.7	9.5	9.1	11.9	−1.1	−1.1	−3.3	−2.6	−3.2	−2.7	11.6	6.1	6.3	9.2
Other manufacturing	10.2	6.7	17.8	10.8	11.4	8.9	16.3	−1.4	−1.4	−3.9	−3.6	−3.8	−3.7	13.9	7.3	7.6	12.6
Arithmetic mean	7.4	7.4	12.5	14.8	13.1	12.9	12.7	−1.2	−1.2	−3.7	−4.1	−3.9	−3.9	8.8	10.8	9.2	8.8

Note to columns 8–13: A minus sign indicates that, net, the tax/subsidy is a tax. A plus sign indicates a net subsidy
* Estimated

(c) The 1963 (1968) input coefficients combined with the 1968 (1963) tariffs and taxes.[13]

(d) The 1963 input coefficients and input tariffs and taxes (t_i and X_i) combined with the 1968 tariffs on final goods (t_j).

RESULTS

The results of the estimation are set out in Table 1. We will first briefly consider 1963 and then 1968, and then go on to a consideration of the changes between 1963 and 1968. The results presented are only for the forty-seven manufacturing commodity groups where the majority of potential imports are visible imports. Thus we exclude service industries such as 'textile finishing' and 'industrial plant and steel work'.

1963 and 1968

Two features stand out. Firstly, effective tariff protection (columns 3 and 4, table 1) and effective excise tax/subsidy protection (columns 10 and 11, table 1) are typically higher than their corresponding nominal tariff and excise tax/subsidy rates (columns 1, 2 and 8, 9, table 1) by a factor which averages 1.69 (1963) and 2.00 (1968) for tariffs and 3.08 (1963) and 3.42 (1968) for excise taxes. Secondly the results confirm the finding of previous papers, e.g. Grubel and Johnson (1967) that the rankings of nominal tariff rates and effective tariff rates are very similar.[14] Data illustrating both these features are set out in Table 2. Details of the range and arithmetic mean of the estimated rates of protection are summarised in Table 3.

Table 2 *Correlations*

	1963	1968
Rank correlation: nominal tariffs/ effective tariff protection	0.943	0.946
Rank correlation: nominal tariffs/ overall effective protection	0.952	0.965
Product moment correlation: nominal tariffs/ effective tariff protection	0.926	0.725

There are, however, enough important exceptions to the generalisations made above that a reliance on nominal tariff rates in any consideration of tariff levels and structure could result in unlooked-for results.[15] Notable exceptions are in 1963, for example, 'paper and board' with a nominal tariff of 2.6% and effective tariff protection of 2.1%, and 'industrial engines', with a nominal tariff of 2.3% and effective tariff protection of − 2.4%. In 1968 the nominal tariff on 'insulated cables and wires' was 16.7% and the effective protection was 132.0%. In both 1963 and 1968 the major factor in the overall level of protection was tariff protection and not excise tax/subsidy protection.

Table 3 Range and averages

Percentages	Effective tariff protection, g_j^1	Effective excise tax/subsidy protection, g_j^2	Overall effective protection $g_i = g_j^1 + g_j^2$
1963 Upper limit	55.1 (motor vehicles)	−1.9 (textile machinery)	51.2 (motor vehicles)
Lower limit	−4.1 (other non-ferrous metals)	−10.0 (cement)	−10.1 (mineral oil refining)
Arith. mean	12.5	−3.7	8.8
1968 Upper limit	132.0 (insulated wire and cable)	2.1 (shipbuilding and marine engineering)	119.9 (insulated wire and cable)
Lower limit	−3.9 (shipbuilding and marine engineering)	−14.6 (mineral oil refining)	−17.4 (mineral oil refining)
Arith. mean	14.8	−4.1	10.8

The changes between 1963 and 1968

The results reported in the previous section seem to confirm the results reported in earlier papers. However, when we compare the years 1963 and 1968 for the UK we have new results. The change in effective tariff protection between the years (table 1, columns 3 and 4) shows no clear pattern; for twenty-four of the forty-seven commodity groups reported the effective tariff protection rose, for twenty-two it fell and in one case it was unchanged.[16] A similar lack of a general change in rates of effective excise tax/subsidy protection (table 1, columns 10 and 11) is also clear with twenty-one rates rising, and twenty-six falling.

When we consider changes in overall effective protection $(g_j = g_j^1 + g_j^2)$ there is again no overall pattern. Out of forty-seven commodity groups there are twenty where the effective tariff protection (g_j^1) changes in the same direction as the effective excise tax/subsidy protection (g_j^2) and twenty-six where g_j^1 and g_j^2 move in opposite directions. Overall protection rose in twenty-two cases and fell in twenty-five.

These changes in effective protection can be viewed in terms of three causative factors, namely, changes in the structure of inputs (a_{ij}) into a commodity group, changes in the rates of nominal tariffs and excise taxes and subsidies $(t_j, t_i$ and $X_j)$, and changes in the proportion of output formed by value added (i.e. changes in $\sum_i a_{ij}$).[17]

In order to investigate the importance of changes in the structure of inputs (a_{ij}) between the years the rates of effective protection were recalculated using the 1963 nominal tariff and excise tax/subsidy rates in conjunction with the 1968 input coefficients.

Effective tariff protection

$$g_j^1 = \frac{t_j^{1963} - \sum_i a_{ij}^{1968} t_i^{1963}}{1 - \sum_i a_{ij}^{1968}}$$

(reported in table 1, column 7).
Effective excise tax/subsidy protection,

$$g_j^2 = \frac{X_j^{1963}(1 + t_j^{1963})}{1 - \sum_i a_{ij}^{1968}}$$

(reported in table 1, column 13).
Overall effective protection

$$g_j = g_j^1 + g_j^2$$

(reported in table 1, column 17).
Comparing columns 3, 4 and 7, and columns 10, 11 and 13, of table 1 it is clear that the changes in the structure of inputs $(a_{ij}^{1963}$ to $a_{ij}^{1968})$ explain very little of the changes in protection between 1963 and 1968.[18]

The changes resulting only from changes in nominal tariff $(t_i$ and $t_j)$ and excise tax/subsidy rates (X_j) (with a_{ij} held constant at a_{ij}^{1963}) are rather more complex as the change in effective tariff protection (g_j^1) can result both from changes in the overall tariffs (t_j) and the changes in the tariffs on inputs (t_i). To isolate the effect of t_j and then of t_i two estimates were made for tariff protection, firstly showing the protection when all tariffs were changed and secondly the protection resulting from a change only in overall tariffs (t_j). We estimate,

$$g_j^1 = \frac{t_j^{1968} - \sum_i a_{ij}^{1963} t^{1968}}{1 - \sum_i a_{ij}^{1963}}$$

(reported in table 1, column 5) and

$$g_j^1 = \frac{t_j^{1968} - \sum_i a_{ij}^{1963} t_i^{1963}}{1 - \sum_i a_{ij}^{1963}}$$

(reported in table 1, column 6).

The effective excise tax/subsidy protection resulting from a change of nominal excise tax/subsidy rates only was estimated using

$$g_j^2 = \frac{X_j^{1968}(1 + t_j^{1968})}{1 - \sum_i a_{ij}^{1963}}$$

(reported in table 1, column 16).

Comparing columns 3, 4 and 5 of table 1 it is clear that for almost every commodity group the majority of the change in effective tariff protection between 1963 and 1968 can be explained by changes in the nominal tariffs (t_j and t_i). Similarly columns 10, 11 and 12 of table 1 show that the changes in effective excise tax/subsidy protection are in almost all cases mainly the result of changes in the nominal excise tax/subsidy rate. Further the results also show that the greater part of the change in effective tariff protection resulting from changed nominal tariffs (t_j and t_i) results from the changes of the overall tariffs (t_j) and not from the changes of nominal tariffs on inputs (t_i) — see columns 3, 4 and 6 of table 1 to confirm the results.

We noted earlier that there seemed to be no pattern to the changes in effective tariff and excise tax/subsidy protection between 1963 and 1968 — some rose and some fell, and we have traced the major cause of the changes to changes in the nominal tariff rates (t_j) and excise tax/subsidy rates ($X_j(1 + t_j)$). The variations in nominal excise tax/subsidy rates with some rising and some falling may not *a priori* surprise us as the rates reflect government policy on taxes and industrial policy, predominantly domestic matters where the treatment of individual industries may differ very much from one industry to another and between one year and another. However, the variations in nominal overall tariffs (t_j), with some rising and some falling, (see columns 1 and 2 of table 1) is surprising, as tariff rates are subject to international agreement and one would expect a general direction and magnitude of change to be apparent between 1963 and 1968. Between these years the only significant change of tariffs was the first cut in tariffs resulting from the Kennedy Round tariff-cutting negotiations. This cut was implemented on 1 July 1968 and averaged approximately 14% over a wide range of manufactured products. Our estimated nominal tariff rates show no such general pattern of cuts by 7 % for the year as a whole.

SOME DIFFICULTIES

We have noted the unexpected pattern of nominal tariff rate changes between 1963 and 1968 and this raises doubts about the methods used in this and previous papers.

The estimation of the tariff rate for a commodity by dividing the total tariff revenue for all items in the group by the total imports of all items in the group means that the individual tariff rates have been averaged using relative imports as weights. Any change in the pattern of imports, whatever the cause, will change the weights.

If the pattern of imports changes in the same way as the pattern of production of items within a commodity group changes then the changes in estimated tariff rates for the commodity group is meaningful. If, however, the change in import patterns reflect short-term disequilibrium fluctuations, then the calculated changes in averaged tariff rates will be inappropriate in the context of effective protection.

We may note (following McAleese) that the changes in the calculated values of t_j and t_i will change the values of a_{ij} calculated and thus the value of $\sum_i a_{ij}$.[19]

The problem of how to average tariff rates has been solved theoretically by Basevi (1971). He demonstrates that the set of weights necessary to remove bias depends upon the use to which the estimates are to be put and the concept of effective protection being used. His analysis produces a theoretical answer which is impractical for empirical work requiring as it does detailed data not normally available or so numerous as to be prohibitively expensive to process. Further, Tumlir and Till (1971) have shown that in practice the choice of weights used does significantly affect the average tariff rates calculated; and this paper has shown that changes in the value of t_j are chiefly responsible for changes in the calculated rates of effective tariff protection.

We must conclude that calculated rates of protection at a highly aggregated level must be treated with considerable caution.

CONCLUSION

The paper confirms that nominal tariff (tax) rates are not sufficiently good proxies for effective protection that we can dispense with effective rates of protection for policy purposes.

When effective protection in 1968 was compared with that in 1963 for UK manufacturing we found no overall pattern of rising or falling protection; some rates fell and others rose, this despite the implementation in mid-1968 of the first tariff cuts resulting from the Kennedy Round tariff negotiations. Further investigation showed that the changes in effective protection resulted almost entirely from the changes in tariffs on finished products (as opposed to intermediate products). The lack of pattern in the changes of these tariff rates led on to a brief discussion of the inadequacy of the method used by this and previous papers to estimate tariff rates — changes in these rates could simply reflect changes in the commodity pattern of imports, all other variables being constant.

The paper presents estimates of effective protection resulting from tariffs and excise taxes/subsidies for UK manufacturing in 1963 and 1968 and suggests that these estimates and the methods used may be less reliable than is desirable.

DISCUSSION: DERMOT MCALEESE

Empirical work of effective rates of protection involves two sets of problems (Corden, 1976). First there are measurement problems. Problems of tariff averaging, tariff redundancy, treatment of non-traded inputs and calculation of the 'implicit' tariff rates for non-tariff barriers, fall under this heading. Second, there are problems of interpretation, which arise when the effective tariff rate has finally been calculated. What do effective tarrifs mean? Do effective tariffs provide all that much more information than nominal tariffs? Can effective tariff rankings shed light on the magnitude and direction of the resource-allocation effects following the elimination of protective barriers to trade?

It is clear that, viewed within this context, Duncan Kitchin's paper adds to the literature on calculation problems, rather than problems of interpretation. His work follows that of Balassa, Baldwin, Barker and Han and Oulton of effective rates of protection in the British economy. He improves on Oulton's study by showing that the latter's estimates of nominal tariffs for 1968, based on provisional import-duty revenue data, are seriously out of line with those constructed with the revised revenue figures.

Kitchin's purpose, however, is not primarily to amend previous estimates of effective tariffs for the UK. Rather, he attempts to show that the practice of calculating nominal tariffs as the ratio of import duty collected to total imports is unsatisfactory and potentially misleading. He does this by comparing the results of tariff calculations in 1963 and 1968 for the United Kingdom. His results suggest that average nominal tariffs, calculated by the import-duty method, oscillate widely between the two years, and completely fail to reflect the average across-the-board reduction which occurred under the Kennedy Round.

Most empirical researchers in the field would agree that the use of import duties as a means of obtaining tariff averages is highly unsatisfactory. This is so particularly in semi-industrialised or less developed countries where duty rebates and exceptions abound and imports are often restricted by means of duty-free quotas. For this reason, other methods of computing average nominal tariffs have frequently been employed. The contributors to Balassa (1971), for example, preferred to use domestic sales data as weights (to the greatest level of disaggregation possible) and then employed international trade weights, rather than import duties, to average the remaining tariffs.

A study of effective protection in the Republic of Ireland (McAleese, 1971) also used very detailed domestic production data as weights, drawn from the input–output table worksheets, and simple arithmetical averages or international trade weights were used to aggregate the tariffs relevant to each activity. To have used the import duty method for each input–output sector would have yielded nonsensical results in this case. While no method of averaging tariffs is perfect, the present paper will confirm many economists' reservations as to the usefulness of the import-duty method.

The downward bias of this method is now well-known. It can also be established that, as the general tariff level falls, the average tariff calculated on the basis of import duties can move either upwards or downwards during the transition to complete free trade. A simple arithmetical example illustrates this.

Suppose there are two goods, A and B, pertaining to a single industry, whose tariffs have to be averaged. Tariffs for A and B are zero and 20% respectively; imports and £100 and £50. The average tariff in this situation on the import duty basis is 10/150 or 6.6%. Now let tariffs be cut by one-half. This leads to a fall in the price of B, which in turn stimulates substitution of B for A, as well as for all other goods whose prices have remained constant. Suppose the new import values are A £50 and B £200. Given the corresponding tariffs of zero and and 10%, the average tariff *rises* by 20/250 or 8%. Thus, when tariff averages are being calculated from import-duty statistics, an across-the-board tariff reduction could lead to either a rise or a fall in the calculated average tariff. Kitchin's finding that the across-the-board reduction in the UK tariffs between 1963 and 1968 is not reflected in a corresponding reduction in his nominal-tariff averages, therefore, does not prove irreconcilable with the fact that the import duty method is downward-biased.

Can all of the difference between Kitchin's 1963 and 1968 effective tariff estimates be attributed to the vagaries of the particular nominal tariff estimation procedure which he employs? As Kitchin himself recognises, the answer is negative. First, the substitution effects referred to above are unlikely to have been sufficiently large to explain the very substantial changes in nominal tariff levels for individual industries between these years. Second, the commodity composition of each industry's output could have changed in the intervening period due to changes in tastes and different income elasticities of demand, apart altogether from substitution effects. Third changes in $(1 - \Sigma a_{ij})$ could also occur, even in the context of a fixed bundle of commodities, if the ratio of profits and wages to gross output changes over time.

Corden (1976) rounds off a discussion of the difficulties involved in calculating effective tariffs with the conclusion that 'these difficulties entitle one to be highly sceptical of greatly disaggregated figures or figures obtained quickly'. Kitchin's paper could be regarded as a striking vindication of this point of view. For Kitchin is not arguing that effective tariffs are useless — on the contrary, he accepts their superiority over nominal tariffs — but he does suggest that much more detailed data are necessary in order to obtain reliable results.

There is surely a need for further work on the UK tariff structure. First, it ought to be possible to obtain more disaggregated production data for the UK than that published in the input — output table, which would help to reduce the bias and inaccuracies inherent in the import-duty method. Second, the more discussion of the individual industry tariffs themselves is needed. Why does the insulated wires and cables effective tariff emerge as 132%? What is the significance of this? One persuasive argument in favour of effective over nominal rates of protection, is that the former provides unexpected results at an individual industry level. Having obtained the unexpected results, it is a pity to see them left unexplored. Third, one would like to see more investigation of industries such as clothing, footwear and textiles where various non-tariff barriers, not taken account of in this or previous studies of the UK effective tariff, are doubtless of considerable importance.

NOTES

1. The author would like to record his grateful thanks for help received from J.L. Ford, R.J. Nicholson, A.A. Sampson, R. Shone, D. McAleese, the UK Central Statistical Office and an anonymous referee. Their help improved the paper and all the remaining inadequacies are the author's responsibility.
2. Early estimates of UK effective protection, Barker and Han (1971) and Oulton (1973) were in error; Barker and Han because of errors in their estimating equations (see Kitchin, 1975) and Oulton because of his use of preliminary data which were subsequently heavily revised.
3. See, for example, Basevi (1966), Grubel and Johnson (1967), Oulton (1973).
4. Product moment correlation between tariff rates and the resulting effective protection was 0.926 (1963) and 0.725 (1968).
5. The importance for policy purposes of effective rates of protection is neatly and clearly discussed in Grubel (1971).
6. Witthans (1973) showed that for the US a relaxation of the assumption of zero elasticity of substitution between inputs resulted in only slight changes. If the value of the elasticity was set at two then the average change (for 135 industries) in the calculated effective protection was only 6%. Additionally,

a priori, we may expect that the elasticities will have low values for the UK because of the high level of aggregation in the input–output tables.
7 The derivation of equation (1) is clearly explained in Corden (1971 pp. 40–2).
8 A full account of the methods and sources used is available from the author on request.
9 The limitations of this weighting method will be discussed in section 5 of this paper.
10 For most commodity groups before aggregation $t_i = t_j$ (when $i = j$). Only in a few cases did the tariff rate charged depend upon the use made of the import.
11 For details of the excise taxes/subsidies involved see *I–O Tables 1963*, pp. 27–8; *I–O Tables 1968*. p.21.
12 The full seventy (1963) and ninety (1968) results are available from the author on request.
13 As explained earlier in this section, for the aggregated analysis a matrix of tariffs on inputs was generated with the deflated input coefficients being used as weights to combine the tariff rates. When applying the 1968 tariffs to the aggregated 1963 coefficients the weights used had to be those of 1968. This is not strictly correct but the 1963 weights are not available. An analogous approximation is necessary when applying the 1963 tariffs to the aggregated 1968 input coefficients.
14 Guisinger and Schydlowsky (1971, p. 279) note, however, 'what a country can learn about its structure of effective protection from the schedule of nominal rates depends critically on the desired level of aggregation'.
15 See Grubel (1971).
16 The product-moment correlation between effective tariff protection in 1963 and 1968 for the forty-seven manufactured commodity groups was 0.407.
17 I am grateful to D. McAleese for pointing out the third possibility. He has found that for the Republic of Ireland the value $\sum_i a_{ij}$ seems to change quite markedly for a commodity group from one year to the next.
18 It must be remembered that the estimation of deflated input coefficients for 1968 (a_{ij}^{1968}) are not entirely independent of the estimated nominal tariff rates (t_j^{1968} and t_i^{1968}) as the published coefficients are deflated by the nominal tariff rates $a_{ij} = a'_{ij}(1 + t_j)/(1 + t_{ij})$.
19 The values of a_{ij} and thus $\sum_i a_{ij}$ may of course change through time simply as a result of changes in the commodity composition of commodity groups. It may not be appropriate to compare 1963 with 1968 as we have done in this paper.

REFERENCES

Balassa, B. *et al.* (1971). *The Structure of Protection in Developing Countries*. Baltimore: Johns Hopkins University Press.

Barker, T.S. and S.S. Han, (1971). Effective rates of protection of United Kingdom production. *Economic Journal* 81, 282–93.

Basevi, G. (1966). The US tariff structure: estimate of effective rates of protection of US industries and industrial labour. *Review of Economics and Statistics* 48, 142–60.

Basevi, G. (1971). Aggregation problems in the measurement of effective protection. In *Effective Tariff Protection*, ed. H.G. Grubel and H.G. Johnson, pp. 115–34. GATT and Graduate Institute of International Studies, Geneva.

Corden, W.M. (1971). *The Theory of Protection*. Oxford: Clarendon Press.

Corden, W.M. (1976). The costs and consequences of protection: a survey of empirical work. In *International Trade and Finance*, ed. P. Kenen. Cambridge University Press.

Grubel, H.G. (1971). Effective tariff protection: a non-specialist guide to the theory, policy implications and controversies. In *Effective Tariff Protection*, ed. H.G. Grubel and H.G. Johnson. GATT and Graduate Institute of International Studies, Geneva.

Grubel, H.G. and Johnson, H.G. (1967). Nominal tariffs, indirect taxes and effective rates of protection: the Common Market countries 1959. *Economic Journal* 77, 761–76.

Guisinger, S. and Schydlowsky, D.M. (1971). The empirical relationship between nominal and effective rates of protection. In *Effective Tariff Protection*, ed. H.G. Grubel and H.G. Johnson, pp. 269–86. GATT and Graduate Institute of International Studies, Geneva.

HM Customs and Excise (1965). *Protective Duties 1963*. London:HMSO.

HM Customs and Excise (1969) *Annual Statement of the Trade of the United Kingdom 1968*. London:HMSO.

HM Customs and Excise (1960–9). *Customs and Excise Tariff 1960 Amendments*. London: HMSO.

Kitchin, P.D. (1975). Effective rates of protection for United Kingdom production: a comment. *Economic Journal* 85, 377.

McAleese, Dermot (1971). *Effective Tariffs and the Structure of Industrial Protection in Ireland*. Dublin: The Economic and Social Research Institute, Paper No. 62.

Oulton, N. (1973). *Tariffs, Taxes and Trade in the UK: The Effective Protection Approach*. Government Economic Service Occasional Papers No. 6. London:HMSO.

Tumlir, J. and Till, L. (1971). Tariff averaging in international comparisons. In *Effective Tariff Protection*., ed. H.G. Grubel and H.G. Johnson, pp. 147–60. GATT and Graduate Institute of International Studies, Geneva.

UK Central Statistical Office (1970). *Input–Output Tables for the United Kingdom 1963*. London: HMSO.

UK Central Statistical Office (1973). *Input–Output Tables for the United Kingdom 1968*. London: HMSO.

Witthams, F. (1973). Estimates of effective rates of protection for United States industries in 1967. *Review of Economics and Statistics* 55, 362–4.

PART FOUR
UTILITY, VALUE AND THE FIRM

11 TRICKS WITH UTILITY FUNCTIONS

W.M. GORMAN[1]

INTRODUCTION

Professor Mary Douglas, the economic anthropologist, has recently become interested in consumer behaviour, which she sees as a sequence of statements about social relationships. Having talked to a number of economists in London and Chicago about the theory of choice, she summarised her conclusions: 'Utility is empty, so we can fill it.' This is exactly what I feel, too, and I was tempted to make it the title of this chapter. I decided not to because it has a missionary fervour. My aim is not to persuade you to go about constructing specific theories of choice within the economist's general framework, but to tell you about a few tricks which you may find useful should you decide so to do.

I had originally intended to range rather widely, considering a variety of theories which might be put forward, and suggesting how each in turn might most simply be modelled within the traditional theory of choice. It soon became clear, however, that this was quite an unrealistic aim in a single chapter. Accordingly I am going to confine myself to two basic ideas, duality and separability, and the tricks they suggest. I will apply them to a number of related hypotheses about consumer behaviour by way of example.

Duality is about the choice of the independent variables in terms of which one defines a theory. Consider an economist building a model of competitive equilibrium. He defines technology and tastes in terms of production and utility functions – that is, in terms of the quantities consumed and produced – and he derives the usual equilibrium conditions for each agent. Now he has to confront his myriad consumers and producers with each other. What they have in common is the *prices* they face, not the quantities they consume or produce, so that these now have to be taken as the independent variables in the problem, and millions of marginal relations have to be solved together to yield the demand and supply functions. This is usually a complicated matter – even to prove the existence of the functions may be difficult, to derive their special properties from those of the production and utility functions underlying them, much more so. Even to find their local properties one commonly has to carry out a complicated Hicksian analysis in terms of substitution matrices and the like. Yet these complicated and sometimes inconclusive manipulations, which take a great deal of the economist's time and intellectual energy, have really very little to do with economics at all, at least in the sense of providing useful insights into economic processes.

How much better it would have been if he could have avoided them by defining everything in terms of the prices from the outset. What duality shows is that this is perfectly possible — indeed we can use the prices of some goods and the quantities of others, should we so wish. They might represent quantities of plant and equipment in a short-run analysis, for instance.

Separability has to do with the structure of a problem. Perfect competition and the absence of external economies, which allow us to examine the behaviour of individual firms in isolation; constant returns, permitting us to discuss the structure of a firm's production plan without knowing its scale; Samuelson's weak independence axiom which says that, in an uncertain world, what we do if it shines is quite independent of what we would have done had it rained; and Bergson's social welfare function based on the sovereignty of self-regarding consumers: all embody separability assumptions, whose function is to allow us to examine one aspect of a problem in at least relative isolation from others

Crudely, then, separability has to do with the 'natural structure' of a problem, duality with the 'natural independent variables'. My contention is that one can simplify one's life a good deal if one thinks explicitly about these matters before setting up a model. Not only is the analysis simpler but its relation to other bits of economics is commonly easier to see.

One difficulty about these two pieces of advice is that they are not always consistent. The 'natural structure' may not be easy to characterise in terms of what would otherwise seem to be the 'natural independent variables'. Quite often one can get around this difficulty by changing one's assumptions slightly, or specialising the analysis a little further. How this may be done is discussed in pages 228–37 and 238–41. When this is impossible, it is best in my experience to follow the 'natural structure' in such cases, and to check one's independent variables as best one can in each particular case.

Because of this one may have to change the *basis* — the set of independent variables — several times in one problem. This is just the kind of activity which I criticised above when indulged in by conventional economists. Once one realises that this problem exists, however, one can often do quite a lot to simplify matters. This is, however, a matter of experience, and knowledge. In this chapter I will have to put such matters aside and keep to the simpler cases where 'structure' and 'basis' go hand in hand. In discussing these I will, however, try to bring out considerations relevant to the more difficult cases in which they do not.

I will be covering a lot of ground in this paper, necessarily superficially. There will be no serious attempt at rigour even in stating results, much less in 'proving' them.

DUALITY AND ITS APPLICATIONS

Duality

To represent tastes in terms of the independent variables' prices we use either the cost function[2]
$$m = g(p, u) = \min\{p.\, x : f(x) \geq u\} \tag{1}$$
or the indirect utility function
$$u = h(p, m) \tag{2}$$
got by solving[3] (1) for u, where the direct utility function
$$u = f(x). \tag{3}$$
The former tells how much money is needed to attain the utility level u, at prices p, the latter what level of utility u is attainable with income m at these prices. Under normal assumptions the two are equivalent, and each in turn is equivalent to (1).

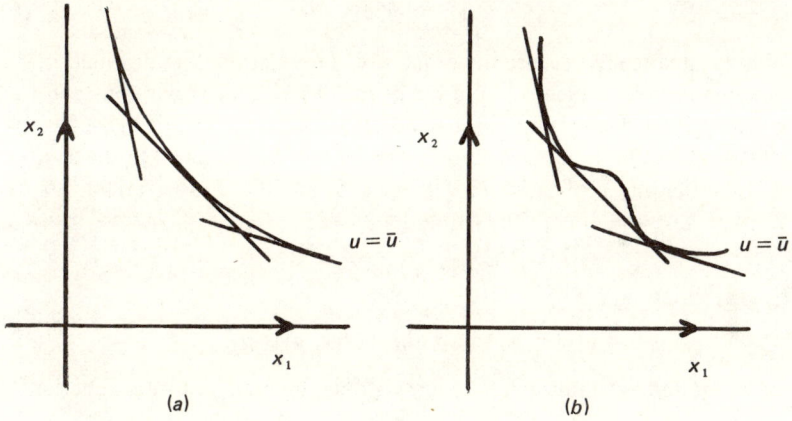

Figure 1 *Deriving the utility function from the cost function.*

It is only the latter statement which gives rise to any difficulty. It is clear that we can calculate how much expenditure is required at given prices p to reach a given level of utility by observing the position of the budget line as in figure 1(a). Similarly, knowing the cost function, one can draw all the budget lines tangent to the indifference curve and hence find it, as their envelope, again as in figure 1(a), as long as the curve is convex — i.e. the utility function is quasi-concave. Figure 1(b) illustrates what happens if it is not: the gaps across the dimples in the curve are bridged and we get the quasi-concave closure of the utility function rather than the function itself. This yields effectively the same predictions about the consumer's behaviour when he faces fixed prices, but not necessarily when he does not.

It can easily be shown that the consumer's compensated demand function

$$x_i = g_i(p, u) = \partial g/\partial p_i, \qquad (4)$$

while his marginal utility of income $\lambda = \partial u/\partial m = (\partial m/\partial u)^{-1} = g_0^{-1}$, where $g_0 = \partial g/\partial u = \partial u/\partial m$, is the shadow price of utility

$$q = g_0 = \partial g/\partial u. \qquad (5)$$

These results in turn yield his uncompensated demand function

$$x_i = -h_i(p, m)/h_0(p, m), \qquad (6)$$

and marginal utility of income

$$\lambda = h_0(p, m) = \partial h/\partial m, \qquad (7)$$

where $h_i = \partial h_i/\partial p_i$, $h_0 = \partial h/\partial m$.

Note that the effect of a compensated change in the price of goods j on the demand for good i is $g_{ij} = \partial^2 g/\partial p_i \partial p_j$. Slutsky's integrability condition therefore becomes

$$g_{ij} = g_{ji} \qquad (8)$$

and holds automatically because the order of differentiation does not matter.[4]

It is sometimes convenient to hold the quantities of some goods constant during this analysis. There may, for instance, be some rationing, or the subject's family responsibilities, house, car, or job may be taken to be fixed in the shortest run. Take the vector of these *fixed goods* as y, and that of the variable goods as x. We then have the direct utility function

$$u = f(x, y), \qquad (9)$$

and the cost function

$$m = g(p, y, u) = \min\{p \cdot x : f(x, y) \geqslant u\}, \qquad (10)$$

giving the required expenditure *on* x, and yielding the indirect utility function

$$u = h(p, y, m). \qquad (11)$$

Here we have compensated demand functions

$$x_i = g_i(p, y, u) = \partial g/\partial p_i, \qquad (12)$$

uncompensated demand functions

$$x_i = -h_i(p, y, m)/h_0(p, y, m), \qquad (13)$$

shadow price of utility

$$q_0 = g_0(p, y, u) = 1/h_0(p, y, m), \qquad (14)$$

and marginal utility of expenditure on x

$$\lambda = h_0(p, y, m) = 1/q_0, \qquad (15)$$

where $h_i = \partial h/\partial p_i$, $h_0 = \partial h/\partial m$.
In addition we have shadow prices of fixed goods

$$q_s = g_s(p, y, u) = \partial g/\partial p_s = -h_s(p, y, m)/h_0(p, y, m). \tag{16}$$

Equation (12) yields a whole series of generalised Slutsky conditions,

$$g_{ij} = g_{ji}, \quad g_{rs} = g_{sr},$$
$$g_{is} = g_{si}, \quad g_{i0} = g_{0i},$$
$$g_{s0} = g_{0s} \tag{17}$$

whose interpretation is left to you.

Finally it is easily shown that cost functions are increasing homogeneous of degree one and concave in p, and the indirect utility functions decreasing, homogeneous of degree zero and quasi concave in p. Effectively any functions with these properties will do as cost or indirect utility functions.[5]

I.f.f. the utility function is strictly quasi-concave in p the cost function is differentiable; i.f.f. the cost function is strictly concave in p, the indifference curves are smooth.

Equivalent adult scales

Statisticians have been using equivalent adult scales for a long time now in analysing budget surveys. 'From a consumption point of view', they say, 'a woman is only half a man, a girl half that again', or some such thing. A schoolmaster I once had put it better: 'When you have a wife and a baby, a penny bun costs threepence.'

There is a complication: babies bulk larger as consumers of nappies than of whisky. We need different scales for different foods. There are said to be economies of scale in catering for large families, too, and we need to allow for this, so that we really need to look at the family as a whole in deciding how many adults it is 'equivalent' to for each good.

Barten (1964) set out to make these ideas rigorous. A family of type θ, he said, is equivalent to $a_i(\theta)$ adults for the consumption of good i, for each i. Let us refer instead to this as a family of type $a = (a_1, a_2, ..)$.

He wrote this family's direct utility function as

$$u^a = f^a(x) = f(x^a), \tag{18}$$

where its adjusted consumption vector

$$x^a = (x_1/a_1, x_2/a_2, ...), \tag{19}$$

corrects for the number of equivalent adults. Its cost function

$$g^a(p, u) = \min\{p_1 x_1 + p_2 x_2 + \ldots : f^a(x) \geq u\}$$
$$= \min\{a_1 p_1 x_1^a + a_2 p_2 x_2^a + \ldots : f(x^a) \geq u\}$$
$$= g(p^a, u), \qquad (20)$$

where $g(., u)$ is the cost function corresponding to the utility function $f(.)$, and the adjusted price vector
$$p^a = (a_1 p_1, a_2 p_2, \ldots) \qquad (21)$$

so that, for a family of three bread-equivalent adults, 'a penny bun costs three-pence'. This immediately yields the adjusted compensated demand function 'per head',
$$x_i^a = g_i(p^a, u), \qquad (22)$$

and thence the ordinary compensated demand functions,
$$x_i = a_i g_i(a_1 p_1, a_2 p_2, \ldots u). \qquad (23)$$

This in turn implies that the compensated elasticities
$$\epsilon_{ij} = \partial \log x_i / \partial \log p_j |_u = \delta_{ij} + \alpha_{ij}, \qquad (24)$$

where compensated elasticities w.r.t. family 'size'
$$\alpha_{ij} = \partial \log x_i / \partial \log a_j |_u \qquad (25)$$

and δ_{ij} is the Kronecker δ.

We can, of course, solve (19) for the indirect utility function
$$u = h^a(p, m) = h(p^a, m), \qquad (26)$$

yielding the adjusted uncompensated demand functions
$$x_i^a = -h_i(p^a, m)/h_0(p^a, m), \qquad (27)$$

and the ordinary uncompensated demand functions
$$x_i = -a_i h_i(p^a, m)/h_0(p^a, m), \qquad (28)$$

implying that the uncompensated demand elasticities
$$\bar{\epsilon}_{ij} = \delta_{ij} + \bar{\alpha}_{ij}, \qquad (29)$$

in the obvious notation.

Equations (24) and (29) are the important results here. Were the theory true, and were the sample to include a great enough variety of family types, we could use them to calculate price elasticities from survey data. As long as everyone faces the same prices, we need not even know what they are.

Barten carried out this important piece of analysis in terms of the direct utility function. The result was a long and difficult discussion. My otherwise obtuse schoolmaster's insight, which reveals everything at one glance, was hidden from him by the scaffolding of his theory.

It is not only that an inappropriate choice of independent variables leads us into a lot of complicated mathematics — it obscures the economic realities, too.

Consumer price indices

Consider a consumer with constant tastes defined by a cost function $g(p, u)$. Let prices be $\bar{p}$ initially and p now. There are many candidates for the title consumer price index

$$I = g(p, u)/g(\bar{p}, u), \tag{30}$$

according to the level of utility u used as a basis for the comparison. The two most obvious are $\bar{h}(\bar{p}, \bar{m})$, $h(p, m)$, where $\bar{m}$, m are the initial and current incomes, and $h(.)$ the indirect utility function corresponding to $g(., u)$.

For a really satisfactory 'true index of the cost of living' to exist, it should be independent of the basis u of comparison. That is, for a true index of the cost of living,

$$g(p, u)/g(\bar{p}, u) = g(p, \bar{u})/g(\bar{p}, \bar{u}), \tag{31}$$

for each $\bar{u}$. Now $g(\bar{p}, u)$ is strictly increasing in u under normal assumptions and so may be chosen as a new utility indicator. Normalize accordingly to get

$$g(p, u)/u = g(p, \bar{u})/\bar{u} = a(p), \tag{32}$$

say, so that

$$m = g(p, u) = ua(p) \tag{33}$$

in this normalisation — that is, utility is produced under *constant average* or *unit costs*. Now

$$x_i = g_i(p, u) = ua_i(p) = ma_i(p)/a(p), \tag{34}$$

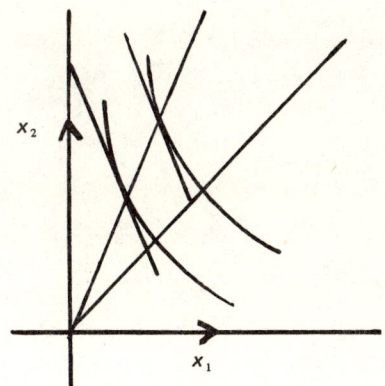

Figure 2 *Homothetic utility function, with Engel curves*

so that we get twice as much utility, at twice as high a cost, if we consume twice as much of each good. Utility is therefore *'produced under constant returns'*. The Engel curves are straight lines radiating from the origin, and the income elasticity of demand for each good is zero (see figure 2).

Preferences like this are called homothetic.[6] They are both necessary and sufficient for the existence of 'true indices of the cost of living' — so that we may conclude that such indices are unlikely to exist. However the problem is of some historical interest, and the results just proved will prove useful below.

Fisher and Shell (1968) considered the altogether more important questions of taste and quality change in their classic paper in the Hicks festschrift. However they did so in terms of the ordinary primal utility function, and were led, in my opinion, into infelicities and mistakes in consequence. I will not attempt to document this belief here, but merely sketch how their approach might have been developed with the aid of the cost function.

First of all consider the case of taste change in general, indexing tastes by parameter a, with $a = \bar{a} = 1$, initially. They ask the question: what income m^* would the consumer need *now* to be as well off at present prices p, as he would be *now* were he faced with the initial budgeting situation $(\bar{p}, \bar{m})$ with his present tastes. That is, they set up the basis of comparison[7]

$$u^* = h^a(\bar{p}, \bar{m}), \qquad (35)$$

in the obvious notation, and define the consumer price index

$$I = g^a(p, u^*)/g^a(\bar{p}, u^*) = g^a(p, u^*)/\bar{m}. \qquad (36)$$

The particular taste change they discuss is one in which the ranking of $x^a = (x_1/a_1, x_2, \ldots, x_n)$ now is the same as that of the x initially. Formally this is a special case of Barten's model in which his vector $a = (a, 1, \ldots, 1)$, so that say,

$$u^* = h(\bar{p}^a, \bar{m}); \quad \bar{p}^a = (a\bar{p}_1, \bar{p}_2, \ldots, \bar{p}_n) = (a\bar{p}, \bar{q}), \qquad (37)$$

$$I = g(\bar{p}^a, u^*)/\bar{m}; \quad p^a = (ap_1, p_2, \ldots, p_n) = (ap_1, q), \qquad (38)$$

and the required income

$$m^* = I\bar{m} = g(ap_1, q, u^*). \qquad (39)$$

These imply that

$$\partial \log I/\partial \log a = \partial \log m^*/\partial \log a =$$

$$= a\{p_1 g_1(ap_1, q, u^*) + g_0(ap_1, q, u^*)\bar{p}_1 \bar{h}_1(a\bar{p}_1, \bar{q}, \bar{m})\}/m^*$$

$$= \{p_1^a x_1^a - \bar{p}_1^a \bar{x}_1^a g_0(ap_1, q, u^*) h_0(a\bar{p}_1, \bar{q}, \bar{m})\}/m^*$$

$$= \{p_1 x_1 - \bar{p}_1 \bar{x}_1 g_0(ap_1, q, u^*) h_0(a\bar{p}_1, \bar{q}, \bar{m})\}/m^*$$

$$= (p_1 x_1 - \bar{p}_1 \bar{x}_1 \partial m^*/\partial \bar{m})/m^*$$

$$= \rho^* - \bar{\rho}\partial \log m^*/\partial \log \bar{m} = \rho^* - \bar{\rho} - \bar{\rho}\partial \log I/\log \bar{m}, \qquad (40)$$

where starred letters refer to behaviour in the 'present' budget situation in (p, m^*), compared to that in $(\bar{p}, \bar{m})$, with present tastes a throughout, and ρ is the proportion of income spent on good 1.

It is therefore not true, as one might have thought, that I increases with a when the good affected bulks more largely in the decision under (p, m^*) than under $(\bar{p}, \bar{m})$.[8] The explanation of the income effect $\bar{\rho}\partial \log I/\partial \log \bar{m}$ is left to you.

In this change of tastes, good 1 has become $b = 1/a$ times as effective, if you like, in satisfying the consumer's wants,[9] possibly because his wife has become a better cook. In the corresponding quality change, the good itself has changed to be just $b = 1/a$ times as effective as before, one unit of the new doing precisely what b of the old would. In terms of the initial good the efficiency price of the new version is $p_1^q = ap_1$. Tastes have not changed so that basis of comparison

consumer price index
$$u^* = h(\bar{p}, \bar{m}) = \bar{u}, \tag{41}$$

and required income
$$I = g(ap_1, q, \bar{u})/\bar{m}, \tag{42}$$

so that
$$m^* = I\bar{m} = g(ap_1, q, \bar{u}); \tag{43}$$

$$\partial \log I / \partial \log a = \partial \log m^* / \partial \log a$$

$$= ap_1 g_1(ap_1, q, \bar{u})/m^*$$

$$= \rho, \tag{44}$$

the share of good 1 in the situation (ap_1, q, m^*). I leave the simple interpretation to you.

I called Fisher and Shell's article classic at the outset, and yet have said very little about their detailed analysis. It is a classic because it defines the problems raised by taste and quality changes clearly and definitively, and constructs models within which their effects might be analysed. These models, moreover, are well motivated and correspond with our intuitive notions of what is going on — or at least with mine. These are important things to have done. In doing them they have put the discussion of taste and quality differences on the right lines.

Their detailed analysis is another matter. Unfortunately, they had set the problem up in terms of the utility rather than the cost function and this made things difficult for them. It has led these skilled practitioners into clumsy arguments, sometimes, in my view, about trivia, or unimportant aspects of their model, and even, I believe, into mistakes. If that is true of Fisher and Shell, what hopes are there for the rest of us when we set up such models in terms of inappropriate variables?[10]

Two generalisations of the equivalent adults model

The equivalent adults model can be written in matrix terms, For a family of type

$$A = \operatorname{diag} a = \begin{bmatrix} a_1 & 0 & \cdots & 0 \\ 0 & a_2 & \cdots & 0 \\ \cdots & \cdots & \cdots & \cdots \\ 0 & 0 & \cdots & a_n \end{bmatrix}$$

its utility function
$$u^A = f^A(x) = f(x^A) \tag{45}$$

where its adjusted consumption vector
$$x^A = {'A^{-1}}x = (x_1/a_1, \ldots, x_n/a_n), \tag{46}$$

and its cost function
$$m = g^A(p, u) = g(p^A, u), \tag{47}$$
where its adjusted price vector
$$p^A = A'p = (a_1 p_1, \ldots, a_n p_n). \tag{48}$$
I leave it to you to verify that (47) and (48) follow from (45) and (46) for any non-degenerate square matrix A. The reason is that
$$p^A \cdot x^A = (A'p) \cdot (A^{-1} x) = (A'p)'(A^{-1} x) = p'AA^{-'}x = p'x = p \cdot x \tag{49}$$
whether or not A is diagonal.[11]

Why we should be interested in this particular collection of household technologies is another matter. I suppose we might postulate a selfish father who nevertheless found it socially necessary to buy his wife flowers and his children toys, for instance, each time he bought himself a new golfclub. An x vector made up of all this would then be equivalent to him of an x^A vector made up of just the golfclub.

For the moment just think of the model as part of the armoury, to be brought into use if and when it seems useful. Think of this section as typifying one of the greatest advantages of a mathematical approach. The economist develops a simple model to fit one case. The mathematician looks at it, asks what is the essential element in the construction which determines the type of results gained, and then finds the widest class of models embodying that essential element. He then hands back this much richer collection of models for the use of the practitioner. Of course, the present is an absolutely trivial example of this type of thing.

The model can be generalised a little further in a direction which we will find ourselves following later. According to (45) and (46) the household of type A transfers inputs x bought in the market into the goods x^A which satisfy its wants through a simple linear technology — which, of course, yields constant returns, or, if you like, incurs constant unit costs. That is, one needs $2x$ to produce $2x^A$.

Introduce overheads b, which have to be incurred before any x^A, or rather $x^{A,b}$, can be produced. That is, consider a family of type (A, b) whose utility function
$$u^{A,b} = f^{A,b}(x) = f(x^{A,b}), \tag{50}$$
where its adjusted consumption vector
$$x^{A,b} = A^{-1}(x - b). \tag{51}$$
Its cost function
$$g^{A,b}(p, u) = p \cdot b + g(A'p, u) = p^A \cdot b^A + g(p^A, u) \tag{52}$$
where we may rather misleadingly define adjusted overheads
$$b^A = A^{-1} b \tag{53}$$
and p^A is defined in (48). Again the proof is left to you.

Equation (52), of course, yields the indirect utility function

$$u^{A,b} = h^{A,b}(p, m) = h(A'p, m - p \cdot b) = h(p^A, m - p^A \cdot b^A) \qquad (54)$$

and, with this yields the compensated demand

$$x = b + A\dot{g}(A'p, u), \quad \dot{g} = (g_1, \ldots, g_n) \qquad (55)$$

and the uncompensated demand

$$x = b - A\dot{h}(A'p, m - p \cdot b)/h_0, \quad \dot{h} = (h_1, \ldots, h_n). \qquad (56)$$

Substituting from (51) into (55) and (56) we get adjusted compensated demand

$$x^A = \dot{g}(p^A, u) \qquad (57)$$

and adjusted uncompensated demand

$$x^A = -\dot{h}(p^A, m^{A,b})/h_0 \qquad (58)$$

where adjusted income

$$m^{A,b} = m - p \cdot b = m - p^A \cdot b^A = g(p^A, u) = g^{A,b}(p, u) - p \cdot b.$$

Note that one does *not* have incorrectly adjusted demands,

$$x^{A,b} = b^A + \dot{g}(p^A, u)$$
$$= b^A - \dot{h}(p^A, m - p^A, b)/h_0$$

as (52) and (54) might make one expect. This is because

$$p^A \cdot x^{A,b} = p \cdot x - p \cdot b \neq p \cdot x \qquad (59)$$

so that the fundamental relation (49) which underlay our previous analysis no longer holds. However (57) and (58) may be derived from the adjusted cost function

$$g(p^A, u) = \min\{p^A \cdot x^{A,b}: f(x^{A,b}) \geq u\} \qquad (60)$$

and the adjusted indirect utility function

$$u = h(p^A, m^{A,b}) \qquad (61)$$

derived from it by solving $m^{A,b} = g(p^A, u)$.

The components model

The most important application of the sort of linear model introduced in the last section is in the analysis of the demand for closely related goods — but its value depends on the fact that the demand, x, for a wide range of n closely related goods is explained by that, y, for a relatively small number, $m < n$, of components or characteristics common to them. In such a model the A^{-1} of the last section is $m \times n$, so that its inverse A does not exist, and the simple dualistic analysis of that section is not available.

In the simplest case we posit that

where
$$u = f(x, z) = F(y, z), \tag{62}$$

$y = Ax + \phi(z)$, so that $y_r = \sum a_{ri}x_i + \phi^r(z)$, each r, (63)

is the vector of common components, and z those of other goods whose demand we are not considering. We will see that $\phi(z)$ drops out of the main analysis, so that no knowledge of it need be assumed, at least for the moment.

Maximising u subject to the usual budget constraint we find that

$$p_i \leqslant \lambda f_i = \sum_r \lambda F_r a_{ri} = \sum_r q_r a_{ri}, \text{ say, each } i, \tag{64}$$

and

$$p_i = \lambda f_i = \sum_r a_{ri} q_r, \text{ each good } i \text{ is consumed}, \tag{65}$$

where q_r is the shadow price of the rth component.

I will assume in this chapter that all the xs are assumed by the relevant people.

This rather old model (see Gorman 1956) has been extensively discussed by Kelvin Lancaster in the last decade, so that I will say rather little about it here. Its advantage for the practical demand analyst is its simplicity, and ease of estimation by regression if the characteristics

$$a^r = (a_{r1}, \ldots, a_{rn}), \tag{66}$$

are known, at least if there are relatively few of them compared with the number of goods x actually being consumed.

The model we estimate is, of course,

$$p_{ti} = \sum_r a_{ri} q_{tr} + u_{ti}, \tag{67}$$

where t refers to the tth time period or region, and the u_{ti} are 'random errors' arbitrarily assumed to be independent of each other in this paper. This can be estimated by least squares if the a^r are known, and by principal component analysis if they are not once we have somehow normalised the goods to get $E(u_{ti}^2) = \sigma^2$, say.

The disadvantage of this model is that it leaves the demand for the actual goods indeterminate — and the elasticity of demand for any one of them, the shadow prices of the *characteristics* being held constant, infinite. Now this definition of the elasticity does differ from the normal one, but not, I feel, sufficiently to explain the relatively low elasticities observed in practice. There are two obvious ways around this difficulty — if difficulty it is.

Specific components. (62)–(65) attempt to explain the interrelations between the demands of the different xs in terms of a few underlying components. There is nothing in this underlying idea which stops us assuming that we value each partly *for itself*, as in

$$p_i = \sum_r a_{ri} q_r + \psi^i(x_i, z), \text{ say,}$$

$$\doteq \sum_r a_{ri} q_r + c_i x_i + d_i + \sum e_{is} z_s, \text{ say,} \qquad (68)$$

as a local approximation.

Here it is assumed that this specific valuation is independent of the consumption of the other xs, since their effect is assumed to come through the common components.

Take one of the zs as numéraire, z_0, and write $\bar{z}$ as the vector of the remaining zs. Then (68) holds i.f.f. the utility function is of the form

$$u = f(x, z) = F(y, z_0, \bar{z}), \qquad (69)$$

where

$$y_r = \sum a_{ri} x_i + \phi^r(\bar{z}), \text{ each } r > 0, \qquad (70)$$

and

$$z_0 = \sum \theta^i(x_i) + \theta^0(z), \text{ say,} \qquad (71)$$

so that z_0 carries all the specific effects in a surprisingly simple way, and one surprisingly like that in which the y_r carry the common effects.

In practice, of course, we assume that very few of the zs occur in (68), and accordingly in $\theta^0(.)$ too. We will expect that $\dot{\theta}^i(x_i) = d\theta^i/dx_i > 0$, and $\ddot{\theta}^i(x_i) < 0$, corresponding to the old-fashioned assumption of the diminishing marginal utility of individual goods.

Components generated differently. (62)–(63) is basically a simple physical model. Each unit of each good contains so much of each component, and these add up. Even chemically they might interact in all sorts of ways. More importantly, we are really interested in the consumer's basic desires — possibly socially determined for instance, rather than physically or biologically.

Given these facts, there is really no reason to confine ourselves to (62)–(63). The simplest alternatives are Cobb–Douglas components

$$y_r = \pi_i x_i^{a_{ri}}, \quad \sum_i a_{ri} = 1 \qquad (72)$$

and CES components

$$y_r = \left(\sum_i a_{ri} x_i^{(1-\sigma)} \right)^{1/(1-\sigma)} \qquad (73)$$

yielding respectively

$$p_i x_i = m_i = \sum_r a_{ri} v_r, \text{ say,} \qquad (74)$$

and

$$p_i x_i^\sigma = \mu_i = \sum_r a_{ri} w_r, \text{ say.} \qquad (75)$$

The analogy with (66) is striking, and similar methods of estimation obviously apply — once one knows σ in the CES case.

Incidentally v_r can be interpreted as the expenditure $q_r y_r$ on y_r in (74), and w_r as $q_r y_r^\sigma$ in (75).[12] (74) is particularly appropriate for cross sectional data where we frequently know m_i, but neither p_i nor x_i.

These results owe their simplicity to the fact that Cobb-Douglas and CES functions are at once additively separable and homogeneous — as, of course, is the original model. Nevertheless, we can get almost as far allowing for overheads as in (51), at least in the Cobb-Douglas case.

Setting generalised Cobb-Douglas components

$$y_r = \pi_i (x_i - c_i)^{a_{ri}}, \quad \sum_i a_{ri} = 1 \tag{76}$$

we get

$$p_i x_i = m_i = \sum_r a_{ri} v_r + c_i p_i, \text{ each } i, \tag{77}$$

so that the c_i can be estimated as in (68).

SEPARABILITY AND ADDITIVE SEPARABILITY

As I mentioned in the introduction many of the normal economic assumptions are essentially separability assumptions, allowing us to treat different aspects of economic problems in at least partial isolation from each other. It is because of the strength of such simplifications, that economists have been able to think of the economy as a great system of interrelated agents and actions without losing themselves completely. The classic locus of the separability idea lies in the structure of the utility function.

We say the vector x is *separable* in the continuous utility function $u = f(x, y)$ if

$$u = f(x, y) = F(\phi(x), y), \tag{78}$$

where $F(.)$ and $\phi(.)$ are continuous and $F(., y)$ strictly increasing.[13]

Suppose now that we know that the vectors $x_1, x_2, \ldots, x_T$ are each separable in

$$u = f(x) = f(x_0, x_1, \ldots, x_T); \tag{79}$$

then and only then,

$$u = f(x) = F(x_0, \phi^1(x_1), \ldots, \phi^T(x_T)). \tag{80}$$

We say that $f(.)$ is *separable* if x_0 is null so that

$$u = f(x) = f(x_1, \ldots, x_T) = F(\phi^1(x_1), \ldots, \phi^T(x_T))$$

$$= F(v), \quad v_t = \phi^t(x_t), \text{ each } t, \tag{81}$$

where each of the functions is continuous and $F(.)$ strictly monotonic. We will call the $\phi^t(.)$ specific satisfaction functions.

Suppose now that we were told for each t how much, m_t, to spend on goods in group t, at prices p_t. Our job, then, would be to

$$\text{maximise } v_t = \phi^t(x_t) \text{ subject to } p_t \cdot x_t \leq m_t, \text{ for each } t. \tag{82}$$

This would yield 'specific satisfaction functions'

$$v_t = \theta^t(p_t, m_t), \tag{83}$$

and conditional demand functions

$$x_i = -\theta_i^t(p_t, m_t)/\theta_0^t(p_t, m_t) \tag{84}$$

$$= \xi^i(p_t, m_t), \text{ say, each } i \in t, \tag{85}$$

in the obvious notation.

Substituting from (83) into (81) we find

$$u = \eta(p, m_1, m_2, \ldots, m_T), \text{ say.} \tag{86}$$

If $m_1, \ldots, m_T$ is the optimal distribution of $m = \Sigma m_t$ over the groups, they maximise u subject to $m = \Sigma m_t$. This yields

$$m_t = \mu_t(p, m), \text{ say, each } t. \tag{87}$$

What all this is saying is that two stage budgeting is capable of being efficient if the utility function is separable. Given that one has budgetted between groups in the right way — that given by (87) — at the first stage, one need only pay attention to the prices of goods in the group in question, when deciding just how to spend any particular group's allocation m_t as in (85). Moreover equations like (85) hold i.f.f. the utility function is separable.

This would be pretty useless were we really to need to know all the prices in detail to calculate m_t in (87). However the situation is not as bad as that. Should we manage to get to an optimum pattern by some stage we can keep optimum from then on with the aid only of a pair of price indices for each group.

If we believe that people do typically budget in two stages, then, there is some reason to try out separable utility functions in practical demand analysis. It certainly reduces the number of parameters drastically, though not drastically enough to allow us to treat more than a few goods at a time.

Econometricians have therefore been driven to more extreme assumptions, typically to additive separability; that is to assume

$$u = f(x) = f(x_1, \ldots, x_T) = \phi^1(x_1) + \ldots + \phi^T(x_T), \tag{88}$$

in an appropriate normalisation where the x_t are typically, though not necessarily, scalars.

It is clear that not only $x_1, x_2, \ldots, x_T$ are separable here with specific satisfaction functions $\phi^1(x_1), \ldots, \phi^T(x_T)$, but also (x_1, x_2) with $\phi^1(x_1) + \phi^2(x_2)$, (x_1, x_5, x_7) with $\phi^1(x_1) + \phi^5(x_5) + \phi^7(x_7)$ and in general

$$\text{any } (x_i)_{i \in s}, S \subset \{1, 2, \ldots T\}, \text{ is separable.} \tag{89}$$

Debreu (1959) proved long ago that this was necessary and sufficient for additive separability under very general conditions.

The important thing here is that different separable vectors *overlap*. To see how this works let (x, y) and (y, z) be separable in

$$u = f(x, y, z) = G(g(x, y), z) = H(x, h(y, z)), \qquad (90)$$

so that y can be associated first with z, in the calculation of u, x only being brought in later, or first with x, z only being brought in later. As we have already seen this is certainly possible with addition — because of the associative law of addition — and also with increasing transformation of addition — such as multiplication. However it is only such operations — essentially only addition — which are associative in this sense. Hence (90) implies the existence of functions such that

$$u = F(\alpha(x) + \beta(y) + \gamma(z)), F(.) \text{ strictly increasing}, \qquad (91)$$

which can, of course be normalised to give $u = \alpha(x) + \beta(y) + \gamma(z)$.

Note that we did not need to be told that x, y, z or (y, z) were separable to get this result. Their separability is implied by that of (x, y) and (y, z).

Similarly, the separability of $(x_1, x_2), (x_2, x_3), (x_{T-1}, x_T)$ in $u = f(x_1, \ldots x_T)$ is sufficient to yield (88) in an appropriate normalisation; though these are only a small proportion of the vectors listed in (89).

In general, what we need is a good deal of overlap, widely spread. The conditions are detailed in Gorman (1968a). The conditions are sufficiently weak, for surprisingly harmless looking assumptions to imply additive separability.

One simple case is as follows. It is normal to assume that an individual facing uncertainty 'should' pay regard only to the possible outcomes, and that his ranking of consumption vectors forthcoming in any given states of the world 'should be' independent of what he would get in others. If so his utility function is separable in the consumption vectors x_s, due to him in states of the world, for each s. This is essentially the *weak independence axiom*.

Consider now society. Its social welfare function, we assume, depends on the consumption x_{st}, of each citizen t, in each state of the world. Suppose it, too, obeys the weak independence axiom. Then $y_s = (x_{s1}, \ldots, x_{sT})$ is separable for each state s of the world.

If we also assume that society is interested only in the welfare of its individual members, as judged by the members, as is also normal, $z = (x_{1t}, \ldots, x_{st})$ is separable, for each citizen t.

Obviously y_s and z_t overlap at x_{st}, for each s, t, so that there is quite a lot of overlapping and it is pretty pervasive. In fact it is more than enough to imply that, in an appropriate normalisation, the social welfare function is

$$W = \sum \phi^{st}(x_{st}) = \sum \theta^t(z_t), \qquad (92)$$

where

$$\theta^t(z_t) = \sum_s \phi^{st}(x_{st}) \qquad (93)$$

is the tth individual's utility function.

The social welfare function is therefore Benthamite and the individual utility functions additively separable — and all this implied by the *joint* assertion of two assumptions which are almost universally made individually, and the overlapping separabilities these generate.

For this reason, and for its simplicity, additive separability is rather frequently used in economic theory. For this reason, too, it is frequently child's play to dream up plausible excuses for it.

Additive separability has a further advantage. As we will see on pages 228–34 it can be expressed simply in terms of the prices by means of the profit function, so that this 'natural structure' typically need not hinder the choice of 'natural independent variables' in this case. In fact, the profit function corresponding to the utility function (88) is

$$g(p, q) = \max\{qf(x) - p \cdot x\}$$
$$= \sum \psi^t(p_t, q), \qquad (94)$$

where $\psi^t(.)$ is that corresponding to $\phi^t(.)$, so that the simple structure is maintained in this dual form.

We would like something similar to hold in the ordinary separable case (81)–(82). For instance, it would be nice were the corresponding cost function to take the form

$$g(p, u) = G(\psi^1(p_1, u), \ldots, \psi^T(p_T, u), u), \qquad (95)$$

particularly were $G(., u)$ to be that corresponding to $F(.)$, and each $\psi^t(., u)$ that corresponding to $\phi^t(.)$.

In fact this is exactly what does happen under quasi-separability, a related concept introduced in the final section. Unfortunately, nothing like it holds in general under ordinary separability. For instance

$$g(p, u) = \min\{p \cdot x \colon f(x) \geq u\}$$
$$= \min\left\{\sum p_t \cdot x_t \colon F(\phi^1(x_1), \ldots, \phi^T(x_T)) \geq u\right\}$$
$$= \min\left\{\sum \min\{p_t \cdot x_t \colon \phi^t(x_t) \geq v_t\} \colon F(v) \geq u\right\}$$
$$= \min\left\{\sum \psi^t(p_t, v_t) \colon F(v) \geq u\right\}, \qquad (96)$$

where $\psi^t(p_t, v_t)$ is the cost function associated with $\phi^t(.)$.

Unfortunately all this simplicity disappears once we attempt to carry out this last minimisation. The reason is simple: there is no 'price' for the tth specific satisfaction. It is the existence of such a price, the marginal cost of this specific satisfaction, that leads to simple dual specifications under homothetic and quasi-homothetic separability in pages 228–34.

RECONCILING SEPARABILITY AND DUALITY

Homothetic, quasi-homothetic and additive separability

As we saw in the previous section, it is often impossible to state the 'natural' structure of a model in terms of the 'natural' independent variables at all simply, This is a real dilemma. The way to escape is to look for special cases in which it does not arise. Quite often they turn out to be interesting. I will discuss some of the possibilities in this section.

Homothetic separability

$$u = f(x, y) = F(\phi(x), y), \tag{97}$$

where (x, y) is the consumption vector, and $\phi(.)$ is homothetic.

Take $\phi(.)$ to be positively homogeneous of degree one without loss of generality. We may then consider it to be a production function yielding $v = \phi(x)$, units of *'specific satisfaction'* from the consumption of x. The corresponding cost function may be written

$$\psi(p, v) = \min\{p \cdot x : \phi(x) \geqslant v\} = v\alpha(p), \text{ say.} \tag{98}$$

The cost function corresponding to (97) may then be written

$$\begin{aligned} m = g(p, q, u) &= \min\{p \cdot x + q \cdot y : F(\phi(x), y) \geqslant u\} \\ &= \min\{\min\{p \cdot x : \phi(x) \geqslant v\} + q \cdot y : F(v, y) \geqslant u\} \\ &= \min\{v\alpha(p) + q \cdot y : F(v, y) \geqslant u\} \\ &= G(\alpha(p), q, u), \end{aligned} \tag{99}$$

where $G(., u)$ is the cost function corresponding to $u = F(.)$.

Solving (99) for u we get the indirect utility function,

$$u = H(\alpha(p), q, m), H(.) \text{ homogeneous of degree zero,} \tag{100}$$

with a similar interpretation.

An exactly similar argument can be applied when

$$\phi(x) = (\phi^1(x_1), \ldots, \phi^T(x_T)), x = (x_1, \ldots, x_T), \tag{101}$$

is a vector of homothetic specific satisfaction functions, normalised to be positively homogeneous of degree one, with the corresponding vector,

$$\alpha(p) = (\alpha^1(p_1), \ldots, \alpha^T(p_T)), \qquad (102)$$

of unit cost functions. It yields (99)–(100) again in the new notation. This is so in particular when y is null, so that

yields
$$u = f(x) = F(\phi^1(x_1), \ldots, \phi^T(x_T)), \qquad (103)$$
$$m = g(p, u) = G(\alpha(p), u), u = h(p, m) = H(\alpha(p), m), \qquad (104)$$

when each $\phi^t(.)$ is homothetic. That is when the utility function is *homothetically separable*, so are the cost and indirect utility functions. So, for that matter, is the profit function where it exists.[14]

Suppose now that the utility function is both homothetic and separable. Then the Engel curves are straight lines radiating from the origin. Hence so are their projections into x_t-space. Hence each $\phi^t(.)$ is homothetic, and the utility function is also homothetically separable. Normalise the specific satisfaction functions $\phi^t(.)$ in the usual way. Then each is positively homogeneous of degree one. So, it can easily be shown, is $F(.)$.

Consider now a separable cost function $G(., u)$ as in (104). Being homothetic and separable it is homothetically separable. In the usual normalisation each component function $\psi^t(.)$ may be taken to be positively homogeneous of degree one. Do so. Then $G(., u)$ is positively homogeneous of degree one. It has the properties of a cost function, each $\psi^t(.)$ of a unit cost function. Interpreting them as such, the utility function is homothetically separable in the form (103) with the $\phi^t(.)$ the production functions with unit cost functions $\alpha^t(.)$.

The separability of the indirect utility function $h(., m)$ and/or the profit function is equivalent to that of the cost function and accordingly yields the same results.

What all this comes to is that, in the homothetic case 'properly' normalized, the unit cost function has all the properties of a price one 'pays' for each unit of specific satisfaction 'produced under constant returns'. Its 'price' is just its unit cost, in fact. Unfortunately homothetic separability is really too narrow an assumption for most cases. Suppose one of the components were 'food' for instance. Then one would consume the different foods in exactly the same proportions however well off one was, which is not really acceptable.

The obvious generalisation of production under constant average or unit costs
$$g(p, u) = ua(p), \qquad (105)$$

is that under constant marginal costs, illustrated in figure 3,
$$g(p, u) = ua(p) + b(p), \qquad (106)$$

where $b(p)$ are the overhead costs. Once they have been looked after, we shall see, the marginal costs $a(p)$ are almost as good aggregates as the unit costs were under homotheticity.

In (105), the Engel curves are given by

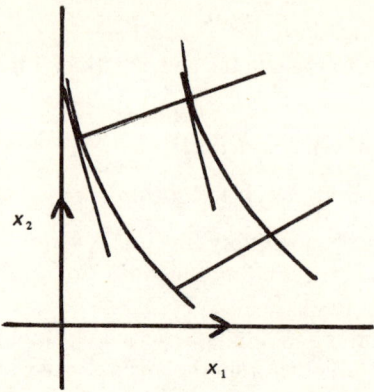

Figure 3 *Quasi-homothetic utility function, with Engel curves*

$$x_i = g_i(p, u) = ua_i(p) = u\mathrm{d}a/\mathrm{d}p_i, \tag{107}$$

so that they are lines radiating from the origin. That this should be so is one definition of homotheticity and is equivalent to assuming that the utility function $u = f(x)$ can be normalised to yield constant returns. or, equivalently, constant unit costs.

(106) yields Engel curves,

$$x_i = g_i(p, u) = ua_i(p) + b_i(p), \tag{108}$$

which are again straight lines. They need not, however, pass through the origin. Let us define a utility function with linear Engel curves as *quasi-homothetic*.

If a utility function can be normalised to have a cost function like (106), it is clearly quasi-homothetic. The converse is also true. To see this, let the cost functions corresponding to $u = 0, u = 1$ be $b(p), a(p) + b(p)$. Then the points of intersection of an Engel curve with these indifference surfaces are $(b_1(p), b_2(p), \ldots, b_n(p)), (b_1(p) + a_1(p), \ldots, b_n(p) + a_n(p))$ and the general point on this straight Engel line is given by

$$x_i = g_i(p, u) = b_i(p) + \theta(p, u)a_i(p), \tag{109}$$

where $\theta(p, u)$ is a current parameter. Multiplying across by p_i and remembering that $g(., u), a(.),$ and $b(.)$ are all positively homogeneous of degree one, we have

$$g(p, u) = \theta(u, p)a(p) + b(p), \tag{110}$$

so that

$$g_i(p, u) = \theta_i a(p) + \theta a_i(p) + b_i(p). \tag{111}$$

Comparing this with (109) and remembering that[15] $a(p) > 0$, we see that $\theta_i(p, u) = 0$, for each i, so that $\theta = \theta(u)$. $\theta(.)$ is clearly strictly monotonic under normal assumptions. We can therefore take $\theta(u)$ as a new utility indicator u^*. u^* is then 'produced' under conditions of constant marginal costs. We will say it yields *constant marginal returns*.

Quasi-homothetic separability

$$u = f(x, y) = F(\phi(x), y), \qquad (112)$$

where (x, y) is once more the consumption vector, but now $\phi(.)$ is only quasi-homothetic. Normalise it so that it yields constant marginal returns. The cost function corresponding to the specific satisfaction function, $v = \phi(x)$, is then

$$\psi(p, v) = \min\{p \cdot x : \phi(x) \geq v\} = v\alpha(p) + \beta(p), \text{ say}, \qquad (113)$$

yielding the cost function,

$$g(p, q, u) = \beta(p) + G(\alpha(p), q, u), \qquad (114)$$

exactly as in the proof of (109), where $G(., u)$ is the cost function corresponding to the utility function $F(.)$. The corresponding indirect utility function is, of course,

$$u = H(\alpha(p), q, m - \beta(p)). \qquad (115)$$

The consumer therefore acts as if his income were $m - \beta(p)$ – 'meets his overheads' that is – and then behaves as if 'specific satisfaction' could be bought at its marginal cost $\alpha(p)$. This is scarcely surprising.

Analogous correlates exist for all the propositions in pages 219–21. We merely replace homothetic by quasi-homothetic, make the 'overheads' the first charge on income, and then treat the marginal costs in the same way as the unit costs were treated above.

In particular we may define

$$u = f(x) = F(\phi^1(x_1), \ldots, \phi^T(x_T)) \qquad (116)$$

to be *quasi-homothetically separable* if each $\phi^t(.)$ is quasi-homothetic. If so we can normalise it to have a cost function $v^t \alpha^t(p_t) + \beta^t(p_t) = \psi^t(p_t, v_t)$. Doing so we find the cost function for $f(.)$ to be

$$m = g(p, u) = G(\alpha^1(p_1), \ldots, \alpha^T(p_T), u) + \sum \beta^t(p_t), \qquad (117)$$

and the indirect utility function

$$u = H\left(\alpha^1(p_1), \ldots, \alpha^T(p_T), m - \sum_t \beta^t(p_t)\right). \qquad (118)$$

Once again analogous results hold for profit functions.

Quasi-homotheticity, like homotheticity above, is inherited by component functions. Thus quasi-homotheticity and separability together imply quasi-homothetic separability— though the converse is of course not true. Either homotheticity or quasi-homotheticity can be followed down a utility tree for this reason, and the results of pages 228–30 generalised accordingly.

Clearly the specification of quasi-homothetically separable preferences in terms of cost, profit or indirect utility functions is nearly as simple as in terms of the utility function. One might even say simpler, because quasi-homotheticity itself is so much more easily expressed in these forms. This is important because sufficiently smooth preferences can always be approximated quasi-homothetically in a given neighbourhood, just as their Engel curves can be by straight lines. I have already pointed out that $\alpha^t(p)$ acts exactly like the price of v_t in the homothetic case, and in the quasi-homothetic case too, once we have taken care of the overheads.

One interesting example of this is that

$$v_t = G_t(\alpha, u) \tag{119}$$

$$v_t = -H\left(\alpha, m - \sum \beta^t(p_t)/H_0(\alpha, m - \sum \beta^t(p_t)\right) \tag{120}$$

in the obvious notation, given (117) and (118) respectively.

To prove (119), note that

$$x_i = g_i(p, u) = \beta_i^t + G_t \alpha_i^t, i \in \{t\}, \tag{121}$$

so that

$$\psi(v_t, p_t) = \sum_{i \in t} p_i x_i = \beta^t + G_t \alpha^t \tag{122}$$

because of the homogeneity of $\beta^t(.)$, $\alpha^t(.)$. Identifying this with $v_t \alpha^t + \beta^t$ below equation (116), we get the desired results.

I leave the proof of (120) to the reader.

Additively separability and duality.

$$u = f(x) = \sum \phi^t(x_t), x = (x_1, \ldots x_T). \tag{123}$$

Additive separability is often assumed or, as we saw on pages 224–28, entailed by apparently harmless postulates. Luckily it can usually be represented quite simply in terms of the profit function

$$g(p, q) = \max\{qf(x) - p \cdot x\}$$

$$= \sum \max\{q\phi^t(x_t) - p_t \cdot x_t\}$$

$$= \sum \psi^t(p_t, q), \text{ say,} \tag{124}$$

where $\psi^t(.)$ is the profit function corresponding to the 'felicity' function $\phi^t(.)$. This in turn yields

$$x_i = -g_i(p, q) = -\psi_i^t(p^t, q), i \in \{t\}, \tag{125}$$

$$u = g_0(p, q) = \sum_t \psi_0^t(p^t, q), \tag{126}$$

if we are lucky.

Let us look a little more closely at these profit functions. Mathematically they are just support functions, and (p, q) are just dummy variables to carry them. However p is a price vector as far as the economist is concerned, and he is tempted to interpret q, too, as the 'price' of utility. To do so, he thinks of utility as a good 'produced' in T independent plants with 'production functions' $\phi^T(.), \ldots, \phi^T(.)$. To do this economically the marginal cost, or shadow price, of 'utility' must be the same everywhere, and it is this constant value which we denote by q.

If a utility, or production, function is to be represented perfectly by a cost function, it must be quasi-concave; if by a profit function, concave. We have already argued that this is not too important a disadvantage in the case of the cost function, because market choices are pretty well represented in any case, and only these matter in many applications. When we represent a utility function by a profit function, the 'market' in question is a purely imaginary one for 'utility', so that this argument is not available. In fact concavity is most important.

To see this, take any consumer with homothetic preferences, and represent them by a utility function of degree two, say. There are rapidly increasing returns to scale, and the competitively efficient way of producing utility will be to consume nothing, or an infinite amount of the goods. That does not give us much of a clue about actual behaviour.

It is normal to assume that utility functions are quasi-concave. Can we not normalise them so as to be concave? Unfortunately not so in general. However, the quasi-concavity of an additive utility function comes close to implying its concavity and that of its component, or felicity, functions.

In fact it implies that at most one of the felicity functions fails to be concave. Suppose, moreover, that there is such a one, and let it be $\phi^s(.)$. Then there exist prices $\bar{p}$ and an income $\bar{m}$, such that expenditure on group s goods rises so rapidly as income increases through $\bar{m}$ that, that on those in *each* other group actually declines. If you like, *all* other groups are inferior.

We will frequently feel able to exclude this case by assumption. If so, each $\phi^t(.)$ will be concave, and with the $\phi(.)$s, $f(.)$, too. Note that this will always be true if, for example $\phi^t(x_t) = a_t \phi(x_t)$, say, $a_t > 0$, for each t, as it frequently is in practice.

By and large, then, the profit function may be expected to give a perfectly good representation of an additive utility function *if it is quasi-concave*. As to why it should be assumed *quasi-concave* in the first case, that is another matter.

Under normal assumptions then the representation of an additive utility function in terms of the profit function is valid and simple. Is it useful?

I personally have found it very useful in many cases, and it underlies much of Ragnar Frisch's work and that of the Rotterdam school, at least implicitly. Yet one must surely feel worried at the mysterious shadow price q of utility appearing in the demand functions (125), even when one realises that, being the marginal cost of utility, it is the inverse of the marginal utility λ of expenditure in general, and in any period.

One answer is that it is exactly this given marginal utility of expenditure which holds the periods together and against which any particular proposal for expenditure would have to be tested.

Another is that $g_{00} \leq 0$ by the concavity[16] of $g(.)$, so that (126) can be solved for q in terms of (p, u) if we wish, to yield the compensated demand equations — and that this is relatively straightforward in principle *because q is after all a scalar*.

Finally

$$m = p \cdot x = -\sum p_i g_i = q_0 g_0 - g$$

$$= \sum (q \psi_0^t(p_t, q) - \psi^t(p_t, q)) \tag{127}$$

is also monotonic in q, and may be solved in terms of (p, m) to yield the ordinary demand equations.

More general homothetic and quasi-homothetic household technologies

There is very little in the last section to stop the same good being used for several different purposes, just as electricity is used both for cooking and lighting. The critical point is that the *same* unit of the good should not contribute to different ends.

Suppose, for instance, that

$$u = f(x) = \max\left\{F(\phi^1(x_1), \phi^2(x_2), \ldots): \sum x_t \leq x\right\}, \tag{128}$$

where the $\phi^t(.)$ yield constant marginal returns, so that their cost functions

$$\psi^t(p, v_t) = \min\{p \cdot x_t: \phi^t(x_t) \geq v_t\} = v_t \alpha^t(p) + \beta^t(p), \text{ say, each } t. \tag{129}$$

The cost function

$$m = g(p, u) = \min\{p \cdot x: f(x) \geq u\}$$

$$= \min\left\{p \cdot \sum x_t : F(\phi^1(x_1), \ldots) \geq u\right\}$$

$$= \min\left\{\sum \min\{p \cdot x_t: \phi^t(x_t) \geq v_t\} : F(v) \geq u\right\}$$

$$= \min\left\{\sum v_t \alpha^t(p) + \sum \beta^t(p): F(v) \geq u\right\}$$

$$= G(\alpha^1(p), \ldots, \alpha^T(p), u) + \sum_t \beta^t(p), \tag{130}$$

where $G(., u)$ is the cost function corresponding to $F(.)$. Solving this for u we get the indirect utility function

$$u = H\left(\alpha^1(p), \ldots, \alpha^T(p), m - \sum \beta^t(p)\right). \tag{131}$$

If each $\alpha^t(.)$ is a marginal cost function[17] and each $\beta^t(.)$ and $G(.,u)$ a cost function, then (130) in turn implies (128) at least over an appropriate domain. Similar results hold for (131).

(128), (130) and (131) look very like (116)–(118). Indeed they are direct generalisations of them.

To see this, consider the case where

$$x_1 = (\bar{x}_1, 0, \ldots 0), \ldots x_T = (0, 0, \ldots, \bar{x}_T) \tag{132}$$

so that

$$x = \sum x_t = (\bar{x}_1, \bar{x}_2, \ldots, \bar{x}_T) = \bar{x}, \text{ say}, \tag{133}$$

$$\phi^t(x_t) = \bar{\phi}^t(\bar{x}_t), \text{ say, each } t, \tag{134}$$

$$\psi^t(p, v_t) = \min\{p \cdot x_t : \phi^t(x_t) \geq v_t\}$$
$$= \min\{p_t \cdot \bar{x}_t : \bar{\phi}^t(\bar{x}_t) \geq v_t\}$$
$$= \bar{\psi}^t(p_t, v_t), \text{ say},$$
$$= v_t \bar{\alpha}^t(p_t) + \bar{\beta}^t(p_t), \text{ say}. \tag{135}$$

Substituting from (133) and (134) into (128) and from (134) into (130) and (131), we get (116)–(118), as required, with a few bars spattered about.

The forward argument from the direct utility function (128) or (116), to the cost function (130) or (118), is the same, then, in each case. However, there is a complication about arguing from a cost function (130) to a utility function (128). Cost functions have special properties. They are closed, concave and positively homogeneous of degree one. For (130) to imply (128), $G(.,u)$ and the $\beta(.)$s have to have these properties, and the $\alpha(.)$s have to be the differences between pairs of such functions.

In the separable case (117) the αs, for instance, depend on different prices. This may allow one to isolate each individual $\alpha(.)$ in turn; for instance by setting the other prices equal to zero. Having isolated it, we may be able to derive the required properties for it in particular problems.[18] No such tricks are available in the more general case (130) now under discussion.

The closed forms (130) and (131) are, of course, a lot simpler to deal with than (128). Why, then, should we wish to derive (128) at all? Commonly, I think, the only real reason will be that we may feel we have a better intuitive grasp of what 'is really going on' when we do so. Partly, of course, this is a culture lag. We are accustomed to direct formulations like (128), and feel more at home with them.

One example of the value of (130) and (131) is that (119) and (120) carry across to this case too, so that

$$v_t = G_t(\alpha, u) = -H_t\left(\alpha, m - \sum \beta^t\right) \Big/ H_0\left(\alpha, m - \sum \beta^t\right). \tag{136}$$

The first follows directly from the fact that, $G(., u)$, the cost function associated with $F(.)$ is given by

$$G(\alpha, u) = \min\left\{\sum \alpha^t v_t : F(v) \geq u\right\}, \tag{137}$$

I leave the proof of the second to the reader.

A similar generalisation is available for the additively separable case (123) and (124).

The profit function corresponding to the utility function

$$u = f(x) = \max\left\{\sum \phi^t(x_t) : \sum x_t \leq x\right\} \tag{138}$$

is

$$g(p, q) = \max\{qf(x) - p \cdot x\}$$

$$= \max\left\{q \sum \phi^t(x_t) - p \cdot \sum x_t\right\}$$

$$= \sum \max\{q\phi^t(x_t) - p \cdot x_t\}$$

$$= \sum \psi^t(p, q), \tag{139}$$

where $\psi^t(.)$ is the profit function corresponding to $\phi^t(.)$. However the argument deriving the crucial concavity of the $\phi^t(.)$ largely from the assumed quasi-concavity of $f(.)$ is not available here. It will have to be assumed explicitly, or derived from other considerations.

One example of this sort of analysis is a variant of the components model discussed above, chosen because it can be estimated in the same way as the original simple model

$$u = f(x, y) = \max\{F(v, y) : \sum x_t \leq x\}, \tag{140}$$

where

$$v = (v_1, \ldots v_T); v_t = \left(\sum_i a_{ti} x_{ti}^{(1-\sigma)}\right)^{1/(1-\sigma)} \tag{141}$$

so that

$$\psi^t(p, v_t) = \min\left\{p \cdot x_t : v_t = \left(\sum_i a_{ti} x_{ti}^{(1-\sigma)}\right)^{1/(1-\sigma)}\right\}$$

$$= v_t \left(\sum_i b_{ti} p_i^{(1-\tau)}\right)^{1/(1-\tau)} = v_t \alpha^t(p), \text{ say,} \tag{142}$$

where

$$\sigma\tau = 1, b_{ti} = a_{ti}^\tau. \tag{143}$$

Hence

Tricks with utility functions

$$g(p, y, u) = \min\{p \cdot x : f(x, y) \geq u\}$$
$$= G(\alpha^1(p), \ldots, \alpha^T(p), y, u), \text{ say,} \quad (144)$$

by an argument similar to that leading to (130). This yields compensated demand functions

$$x_i = g_i(p, y, u) = \sum_t G_t \alpha_i^t$$

so that

$$= \sum_t v_t b_{ti}(p_i/\alpha^t(p))^{-\tau} \quad (145)$$

$$p_i^\tau x_i = \sum_t b_{ti}(\alpha^t(p))^\tau v_t). \quad (146)$$

Assume τ known and set

$$p_i^\tau x_i = m_i, \; \alpha^t(p)^\tau v_t = M_t, \quad (147)$$

to get

$$m_i = \sum_t b_{ti} M_t. \quad (148)$$

Adding a disturbance term, we estimate the bs and Ms from time series or cross-sectioned data by, for example, component analysis.

Note that v_t and α^t are the 'quantity' and 'price' of the tth component respectively — so that the definitions of M_t and m_i in (147) are in line with each other.

As $\sigma \to 0$ we approach the limiting Cobb–Douglas case, where we analyse the expenditures $m_i = p_i x_i$ into components. This is a useful model because prices and quantities may not be available in surveys, while expenditures frequently are.

Note that the analysis of the Cobb–Douglas case here is precisely the same as on pages 221–4, even though the same unit of a good ministers to several different ends there, and to one here. This is an interesting case of non-identifiability, but I will not discuss it here.

The components v_t in (142)–(146) were both additively separable and homothetic. Each quality contributed to the simplicity of the analysis. However, we can replace homotheticity by quasi-homotheticity here, too. We normalise to write the components

$$v_t = \left(\sum_i b_{ti}(x_{ti} - e_{ti})^{1-\sigma} \right)^{1/(1-\sigma)}, \text{ each } t \quad (149)$$

instead of (141) and find

$$g(p, y, u) = \sum e_i p_i + G(\alpha^1(p), \ldots, \alpha^T(p), u) \quad (150)$$

instead of (144) where $e_i = \Sigma_t e_{ti}$ is the essential minimum of good i in the obvious interpretation of the model.

Quasi-separable, pseudo-separable, and related household technologies

By now you will have noticed how very much easier it is to move back and forward between primal and dual representatives if the original utility function is homothetic, and how much more easy to apply dualistic arguments to separable utility if its components are positively homogeneous of degree one.[19] Noticing that the dualistic representations are necessarily homogeneous of degree one, suggests one possible reason for this phenomenon, especially when we remember the symmetry of the relation $p \cdot x = m$ connecting the two.

This suggests that we should seek a homogeneous representation of tastes in x-space, and found a separability concept on it.

Consider a utility function
$$u = \theta(x), \tag{151}$$
and define
$$f(x, u) = k \quad \text{if} \quad u = \theta(x/k). \tag{152}$$

Then $f(., u)$ is clearly positively homogeneous of degree one, and the consumer's preferences are represented by
$$f(x, u) = 1. \tag{153}$$

The interpretation of $f(x, u)$ is also clear — it tells us proportionately how much more of each good we have than we need to reach the given level of utility. Thus $f(x, u) = 2$ means that we could throw away just half of our supplies and still reach u. It is therefore an acceptable index of quantity, *given u*.

The corresponding cost function is
$$g(p, u) = \min\{p \cdot x : f(x, u) = 1\}, \tag{154}$$
which is equally satisfactory as a price index, *given u*. Moreover
$$f(x, u) = \min\{p \cdot x : g(p, u) = 1\}. \tag{155}$$

The easiest and most revealing way to see (155) is to look at the product
$$f(x, u) g(p, u) = k g(p, u) \leq k p \cdot x^* = p \cdot x, \text{ each } k \geq 0, \tag{156}$$
where
$$f(x^*, u) = 1, \quad x^* = x/k. \tag{157}$$

Now let us say that p and x are *conjugates at the level of utility u* if the cheapest way to reach u when prices are of the form ap is $x^* = x/k$, say.

Suppose $\bar{p}, \bar{x}$ are conjugates at u. Then
$$f(\bar{x}, u) g(\bar{p}, u) = k g(\bar{p}, u) = k \bar{p} \cdot x^* = \bar{p} \cdot \bar{x}. \tag{158}$$

(156) and (157) yield (154) if we set up $p = \bar{p}$, and (155) if we put $x = \bar{x}$.

The notable symmetry to be observed in (154) and (155), (156) and (158) is the strength of this representation. It allows one to move back and forth between the primal and dual representation effortlessly.

Moreover
$$p_i = f_i(x, u) \quad \text{when} \quad m = g(p, u) = 1 \tag{159}$$
follows from (155) in exactly the same way as $x_i = g_i(p, u)$ did from (4) on page 214, when $f(x, u) = 1$, that is $u = \theta(x)$.

Tricks with utility functions 239

Let us now say that preferences are *quasi-separable* if

$$f(x, u) = F(\phi^1(x_1, u), \ldots, \phi^T(x_T, u), u), \quad (160)$$

where we can without loss of generality take each $\phi^t(., u)$, and hence $F(., u)$, to be positively homogeneous of degree one. Then

$$\begin{aligned}
g(p, u) &= \min\{p \cdot x : f(x, u) \geq 1\} \\
&= \min\left\{\sum p_t \cdot x_t : F(\phi^1(x_1, u), \ldots, u) \geq 1\right\} \\
&= \min\left\{\sum \min\{p_t \cdot x_t : \phi^t(x_t, u) \geq v_t\} : F(v, u) \geq 1\right\} \\
&= \min\left\{\sum \min\{p_t \cdot v_t x_t^* : \phi^t(x_t^*, u) \geq 1\} : F(v, u) \geq 1\right\} \\
&= \min\left\{\sum v_t \psi^t(p_t, u) : F(v, u) \geq 1\right\} \\
&= G(\psi^1(p_1, u), \ldots, \psi^T(p_T, u), u), \quad (161)
\end{aligned}$$

where $\psi^t(., u)$ is the cost function corresponding to $\phi^t(., u)$, for each t, and $G(., u)$ that corresponding to $F(., u)$.

This is a very pleasant result, maintaining the structure of $F(., u)$ in the simplest possible way. Moreover the symmetry of (154) and (155), (156) and (158), implies that we can argue from (161) to (160) in exactly the same way.

Equation (161) implies that

$$x_i = g_i(p, u) = G_t(\psi^1(p_1, u), \ldots, \psi^T(p_T, u), u) \, \psi_i^t(p_t, u), \quad (162)$$

$$m_t = p_t \cdot x_t = G_t(\psi^1(p_1, u), \ldots \psi^T(p_T, u), u) \psi^t(p_t, u). \quad (163)$$

Now p_t and x_t are clearly conjugate at u,[20] so that

$$p_t \cdot x_t = \phi^t(x_t, u) \psi^t(p_t, u) = v_t \psi^t(p_t, u). \quad (164)$$

Hence

$$v_t = G(\psi^1(p_1, u), \ldots, \psi^T(p_T, u), u), \quad (165)$$

and

$$x_i = v_t \psi_i^t(p_t, u) = m_t \psi_i^t(p_t, u)/\psi^t(p_t, u). \quad (166)$$

How should (163), (165) and (166) be interpreted?

First notice that $\psi^t(., u)$ and $\phi^t(., u)$ being positive, increasing and positively homogeneous of degree one, provide rather acceptable price and quantity indices for group t. That they should depend on the consumer's overall standard of living u is rather acceptable, too.

Equations (163) and (165) then say that, given his overall standard of living, the consumer's money, m_t, and real expenditure, v_t, on goods in group t depends only on these price indices, so that allocation between groups depends only on the price levels in them.

Equation (166) refers to allocation within group t. It says that, given real expenditure v_t, or money expenditure m_t, then consumption of the individual goods in group *t* depends only on *their* prices p_t and the consumer's overall standard of living. Once more a very acceptable notion of separability. So far so good.

Unfortunately (166) does have one less acceptable implication.

Hold the consumer's general standard of living u constant and vary the prices in *other* groups in such a way as to increase m_t — say double it. The consumption x_i of each good in group t will then double too. It is not fair to say that we cannot group luxury and utility versions of the same good together. After all, the x_i, $i \in t$, may vary in quite a different manner as u increases. Nevertheless this proportional variation in the x_i, $i \in t$ is something one must bear in mind in deciding whether or not to use models based on quasi-separability.

The property referred to in the paragraph beginning '(163) and (165) . . .' above is equivalent to quasi-separability, as is that referred to in that beginning '(166) . . .'. Hence one cannot have either of these rather desirable properties without the less desirable one which we have just been discussing.

There is nothing in the discussion above which implies that u is a scalar.[21] We can apply it, for instance, to a short run technology in a firm with a fixed equipment vector u. Or u may be replaced everywhere[22] by a vector (u, y) where y is a vector giving the consumption of some goods which we do not want to represent by their prices.

We can generalise this concept in much the same way as we did homothetic and quasi-homothetic separability on pages 228-34.

Define the homogeneous representation

$$f(x, u) = \max \left\{ F(\phi^1(x_1, u), \ldots, \phi^T(x_T, u), u) : \sum x_t = x \right\}, \quad (167)$$

where each $\phi^t(., u)$, thence $F(., u)$ too, is positively homogeneous of degree one. Let $\psi^t(., u)$, $F(., u)$ be the corresponding cost function. Then, easily, that corresponding to $f(., u)$ is

$$g(p, u) = G(\psi^1(p, u), \psi^2(p, u), \ldots, \psi^T(p, u), u), \quad (168)$$

and it can also be shown that

$$v_t = \phi^t(x_t, u) = G_t \quad (169)$$

while, as before,

$$x_i = \sum G_t \psi_i^t = \sum v_t \psi_i^t. \quad (170)$$

An alternative generalisation, which I have found quite helpful in taking a preliminary glance at the housing market, can be constructed in the following manner.

There are, of course, many representations of the form

$$f(x, u) \gtreqless 1, \text{ according as } \theta(x) \gtreqless u, \quad (171)$$

for any given utility function $u = \theta(x)$ as long as we do not require homogenity. If $\theta(x) > 0$, $\theta(x)/u$ is one. Let us say that the preference field is *pseudo-separable*

if
$$f(x, u) = F(\phi^1(x_1, u), \ldots, \phi^T(x_T, u), u) \tag{172}$$

for such a representation, where $x = (x_1, \ldots x_T)$, is a partitioned consumption vector and $f(., u)$, $F(., u)$ and the $\phi^t(., u)$ need not be homogeneous.

Pseudo-separability includes both quasi-separability — use the homogeneous representation — and ordinary separability — use $\theta(x)/u$. Its defining characteristic is that the marginal rate of substitution in between two goods in the same group t, depends only on each t.

Quasi-separability bears the same relation to pseudo-separability as homothetic separability to separability proper. We saw on pages 228–34 that quasi-homothetic separability has effectively the same simple properties as homothetic separability. The same is true of *quasi-homothetic pseudo-separability* as defined by

$$g^t(p_t, v_t, u) = \min\{p_t \cdot x_t : f^t(x_t, u) \geq v_t\} = v_t a^t(p_t, u) + b^t(p_t, u), \tag{173}$$

and quasi-separability equals homothetic pseudo-separability. Note that u is treated as a parameter in (173).

Using quasi-homothetic pseudo-separability instead of quasi-separability relaxes (166) in an obvious manner. Since we found (166) rather disquieting, this is reassuring.

Quasi-separability and quasi-homogeneous pseudo-separability can be generalised in much the same manner as homothetic and quasi-homothetic separability was on pages 234–37.

NOTES

1 I have been brooding over the general ideas in this paper off and on over the last 25 years, and have discussed them with too many people to mention — though I would like to thank in particular, Sydney Afuat, whose own work in this field is grossly undervalued, for many stimulating discussions.
   May I thank the British Social Science Research Council, whose support has led to me getting some of these notions into print at last, and attempting to apply them to practical problems.
2 Strictly 'inf' rather than 'min', since the minimum might be unattainable. I will neglect this nicety throughout this paper.
3 Note that $g(p, .)$ will be strictly increasing under normal assumptions, certainly when $p > 0$.
4 Given a little weak continuity. In fact this holds almost everywhere in general, and everywhere in most practical examples.
5 Strictly, the cost function is closed concave, but the distinction need not worry us here. In most cases, only positive consumption will be possible, so that we will tend to assume $g(., u)$ increasing, too.
6 There are several possible definitions of homotheticity. The most common is that a function is homothetic if it is a function of a homogeneous function. All such functions are either themselves homogeneous of degree zero or functions of functions which are homogeneous of degree one. In many economic interpretations we have reason to reject homogeneity of degree zero — for

example, because our functions are strictly increasing. The alternative definition therefore is that a function is homothetic if it is a function of a function which is homogeneous of degree one. Equivalently we can define it as having Engel curves which are straight lines radiating from the origin, or ruled surfaces generated by such lines.

7 This might be called a Laspeyres type approach. It probably does represent the idea which underlies wage negotiations for instance. An alternative Paasche type approach would yield a basis $u^{**} = h(p, m)$ of comparison and an index number $I = m/g(\bar{p}, u^{**})$, telling how much money $m^{**} = g(\bar{p}, u^{**})$ the consumer would have needed with initial prices $\bar{p}$ and initial tastes, to have been just as well off as he would have been facing the present budgetary situation $(p \cdot m)$ with these initial tastes.

Fisher and Shell point out quite rightly that this type of approach is appropriate even if the preference ordering has not changed, because there is no reason to believe that one's capacity for innocent enjoyment has not. Of course, it gives the same result as the conventional approach in such cases.

8 Each assumed taken under the present taste regime a, of course.
9 That is the preference ordering over the $x^a = (x_1/a_1, x_2, \ldots x_n)$ is the same now as that over the x was initially.
10 I had planned to discuss their work in detail but unfortunately it would have led to this section dominating the chapter. It turned out to be uneconomic to consider just one or two points: the common overheads are too large.
11 The first economist to write down (49) seems to have been Samuelson in his *Foundations*. Of course any economist who had read any relativity theory must have realised its existence and import before that.
12 Remember that only the xs are needed in the production of the ys in (73).
13 The preference ordering indicated by $\phi(.)$ over x space is thought of as being derived from that indicated by $f(.)$ over (x, y) space holding y constant. This is why $F(., y)$ is strictly increasing.
14 Or, if you prefer, is finite.
15 Assuming it costs more to attain $u = 1$ than $u = 0$!
16 We would really need strict concavity — corresponding to the smoothness of the preference relation.
17 That is, the difference between two increasing closed concave functions, each positively homogeneous of degree one.
18 See, for example, Gorman (1968b, section VII).
19 However quasi-homotheticity — yielding a marginal cost function — proved the really important thing. This is taken up on page 241 below.
20 Since x_t would be the cheapest way of acquiring utility u at prices p, were u defined implicitly be $\phi^t(x_t, u) = 1$.
21 Admittedly we did write $u = \theta(x)$, but this was purely incidental. It might, for example, have been $u = \theta(x, y)$, and $f(x, y, u) = 1$ where $f(., y, u)$ is homothetic. Then (u, y) would be the vector u.
22 The statements $u = \theta(x)$ in that argument are purely incidental as in note 21.

REFERENCES

Anton Barten, 1964: 'Family composition, prices and expenditure patterns' in *Econometric analysis for national economic planning* edited by P.E. Hart, G. Mills and J.K. Whitaker, Butterworths, 1964.

Franklin Fisher and Karl Shell, 1968: 'Taste and quality changes in the pure theory of the true cost of living index' in *Value, capital and growth, papers in honour of Sir John Hicks* edited by J.N. Wolfe, Edinburgh University Press, 1968.

G. Debreu, 1959: 'Topological Methods in Cardinal Utility Theory', in Arrow, Karlin and Suppes: *Mathematical Methods in the Social Sciences*, 1959 (Stanford University Press, 1960).

W.M. Gorman, 1956: 'The demand for related goods: a possible procedure for analysing quality differentials in the egg market', Journal paper no. J3129, Iowa Agricultural Experiment Station, November 1956.

W.M. Gorman, 1968a: 'The structure of utility functions'. *Review of Economic Studies* 35, 367–90.

W.M. Gorman, 1968b: 'Measuring the quantities of fixed factors' in *Value, capital and growth, papers in honour of Sir John Hicks* edited by J.N. Wolfe, Edinburgh University Press, 1968.

Kelvin Lancaster, 1967: 'A new approach to consumer theory.' *Journal of Political Economy* 74, 132–57.

12 WHATEVER HAPPENED TO THE LABOUR THEORY OF VALUE ?

RONALD L. MEEK[1]

The title I have chosen for this paper is of course misleading and meretricious. What I am actually going to do is to deliver some random reflections on the current controversy over the so-called 'transformation problem' — i.e. the problem of the conversion or transformation of Marx's volume I 'values' and surplus values into his volume III prices of production and profits. During the last few years this seemingly rather esoteric problem has assumed a degree of importance which those of us who dabbled in it in the 1940s and 1950s never dreamed possible. For most of us in those innocent days the problem appeared to be at bottom a purely formal one, and once it had been shown to be technically soluble we breathed a sigh of relief and turned our attention to higher things. But with the recent revival of interest in Marxian economics the whole business of the transformation problem has come on to the agenda again. Every other journal that you open these days contains an article on some aspect or other of the transformation problem; symposia have been conducted on it in a number of countries; and there have been colloquia on it in the *Journal of Economic Literature* and the *Bulletin of the Conference of Socialist Economists*. The odd thing is that nowadays everyone treats the issues involved as immensely serious: the particular attitude you take towards it is widely supposed to be indicative of your position on a whole number of other quite different issues. It has got all mixed up with Sraffa's commodity-production models, with the capital controversy, and with the associated question of the so-called Ricardo—Marx tradition in the history of economic thought, forming a witch's brew of considerable potency which Samuelson periodically emerges to sniff and stir.

In this paper, I am not going to try to *analyse* these recent contributions — many of which I have not read, and most of which I am sure I do not fully understand — but rather to steer my way through them as quickly as possible in order to get around to one of the most important of the problems which the debate has brought into relief: the problem of why Marx thought it necessary to 'start with values'. Why did he think that *anything* had to be 'transformed' in order to arrive at prices? And if something *did* have to be 'transformed' in order to arrive at them, why did it have to be these mysterious, non-observable, volume I 'values'?

Let us go right back to the beginning and try to describe, as briefly and simply as possible, what the famous transformation problem is all about. Marx started off in volume I of *Capital* with a definition[2] of the 'value' of a commodity as the total quantity of labour which was normally required to produce a unit of it, and proceeded with his analysis on the assumption that the prices at which commodities sold on the market would normally be proportionate to their 'values' in this sense.[3] In particular, this assumption was retained in his famous analysis of surplus value in parts III and IV of volume I, in which he laid the theoretical foundations for his explanation of the origin, persistence, and level of capitalist profit. Then, much later, in volume III of *Capital*, he endeavoured to bring his volume I analysis into closer contact with reality by means of an operation which he described as the 'conversion' or 'transformation' of surplus values into profits and (consequentially) of 'values' into prices of production. The easiest way of explaining this operation of Marx's is in terms of the following very simple three-industry 'value' schema:

	c	v	s	a
I	20 +	80 +	80 =	180
II	50 +	50 +	50 =	150
III	80 +	20 +	20 =	120

Here the economy is assumed to consist of three industries, I, II, and III, each of which employs a capital of 100 (in 'value' terms). The symbols have their usual Marxian meanings: c is constant capital, v is variable capital, s is surplus value, and a is simply the sum of these three quantities. The exploitation ratio s/v is assumed to be the same in each industry, but the organic composition of capital c/v is assumed to be different in each. Now in volume I of *Capital*, as we have just seen, Marx assumes throughout that all commodities sell at prices which are equal to (or proportionate to) their 'values'. If this were in fact true in the present case, it would mean that the whole of the surplus value generated in the production of each of the three commodities would accrue directly to the capitalist producer *of that commodity* in the form of a net gain when he sold the commodity on the market. An implication of this, of course, is that since the organic composition of capital differs from one industry to another, the ratio of net gain to capital (i.e. roughly the rate of profit) would also differ. But such a situation would in fact be impossible under capitalism, at any rate if we assume a reasonably high degree of mobility of capital between different industries. In that case, clearly, prices would have to adjust, diverging from 'values' to the extent necessary to equalise the rate of profit over the economy as a whole.

What this process of adjustment in effect amounted to, Marx argued in part II of volume III, was the sharing-out of the *total* amount of surplus value generated in the economy among the different industries in accordance with the ratio which the capital employed in each industry bore to the total capital employed in the economy as a whole. In the simple economy of our three-industry schema, a total of 150 surplus value is produced. Each industry employs $\frac{1}{3}$ of the total capital, so each receives ⅓ of the total surplus value, i.e. 50, in the form of profit. This 50 profit is added to the 100 capital employed in each industry to form in each case a 'price of production' of 150. Thus the price of the product of industry I will be ⅚ of its 'value'; that of the product of industry II (where the organic composition of capital equals the social average) will be equal to its 'value'; and that of the product of industry III will be $1\frac{1}{4}$ times its 'value'. The rate of profit in each industry will be $\frac{1}{2}$ (i.e. 50%).

Now, it will help to pave the way for what will shortly follow if we stretch an ideological point or two and allow ourselves to say that what Marx's procedure *in effect* amounted to was the setting-up and solution of a system of simultaneous equations of the general form:

$$c_1 + v_1 + r(c_1 + v_1) = a_1 p_1,$$
$$c_2 + v_2 + r(c_2 + v_2) = a_2 p_2,$$
$$c_3 + v_3 + r(c_3 + v_3) = a_3 p_3,$$
$$r\left[\sum(c+v)\right] = \sum s.$$

Here c, v, s, and a have the same meanings as before; r is the average rate of profit; and p_1, p_2, and p_3 are what may be called the price-value coefficients — i.e. the numbers by which the 'values' of the three products have to be multiplied in order to arrive at prices which satisfy the conditions of the problem. The fourth equation, of course, embodies the postulate that the sum of the profits is equal to the sum of the surplus values. Substituting the values for the cs, the vs, the ss, and the as which we used in our numerical example, we naturally get the same results for the unknowns as we did before: p_1 works out at $\frac{5}{6}$, p_2 at 1, p_3 at $1\frac{1}{4}$, and r at $\frac{1}{2}$.

The particular aspect of Marx's method of transformation upon which most attention has been concentrated is the fact that he transformed only outputs, and not inputs, from 'values' into prices. Once again let us put the problem as simply as possible. Suppose that industry I produces capital goods and industry II produces workers' consumption goods. Then, surely, if you apply a particular price-value coefficient to one of these commodities when it appears in the equations as an *output*, you ought also at the same time to apply it to this same commodity whenever it appears as an *input*. If you in fact did this, would you or could you get a determinate solution? This was the form in which the problem usually presented itself to my generation. There was a certain amount of debate about it, but it was not too long before everyone was (or appeared to be) satisfied that the problem was really a very trivial one indeed. One of the landmarks in the debate was Bortkiewicz's solution; but the two really decisive ones — and the only ones I shall have time to say anything about in this paper — were those of Winternitz and Seton.

Winternitz (1948) used a simple three-industry model, in which industry I was assumed to produce capital goods and industry II workers' consumption goods. This meant that the price-value coefficient p_1, applied in Marx's method only to the output a_1, would also have to be applied to the inputs c_1, c_2, and c_3; and that the price-value coefficient p_2, applied in Marx's method only to the output a_2, would also have to be applied to the inputs v_1, v_2, and v_3. Thus Winternitz began with a 'transformed' schema consisting of the three equations:

$$c_1 p_1 + v_1 p_2 + r(c_1 p_1 + v_1 p_2) = a_1 p_1,$$
$$c_2 p_1 + v_2 p_2 + r(c_2 p_1 + v_2 p_2) = a_2 p_2,$$
$$c_3 p_1 + v_3 p_2 + r(c_3 p_1 + v_3 p_2) = a_3 p_3.$$

For full determinacy a fourth equation was needed. Winternitz used

$$a_1 p_1 + a_2 p_2 + a_3 p_3 = a_1 + a_2 + a_3$$

which embodies the postulate that the sum of the prices is equal to the sum of the 'values'. Alternatively, of course, he could have used an equation embodying the equality of the sum of the profits and the sum of the surplus values; or he could have employed the *numéraire* trick and set the price-value coefficient in the case of one of the industries as equal to 1. In any event, when the problem was posed in this way the solution was obviously simple.

Once the technical job had been done, it was difficult to understand why the transformation problem had seemed such a great one. It remained only to generalise the analysis. Why should the number of industries in the model be restricted to three? Why should it be assumed that the ultimate use of each product in the economy was invariable and predetermined by its industry of origin? Seton (1957), in what I myself still regard as the most distinguished of all the contributions to the debate, generalised the analysis on the basis of a kind of Leontief input–output model, assuming an n-fold subdivision of the economy, in which each product might be allocated among several or all possible uses. Everything was solved. You still needed the counterpart of a fourth equation in order to get the model to yield absolute as distinct from relative prices, and there was no good reason for selecting any one of the various candidates for this equation rather than any other; but with this limitation the problem was technically soluble.

I must apologise for introducing an element of autobiography here. In 1956 I had published a modest piece on the transformation problem (Meek, 1967, pp. 143–57), which had taken me a long time to write but which contained two or three rather egregious errors. These errors were taken up by Seton and exposed (in the nicest possible way) in his article — which seemed indeed to have been in part inspired by them. So I comforted myself with the reflection that there were more ways than one of going down in history, and turned my attention to other things. It was not until 1971 that I realised that the issue was by no means as dead as I had thought. In that year Samuelson (1971) published a very long and involved piece on the transformation problem, in which he had the bad taste to resurrect this old article of mine and commend it to his readers. But worse than this, he had the temerity to fling out a challenge in one place in the article to 'Dobb and Meek' and in another to 'Marx and Meek'. To be placed second in these pairs was of course quite infuriating, and I decided that I ought to give at any rate a *little* attention to what had been and apparently still was going on in this field.

I found that a number of very curious things had been going on, and as the 1970s proceeded they became curiouser and curiouser. Seton, having already successfully solved the transformation problem forwards, as it were, had joined with Morishima (1961) to solve it backwards as well, just for good measure – an exercise which I could not help applauding, even if only as an acrobatic feat. Morishima (1973) then went on to demonstrate that positive profits will be yielded if and only if there is positive surplus value in Marx's sense, and proclaimed this, with portentous capital letters, as the 'Fundamental Marxian Theorem', thereby implying (at any rate to one untutored and unmathematical reader) that this was all that really mattered, and that attempts at the quantitative derivation of a specific rate of profit from a pool of surplus value of a determinate size were at the best merely of heuristic value. I was a little more worried about this, since it seemed to leave a great deal of Marxian economics as I understood it resting on a very slender pediment indeed – and a pediment which I felt might well disappear entirely if one dropped two or three of Morishima's less realistic assumptions. But I was cheered by the fact that at about the same time a number of other writers were beginning to ask what Marx's reproduction schemes, and his law of the falling tendency of the rate of profit, would look like if you redid his analysis in terms of prices of production instead of in terms of 'values' – which seemed to me to be a very useful question to ask.

During the last two or three years, the transformation problem seems to have become the focus of a rather bitter quarrel between two rival groups of radical economists – those who see Marx as having worked within a broad tradition or stream of thought with Ricardo at one end and Sraffa at the other, and those who see Marx as standing more or less outside this (and every other) stream of thought. Members of the latter group, so far as I can gather, usually tend to reject all the traditional methods of solving the transformation problem as being not only unacceptable but also unnecessary, and to anathematise them, along with Sraffa and all his wicked works, as 'neo-Ricardian'. In contrast, members of the former group usually tend to accept one or another of the traditional methods of solution (although for some of them a great deal seems to hang on choosing the *right* method from among the various alternatives), and to stress the strong analogy which they believe exists between Marx's work and Sraffa's in this respect. This debate has become very fierce, particularly when it impinges on the capital controversy (which of course it frequently does); and the word 'logical' is used so very often by the participants that one senses immediately that religion is heavily involved. Personally, although I have some sympathy for both points of view, and am no longer at all religious about these matters, I find myself leaning rather more towards the 'neo-Ricardians' than towards their critics. I think that it *is* useful to talk in terms of a broad Ricardo–Marx–Sraffa tradition or stream of thought, in which the question of the relation between the social surplus and the rate of profit has always been (and still is) a central theme; and I shall be returning to this point at the end of this paper.

But having said all this, one still has an uneasy feeling that in this great whirlwind of debate the really essential question is in danger of getting blown away. This question, as I have already said, is simply whether Marx's journey from volume I to volume III was really necessary. Why, to put the question in yet another way, did Marx start with the assumption that commodities sold 'at their values' when he was very well aware right from the beginning that in actual fact under competitive capitalism they sold at prices which in most cases diverged widely from their 'values'? And why did he think it necessary, in his analysis of these real-world competitive prices, to *derive* them from 'values' by means of this rather odd transformation process?

Let me first of all try to deal with some of the less convincing answers which are sometimes given to this question.[4] Some writers, particularly those who are anxious to sociologise Marx (and sociologising him is almost as bad as mathematising him), are apt to say that Marx was not really interested in prices, and that his theory of value was not intended to explain the level of prices at all: it was rather the embodiment or crystallisation of a basic methodological principle. And there is of course something in this. It is true that Marx was not *very* interested in prices, or at any rate in the prices of individual commodities as distinct from broad groups of commodities. And it is also true, and in my opinion very important indeed, that his theory of value *did* embody or crystallise a basic methodological principle – the principle that relations of exchange should properly be analysed in terms of relations of production. But there is surely little doubt that he wanted his theory of value not only to embody this principle, but also to do another and more familiar job as well – the same job which theories of value had always been employed to do in economics, that is, to determine prices. When one recalls the strenuous efforts that Marx made in volume III to show that prices of production, although they normally diverged from 'values', did so in an orderly law-governed manner, and that they could in fact be said to be ultimately derived from or determined by 'values', one must surely come to the conclusion that this first attempt at an answer to our question simply will not stand up.

Other writers have argued that in volume I, for the sake of simplifying his analysis, Marx assumed as a first approximation to reality that organic compositions of capital were equal in all industries – which, if it were true, would of course mean that under competitive conditions prices would tend to coincide exactly with 'values'. Then in volume III, they argue, he proceeded to a second approximation to reality in which he dropped this initial simplifying assumption and showed that the modifications which resulted were of a relatively minor character. But once again this just will not stand up. Throughout volume I Marx very carefully and repeatedly sets out the simplifying assumptions he is making; and so far as I can see there is not a single word anywhere which suggests that included among these was this alleged assumption of equal organic compositions of capital. Nor does this interpretation seem to me to tally with Marx's insistence in volume III that the analysis of prices must not simply be *juxtaposed* to the analysis of 'values' but rather in some meaningful sense *derived* from it.

A third possible answer, which is sometimes combined with a version of the first, is that Marx's procedure was designed primarily to expose the real source of capitalist profit — i.e. to show that profit was the result, not of anything which the capitalist or his capital did, but of the exploitation of the workers. What better way of showing this, it is argued, than to begin (as did Marx) by abstracting from certain aspects of the competitive process which disguise the exploitative origin of profit, and by analysing the way in which, as a result of the class monopoly possessed by the capitalists, the work-force *in each individual industry* is compelled 'to do more work than the narrow round of its own life-wants prescribes' (Marx, 1954, p. 309), thereby producing for the capitalists in that industry a kind of free net gain or 'surplus value' whose magnitude depends upon the *amount* of extra work it is compelled to do. Then, later on, having started off on the right foot in this way, you can as it were put the competitive disguise back on again, and show how competition redistributes the *total* pool of 'surplus value' produced over the economy as a whole, so that some capitalists in fact finish up with more net gain than their own workers produce and some finish up with less.

Let me say at once that I think there is quite a lot in this: it is much closer to the truth than either of the other possible explanations of Marx's procedure which we have considered. There is abundant textual evidence to the effect that Marx was indeed anxious that his theory of 'value' and price, whatever else it did, should highlight (and on no account obscure) the exploitative character of profit as a class income. He speaks again and again of the way in which bourgeois economists are blinded by competition; how, by failing to 'start with values', they fail to penetrate through the outward (competitive) disguise into the internal (exploitative) essence; and how, for the same reason, they are deluded into accepting various apologetic theories of price which at the best are mere 'adding-up' theories and at the worst imply that profit and rent are in some way produced by capital and land respectively. And in the very important final chapters of *Capital* (1959, part VII, pp. 794–863), which few people read, he explains how necessary it is, in order to counteract all this vulgar nonsense, to begin by postulating the existence of some prior concrete magnitude — i.e. roughly some magnitude which is independent of market prices — which can plausibly be regarded as constituting the ultimate source of profit and rent and as limiting their aggregate level.[5] In Marx's system, this prior concrete magnitude consists precisely of the sum of the 'values' of the commodities. Given this magnitude, Marx argues, and given all the cs and vs, the quantitative limit of the aggregate level of profit and rent over the economy as a whole is determined.

I have done my best to make this third answer appear as plausible as possible, because I believe that it does get us some way towards the truth. But it does not get us all the way by any means. A moment's thought will surely show that quite a lot still remains to be explained. *Given* the necessity, as Marx saw it, of postulating some kind of prior concrete magnitude which limited the aggregate level of profit and rent, why exactly did he decide to constitute it of the 'values' of commodities — those 'values' at which he knew very well that commodities hardly ever in fact sold, at any rate under developed capitalism? What *sense* does it make, to put the question in a more provocative way, to say that profit and rent are derived from, or paid out of, or limited by, the sum of individual surplus values like the ss in our illustrative schema, which can perhaps not *too* unfairly be described as abstract, unrealised, non-observable, or even imaginary quantities?[6] And critics of Marx like Samuelson can give what they believe to be the turn of the screw at this point by arguing that Marx's procedure not only made no sense but was also quite unnecessary, since you can easily get the main results which Marx wanted to get — i.e. prices and profits uniquely determined, in a model in which it is assumed that profits are paid out of and limited by a pre-existing concrete social surplus — by using commodity-production models *à la* Sraffa.

Why then did Marx, who was certainly no fool, believe that 'starting with values' in fact made perfectly good sense? It is time for us to try and give a direct answer to this question. And now that we have allowed Samuelson to get his word in, we must also before we conclude try to answer another question: is it in fact possible to do Marx's job, and perhaps to do it better, on the basis of Sraffian commodity-production models? Let us deal with these two questions in order.

The *main* reason why Marx thought that 'starting with values' made good sense, I would suggest, has to be sought in certain features of his economic methodology. Marx's chief concern in his economic work, speaking very broadly, was with the analysis of what he called *the system of commodity production* — 'commodities' in his terminology being goods which were produced for sale on some kind of market by individual producers or groups of producers operating more or less independently of one another. The system of commodity production, as he conceived it, constituted the 'second great form' or 'second stage' in the development of society. It grew up within, and gradually dissolved and replaced, the 'first social forms', which were based on 'relations of personal dependence'. It underwent a process of internal development, assuming different forms and eventually reaching its apogee under capitalism. And it was destined, sooner rather than later, to give way to the 'third stage' in the development of society, which would be based on socialist relations. Marx (1973, p. 158) very clearly sketched out this stadial scheme, which of course cuts across the other more familiar one of which he also made extensive use, and there are many echoes of it in Marx's later economic work.

Now the particular type of economic organisation upon which Marx concentrated most of his attention was of course *capitalism*. But, looking at capitalism as he did in the perspective of the stadial scheme just outlined, he believed that it was very important to visualise it first and foremost as *a particular form of the system of commodity production* — that form in which the great majority of products were commodities and the great majority of commodities were the products of capital, and in which the direct aim of capital was the production of surplus value through the exploitation of labour power, which had itself become a commodity. 'Already implicit in the commodity', wrote Marx (1959, p. 858), 'and even more so in the commodity as a product of capital, is the materialization of the social features of production and the personification of the material foundations of production, which characterize the entire capitalist mode of production.'[7] Thus Marx believed that an analysis of the commodity as such was a necessary prerequisite of the analysis of capitalism. The logical starting-point, as he saw it, had to be an analysis of 'simple' (i.e. non-capitalist, or a-capitalist) commodity production and circulation; and the subsequent analysis of *capitalist* commodity production and circulation could not just be juxtaposed to this, but in some way or other had to be *developed out of it*. It was this methodological consideration, I believe, which was largely responsible for the way in which Marx posed the problem of the determination of prices. The great question here, Marx said in effect, was what happened to the 'law of value' appropriate to simple commodity exchange when you passed from this to capitalist commodity exchange. In other words, what kind of changes does the mode of price determination undergo when the simple commodity becomes capitalistically modified? Let us note in passing that there was nothing particularly metaphysical or un-English about this way of posing the problem: up to a point, Marx was fairly obviously carrying on here in the tradition of Smith and Ricardo. And he was also carrying on in this same tradition when he 'started with values' — i.e. when he postulated that under simple commodity exchange prices would tend to be proportional to quantities of embodied labour.

It is important to add here, however, that in the case of Marx this procedure, although it assumed a logical form, had a significant 'historical' dimension, which was present only in embryo (if indeed at all) in the work of Smith and Ricardo. Not nearly enough attention has been paid in recent years to what I have called Marx's 'logical–historical method' (Meek, 1973, p. 148), one of the most interesting and significant fruits of his early Hegelian studies, in spite of the fact that it must surely be an important ingredient of any plausible explanation of why he 'started with values' and is therefore of special relevance to the whole question of the transformation problem. I am not going to say very much about this at the present juncture: there is shortly to be a debate on it in the *Economic Journal*. Let me just say this: Marx, I believe, visualised the logical method of treatment which he adopted in his economic analysis — proceeding as it did from the most simple to the most complex categories and relations — as a kind of 'corrected mirror-image' (to use Engels's phrase) of the historical course of development of these categories and relations. Unfortunately, the passages in which Marx emphasised the exceptions to this — the corrections which had to be made in the 'corrected mirror-image' — are more accessible and better known than the much more numerous ones in which he noted certain interesting correspondences between the course of his logic and the course of history. But at any rate so far as the analysis of 'value' is concerned, there are several places in which this question is directly broached by Marx — for example chapter X of volume III, where, in the context of his treatment of the transformation problem, a very interesting and extended discussion culminates in the statement that 'it is quite appropriate to regard the values of commodities as not only theoretically but also historically *prius* to the prices of production' (Marx, 1959, p. 174). This applies, Marx explains, to conditions in which the labourer owns his own means of production, and also to the guild organisation of handicrafts, so long as the mobility of capital between different branches of production is low. The fact that Engels in his famous *Supplement* to volume III of *Capital* went overboard a bit in commenting on this passage[8] should not lead us to underestimate its significance, particularly since there are at least half a dozen other passages of the same import in Marx's work. Nor should it lead us to believe that Engels never said anything sensible on this issue. He did — and by no means least in his preface to volume III, where he speaks as follows of Marx's economic method and its application to the analysis of 'values' and prices:

It is self-evident that where things and their interrelations are conceived, not as fixed, but as changing, their mental images, the ideas, are likewise subject to change and transformation; and they are not encapsulated in rigid definitions, but are developed in their historical or logical process of formation. This makes clear, of course, why in the beginning of his first book Marx proceeds from the simple production of commodities as the historical premise, ultimately to arrive from this basis to capital — why he proceeds from the simple commodity instead of a logically and historically secondary commodity — from an already capitalistically modified commodity (Marx, 1959, pp. 13–14).

What Engels is saying here, to put it in a nutshell, is that Marx conceived the state of 'simple' commodity production with which he started not only as noncapitalist or a-capitalist, but also in a certain sense as *pre*-capitalist.

One has to be very careful here, of course. If one tries to justify Marx's procedure in 'starting with values' by referring to his logical–historical method, one runs the risk of getting the reply that this is no justification at all, since there never in fact was an identifiable historical period characterised by the fact that commodities sold at their 'values'. I think, however, that such a reply would embody a misunderstanding, if not a trivialisation, of the rather sophisticated concept of historical stages which Marx employed. And I think, too, that such a reply would beg one of the most interesting questions of all — which is, what *kind* of conformity between logic and history would it be necessary to demonstrate in order to help justify Marx's proceeding from 'values' to prices, rather than the other way round or not at all? With which gnomic remarks I shall leave this important issue, and proceed to the second of my two final questions.

This was whether it is in fact possible to do Marx's job, and perhaps even to do it better, on the basis of Sraffian commodity–production analysis. Well, I now have a vested interest in an affirmative answer to this question: my own set of five Marxian–Sraffian commodity–production models is on record (Meek, 1973, pp. xxxiiff). Although I have called these models 'my own', I must in due honesty confess that all I have really done is to plagiarise Sraffa's three basic models, adding another two and linking the sequence of five together with a kind of logical–historical analysis similar to that employed by Marx. We begin with a pre-capitalist subsistence economy (model 1), which eventually becomes capable of producing, and does in fact produce, a surplus product (model 2). A number of separate groups of capitalists now emerge, each taking over one of the industries in the economy and appropriating the whole of the surplus produced there as profit (model 3). We then assume that as a result of competition between the capitalists, and the consequent migration of capital from one industry to another, the rate of profit on capital is equalised over the economy as a whole (model 4). Finally, we assume that the workers combine and force the capitalists to return some of the surplus to them (model 5). Essentially, the models consist of a series of sets of input–output equations expressing the conditions of production in each industry in the economy, which determine mutually and simultaneously the prices of all the commodities concerned and also (where appropriate) the level of the average rate of profit.[9] Or, looking at the models from another point of view, we can say that they demonstrate the way in which the mode of price and income determination changes as we imagine ourselves proceeding in five successive logical–historical stages from a pre-capitalist subsistence economy at the bottom to an advanced capitalist surplus economy at the top.

In Sraffian commodity-production models, of course, the inputs and outputs are not expressed in terms of the 'values' (in embodied labour terms) of the commodities concerned, but rather in terms of the quantities (in physical units) of these commodities themselves. The use of these models may therefore worry some Marxists for whom the word 'labour' (and even more the words 'labour theory of value') still have a kind of halo over them, and for whom the notion that profit 'resolves itself into a surplus value created by labour', or represents 'a deduction from the product of labour', still appears as the whole essence of the matter. But certain harsh realities have to be faced. First, if the technical difficulties standing in the way of the reduction of inputs to quantities of (dated) labour are really as great as Sraffa (1960, pp. 58–9, 67–8) maintains, then we just do not have any option: whether we like it or not, we simply *must* replace embodied-labour models by commodity-production models. Secondly, the notion that profit is produced exclusively by living labour, or that it is 'a deduction from the product of labour', does not possess a great deal of scientific substance. If you *define* input and output as products of labour (or, to put it another way, if you decide to *measure* input and output in terms of labour), then obviously whenever there is a surplus of output over input its exclusive source will appear to be labour.[10] We should not worry too much, then, if the models we use do not enable us to make statements of this rather unsatisfactory kind about exploitation.

But let us be careful not to concede too much. Obviously we must be able to make statements of *some* kind about exploitation, and they must be statements which go to the heart of the matter. For Marx the heart of the matter undoubtedly lay in the fact (already mentioned above) that the work-force in a capitalist economy, as a result of the class monopoly possessed by its employers, is compelled 'to do more work than the narrow round of its own life-wants prescribes'. It is true, I think, that if one drops this one drops Marxism; and it is also true that there is nothing in Sraffa's models of a surplus economy, as they stand, which clearly implies that such a state of affairs exists.[11] But I cannot see that any great ideological sin is involved in taking Sraffa's models as constituting the general technical basis (as it were) of our analysis, and where necessary simply specifying any additional institutional datum that is required. *After all, this is very much the kind of thing which Marx himself did*. In the important chapter XVI of volume I, Marx (1954, p. 511) emphasised that there is a significant sense — even if only a 'very general' one — in which surplus value rests on a 'natural' basis:

> If the labourer wants all his time to produce the necessary means of subsistence for himself and his race, he has no time left in which to work gratis for others. Without a certain degree of productiveness in his labour, he has no such superfluous time at his disposal; without such superfluous time, no surplus-labour, and therefore no capitalists, no slave-owners, no feudal lords, in one word, no class of large proprietors.

Here, in effect, Marx is outlining a 'model' of an economy in which the natural and technological conditions are such that the production of a surplus product, and therefore the appropriation of this product by one or another 'class of large proprietors', is *possible*. But will the potential surplus product in fact be produced? If it is produced, will it in fact be appropriated by such a class, or will it be consumed by the direct producers? And if it is in fact appropriated by such a class, which class will it be and how will it manage to get away with it? To go from the *possible* to the *real*, in other words, requires in every case the specification of a particular institutional datum.[12] In my own series of models, as in Marx's, a different institutional datum is specified for each. After the production of a surplus product becomes technically possible, I assume that it is in fact produced, but that at first it is consumed by the direct producers.[13] Then the crucial change occurs: a capitalist class emerges, and manages to appropriate the surplus product for itself by dispossessing the direct producers of their means of production, reducing their wages to subsistence level, and using its monopoly of capital (in effect) to force them to 'work gratis' for it during their 'superfluous time'. If this is not exploitation in the true Marxian sense, then I do not know what is.[14]

With the specification where necessary of the appropriate institutional datum, then, and with remarkably little modification and development, a sequence of Sraffian models can be made to do essentially the same jobs which Marx's labour theory of value was designed to do. We can start, as Marx's system did, with the postulation of a prior concrete magnitude which limits the levels of class incomes. We can adopt the same kind of view about the order and direction of determination of the variables as Marx did. The same kind of quantitative predictions about the relation between price ratios and embodied-labour ratios can (if we wish) be made, and the analysis based on the models can readily be framed in logical–historical terms. The same kind of scope can be left for the influence of social and institutional factors in the distribution of income, and the transformation problem can be solved in passing, as it were, without any fuss whatever. In the light of all this, the fact that we do not need to tell our Sraffian equations anything at all about Marxian 'values' seems superbly irrelevant.

That is the end of what I have to say, but it is only the beginning of what I think ought to be said. Given the perspective in which Marx viewed capitalism, the methodology which he thought appropriate to employ in its analysis, and the techniques which were available to him, he virtually *had* to 'start with values' and transform them into prices: he could do no other. Given the new techniques which are available to us today, we can do Marx's job more effectively. But the great question is, of course, whether that job is still worth doing – in other words, whether Marx's perspective and methodology are still worth our serious attention today. It is high time that this question became the main focus of the debate.

NOTES

1 In preparing this paper for publication, I have left the text more or less in the form in which it was delivered at the AUTE Conference, without making much attempt to remove the colloquialisms. I have, however, amended the concluding paragraphs in order to deal with a rather important question which was raised by Mark Blaug in the discussion.
2 To use the word 'definition' here is of course to beg a number of important interpretative questions. Marx (1954, p. 38), however, when he first introduced his notion of 'value' in volume I of *Capital*, had no hesitation in going on immediately to speak of 'Value as defined above'.
3 Once again this statement begs a number of questions, but it seems to correspond fairly closely to what Marx (e.g. 1954, p. 220n) meant by the assumption, so often explicitly made in volume I, that 'prices = values'.
4 Cf. Baumol (1974, pp. 53–5).
5 Marx's main discussion of this crucial point will be found in chapter L, entitled 'Illusions Created by Competition' (1959, pp. 831–54).
6 This, as I understand it, was the real point at issue in the exchanges between Baumol and Samuelson in the colloquium on the transformation problem in the March 1974 number of the *Journal of Economic Literature*. Baumol felt

that the third answer discussed above was sufficient to explain why Marx thought it necessary to 'start with values'; Samuelson felt that it was not in fact sufficient, since it made no sense to describe 'surplus value' as the source of profit; and neither of them came anywhere near to understanding what the other was trying to say.

7 Cf. also Marx (1954, p. 82), 'The mode of production in which the product takes the form of a commodity, or is produced directly for exchange, is the most general and most embryonic form of bourgeois production.'

8 I am mainly referring here to Engels's statement, at the end of his discussion of this question in the *Supplement*, that 'the Marxian law of value... has prevailed during a period of from five to seven thousand years' (Marx, 1959, p. 876).

9 Strictly speaking, 'profit' in the technical sense appears only in models 3, 4, and 5. In model 3 there are in effect different rates of profit in each industry; and in model 5 the rate of profit (and of course the prices) are indeterminate unless we postulate that the wage is known.

10 Cf. Rowthorn (1974, p. 82).

11 Cf. *Ibid.* pp. 84–5.

12 Cf. Marx (1954, p. 514): 'Favourable natural conditions alone, give us only the possibility, never the reality, of surplus-labour, nor, consequently, of surplus-value and a surplus-product.' Also (1969, p. 406): 'It is clear that though the existence of *surplus-labour* presupposes that the productivity of labour has reached a certain level, the mere *possibility* of this surplus-labour ... does not itself make it a *reality*. For this to occur, the labourer must first be *compelled* to work in excess of the [necessary] time, and this compulsion is exerted by capital.'

13 Marx (e.g. 1959, pp. 172–4) quite frequently postulates a situation of this kind.

14 Another kind of link between profit and surplus value can be established on the basis of commodity-production analysis if we work in terms of Sraffa's 'standard commodity'. It can readily be shown that there is a simple relationship between the average rate of profit in the economy as a whole on the one hand, and the rate of surplus value *in the production of the standard commodity* on the other hand (cf. Eatwell, 1974, p. 301). It can plausibly be argued that this is essentially the same kind of relationship as that which Marx postulated between the average rate of profit in the economy as a whole and the rate of surplus value *in the production of the commodity produced by capital of average organic composition*. Far be it from me to object to Mr Eatwell or anyone else coming through this particular door, since I rather think that I am the one who originally opened it (cf. Meek, 1967, pp. 175–8). But before too much emphasis is given to the point, I think it should be borne in mind that the model with which Marx himself initially explained the transformation of 'values' into prices was one in which the organic composition of *none* of the capitals concerned was equal to the social average. It was only later in his exposition, after he had done all the donkey-work, that he drew attention to the relationship just mentioned.

REFERENCES

Baumol, W.J. (1974). The transformation of values: what Marx 'really' meant (an interpretation). *Journal of Economic Literature* 12, 51–62.
Eatwell, J. (1974). Controversies in the theory of surplus value: old and new. *Science and Society* 38, 281–303.
Marx, K. (1954). *Capital*, vol. I. Moscow: Foreign Languages Publishing House.
Marx, K. (1959). *Capital*, vol. III. Moscow: Foreign Languages Publishing House.
Marx, K. (1969). *Theories of Surplus Value*, part II. London: Lawrence & Wishart.
Marx, K. (1973). *Grundrisse*, tr. M. Nicolaus. Harmondsworth: Penguin Books.
Meek, R.L. (1967). *Economics and Ideology and Other Essays*. London: Chapman & Hall.
Meek, R.L. (1973). *Studies in the Labour Theory of Value*, 2nd edn. London: Lawrence & Wishart.
Morishima, M. (1973). *Marx's Economics*. Cambridge University Press.
Morishima, M. and Seton, F. (1961). Aggregation in Leontief matrices and the labour theory of value, *Econometrica* 29, 203–20.
Rowthorn, R. (1974). Neo-classicism, neo-Ricardianism, and Marxism, *New Left Review*, no. 86, 63–87.
Samuelson, P.A. (1971). Understanding the Marxian notion of exploitation: a summary of the so-called transformation problem between Marxian values and competitive prices, *Journal of Economic Literature* 9, 399–431.
Seton, F. (1957). The 'transformation problem', *Review of Economic Studies* 24, 149–60.
Sraffa, P. (1960). *Production of Commodities by Means of Commodities*. Cambridge University Press.
Winternitz, J. (1948). Values and prices: a solution of the so-called transformation problem, *Economic Journal* 58, 276–80.

13 THE FIRM, FINANCE AND EQUILIBRIUM IN ECONOMIC THEORY

S. J. MOSS

A number of eminent economic theorists have recently evinced a certain disquiet over the state of Walrasian general equilibrium theory as it has developed out of the Arrow–Debreu model (1954). In this volume, for example, Professor Fisher raises a number of points about the difficulty of analysing disequilibrium processes within the Arrow–Debreu framework. Several years ago in this series of conferences, Professor Hahn (1973) considered a slightly different problem first raised in a formal model by Roy Radner (1968). Radner pointed out that the existence of a full-blown general equilibrium cannot be proved if individual traders are not assumed to be omniscient and if trading takes place and transactions are agreed at every one of a long sequence of dates.

Both Professor Fisher and Professor Hahn suggest that the problem may be one of mathematical tractability which could be solved in one of two ways. Either the Arrow–Debreu theory might be restated in a different form or new mathematical techniques might be found to overcome the difficulties in a theory which is fundamentally sound. There is, of course, the third alternative: it may be that the problems are inherent in the Arrow–Debreu theory of general equilibrium and are not just the result of particular analytical techniques or particular formulations of that theory.

The purpose of this paper is to argue the last alternative. In particular, it will be argued that a Keynesian analysis of investment together with certain managerial theories of the firm provide a mutually exclusive alternative to the neoclassical conception of the firm and one which, in an alternative model of general equilibrium, does not raise the problems which have been found in the neoclassical versions. It will also be suggested that these same problems ramify quite widely through the corpus of modern, neoclassical theory and are not restricted to general equilibrium models.

The managerial theories which we shall consider are primarily those of Andrews (1949), Penrose (1959) and Chandler (1962). The alternative general equilibrium framework which I shall suggest entails elements from a theory which has been called variously 'neo-Marxian', 'neo-Ricardian', and 'neo-Keynesian'. These appear to me to be three streams of a single theory; the best known progenitors of each of these streams perhaps being Joan Robinson (e.g. 1956, 1962), Piero Sraffa (1960) and Nicholas Kaldor (e.g. 1956, 1966), respectively. For purposes of exposition and without prejudice to other sources of inspiration, we shall call this 'Cambridge' approach neo-Keynesian since we shall use it to further an argument of Keynes.

The relevant aspects of the managerial theory and the nature of its solution to neoclassical problems will be outlined in the first section. In the second section we shall develop our neo-Keynesian general equilibrium model of growth and income distribution. The relevance of that model to the managerial theory of the firm and its incompatibility with neoclassical theory and, in particular, the neoclassical view of the firm will be demonstrated. The final section will be taken up with comments about the usefulness and the shortcomings of our equilibrium analysis given that it solves or eliminates difficulties of the sort alluded to by Professors Fisher and Hahn.

NEOCLASSICAL PROBLEMS AND MANAGERIALIST/KEYNESIAN SOLUTIONS

Of the two problems mentioned in the introductory paragraph, we shall consider first the Radner problem since it has to do with the existence rather than the stability of equilibrium.

Radner considers the Arrow–Debreu model with the usual forward markets in every dated, located commodity. But he adds two twists. First, he assumes that there exist spot markets, i.e. markets in commodities dated 'today' where trades in these commodities can be agreed today. Second, he assumes that there will be spot and forward markets not only today, but tomorrow and the day after and every day on into the infinite future. Whatever other sources of information entrepreneurs and households may have (*vide*, Kornai, 1971), the equilibrium prices at every date will certainly convey information to traders which was not available at any earlier date. In Radner's words (1968, p. 35),

An agent may choose a strategy determining how his inputs and outputs will depend upon his information, including the 'spot' prices in later markets, but such a strategy will not independently determine an act [i.e. actual inputs and outputs]! The acts of all agents will be determined jointly by their choice of strategies. In this sense, the introduction of spot markets introduces 'external effects' among the acts of the several agents in the economy [and so] destroys one of the important conditions for the 'classical' analysis of competitive equilibrium. In particular, an agent will no longer be able to assign a definite value to a strategy for given prices in the futures market. *There would arise a demand for liquidity, but unless agents could correctly predict the strategies of others, and calculate the consequences, he could not determine his optimal demand for liquidity!*... The Arrow–Debreu world is strained to the limit by the problem of choice of information. It breaks down completely in the face of limits on the ability of agents to compute optimal strategies. [Emphasis added]

It is perhaps curious, if it is not surprising, that the same point which Radner wrested from the internal logic of the Arrow–Debreu system, Keynes adduced in support of the *General Theory* in the 1937 *Quarterly Journal of Economics* symposium. After discussing properties of what, in neoclassical general equilibrium theory, would be called 'states of the world', Keynes argued,

> About these matters there is no scientific basis on which to form any calculable probability whatever. We simply do not know. Nevertheless, the necessity for action and for decision compels us as practical men to do our best to overlook this awkward fact and to behave exactly as we should if we had behind us a good Benthamite calculation of a series of prospective advantages and disadvantages, each multiplied by its appropriate probability, waiting to be summed. (Reprinted in Keynes, 1973, pp., 113–14.)

That Keynes recognised this to be the case was, he said, his principal advance over the orthodoxy of his (and, apparently, our) day. This led him to the same point that Radner reached thirty-one years on. Again in Keynes' words,

> It is a recognised characteristic of money as a store of value [i.e. liquidity] that it is barren; whereas practically every other form of storing wealth yields some interest or profit. Why should anyone outside a lunatic asylum wish to use money as a store of wealth? Because, partly on reasonable and partly on instinctive grounds, our desire to hold money is a barometer of the degree of our distrust in our own calculations and conventions concerning the future. (1973, pp. 115–16).

In effect, these 'calculations and conventions' are an exceedingly flimsy foundation on which to take decisions and are, therefore, subject to 'sudden and volatile changes'. 'At all times the vague panic fears and unreasoned hopes are not really lulled, and lie but a little way below the surface.' (Keynes, 1973, p. 115.) The optimal liquidity for any individual at any one moment is not some stable function of prices or anything else which can be quantified. It depends on his mood of the moment and his general disposition towards optimism. Where Radner proved that, in the absence of omniscience and omnipotence, the future is uncertain in the sense of Keynes and Knight, Keynes assumed it as an obvious induction from the facts of the world in which he lived.

The alternative to holding liquidity, of course, is holding earning assets. Among these assets are the plant, equipment and materials of manufacturing and service industries. The decisions of each entrepreneur to invest in such resources depends on the same expectations as their decisions to hold liquidity and therefore not to invest. We know from the marriage of input–output analysis and multiplier accelerator theory (Goodwin, 1949) that the investment decisions of any firm ramify throughout the economy. If the expectations of each entrepreneur are affected by present states of demand and, therefore, by the expectations of other entrepreneurs, expectations are interdependent and we can expect conventional opinions to hold wide sway. But even then, changes in expectations cannot be viewed as stable functions of standard economic variables. In effect, the accelerator coefficients are volatile functions of the state of demand for given commodities, the general state of the economy and the state of the news as well as a host of other non-quantifiable and non-economic phenomena. Judging by his comments in his article (1973), this is the basis of Keynes' theory of effective demand as well as his theory of liquidity.

This approach solves Radner's problem, at least insofar as it relates to optimal liquidity, by the simple expedient of denying its relevance. And, as Radner pointed out, by proving that a theory of optimal liquidity is impossible whenever there is likely to be a demand for liquidity, the whole Arrow–Debreu model and its derivatives are left in tatters.

Can anything be saved from this wreckage? If so, one prerequisite is to replace the maximiser of discounted, expected profits and pleasures with one who, whatever his liking for profits and sybaritic pursuits, can exist in a world where there is a demand for liquidity and where his obsessions may lead him to hold money as a store of wealth. It is here that the managerial theory of the firm can step boldly to the rescue.

The firm of the managerial theory is a collection of resources which evolve over time. Among the employees of the firm is a group which can be identified as its 'management team' (Penrose, 1959, pp. 45–9). The members of this team take the decisions which involve important alterations in the composition or utilisation of the resources comprising the firm. There is no lack of empirical evidence for the existence of such groups and their role within the firm. A representative list includes Alexander (1960, 1966), Didrichsen (1972), Penrose (1960) and Snooks (1973). Chandler (1962) in particular has provided exhaustive documentation of the importance of an appropriate organisational structure for the efficient utilisation of resources and of the role of the management team in devising and implementing that structure.

The managerial limitations on any firm's investments have been most extensively analysed by Professor Penrose. The kinds of resources which the management team will add and the methods of utilisation depend on the human limitations of the members of the team; in particular on the limitations which Radner showed to be anathema to Arrow–Debreu theorising. Managers have limited time in which to consider potential investment projects and limited knowledge and expertise with which to evaluate the likely outcomes of alternative projects. The time limitation means that entrepreneurs cannot consider every feasible project known to man at any date. Professor Penrose suggests that managers will feel less uncertain about the outcomes of investment projects the more they know of the markets in which the outputs are to be sold, the technological characteristics of the processes by which they are to be produced and the sources of supply of the inputs to the production processes. To some extent knowledge can be bought in the form of consultants' services or additions to the management team or labour force. What cannot be bought is experience with the technology and markets and the long-standing manager's knowledge of the abilities of the firm to expand in any particular direction. This experience is derived in large part from the existing resources of the firm and the uses to which they are put. As a result, the nature of the investment projects which managers will consider, and those about which they are likely to feel most confident, will be directed by the past activities of the firm and past development of the firm's resource base. (Cf. Penrose, 1959, pp. 51–3, 56–60.)

There nowhere exists a list of all feasible investment projects. It is likely therefore that possible projects will be suggested to managers by their knowledge of and experience with particular markets and technologies. Much of the information about markets originates with comments or complaints garnered by the firm's sales force. Alterations in the technological base of the firm may be suggested by obvious limitations of the existing technology, shortages of some types of inputs or the existence of by-products when disposal is not free (Rosenberg, 1969). The empirical evidence of wide-ranging increasing returns to scale suggests that investment projects involving increased utilisations of existing capacities will increase the profitability of existing lines of production in addition to any profits generated by the new outputs (Pratten, 1971; Silberston, 1972). Moreover, expanding a labour force of given skills or a sales force in given markets is, in practice, less costly than training an entire labour force in new skills and eliminates the time required by sales personnel to make new contacts and 'build their territory' from scratch. Not only are investments which mesh with the existing resources of the firm more likely to be defined by the firm, they are also more likely to entail a smaller opportunity cost to the firm than investment projects which do not.

It is only a small step from this account of the determinants of the direction of investment to Keynes' account of the determination of the magnitude of investment. For whether a management team will invest in additional resources or sanction changes in the utilisation of existing resources depends on the team's evaluation of the prospects for success. Even if the team is more likely to feel confident about investments which, for reasons given above, they understand better or which entail lower opportunity costs, there is no necessary presumption that the team's members will feel very confident about the profitability of any investment project. Indeed, their experience and knowledge, the information they receive about competitors' activities, recent states of demand, order book lengths, and so on may give their 'vague panic fears' a decided edge over their 'unreasoned hopes'. If this psychological state ramifies through the economy, investment declines and employment and output growth fall away.

This seems a perfectly obvious possibility within a managerial theoretic framework and does no obvious violence to the facts of the real world. Why does the same conclusion not arise naturally in a Walrasian, Arrow–Debreu or any other neoclassical framework? One possibility is that the relationship between the firm and the market is specified differently in the managerial theory. We consider this possibility first for commodity markets, and secondly for financial markets.

The firm of neoclassical theory is confronted with an opportunity set which may be represented as a set of feasible production plans as in Arrow–Debreu models or, in partial equilibrium theory, as a cost curve. When the optimising neoclassical entrepreneur goes to the market, therefore, he will only agree trades which put him on the boundary of his opportunity set. At any interior point, he knows he could do better since he knows this exogenously given, objective boundary. In the managerial theory, however, there is no such exogenous set. The perceived set of opportunities we have seen to be determined endogenously and within the firm. It depends on the entire past history of the firm's investment, personnel and managerial policies. It is expanded with the vision of the firm's managers and contracted by their short-sightedness and narrow-mindedness. Managers' perceptions of their opportunities in any given state of things depends on their expectations and optimism. Thus, where the neoclassical entrepreneur cannot perceive himself to have exhausted all of his market and/or technological opportunities unless he has in fact done so according to an absolute and exogenous standard, the corporate manager can miss opportunities without knowing it. He can fail to define a relevant investment project and he can misread signals since no-one provides the same objective, external standard for him that the neoclassicals provide for their entrepreneur. If the managers of a significant number of firms fail to exploit opportunities or fail to find them, then their decisions will be self-justifying as we know from the most elementary textbook accounts of Keynesian theory.

The same line of argument cannot be extended directly to the financial markets. The reason is that the nature of financial assets differs from the nature of real assets (or capital goods) in an important manner which is usually overlooked by neoclassical theorists.

On the organised financial markets, securities have unambiguous market valuations since their prices are continuously quoted. There are no such unambiguous market valuations of the real assets of firms. The managerial conception of the firm implies that real assets are components of integrated collections of resources. If they were not, if this conception of the firm were false, *and* if there were sufficiently well organised markets for real assets, only then would they have a current market value. This is not to suggest that no commodities exist which are traded on organised markets. But typically these are agricultural and mineral produce which can be highly standardised and which are valuable in relation to their carrying costs (Kaldor, 1960). Nonetheless, there are no such perfect markets for second-hand production plants or specialised equipment although from time to time these are traded on very thin markets indeed.

As a result, the cash flows of manufacturing and non-financial service enterprises are independent of any values which may be placed on their stocks of earning assets. For financial institutions and other rentiers, however, cash flows are generated on the turn by borrowing at one rate of interest and lending at another, higher rate. Their cash flows are thus largely determined by the values of their earning assets. In buying securities, therefore, rentiers are concerned with qualitatively different sources of return than are the managers of non-financial companies in buying investment goods. Moreover, without discontinuous alterations in resource compositions of a sort which is unlikely in the context of the managerial theory, rentiers will not arbitrage between real and financial assets. For one thing, they will lack the appropriate organisation and supporting services to operate (say) a blast furnace or a sugar refinery and, for another, their experience with markets where the conventional view of asset valuations is paramount will not suit them to taking decisions in markets where such conventional views are irrelevant.

If this argument is right, it directly undercuts several well-known neoclassical theories of finance such as Tobin's (1958) and the Modigliani–Miller (1958) theory, together with their extensions to general equilibrium models (Tobin, 1961; Stiglitz, 1974). It also suggests that there will be nothing to eliminate persistent differences between rates of return on real assets and rates of return on financial assets.

To demonstrate these points, we consider a firm which has issued S equity shares which are trading at price q, but no bonds, debentures or other forms of debt. Suppose that we can assign some value K to the real capital of the firm and that the firm's rate of return on K is r. We shall see presently what the value of real capital means in this context. Title to every dollar's worth of real capital can be purchased on the stock exchange for $qS/K = v$ dollars, where v is the valuation ratio (Marris, 1964).

In the Tobin theory, real capital has a value and is interchangeable with titles to that real capital. That is $qS = K$ and so $v = 1$. In the Modigliani–Miller theory, the rate of return on real assets and the rate of return on share-holdings are the same — both equal to r. The price–earnings ratio is assumed to be the stock market price of an infinite stream of earnings of one dollar discounted at rate r. That is, the price–earnings ratio is assumed to equal $1/r$. At the same time, firms are divided into risk classes on the basis of their price–earnings ratios. Taken together, these assumptions amount to assuming that the value of shares are identical to the value of real capital for every firm since the price–earnings ratio is

$$\frac{q}{rK/S} = \frac{qS}{rK} = \frac{vK}{rK} = \frac{v}{r}.$$

We shall see in the next section that, except for one limited case, the valuation ratio is unity if and only if the rate of return on shares and the rate of return on the equilibrium value of investment good stocks are identical. Moreover, it will be seen to be crucial to the entire neoclassical view of market relations that the valuation ratio should be unity whereas, as we argued above, the managerial theory as developed here suggests that any such presumption is unwarranted.

A MODEL OF NEO-KEYNESIAN GENERAL EQUILIBRIUM

If the managerial theories of the firm are incompatible with the market relations of neoclassical theory, it will be useful to see what sort of economy-wide relations are justified by those theories. The framework we shall employ is neo-Keynesian in the sense suggested in the introduction. In comparing this framework with neoclassical general equilibrium we shall be able to give a relatively simple formal expression to the verbal argument of the preceding section.

In building an equilibrium model which doesn't do gross violence to Keynes' argument about the role of expectations and their lack of a scientific, probabilistic basis, we require to specify a situation in which there is never cause to revise expectations at all. In other words, we require an undisturbed balance between the vague panic fears and unreasoned hopes of entrepreneurs and rentiers alike. Such cases are hard to find and none are plausible representations of the real world. Of all the implausible cases which have been suggested, steady-growth equilibrium is perhaps the least unlikely. We simply suppose that prices have been set to yield a uniform, constant rate of profit on costs and, at these prices, demands have been growing at the constant rate g since time out of mind. If every enterprise believes that its demands will grow at this rate and increases its purchases of inputs at that rate, income will grow at the same rate but, with the labour force also growing at that rate, income per worker will be constant. There will, therefore, be no income effects on the demand for consumption goods or, in the absence of technical change, substitution effects in the demands for investment goods.

In a world such as this, it will be sufficient to model a closed economy, with no government spending or taxation and in which a single consumption good and a single investment good are produced. Each unit of investment good is produced by b workers equipped with a units of previously produced investment goods. Each unit of the consumption good is produced by β workers equipped with α investment goods. In each of these production processes, the investment good input is used up and leaves no residue. We denote the rate of profits r and the wage rate (i.e. wage per worker per period) w. The investment good is assumed to be paid for at the beginning of the unit time period and wages at the end. The investment good price p then is

$$p = (1 + r)pa + wb \tag{1}$$

and the consumption good price is

$$\pi = (1 + r)p\alpha + w\beta. \tag{2}$$

As we are only interested in relative prices, we take the consumption good as numéraire and

$$\pi = 1. \tag{3}$$

Let X be the stock of investment goods at the start of the period so that at growth rate g the output at the end of the period is $(1 + g)X$. c is the output of consumption goods at the end of the period. In steady-growth equilibrium,

$$X = (1+g)X + \alpha c. \tag{4}$$

The employment of labour N is

$$N = b(1+g)X + \beta c. \tag{5}$$

That N is both the supply of and demand for labour follows from our strictures on the nature of steady-growth equilibrium. But the size of N need not be the size of the available labour force. The real wage w/π can be taken to be the subsistence wage at which workers will not riot and run amuck. So long as the size of the labour force exceeds N, the existence of a pool of unemployed workers need not disturb the equilibrium in which case we have a 'bastard golden age' (Kahn, 1959). Of course, labour unrest or any change in the wage rate will destroy the equilibrium.

The firm is represented in this model in the equations for saving–investment equilibrium. Adopting a construction of Kaldor (1966), we suppose that there exist limited liability corporations which issue ordinary shares but no bonds or other debt instruments. The fraction s_c of net corporate profits rpX is retained, the remainder being distributed as dividends. The fraction f of the cost of net investment gpX is financed by issues of new shares. Kaldor assumes that net investment in each period just exhausts retained profits *plus* the proceeds of that period's share issues. Formally,

$$gpX = s_c rpX + fgpX$$

or

$$r = \frac{1-f}{s_c} g. \tag{6}$$

If profit retentions and external finance were to exceed net investment, the excess would be unused purchasing power held by corporations, i.e. liquidity. If there were a deficiency, then corporate liquidity would fall by the value of the deficit. In steady-growth equilibrium, uncertainty is lulled and liquidity has no role to play. Alternatively, we could assume that so long as the balance between fear and hope is maintained, corporate managers neither increase nor diminish their liquid assets. In either case, the value of liquidity will be ignored to avoid having to introduce a money supply. Equation (6) is our warrant for this approach.

Having determined the supply of new shares, it remains to determine the demand for them. Shares yield two kinds of return: dividends and capital gains. The value of dividends, of course, is $(1-s_c)rpX$. The value of capital gains is the total increase in the value of all shares *minus* the value of new share issues. The value of all shares at the beginning of the period is vpX, where, as before, v is the valuation ratio. In order to avoid speculation in shares with the consequent uncertainty, the valuation ratio is assumed to be constant so that the growth in share values during the period is $vgpX$ and the value of capital gains is $(v-f)gpX$. The total rate of return on shares then is

$$i = \frac{(1-s_c)r + (v-f)g}{v} \qquad (7)$$

The general practice in neo-Keynesian modelling is to characterise savings behaviour by macroeconomic savings ratios where each ratio is the fraction saved out of each functional class of income (wages or profits) (Kaldor, 1956, for example) or the fraction saved out of the income of different groups of households (e.g. 'pure capitalists' and 'worker-capitalists') (Pasinetti, 1962). Although these savings ratios are usually assumed to be exogenous constants, there is no difficulty in deriving them endogenously from elementary utility theory. It may be worthwhile to do so in passing since the absence of utility theory from neo-Keynesian analyses seems to worry some economists, particularly writers of Hobart papers.

If there are H households, all seeking to maximise their own utility functions with the usual convexity and continuity properties, the problem for the hth household will be to maximise $U_h(c_h, s_c, N_h)$, where c_h is the magnitude of the hth household's consumption basket, s_h is the fraction of household income which is saved and N_h is its provision of labour services. The constraint is

$$\pi c_h = (1-s_h)(wN_h + j_h ivPX), \qquad (8)$$

where j_h is the fraction of the value of outstanding shares held by the hth household. This maximising problem is the same as that used by Clower (1965) to obtain income-constrained demand functions of the form

$$c_h = U_h^{(c)}(\pi, w, i, y_h) \qquad (9)$$

$$N_h = U_h^{(n)}(\pi, w, i, y_h) \quad (h = 1, \ldots, H), \qquad (10)$$

where

$$y_h = wN_h + j_h ivpX \qquad (11)$$

Savings and, hence the savings ratios s_h are treated here as residuals. Having determined the consumption good demand and labour supply from the maximising algorithm, the savings ratio is determined as well.

The use of utility theory forces us to assume that there is a constant number of households if each has a different utility function. In order to avoid income effects in consumption, we will assume that the working population of each household is growing at rate g. If savings is then to grow at the same rate as investment, the income and capital gains, hence the wealth, of each household will also have to grow at rate g. That is

$$g = \frac{s_h(wN_h + j_h ivpX)}{j_h vpX} \quad (h = 1, \ldots, H). \qquad (12)$$

Of course, all wealth must be owned so that

$$\sum j_h = 1. \tag{13}$$

A version of the Pasinetti (1962) distribution theorem follows easily from equation (12). Suppose that one household, the 1st, supplies no labour — its maximising algorithm yields a corner solution. Then $N_1 = 0$ and

$$g = s_1 i.$$

Given the growth rate, which, as we shall see, is determined in the corporate sector, the rate of return on financial assets will be determined by the behaviour of rentiers who do no work no matter what may be the saving behaviour of workers who save.

As in any equilibrium system, all markets must clear. Equation (4) implies that the investment good market clears. For the consumption good market to clear,

$$\sum c_h = c. \tag{14}$$

Writing equation (12) in full, summing over h and substituting from the summation identity (13), we find that

$$fgpX = s_w wN + s_r(1 - s_c)rpX - (1 - s_r)(v - f)gpX,$$

where $s_w = \Sigma s_h N_h/N$ and $s_r = \Sigma s_h j_h$. In words, equations (12) and (13) imply that the excess of household saving out of income over consumption out of wealth, i.e. *the demand for new securities*, is just equal to the supply of new securities by the corporate sector. In short, the financial market clears. There remains only the labour market; but since the product and financial markets all clear, by Walras' Law, the labour market must clear as well.

We therefore have $(5H + 10)$ unknowns in the $(5H + 9)$ independent equations (1)–(14). The remaining degree of freedom is a characteristic of neo-Keynesian models and, we shall argue, it is crucial to any interpretation of the present model.

The degree of freedom is a confession of ignorance. A theory of investment would determine g or, alternatively, a theory of distribution would determine r or w. But that confession of ignorance provided the rationale for considering steady-growth equilibrium in the first place and has been a principal tenet of the entire argument of the paper. Indeed, by appeal to that earlier argument, we will set g exogenously.

No matter what variable is set exogenously, the model has a recursive structure. In the present case, the rate of growth determines the profit rate in equation (6) and, in equation (1), the profit rate, determines the price of the investment good relative to the wage rate. The relative price of the consumption good is then determined in equation (2). In effect, the investment and financial policies of firms, as given in equation (6) determine firms' mark-up on cost rather as Andrews (1949) and, in a different model, Eichner (1973) have suggested. That the distribution of income within the investment good sector is determined by the rate of profit (or mark-up) and the technical conditions of investment good production follows from the status of the investment good as a 'basic' commodity (Sraffa, 1960). The wage rate follows from the distribution of income and the technical conditions of production in basic commodity production irrespective of the technical conditions of non-basic commodity production — in this model, the consumption good.

The growth rate also determines the output of consumption goods relative to the stock of investment goods in the economy as well as the demand for labour in, respectively, equations (4) and (5). In other words, the growth rate and the technical conditions of production determine outputs per worker.

In equilibrium, the distribution and value of wealth (the j_h and v, respectively) must be such that net household saving grows at the same rate as the demand for that saving. Thus, the distribution of wealth and its value relative to the cost of circulating capital goods are determined endogenously in equations (12) and (13). Of course, the financial and consumption good markets do not clear independently of one another and the value of savings will equal the value of new share issues only if *ex ante* consumption just exhausts consumption good output (equations (8) and (14)). Our utility theoretic construction enables households to have some part in determining the distribution of employment among households and the scale of the system at the beginning of the period. They do not enter into the determination of the time path of the economy or the distribution of income between profits and wages except insofar as they ratify the prior investment and financial decisions of the corporate sector.

The difference between this neo-Keynesian model and Walrasian/Arrow–Debreu equilibrium could hardly be sharper. Our neo-Keynesian model entails corporate power to determine the rate of growth and the share of wages in income and the power of pure rentiers, those who contribute no labour to the production of commodities (e.g. banks and insurance companies) to determine the rate of return on financial assets given the investment policies of corporations. The neoclassical models of general equilibrium analyse only those economies in which all economic agents meet in the market-place on an equal footing. Whereas each individual's decisions in the neoclassical world must be mutually compatible with the decisions of every other individual, in the neo-Keynesian world described here, workers (whether they save and thus own titles to real capital or not) can only ratify the prior decisions of those who control corporations and those who own but do not work for them.

This line of argument may seem to put a greater weight of interpretation on the recursive structure than it can bear. There is, however, some precedent for this approach in a seminal paper by Simon (1953). In the second place, without this recursiveness the model becomes simply a special case of Walrasian equilibrium. If the entire system must be solved simultaneously, then all markets, including the market for investment goods, stand on the same footing. Decisions to invest and, therefore, the rate of growth are determined simultaneously with decisions to purchase consumption goods or supply labour services. So much is clear from the foregoing argument. In addition, the financial markets and the markets for investment goods become indistinguishable, as we will see presently. But we have already seen that the determination of the direction and magnitude of investment takes place within firms but not within markets in the managerial theory of the firm *and* the managerial conception of the firm implies that the market for real assets (or real capital) and the market for financial assets are essentially different. We shall now argue that these two properties of the managerial theory depend intimately upon one another in neo-Keynesian equilibrium.

From equations (6) and (7) we have

$$i = \frac{r - (s_c r + fg)}{v} + g = \frac{r - g}{v} + g.$$

Solving for v we have the Kahn (1972) formula for the valuation ratio,

$$v = \frac{r - g}{i - g}.$$

Because it is endogenously determined in the neo-Keynesian model, the valuation ratio is unlikely to be unity and will take that value only by an unlikely accident. Excepting the case of golden rule growth ($r = g$), when the valuation ratio is indeterminate, the rates of return on shares and on real assets will almost certainly differ. This conclusion is, of course, compatible with the managerial view of the firm and is incompatible with neoclassical theories of finance.

If a neoclassical view were adopted, we should have to add another independent equation to our neo-Keynesian model; either $r = i$ or $v = 1$. This equation would take up the remaining degree of freedom and would also destroy the recursive structure of the model. For the rate of profit r would then be determined in the various markets rather than by corporate policies and so, therefore, would the growth rate and prices as well as all supplies and demands. With the rate of profits and the rate of growth determined in the financial and product markets, corporate managers could do what they liked about financial policies without affecting any prices, rates of return, supplies or demands.

Either the neoclassical view of markets hangs together or the elements of neoclassical theory hang separately. Once the decision to invest is taken out of the market place and given without reservation to the entrepreneur, the labour market works in a way which can throw up Keynesian involuntary unemployment and the markets for financial assets cease to have the effects generally supposed in neoclassical theory.

CONCLUSION: THE ROLE OF EQUILIBRIUM ANALYSIS.

If stability analysis is difficult in the context of neoclassical general equilibrium theory, it is impossible in neo-Keynesian theory. For the neo-Keynesian model requires a delicate balance between mania and depression in a world of manic depressives. The difficulty which this raises is not one of Harrodian instability where the warranted growth rate continues to exist even if the actual growth rate differs from it. Equilibrium is destroyed by any movement away from it and no other can be expected to replace it. Such is a necessary consequence of the volatility of expectations in a world where there is no scientific basis on which to calculate the probabilities of future events. In this circumstance, notions of stability cease to have any economic relevance.

What then is the use of neo-Keynesian equilibrium? Its principal use so far has been as the basis of the 'Cambridge' attack on orthodox theory. Certainly, the capital theory and distribution debates are very well known. More recently, Hollis and Nell (1975) have suggested that models of the sort employed here, which specify institutions and social classes, avoid the methodological conundrums to which neoclassical models are subject. Neoclassical models require positive methodology for any claim to relevance and that methodology is philosophically untenable.

One of the difficulties with these theoretical and philosophical arguments is that neoclassical and applied economists dismiss them as a curious form of religious warfare. To be sure, the ideological overtones will not be denied here. Nonetheless, the principal use of equilibrium concepts in economics has been to write models, either mathematical or verbal. But one hopes that modelling is not an end in itself. As Keynes had it, 'The object of our analysis is not to provide a machine, or method of blind manipulation, which will furnish an infallible answer, but to provide ourselves with an orderly and organised method of thinking out particular problems' (Keynes, 1936, p. 297). The problems which we have considered here turn on the effect of genuine uncertainty in a world where decision makers lack omniscience and omnipotence. We have argued that neoclassical theory in general and general equilibrium theory in particular cannot encompass the problems inherent in such a world because of their specification of the firm and other economic agents. This specification is bound up with the neoclassical conception of the market. Our account of managerial theory and our neo-Keynesian equilibrium model have been used to argue that institutions such as the corporation can be specified as organisations whose function is to produce goods and services in the face of an unknown future and that such a specification implies that markets do not work as neoclassical theory would have it.

We have proposed that the managerial/neo-Keynesian alternative to neoclassicism is one with a sound logical basis and considerable empirical support. At the same time, it is not burdened with the mathematical and philosophical difficulties which afflict neoclassical analysis. If this proposition is correct, surely the theory deserves consideration on grounds which are not simply ideological.

NOTES

1 I am grateful to J.A. Kregel, A.R. Nobay and an unknown referee for their comments.

REFERENCES

Alexander, A.P. (1960). Industrial entrepreneurship in Turkey: origins and growth. *Economic Development and Cultural Change* 8, 349–65.
Alexander, A.P. (1966). *Strategy and Structure*. Cambridge, Mass.: MIT Press.
Andrews, P.W.S. (1949). *Manufacturing Business*. London: Macmillan.
Arrow, K.J. & Debreu, G. (1954). Existence of an equilibrium for a competitive economy. *Econometrica* 22, 265–90.
Chandler, A.D. jnr (1962). *Strategy and Structure: Chapters in the History of the American Industrial Enterprise*. Cambridge, Mass.: MIT Press.
Clower, R.W. (1965). The Keynesian counter-revolution: a theoretical appraisal. In *The Theory of Interest*, ed. F.H. Hahn and F. Brechling, pp. 103–25. London: Macmillan.
Didrichsen, J. (1972). The development of diversified and conglomerate firms in the United States, 1920–1970. *Business History Review* 46, 202–19.
Eichner, A.S. (1973). Theory of the determination of the mark-up under oligopoly. *Economic Journal* 83, 1184–1200.
Goodwin, R.M. (1949). The multiplier as matrix. *Economic Journal* 59, 537–55.
Hahn, F.H. (1973). On the foundations of monetary theory. In *Essays in Modern Economics*, ed. M. Parkin & A.R. Nobay, pp. 230–42. London: Longman.
Hollis, M. & Nell, E.J. (1975). *Rational Economic Man*. Cambridge University Press.
Kahn, R.F. (1959). Exercises in the analysis of growth. *Oxford Economic Papers*, 2nd Series, 11, 143–56.
Kahn, R.F. (1972). Notes on the rate of interest and the growth of firms. In *Selected Essays on Employment and Growth*, pp. 208–32. Cambridge University Press.
Kaldor, N. (1956). Alternative theories of distribution. *Review of Economic Studies* 23, 83–100.
Kaldor, N. (1960). Speculation and economic stability. In *Essays on Economic Stability and Growth*, pp. 17–58. London: Duckworth.
Kaldor, N. (1966). Marginal productivity and the macro-economic theories of distribution. *Review of Economic Studies* 33, 309–19.
Keynes, J.M. (1936). *The General Theory of Employment, Interest and Money*. New York: Harcourt, Brace and World.
Keynes, J.M. (1973). *The General Theory and After: Part II, Defence and Development. The Collected Writings of John Maynard Keynes*, vol. 14, ed. D. Moggridge. London: Macmillan.
Kornai, J. (1971). *Anti-equilibrium*. Amsterdam: North-Holland.

Marris, R.L. (1964). *The Economic Theory of 'Managerial' Capitalism*. London: Macmillan.
Modigliani, F. & Miller, M.H. (1958). The cost of capital, corporation finance and the theory of investment. *American Economic Review* **48**, 261–97.
Pasinetti, L.L. (1962). Rate of profit and income distribution in relation to the rate of economic growth. *Review of Economic Studies* **29**, 267–79.
Pratten, C.F. (1971). *Economies of Scale in Manufacturing Industries*. Department of Applied Economics Occasional Papers, no. 28. Cambridge University Press.
Penrose, E.T. (1959). *The Theory of the Growth of the Firm*. Oxford: Basil Blackwell.
Penrose, E.T. (1960). The growth of the firm: a case study: the Hercules Powder Company. *Business History Review* **34**, 1–23.
Radner, R. (1968). Competitive equilibrium under uncertainty. *Econometrica* **36**, 31–59.
Robinson, J. (1956). *The Accumulation of Capital*. London: Macmillan.
Robinson, J. (1962). *Essays in the Theory of Economic Growth*. London: Macmillan.
Rosenberg, N. (1969). The direction of technical change: mechanisms and focusing devices. *Economic Development and Cultural Change* **18**, 1–24.
Silberston, A. (1972). Economies of scale in theory and practice. *Economic Journal* **82**, 369–91.
Simon, H.A. (1953). Causal ordering and identifiability. In *Studies in Econometric Method*, ed. W. Hood & T.C. Koopmans, pp. 49–74. New Haven and London: Yale University Press.
Snooks, G.P. (1973). The growth process of the firm: a case study. *Australian Economic Papers* **12**, 162–74.
Sraffa, P. (1960). *Production of Commodities by Means of Commodities*. Cambridge University Press.
Stiglitz, J.E. (1974). On the irrelevance of corporate fiscal policy. *American Economic Review* **74**, 851–66.
Tobin, J. (1958). Liquidity preference as behavior towards risk. *Review of Economic Studies* **25**, 65–86.
Tobin, J. (1961). Money, capital and other stores of value. *American Economic Review* **51**, 26–37.

INDEX OF NAMES

(italicised numbers indicate bibliographical references)

Afuat, S., 241
Alchian, A.A., 38
Alexander, A.P., 264, *275*
Andrews, P.S.W., 261, 272, *275*
Anthony, D.W., 125
Arrow, K.J., 3, 8, 9, 14, 15, 18, 24, 26, *27*, 35, 36, 37, *48*, 62, *243*, 261, 262, 264, 265, 266, 272, *275*
Auernheimer, L., 52, 54, *66*

Bailey, M., 65
Bailey, R.E., 62–4
Balassa, B., 189, *190*, 203, 204, *206*
Baldwin, R.E., 203
Barker, T.S., 195, 203, 205, *206*
Barro, R.J., 46, 47, 48, *48*, 64, *66*, 96, *96*, *170*
Barton, A., 215, 216, 218, *242*
Basevi, G., 202, 205, *206*, *207*
Baumol, W.J., 48, *48*, 64, *66*, 257–8, 259
Bentham, J., 227
Berglas, E., 190, *190*
Bergson. A., 212
Bergstrom, A.R., 158, 159, 165, 166, *170*
Bhatia, R.J., 39, *48*
Blaug, M., 257
Blinder, A.S., 81, 90, 92, 95, *96*
Bliss, C., 100, *125*
Block, H.D., 8, 9, 26, *27*
Borchardt, K., *126*
Bortkiewicz, L. von, 247
Boyer, R.S., Ch.9 (173–91), *190*
Bradford, D.F., 64, *66*
Brainard, W., *171*
Branson, W.H., *170*
Brechling, F.P.R., *28*, *48*, *170*, *275*
Brown, E.H. Phelps, 122, *125*
Brumberg, R., 82, *97*
Brunner, K., *96*, *96*, *170*
Bushaw, D.W., 47, 48

Cagan, P., 64, 65

Cassel, G., 189, 190, *190*
Cathcart, C.D., 64, *66*
Chandler, A.D. jnr., 261, 264, *275*
Christ, C.F., 81, 90, *96*, *170*
Clower, R.W., 4, *28*, 38, 47, *48*, *170*, 270, *275*
Connolly, M.B., *170*
Cooper, R.N., *151*, *170*, *190*, *191*
Corden, W.M., Ch.7 (129–51), *151*, 193, 203, 205, 206, *207*
Cournot, A., 58, 61, 64

Debreu, G., 26, *28*, 62, 65, *66*, 226, *243*, 261, 262, 264, 265, 266, 272, *275*
Denison, E.F., 112, *125*
Didrichsen, J., 264, *275*
Dixit, A.K., 58, 59, 64, *66*
Dobb, M.B., 249
Dornbusch, R., *171*, 190, *190*
Douglas, M., 211
Ducros, B., *126*

Eatwell, J., 258, *259*
Eichner, A.S., 272, *275*
Eltis, W.A., 100, 101, 123, *125*
Engels, F., 253, 254, 258

Fisher, F.M., Ch.1 (3–29), *28*, 169, 218, 219, 242, *243*, 261, 262
Fisher, G.R., 166–9
Foley, D.K., 95, *96*
Ford, J.L., 125, 205
Frenkel, J., 64, *66*
Friedman, M., 76, *76*, 80, 81, 88, 96, *97*, *170*
Frisch, R., 233

Goodwin, R.M., 263, *275*
Gorman, W.M., 150, Ch.11 (211–43), *243*
Grandmont, J.M., 65, *66*
Gray, M.R., 48
Grossman, H.I., 47, 48, *48*, *170*

Index of names

Grubel, H.G., 193, 198, 205, 206, *207*
Guisinger, S., 193, 206, *207*

Hahn, F.H., 8, 11, 12, 13–19, 19, 20, 22, 23, 24, 26, 27, 27, *28*, *48*, 65, *66*, *170*, 261, 262, *275*
Hall, R.L., 34, *48*
Hallett, G., 125, *125*
Han, S.S., 195, 203, 205, *206*
Hanser, K., *126*
Harrod, R.F., 100, 102, 116
Hart, P.E., 242
Hegel, G.W.F., 253
Helmstader, E., 115, *126*
Henderson, J.M., 48, *48*
Henry, C., 26, *28*
Henry, E.W., *126*
Hicks, J.R., 5, 7–8, *28*, 35, 48, *48*, 211, 218
Hindley, B., 189
Hitch, C.J., 34, *48*
Hollis, M., 274, *275*
Holmes, P., 150
Hood, W., *276*
Hurwicz, L., 3, 8, 9, 26, *27*

Intiligator, M.D., *66*

Jackman, R., 189, 190
Johansen, L., 100, *126*
Johnson, H.G., 76, *76*, 162, *170*, 189, 190, *191*, 193, 198, 205, *207*
Jonson, P., 189
Jorgenson, D., 80, *97*

Kahn, R.F., 269, 273, *275*
Kaldor, N., 261, 266, 269, 270, *275*
Karlin, S., *243*
Kaspura, A., 189, *191*
Kendrick, D.A., *66*
Kenen, P., *207*
Keynes, J.M., 4, 33, 38, 39, 48, *48*, 261, 262–4, 268, 270–4, *275*
Kitchin, P.D., Ch.10 (193–207), *207*
Knight, M.D., Ch.8 (153–71), *170*, 189, 263
Koopmans, T.C., 26, *28*, 65, *276*
Kornai, J., 262, *275*
Kregal, J.A., *275*
Kurihara, K., *97*

Laffer, A., 190, *191*
Laidler, D.E.W., 42, 47, *48*, Ch.4 (67–77), *76*, 188–9
Lancaster, K., 222, *243*
Laursen, S., 190, *191*
Leacy, F.H., *126*
Leijonhufvud, A., 34, 38, 42, 47, 48, *48*, *49*
Leontief, W., 248

Lerner, A., 64, *66*
Lyapounov, A., 26, *28*

McFadden, D., 8, *28*
Marchal, J., *126*
Marris, R.L., 267, *276*
Martin, J., 150
Marty, A.L., Ch.3 (51–66), *66*, 75, 76, *76*, 77
Marx, K., 245–57, *259*, 261
McAleese, D., 202, 203–5, 205, 206, *207*
Meek, R.L., Ch.12 (245–59), *259*
Meenan, J., *126*
Meltzer, A.H., 96, *96*
Metzler, L., 26, *28*, 86, 87, 92, 93, *97*, 174, 190, *191*
Miller, Marcus, H., 92–6, 96
Miller, Merton, H., 267, *276*
Mills, G., 242
Minami, R., 99, 110, 111, 125, *126*
Modigliani, F., 82, *97*, 267, *276*
Moggridge, D., *275*
Morishima, M., 47, *49*, 249, *259*
Moss, S.J., Ch.13 (261–76)
Mundell, R., 65, *66*, 86, 87, 92, 93, 94, *97*, *170*, 174, 178, 180, 190, *191*
Mussa, M., 150, *151*

Negishi, T., 8, 12, 26, 27, *28* Ch.2 (33–49), *49*
Nell, E.J., 274, *275*
Nicholson, R.J., 205
Nixon, J., 189
Nobay, A.R., 169, 189, *191*, 275, *275*

Ohkawa, K., 99, 107, *126*
Ono, A., 99, 111, *126*
Oppenheimer, P., 149, 150, *151*
Ott, A., 81, 90, *97*
Ott, D.J., 81, 90, *97*
Oulton, N., 203, 205, *207*

Parkin, J.M., 42–7, 47, *48*, *49*, *170*, *191*, *275*
Pasinetti, L.L., 270, 271, *276*
Patinkin, D., 38, 47, *49*, 65, *66*, *170*, *191*
Penrose, E.T., 261, 264, 265, *276*
Pesek, B.P., 76, 77
Peters, W., 48
Phelps, E.S., 45, 46, 48, *49*, 52, 53, 62, 63, 64, 65, 66, *66*, 80, *97*, 100, *126*
Phillips, A.W., 39, *49*, 163, *170*
Poncet, J.F., 114, *126*
Posner, M., 150, *151*
Powell, A.A., *170*
Pratten, C.F., 265, *276*

Quandt, R.E., 48, *48*

Radner, R., 65, *66*, 261, 262, 263, 264, *276*

Index of names

Rasche, R.H., 96, *97*
Razin, A., 190, *190*
Ricardo, D., 249, 250, 253, 261
Robinson, J., *48*, 261, *276*
Rosenberg, N., 265, *276*
Rosovsky, H., 99, 107, *126*
Rothschild, M., 24, 27, *28*
Rowan, D.C., 123–4
Rowthorn, R., 258, *259*
Rybczynski, T.M., 150, *151*

Sampson, A.A., 205
Samuelson, P.A., 5, 7, 26, *28*, *29*, 212, 242, 245, 248–9, 252, 257–8, *259*
Sandmo, A., 58, 59, 64, *66*
Sargent, J.R., 123, *126*
Saving, T.R., 76, *77*
Scarf, H., 10, *29*
Schmeidler, D., 27
Schydlowsky, D.M., 193, 206, *207*
Seton, F., 247, 248, 249, *259*
Sheen, J., 189
Shell, K., 218, 219, 242, *243*
Shinkai, Y., 189, *191*
Shone, R., 205
Sidrauski, M., 95, *96*
Silber, W.L., 83, 89, *97*
Silberston, A., 265, *276*
Simon, H.A., 272, *276*
Smith, A., 253
Snooks, G.P., 264, *276*
Solow, R.M., 81, 90, 92, 94, 95, *96*, *97*
Sonnenschein, H., 26, *29*
Sparks, G.R., Ch.5 (79–96)
Spencer, R.W., 96, *97*
Sraffa, P., 245, 249, 250, 252, 255, 256, *259*, 261, 272, *276*
Stein, J., 65, *66*
Stiglitz, J.E., 267, *276*
Stolper, G., *126*
Sumner, M.T., 48
Suppes, P., *243*
Surrey, M.J.C., 96, *97*
Sutton, J., Ch.6 (99–126)
Sweezy, P.M., 34, 35, *49*
Swoboda, A.K., *170*, *171*, 189, 190, *191*

Till, L., 202, *207*
Tobin, J., 83, 88, 89, 94, *97*, *170*, 267, *276*
Tower, E., 64, *66*
Tumlir, J., 202, *207*
Turnovsky, S., 189, *191*

Uzawa, H., 11, 12, 26, 27, *29*

Wallich, H.L., 114, *126*
Walras, L., 5, 261, 265, 272
Whitaker, J.K., 242
Wicksell, K., 63
Williams, R.A., *170*
Williamson, J., 147–50
Winternitz, J., 247, *259*
Witthans, F., *207*
Wolfe, J.N., *243*
Wymer, C.R., Ch.8 (153–71), *170*

Yeager, L., 189, *191*
Yohe, W.P., 96, *97*
Younes, Y., 65, *66*

Zis, G., *191*

SUBJECT INDEX

accelerator 86, 158, 263
adaptive expectations 80, 81
aggregation problems 6–7, 33, 96, 202

balance of payments 129–51, 159–60, 161–2, 177
    monetary approach to 153–71
banking 64, 72, 139–40, 154, 160

capital
    international flows of 134, 173
    marginal product of 67, 158
capital theory 74, 99–126, 246–58
Central Bank 154, 161
Club of Rome 131
competition 3, 4, 25, 26, 34, 35, 42, 76, 141, 211, 251
consumers' surplus 58
consumption 70, 90, 148–50, 162, 247–8
    composition of 82, 215
    determinants of demand for 53, 83, 85, 91, 134, 138, 268
    as a component of National Income 54, 56, 70, 158
consumption function 94, 96, 270

deflation 135, 144–5, 146, 147, 148
devaluation 141, 145, 161, 190
disequilibrium 153–71, 189

econometric estimation 153
economic growth 99–125, 160, 163–4, 271
    international comparisons of 112–15, 122
EEC 4
elasticity
    of demand 34, 35, 36, 41–2, 43, 129–30, 143, 205, 216, 222
    of demand for labour 38
    of supply of labour 102–6, 108, 110–11, 123, 124, 125
    interest elasticity of expenditure 48
    of substitution 100, 101, 106, 121, 123, 137, 159, 205–6

    of supply of imports 194–5
Engel curves 217, 229–30, 232, 242
equilibrium 100, 137, 141, 154, 162, 211, 261–75
    general 3–26, 61, 62, 65, 71, 131, 261, 267, 268–73, 274
    partial 4, 23, 25, 61, 71, 158, 266
estimation problems 165–6, 167
excess demand 5–22, 42–7, 153–4, 162, 177, 179, 185
    for assets 175
    for exports 159
exchange rate 173, 177, 182, 185, 193
exchange rate regime 136, 141, 149, 153, 161, 166, 169, 173–4, 175, 178–81, 183–4, 186–90
expectations 33, 40, 263, 266
    and investment decisions 100, 101, 108–9
    irrational 268
    unfulfilled 63
    see also adaptive expectations; inflation, expected; unemployment, expected; utility, expected

fiscal policy 43–4, 79–96, 135, 153, 163, 178, 180
fixprice/flexprice industries 35
full employment 4, 80, 90, 93, 136–8, 144, 146–7

government intervention 3

import quotas 193
income distribution 99–125, 136, 138, 140, 148, 262
income effect (on demand) 26, 131–3
indexation 91
inflation 72, 93, 160
    accelerating 42, 86, 173
    and recession 4, 33
    cost inflation 135
    expected 42–54, 64, 80, 86, 188–9
    government revenue from 52–64, 88, 94

Subject index

international transmission of 173–89
theory of 33–47
interest rate
  adjusment 138
  and borrowing 161
  and consumption 96
  and demand for bonds 134, 163
  and demand for money 5, 56–8
  and IS–LM model 85, 150
  and monetary expansion 73, 86–7, 94
  and savings 135–6
  and speculation 38
  as a determinant of investment 31, 139
  determination of 154
  real 51, 53–5, 61, 75, 93, 136, 158
investment
  and accelerator 86
  and Capital Theory 99, 101–8, 117, 272
  and multiplier 85
  and international capital movements 133–7, 149–50
  decisions 264–5
  determinants of, 41, 269
  goods 54, 267
  in IS–LM model 83
  keynesian theory of 261
  neoclassical theory of 80
IS–LM model 82–3, 84–5, 88–9, 91, 150–1

Kennedy-round talks (on tariffs and trade) 193, 202, 203, 204
Korean war 109–10

labour theory of value 245–57
labour unrest 269
LDCs (less developed countries) 131–2, 138, 148
Lipschitz conditions 21, 26
liquidity trap 48
Lyapounov functions 8–9, 11–13, 17

managerial theory of the firm 261–75
'monetarism' 79, 88, 92, 96, 136
monetary expansion 58, 65, 67–76, 136, 147, 159, 179–80, 186
monetary policy 43–4, 79–96, 109, 129, 135, 136, 153, 163, 168
money 15, 17, 24, 213, 242, 263
  demand for 41, 68, 75, 88, 91, 161, 177: income elasticity of 51–5, 76; interest elasticity of 52–7, 72, 88, 91; speculative 38; tax elasticity of 59–60, 65
  'inside'–'outside' 70–1, 76
  neutrality of 67, 74, 75, 86, 88
  quantity of 40, 94, 181: optimum 67, 75
  quantity theory of 79–96
  supply of 51–6, 79, 84–5, 87–91, 145, 153, 186: and IS–LM model 151
monopoly 25, 35, 42, 48
multiplier 83, 85, 88, 90, 95, 188, 263

'new' microeconomics 33–47

OECD 129–42, 147, 150
oil price rise 129–51
oligopoly 34–7
OPEC 129–42, 147–9, 151

Pareto optimality 4, 12, 61–2, 130
permanent income 79, 80–3, 84, 88, 90, 91, 94
Phillips curve (unemployment–inflation trade-off) 80, 86
  loops around 38
portfolio choice 83, 88–9, 90, 140, 162, 174, 178–9, 180, 183
price
  adjustment 5, 6, 8–9, 10, 12, 17, 20–1, 23–6
  expected 20
  relative 17, 39, 173, 177, 179, 184, 268
  rigidity/flexibility of 34, 39, 43, 82, 90, 129, 136–7, 138, 145–6, 189
production 7, 11, 18, 19–23, 24, 68, 154, 211
production function 106, 121, 123
  Cobb–Douglas 79, 223–4, 237
  CES 100, 101, 158, 223–4
profits
  and devaluation 145
  and factor shares 102, 104, 107, 246, 272
  and the individual firm 15, 16, 268
  determinants of 232–3, 236, 252, 255, 258
  maximisation 16, 18, 19, 25, 36, 45, 72–3, 80
purchasing power parity doctrine 173, 189

rent 252
resource depletion 18
returns to scale
  constant 6, 18, 68, 76, 107, 217
  increasing 265
revealed preference 9
revenue maximisation 72

savings 72, 149
  as a function of income 70, 270, 271
  composition of 56
  neoclassical theory of 67
  sources of 41, 135
search models 23, 25, 27
seignorage 55, 57, 58, 63
simulation 166, 167
social welfare function 58, 212, 226–7
sterilisation (of international money) 179, 190

subsidies 137, 193–205
substitution 7, 8, 26, 64, 131, 133, 149, 204–5, 211, 268

tariffs 132, 141, 193–205
tastes (as a partial determinant of demand) 132–3, 205, 211, 219
tâtonnement 5–10, 11, 20, 27, 40, 47, 154
taxes
    indirect 131–2, 137, 193–205
    on income and wealth 86–91, 94–6, 137, 139
    in national income 268
    optimal structure of 51–66
technical progress 75–6, 100, 102, 116, 121, 158, 269
technology 6, 16, 18, 19, 22, 99–101, 123, 211, 264–5, 266
terms of trade 129–35, 159, 160
time lags 154, 168
time preference 68, 73, 74–6
trade unions 45
traded/non-traded goods distinction 173–9, 181–5, 187, 188, 190
transfer problem 131
transformation problem 245–6, 248–50

unemployment 33–47, 114, 125, 138, 141, 149, 269, 273
    expected 38
    frictional 39
    probability of 37
utility
    diminishing marginal 65, 67, 76
    expected 13, 37–8
    functions, properties of 11, 18, 19, 26, 63, 211–41, 272
    maximisation of 16, 58–9, 270

wage cuts 38, 40
wage rigidity/flexibility 39, 43, 82, 138
Walras' law 5, 7, 8, 10, 14, 16, 27, 58–9, 271
Walrasian auctioneer 6, 21, 23, 71
wealth
    as a determinant of demand 11, 53–4, 177, 271
    and inflation 65, 181
    and monetary and fiscal policy 79–96, 157, 162
    and time preference 74, 76
welfare 3–4, 51, 58, 64, 69, 129–31, 147, 149, 150

Soc
HB
21
A81

DATE DUE